*The Immigrant Heritage of America Series*

Cecyle S. Neidle, *Editor*

New Amsterdam Now New York on the
Island of Man(hattan) 1650–1653.

# The Dutch in America, 1609-1974

### By GERALD F. DE JONG
*University of South Dakota*

TWAYNE PUBLISHERS
A DIVISION OF G. K. HALL & CO., BOSTON

**Library of Congress Cataloging in Publication Data**

De Jong, Gerald Francis, 1921–
 The Dutch in America, 1609–1974.

 (The Immigrant heritage of America series)
 SUMMARY: Traces the history of Dutch-Americans dis-
cussing why each wave of immigrants left Holland, where they
settled, and their way of life in and contributions to their new
country from colonial times to the present.
 Bibliography: p.
 1. Dutch in the United States—History. [1. Dutch in the
United States—History] I. Title.
E184.D9D44          917.3'06'3931          74-13738
ISBN 0-8057-3214-4

To Jeanne and the six "little" De Jongs:
Owen, Gerald II, Drew, Nanette, Chester, and Karl

# Contents

# About the Author

Gerald Francis De Jong was born in 1921 near the Dutch community of Orange City, Iowa, where his grandparents had settled during the 1880's after emigrating from the Netherlands. He attended Northwestern Classical Academy and served in the Navy for thirty-eight months during the Second World War. Graduating from Morningside College with honors in 1950, the author completed his education at the University of Wisconsin, where he received a Ph.D. in history in 1956. At Wisconsin, he received several academic awards, including a University Fellowship. Dr. De Jong has held teaching and administrative positions at various colleges in the Middle West, and is currently Professor of History at the University of South Dakota.

Professor De Jong's Dutch ancestry stimulated his interest in the history of the Netherlands and in the story of the Dutch in America. He wrote his doctoral dissertation on the Dutch revolt against Spain, and spent a year (1953–1954) as a Fulbright Scholar at the University of Utrecht, where he studied under the late Professor Pieter Geyl, one of Holland's most distinguished historians. The summers of 1968 and 1971 were also spent in the Netherlands doing research. Articles written by him on the Dutch experience in America have appeared in journals and magazines in the United States and in the Netherlands.

# Preface

HOLLANDERS HAVE BEEN MIGRATING TO AMERICA EVER SINCE Henry Hudson's famous voyage aboard the *Halve Maen* in 1609, which gave the Netherlands a claim to present-day New York and New Jersey. Although the Dutch have never been as numerous in the United States as the Irish, Germans, Italians, and several other ethnic groups, their influence on American history at certain times and in specific regions has been significant. In the seventeenth century, for example, New York City was known as New Amsterdam, and during the colonial period persons of Dutch descent were the dominant ethnic group in various communities in the Hudson Valley and northern New Jersey. Similarly, during the latter half of the nineteenth century, tens of thousands of Hollanders came to the United States and established numerous rural settlements throughout the Middle West and West, while others located in Dutch enclaves in the cities. Most of these communities still exist today, and have only recently given up their Old World traditions. Moreover, nearly ninety thousand Dutch citizens have emigrated to the United States since the Second World War.

This study of the Dutch-Americans follows primarily a chronological approach by noting why Hollanders left their native land at various times in history and describing where each wave of immigrants settled. The problems they faced in their new homes and the activities in which they engaged, as well as the later resettlement of many of their descendants at new locations in the United States, are discussed. The book occasionally reverts to a topical approach by examining the role that persons of Dutch descent played in certain aspects of American life, such as religion and politics. Chapter XIII is a kind of Dutch-American *Who's Who*, summarizing the contributions made by specific persons of Dutch descent in various fields during the last hundred years. The final chapter, entitled "Epilogue," points out some of the major conclusions reached by the study.

The reader should be cognizant of a special problem pertaining to the Dutch during the colonial period, namely, the difficulty of determining what constitutes a Dutchman. Family names give some indication, but they are by no means definitive. By the time of the American Revolution, for example, there were many colonists with names having the Dutch prefix "Van" whose ancestry could be traced to the New Netherland period, but whose Dutch lineage had been greatly diluted because of several generations of intermarriage. On the other hand, because women do not perpetuate family names, there were many colonists with non-Dutch-sounding names who nevertheless had considerable Dutch blood. These problems, which become increasingly complex the further one moves from the New Netherland period, can only be solved by doing considerable genealogical research on each family name.

Even after determining the degree of Dutch purity in the bloodlines of various colonial families, it is often doubtful that the result is worth the effort. Generally speaking, the cultural background and surroundings of a colonist are more important in determining "Dutchness" than is biological makeup. Indeed, it frequently happened that colonists of German, Scandinavian, Walloon, and other extractions living in Dutch communities in the Hudson Valley and northern New Jersey were hardly distinguishable from "pedigree" Dutchmen. They attended Dutch church services, spoke Dutch as their everyday language, and observed Dutch customs and traditions. In view of these difficulties and considerations, this study, as it pertains to the colonial period, describes the Dutch and their influence in rather broad terms, with only limited references to specific Dutchmen or Dutch families.

In composing a general history of the Dutch in America covering more than three and a half centuries, I naturally relied on the scholarship of a host of other historians. Two extensive works on this subject have been written in which few details have been omitted. These are J. Van Hinte, *Nederlanders in Amerika: Een Studie over Landverhuizers en Volkplanters in*

# Preface

*de 19<sup>de</sup> en 20<sup>ste</sup> Eeuw* (2 vols., Groningen, The Netherlands, 1928), and Henry S. Lucas, *Netherlanders in America: Dutch Immigration to the United States and Canada, 1789–1950* (Ann Arbor, Mich., 1955). Why, then, write another history of the Dutch in America? Van Hinte's work has long been out of print and has a limited use because it is in Dutch. Lucas's work, in addition to being somewhat dated, is too massive and encyclopedic for the general reader. Moreover, both of these studies virtually ignore the colonial period.

My research was also greatly facilitated by numerous monographs and by published documentary material. A special recognition is due those scholars of yesteryear, such as Edmund O'Callaghan, Arnold J. F. Van Laer, and Edward T. Corwin, who labored through dusty archival material of the colonial period, deciphering difficult handwriting, and translating into English from a Dutch language that often differed markedly from what is in use today. Without the painstaking work of these men, my task would have been more difficult.

I am grateful to many persons, most of them professors and clergymen, on both sides of the Atlantic who read parts of the manuscript and offered constructive criticism. Particular thanks in this regard are given to John W. Beardslee III, Frederick W. Bogert, J. C. Boogman, Herbert Brinks, Elton J. Bruins, Peter Y. De Jong, Herman Harmelink III, R. Alton Lee, John P. Luidens, Robert P. Swierenga, H. A. Van Luyk, and Willard C. Wichers. In addition, appreciation is expressed for the candid responses received from dozens of inquiries sent to Dutch-Americans scattered throughout the United States. Repeated courtesies have also been extended me by staff members of numerous libraries, especially those of the University of South Dakota, Northwestern College, Dordt College, Hope College, Calvin College, Rutgers University, and New Brunswick Seminary, as well as the New York Historical Society Library, the New York Public Library, the Royal Library in The Hague, and the library of the Netherlands Immigration Service in The Hague. As the manuscript reached various stages of completion, I profited greatly from the many suggestions given by Cecyle S. Neidle, general editor of the Twayne series on immigration.

Last, but above all, a special word of thanks is due my wife,

Jeanne, whose assistance and encouragement helped make writing this book a labor of love.

GERALD F. DE JONG

*University of South Dakota*

# The Dutch in America,
# 1609-1974

CHAPTER I

# The Dutch in the Old World

THE IDEAS AND CUSTOMS OF IMMIGRANTS ARE DERIVED IN PART
from their "mother country" and are frequently passed on to
their descendants. It is for this reason that a knowledge of the
history of the Netherlands is useful for understanding the
Dutch in America. Such information is also necessary for placing
the periods of Dutch emigration to the United States in their
proper historical perspective, especially with relation to why
Hollanders decided to leave their ancestral home and seek a
new life overseas. Moreover, a survey of Dutch history is helpful
for correcting mistaken views held in the United States about
the Netherlands.[1]

Millions of Americans today still think of Holland as a land
of windmills and dikes, of tulips and wooden shoes, and of
slow-moving canals and sleepy villages. These impressions are
in part the result of reading in one's youth such stories as
*Hans Brinker,* or viewing the paintings of the old Dutch masters,
or seeing tourist literature about places in the Netherlands like
Volendam, Marken, and Alkmaar. "Tulip festivals" that are
celebrated in some Dutch communities of the United States
have also helped perpetuate these impressions. Anyone who
has recently visited the Netherlands, however, knows that it
no longer resembles the landscapes depicted on the canvases of
Vermeer and Van Ruysdael, and that its inhabitants no longer
look like the peasants and burghers shown in the paintings of
Brueghel and Rembrandt. As one of the most densely populated
countries in the world (thirteen million people living on about
fourteen thousand square miles), the Netherlands is teeming
with activity and motion.

Even before the rapid industrialization and urban growth of
recent decades, life for many Hollanders was anything but
simple. The Netherlands, as much as any European country,

was affected by all the great movements of modern times, including the rise of capitalism, the Renaissance, the Reformation, and the Industrial Revolution, as well as the interminable wars that have plagued mankind during the past five centuries. Moreover, the Netherlands, like the United States, achieved its independence after a revolution against what was considered tyrannical rule. The leader of this revolt, William the Silent, Prince of Orange (1533–84), is looked upon by the Dutch today in much the same manner as Americans regard George Washington.

The Low Countries, as present-day Netherlands, Belgium, and Luxemburg are often called collectively, were quite primitive during the early Middle Ages, especially in the north, which had been little influenced by Roman civilization. Gradually, however, political and economic links with neighboring lands, together with the leavening work of the Christian Church, made their influence felt. The region slowly matured politically, as did its economic and cultural life. Many small principalities were merged to form larger political units, such as the counties of Flanders, Holland, and Gelderland, and the duchies of Brabant and Limburg. There were also episcopal territories, such as Utrecht and Liège.

Stimulated by the expansion of commerce and industry, the Low Countries witnessed considerable urban growth during the late Middle Ages. The most important towns—Antwerp, Bruges, Brussels, Ghent, Mechelen, and Ypres—were established first in the south, but eventually the north, too, could boast of such enterprising places as Amsterdam, Delft, Haarlem, Dordrecht, Utrecht, Leiden, and Middleburg. Simultaneously, a rich cultural life developed. This is evidenced in art by such painters as the brothers Van Eyck and Roger Van der Weyden. In literature, animal fables centering on Reynard the Fox and numerous mystery and morality plays were written. Similarly, the activities of the Brothers of the Common Life attested to a deep spiritual life.

At the close of the fourteenth century, the dukes of Burgundy began the political unification of the innumerable principalities, territories, and autonomous cities that made up the Low Countries. Most of the Burgundian holdings were transferred to the House of Hapsburg as a result of the marriage in 1477 of Mary of Burgundy and Maximilian of Hapsburg. The Hapsburgs were rulers of Austria and later also of Spain. In 1506, the Low Countries were given to Charles, a grandson of Maximilian and Mary. Later, he inherited the remainder of the Hapsburg lands, and in 1520 became Charles V, Holy Roman Emperor. During the 1550's, when the Hapsburg Empire was broken up, Spain and the Low Countries were transferred to his son Philip II.

During the time of Charles V, the Low Countries were frequently referred to as the "Seventeen Provinces," the idea being that there were seventeen principalities joined together under one rule. The government, however, was not strongly centralized. Each of the provinces jealously guarded and preserved its special privileges and customs, a practice that was continued long into the modern period. Even today, although the total land area of the Netherlands comprises only fourteen thousand square miles, there are noted differences among the various sections of the country in dialect and social customs. These same differences were frequently transferred to the Dutch settlements in America, thereby reflecting the locality from which each group of immigrants came in the Netherlands.

The unification movement that had been started by the Burgundians and continued by the Hapsburgs was of short duration. Heavy financial demands on the populace, persecution of the Protestants, and the centralizing governmental policies of Philip II produced considerable unrest and led to full-scale revolt in the 1560's. Although most of the Low Countries participated in the revolt, it succeeded only in the north. By the time of the Twelve Years' Truce in 1609, the seven northern provinces had achieved *de facto* independence, which became *de jure* by the Treaty of Münster in 1648. The new northern state was officially called the United Provinces, but was popularly known by such names as the Netherlands, the Dutch Republic, and Holland.

The government of the new state was a loose confederation of seven provinces: Holland, Zeeland, Utrecht, Gelderland, Overijssel, Groningen, and Friesland. In addition, there were state lands, or *generalitietslanden,* as they were called, in Brabant and Limburg, which were not given provincial status until many years later. In theory, during the period of the Republic, which lasted until 1795, the States General governed the country. Delegates to this body, however, were powerless to act on major issues without first seeking the approval of their provincial estates; the latter, in turn, were accountable to the town oligarchies, made up largely of wealthy merchants and a few landed aristocrats. Thus, in a sense, the States General was a senate of delegates representing quasi-independent provinces and towns. It is not surprising, therefore, that one historian described the Dutch Republic as "one of the most strangely complicated systems of government the world has ever seen—especially strange because no one could ever say positively where or with whom the sovereignty really resided."[2]

Although the government had its shortcomings, two factors helped give it stability and enabled it to last for about two centuries. One of these was the prestigious House of Orange, which traditionally furnished the stadtholders of the provinces. Under the Burgundian and Hapsburg rulers, these officials served as provincial governors or viceroys, representing the alien overlords. The office was retained after Spanish rule had been overthrown, although there were occasional stadtholderless periods in most of the provinces. Generally speaking, the stadtholder was the executive officer of the provincial estates and had various powers relative to the appointment of municipal magistrates and judges. The stadtholder of the House of Orange also served as commander in chief of the country's army and navy.

The economic preponderance of the province of Holland as compared to the other provinces also helped give unity to the fragmented state. Because most of the Dutch financial and commercial enterprises were located in that province and because it regularly contributed over half of the national budget, its delegates to the States General were given, although sometimes grudgingly, a commanding voice in the conduct of government. It was the great importance of this province that made it commonplace to refer to the whole of the Netherlands as Holland, in much the same manner that it became customary to refer to Great Britain as England.

When the first Hollanders began moving to America after Hudson's voyage of 1609, the Dutch Republic was just entering its Golden Age. This period, which lasted until the close of the seventeenth century, was characterized by extensive economic growth and a rich cultural life—accomplishments which can only be considered phenomenal in view of the country's small size. Ship building, fishing, cloth making, brewing, tanning, and soap making became major industries, while improvements in agriculture never failed to impress foreign visitors. But it was especially in the field of commerce that the Dutch distinguished themselves during the seventeenth century. They founded colonies in Brazil, the West Indies, North America, Africa, Ceylon, the East Indies, and Formosa. They also carried on trade with the Levant, Russia, Japan, and especially the Baltic.

Along with this economic growth, the country enjoyed a rich cultural life during the Golden Age. Space permits mention of only a few of the great Hollanders of this period. The paintings of Frans Hals, Jacob Van Ruisdael, Jan Steen, Jan Vermeer, and the great Rembrandt Van Rijn are masterpieces. Literary figures included Gerbrand Adriaanszoon Bredero, Jacob Cats, Pieter Corneliszoon Hooft, Constantijn Huygens, and Joost Van den Vondel. In science, outstanding biologists such as Antonie Van Leeuwenhoek and Jan Swammerdam, physicians like Herman Boerhaave, mathematicians of the stature of Simon Stevin, and physicists such as Christian Huygens made significant contributions. Other men of learning included Hugo De Groot (Grotius), the "father of international law," and Baruch Spinoza, the noted philosopher.

A country as small as the Netherlands could hardly expect to maintain a dominant economic position once the larger neighbors decided to challenge it. The Netherlands also had the disadvantage of the weak political structure noted earlier. Increasingly, too, the ruling patrician families placed their own selfish interests ahead of the best interests of the state, while Dutch shippers and manufacturers were inclined to rest on their laurels and did not modernize their ships and industrial plants. Moreover, a series of wars with England and France exhausted the country. By the time of the Peace of Utrecht (1713), the Golden Age of the Dutch Republic had practically ended.

Economic decline during the eighteenth century was accompanied by various political problems. The stadtholderate lost some of the popularity it once enjoyed, and the patrician oligarchy was unable to regain its former prestige. A new political party arose known as the *Patriotten,* which was interested in reforming the Dutch government, especially by increasing the influence of the well-to-do burghers. The period from 1785 to 1813 witnessed considerable political confusion. Governmental changes were frequent, and the country became more and more tied to the destinies of France. For a time (1806–10), Napoleon's brother Louis even ruled the country as King of Holland, and in 1810, the Netherlands ceased to exist as an independent country when it became part of the French Empire.

After the defeat of Napoleon in 1813 and the meeting of the Congress of Vienna in 1814–15, the Netherlands not only regained its independence, but the country nearly doubled in size. In an effort to create a strong buffer state to deter France from future aggression, the southern Low Countries were joined with the Netherlands to form the United Kingdom of the Netherlands. Political and religious differences between the two sections, however, made this a union of short duration. During the revolutions which swept over Europe in the 1830's, the people of the south rose in revolt. Their efforts succeeded, and the modern state of Belgium was created. A more permanent change after the Napoleonic era came with the elevation of the stadtholderate family to the position of kingship. In 1815, William, the son of the last stadtholder, William V, was given the title King William I.

Numerous internal problems plagued the Netherlands during the decades after Napoleon. The constitution under which William I (1815–40) ruled was not very democratic with respect to ministerial responsibility and suffrage. Under his successor, William II (1840–49), a new constitution was promulgated in 1848 which was much more liberal, although it gave less than 20 percent of the adult male citizens the right to vote. The economic situation was particularly bad by the middle of the nineteenth century. Industrial growth was still hampered by the decline of the staple market during the previous century. In 1850, there was only one factory in the Netherlands that employed more than a thousand workers. Pauperism was commonplace; during the 1840's, one-third of the people was dependent on outside help. One writer described the masses at this time as being "economically poor, politically powerless, socially subordinate, and culturally unenlightened."[3]

Domestic policies during the second half of the nineteenth

century centered primarily on the effort to make the government more responsive to the will of the people. Increasingly, too, political groups concerned themselves with various social problems. Liberal and Socialist parties appeared, as did organizations that catered to the aspirations of the Calvinists and the Catholics. As a consequence, there was steady progress toward parliamentary democracy and the economic situation gradually improved. Industries expanded, agriculture showed steady gains, and Rotterdam and Amsterdam grew as shipping centers. Commercial interests in the East Indies, which in the past had been limited to the island of Java and some coastal areas, multiplied.

This is not to say that economic growth in the Netherlands after 1850 was an unmixed blessing. Severe economic depressions plagued Holland about once every two decades, and the replacement of hand labor by steam-powered machinery created periodic unemployment. The Industrial Revolution also caused grave social problems, including long working days, child labor, and slum conditions. Agriculture, too, was not without its difficulties, especially as a result of foreign tariff barriers. In addition, the rapid growth in population after 1870 not only cut down the size of the family farm, but made it difficult, because of land costs, for a young man to start farming on his own. Needless to say, these problems, when they occurred, had an impact on Dutch emigration to the United States.

The period between World Wars I and II was also one of mixed blessing. Although the Netherlands maintained a strict neutrality during World War I, the country suffered economically. Severe restrictions were placed on Dutch commercial activities not only by the Netherlands government but also by the belligerent powers. After the war, the major political issues revolved around questions of defense, meeting the demands of Indonesian nationalists, and social legislation. Generally speaking, the Netherlands prospered during the 1920's, but the worldwide depression of the 1930's caused considerable unemployment and serious social unrest. The attempt to maintain strict neutrality, which had succeeded in World War I, failed in the Second World War. The German army, and especially the air force, struck suddenly and without mercy on May 10, 1940. Although the Dutch fought valiantly, organized resistance came to an end after only a week of fighting.

Reconstruction was the major problem facing the Netherlands after World War II, the country having suffered terribly from five years of Nazi occupation.[4] Fortunately, the United States gave considerable help through the Marshall Plan, by which the Netherlands received more than one billion dollars, or about a hundred dollars for each man, woman, and child. Economic recovery was also aided by strenghening the ties of Holland with western Europe, especially through membership in the Benelux Customs Union, the European Coal and Steel Community, and the European Economic Community (Common Market). In foreign affairs, the Netherlands did not resume the traditional policy of neutrality it had followed before World War II. It became a charter member of the United Nations and entered immediately into several alliances with the Western powers, including the North Atlantic Treaty Organization (NATO).

The Netherlands was unsuccessful in maintaining its extensive colonial holdings after the war. Indonesian nationalists proclaimed the independence of the East Indies in 1945, and after intermittent but sometimes serious fighting, the Dutch agreed to most of their demands at the Round Table Conference in 1949. Today Surinam, on the South American continent, and the Netherlands Antilles, consisting of the Leeward and Windward islands in the Caribbean, are all that remain of Holland's once far-flung empire. In 1954, these holdings were given full responsibility for their internal affairs and made equal partners with the Netherlands within the Kingdom.

Despite the pessimism that existed among the Dutch people about their country's future immediately after World War II, when one in three Hollanders seriously considered emigrating,[5] the Netherlands today is enjoying another Golden Age in terms of economic development. To deal with population pressure, the government embarked upon an ambitious industrialization program, encouraging native industries in whatever way possible, and also inducing foreign firms to locate in the Netherlands. As a consequence, it is one of the most highly industrialized countries in the world today. Nearly half its population is engaged in industry and a third of its people live in cities of over a hundred thousand. The country's major industries are metalworking, electrical goods, textiles, and food processing. Firms such as Unilever, Royal Dutch/Shell, and Philips have production and exporting plants in dozens of countries throughout the world. Transportation and shipping are thriving, as Rotterdam—the busiest port in the world—and the extensive airline operations of KLM indicate. Agriculture, too, despite tremendous problems, remains important in the Dutch economy. Through government assistance and intensive cultivation of the soil, agricultural products represent about one-sixth of Holland's total exports.

Steady economic growth has caused Dutch interest in emigration to decline considerably since the immediate post–World War II years, when it reached an all-time high of about fifty thousand in 1952. During the decade of the 1960's, Dutch emigration averaged fewer than ten thousand annually. Only time can tell whether it will be awakened again at some later date. Future Dutch departures will depend in part upon whether the Netherlands can maintain its rapid rate of industrialization. As any student of this subject knows, however, emigration is a two-way procedure—it depends not only on conditions at home, but also on conditions in the country of destination. The countries to which the vast majority of Dutch emigrants have gone since World War II—Canada, Australia, and the United States—are no longer as willing to accept new immigrants.

CHAPTER II

# The First Dutch Settlements in the New World

WHEN THE DUTCH ESTABLISHED THEIR HUGE MARITIME EMPIRE during the seventeenth century, they were at first not greatly attracted to North America. Although some trade and privateering were carried on during the late sixteenth and early seventeenth centuries by Dutch ships operating off the coast of Newfoundland and French Canada, these ventures were very limited. The Netherlands, being engaged in a war with Spain and more interested in the Baltic trade and in tropical products, tended to ignore North America. Nor did fishing in American waters have a particular appeal, largely because the cod season off Newfoundland coincided with the herring season nearer home.[1]

Even after Henry Hudson's memorable voyage in 1609, the Dutch showed only a moderate interest in North America. Hudson, although of English birth, was engaged by the Dutch East India Company to search for a passage to the Far East by going north and east, around Asia. The Company undoubtedly selected him because he had attempted twice before, while in the service of English merchants, to find a northeast passage. Hudson set sail from Holland on April 6, 1609, in the Company ship the *Halve Maen*, a vessel of eighty tons with a mixed crew of about eighteen Dutch and English sailors. Calm seas, a rebellious crew, and impassable ice forced him to give up the search for a northeast passage after his ship had reached the vicinity of Novaya Zemlya. He thereupon sailed the *Halve Maen* westward, passing Newfoundland on July 3, and then southward down the coast of North America almost as far as Chesapeake Bay. Hudson then turned the vessel around and explored the coast northward, reaching Sandy Hook Bay on September 4.

After sailing about one hundred fifty miles up the Hudson, during which time a small amount of trade was carried on with the Indians, he came to realize that this river was not the fabled passage and shortcut to the Far East. Consequently, on October 4, 1609, the *Halve Maen* again stood out to sea and began its long journey home.

The information brought to Holland by crew members of the *Halve Maen* awakened some interest among Dutch entrepreneurs in the possibilities of trade with the Indians. As a consequence, although Dutch commerce continued to be directed primarily toward the Baltic and the tropical regions, several exploring and trading voyages were made to North America under Dutch auspices between 1609 and 1614. On the basis of these voyages and that of Henry Hudson, the Dutch laid claim to all the land between the Delaware and Connecticut rivers. This territory, approximately one hundred seventy-five miles in width at the coastline, soon became known as New Netherland, after the parent country.

On October 11, 1614, the States General granted a charter to several Dutch merchants, authorizing them to form the New Netherland Company with exclusive trading rights in the territory "situe in America between New France and Virginia, whereof the sea coasts lie between the fortieth and forty fifth degrees of Latitude, now named New Netherland."[2] A trading post, Fort Nassau, was constructed on the upper Hudson at Castle Island. When floods destroyed this settlement in the spring of 1617, a new post, Fort Orange, was built nearby on the west bank of the river. It became the nucleus for present-day Albany. A few smaller posts of a makeshift nature were also established at strategic locations for carrying on trade with the Indians. When the monopoly of the New Netherland Company expired in 1618, Dutch trade in North America was again opened to everyone until the creation of the famous West India Company in 1621.

The charter of the West India Company granted stockholders a monopoly of Dutch trade over a wide area of the world, including the west coast of Africa from the Tropic of Cancer southward and the western hemisphere as far north as Newfoundland, thus including New Netherland. Within this vast territory, the officials of the Company were permitted to establish and govern colonies as they saw fit, subject only to the supervision of the States General. Management of the organization rested in a board of nineteen directors, usually sitting at Amsterdam.[3]

The West India Company was prevented from paying immediate attention to New Netherland because of an initial shortage of funds. The directors at first were also primarily interested in trade with West Africa and in wresting Brazil from the Portuguese. It was therefore not until November 3, 1623, that authorization was made "to send a ship to the Virginias ... with V or VI families of colonists in order to make a beginning of settlement there."[4] This authorization resulted from a request made by several refugee families from the Spanish Netherlands for permission to go to New Netherland as colonists.[5]

On the basis of the documents which have thus far come to light, it is impossible to state exactly when the resolution of November 3 was carried out. The first concrete evidence of settlers being sent to New Netherland under the auspices of the West India Company is the dispatch of a ship in the early spring of 1624. It was appropriately named the *Nieu Nederlandt* and carried about thirty families and some single men. Most of the passengers were Protestant refugees—Walloons from the Spanish Netherlands and Huguenots from France. The *Nieu Nederlandt* also carrried livestock, seed grain, and farm implements for the colonists. Cornelis Jacobsen May, who had visited the region at least twice before, was placed in charge of the expedition and was designated the colony's first provisional governor.[6]

Upon their arrival in New Netherland in May, 1624, most of the colonists settled on the upper Hudson at Fort Orange, but some located on Governor's Island, off the tip of Manhattan Island, and a few settled to the south on the Delaware River. The Dutch later built a fort and trading post, Fort Nassau, on the Delaware near the present site of Gloucester, New Jersey. It is possible that Governor May also dispatched a few settlers to the Connecticut River.[7]

More colonists and additional livestock and implements were sent during the months that followed. Thus, in early 1625, the

*Orangenboom* arrived in New Netherland with more settlers
and a new governor, Willem Verhulst, who replaced May.
Verhulst made the Delaware settlement his place of residence,
as probably May also had done. It is possible that at this time
the directors in Holland had greater interest in the Delaware
settlement than in the settlements to the north at Fort Orange
and Governor's Island. Verhulst was instructed, for example, to
distribute among the three settlements the colonists who had
accompanied him but to "strengthen the population of the
southern colony most."[8]

A few months after Verhulst's arrival, forty-two additional
settlers came to New Netherland aboard the *Mackreel*. Three
other vessels also arrived carrying about a hundred head of
livestock—horses, cows, sheep, and hogs—and a variety of agricultural implements. A contemporary writer described as follows
the care that was shown in transporting the livestock:

Each animal has its own stall, with a floor of three feet of sand,
arranged as comfortably as any stall here [in Holland.] Each animal
has its respective servant who attends to it and knows what he is
to get if he delivers it there alive. All suitable forage is there, such
as oats, hay and straw, and what else is useful.[9]

As a result of this attention, only two animals died during the
voyage.

A surveyor and engineer named Cryn Fredericksz also arrived
on the *Mackreel*, with orders from the directors to build a
fortification somewhere near the mouth of either the Hudson
or Delaware River, the exact site to be chosen by him in con-
sultation with Verhulst and other officials in the colony.[10] Manhattan Island was chosen as the site for the fort, which was
called Fort Amsterdam in accordance with the instructions from
the Company officials in Holland. It was intended to serve
several purposes: protect the colonists from the Indians, guard
the entrance to the Hudson River from other European nations,
and serve as headquarters for Company operations in New
Netherland. The settlement which grew up around the fort
became known as New Amsterdam. In order to safeguard the
settlers from Indian attacks and to acquire additional workmen

to speed the construction of Fort Amsterdam, Governor Verhulst moved the Delaware colonists to Manhattan Island. Except for a token force of about sixteen men, the colonists at Fort Orange were relocated in a similar manner.[11]

A house for the governor of the colony and lodging for other Company officials, as well as barracks for the soldiers and some storehouses, were constructed within the walls of the fort. The adjoining dwellings were at first very crude, many of them being partly in the ground and resembling cellars. Dominie Jonas Michaelius, who served as the colony's first ordained minister, described these early houses as nothing more than "hovels," in which the colonists "nestled rather than dwelt."[12] Beyond the fort and the surrounding houses were the Company farms, as well as the lands belonging to some of the public officials and to the so-called free-farmers. A report of late 1626 from Manhattan Island declared that the colonists "are in good heart and live in peace there" and that the grain which had been sown in middle May was harvested with good results by middle August.[13]

In 1626, the West India Company appointed Pieter Minuit as successor to Verhulst. Beginning with this appointment, the highest ranking official in New Netherland was henceforth officially designated director general, although the title of governor was also frequently used. One of Minuit's first official acts was the purchase of Manhattan Island in 1626 from the Indians, thereby legalizing Dutch occupation of the island and the construction of Fort Amsterdam. The price was some blankets, kettles, and trinkets, whose total value was sixty guilders—one of the greatest real estate bargains ever made in the history of man. Although the settlement on Manhattan Island was called New Amsterdam, it compared in few respects to its namesake in Holland. By the end of 1626, it consisted of about thirty houses and two hundred inhabitants, a figure which had increased to only two hundred seventy by 1628.[14]

Bastiaen Jansz Krol, a former lay preacher and minor Company official, succeeded Minuit as governor in 1631, and served until 1633. Nothing of great significance pertaining to the colony occurred during Krol's administration, but under his successor, Wouter Van Twiller (1633–37), there was considerable interest in colonizing New Netherland. In 1633, the Dutch constructed a trading post and blockhouse, Fort Good Hope, on the Connecticut River near the present site of Hartford, and two years later they regarrisoned Fort Nassau on the Delaware River. A trading post was also established at the present site of Philadelphia, but was abandoned a short time later.

The Dutch also began settling Long Island during Van Twiller's administration, and continued to do so under succeeding governors. In 1636, several New Netherlanders, including Van Twiller himself, purchased land from the Indians in the southwestern corner of the island. These patents became the nucleus for the settlement of New Amersfoort, which was renamed Flatlands after the English occupation of New Netherland in 1664. Other colonists at this time settled just across the East River from New Amsterdam at Gowanus and Wallabout. When a ferry was established about 1640 between New Amsterdam and Long Island, a small settlement arose near the landing place on the Long Island side. It soon became known as "the Ferry." About 1646, the village of Breuckelen—now called Brooklyn—was established "about two thousand paces" from the Ferry.[15]

The authorities in Holland, worried about the sparse settlement of New Netherland, declared that more colonists had to be sent out to protect the small and widely scattered communities against possible Indian attacks, and to offset, on the basis of occupation, the claims that England was making to the region. An increasing number of critics in Holland were also demanding that less emphasis be placed on the fur trade, and greater priority be given to agriculture. Consequently, various steps were taken beginning as early as 1629 to increase emigration to New Netherland and to develop its agricultural potential.

The most elaborate scheme for attracting colonists was the so-called patroon system, which was established in 1629 by the "Charter of Freedoms and Exemptions." By this plan, a qualified entrepreneur, or patroon, was given a tract of land extending sixteen miles along the seacoast or the bank of a navigable river, or eight miles along both river banks, and extending as far "into the country as the situation of the occupiers shall permit." To qualify as a patroon, a person had to have been a major stockholder since the time the West India

Company was founded. In return for a grant of land, the patroon promised to settle on his estate, within four years, fifty colonists over fifteen years of age. The settlers, on their part, had to pay the patroon a fixed rent for the land they worked as well as a share of the profits. The patroon was also given certain rights over his settlers with respect to fishing, hunting, milling, and justice.[16]

At least six patroonships were registered in accordance with the plan, but only three were settled. One of them was named Pavonia, after the Latinized form of its owner's name, Michiel Reyniersz Pauw. It was located on the west bank of the lower Hudson River just across from New Amsterdam, but also included Staten Island. Another patroonship was founded by Samuel Godyn and Samuel Blommaert. It was called Swanendael, meaning "Valley of the Swans," and was located on the west bank of Delaware Bay, near the present site of Lewes, Delaware. A third patroonship, called Rensselaerswyck, was located in the vicinity of Fort Orange.

Swanendael initially gave some hope for success when, in the spring of 1631, twenty-eight men and a shipload of supplies were deposited there. These settlers were soon joined by several men from New Amsterdam. A fort was built, and about one hundred fifty square miles of land were purchased from the Indians. Farming prospered, as shown by a report of July, 1631, stating that the "cows had calved" and the "lands were sewn and adorned with beautiful crops."[17] Because of numerous accounts that whales had been sighted in Delaware Bay, whaling, too, became one of the principal objectives of the Swanendael colony.

Despite the prospects for farming and whaling, Swanendael lasted only four years. As the result of a misunderstanding with the Indians, the colony's settlers were massacred and the buildings and palisades destroyed. Although Dutch trading ships continued to visit the region, no immediate attempt was made to resettle Swanendael, and in 1635, it was sold back to the West India Company. By this time, the patroonship called Pavonia had also failed, and it, too, had been repurchased by the West India Company.

Kiliaen Van Rensselaer, a diamond merchant and wealthy

landowner of Amsterdam and a director of the West India Company, established the only successful patroonship. Van Rensselaer obtained a tract of land along the Hudson River above and below Fort Orange. The tract lay on both banks of the river, and eventually totaled several hundred thousand acres. In conformity with the "Charter of Freedoms and Exemptions," the Indian title to the land was invalidated by purchase, and steps were taken to bring in settlers.

Rensselaerswyck, as the patroonship was called, survived for several reasons. It was favorably located for trade and already had the nucleus of a colony at Fort Orange. Furthermore, although Kiliaen van Rensselaer was an absentee landlord and never visited America, he personally took a deep interest in his plantation and even resettled some tenants there from his estates in the Netherlands. Fortunately, too, the patroon had a very capable agent, his grandnephew, Arent Van Curler, to look after his interests at Rensselaerswyck.[18]

In a renewed effort to bring more settlers to New Netherland, the West India Company issued a revised "Charter of Freedoms and Exemptions" in 1640. Some of its clauses were designed to encourage persons of limited economic means to settle in New Netherland by promising one hundred morgens (two hundred acres) of land to each person who went to the colony "with five souls above fifteen years." The revised plan also contained provisions for erecting new patroonships, but under different terms than those given in 1629. To qualify as a patroon under the new charter, it was no longer necessary to be a major stockholder of the West India Company. Moreover, the size of the grants were cut by about one-fourth, and the period during which a patroon had to settle the required number of fifty colonists was shortened from four to three years. The patroon's rights over his colonists were also more limited.[19]

Once again several patroonships were registered, but none was successful. One of the most promising was founded in 1641 by David Pietersz De Vries and named, in his honor, Vriesendael, meaning "De Vries' Valley." It was located on the west bank of the Hudson River not far north of the former patroonship of Pavonia. De Vries described the site of his plantation as a fine place, situated along the river, under a mountain. There is a flat [section of land] there, a hour and a half's journey in extent, where hay can be raised for two hundred head of cattle, and where there is thirty morgens of corn-land, where I have sown wheat which grew higher than the tallest man in the country. Here were also two fine falls from the mountains, where two good mills could be erected for grinding corn and sawing plank. It was a beautiful place for hunting deer, wild turkeys, and pigeons.[20]

The patroonship of Myndert Myndertsen Van der Horst of Utrecht, the Netherlands, was located near Vriesendael—so close, in fact, that De Vries said it was only an hour's walk from his own settlement. A third patroonship governed by the revised regulations was established by Cornelis Melyn on Staten Island.

Although only Rensselaerswyck could be considered a success, the patroonships did contribute to the settlement of New Netherland. A few officials and settlers frequently stayed on the land as independent farmers after the estates were repossessed by the West India Company, and their dwellings sometimes became sites for villages. Thus, a small hamlet of buildings that had been part of Pavonia gradually grew into the settlement later known as Bergen. By 1661, Bergen consisted of about thirty families and had a school, a ferry which ran thrice weekly to New Amsterdam, and a *voorlezer*—meaning "sermon reader"—to look after the religious needs of the people and to teach school. The villages of Hoboken and Paulus Hook were founded in a similar manner.[21]

The patroon system was the most elaborate scheme for colonizing New Netherland, but there were other developments from time to time which helped bring Dutch settlers to American shores. In 1644, about two hundred soldiers and refugees arrived in New Amsterdam from Brazil, where Dutch influence had been steadily losing out to the Portuguese. Refugees continued to arrive in New Netherland until Portugal completely regained its former colony in 1654. Although many of them remained in New Netherland only briefly and then continued their journey to Holland, some settled there permanently.[22] It was as a refugee from Brazil that New Netherland received its first Jewish settler, Jacob Barsimon, in August, 1654—perhaps the first Jew to locate in the North American colonies. In September of that same year, twenty-three more Jews arrived from Brazil and settled in New Netherland.[23]

Another scheme for increasing the population of New Netherland was initiated about 1650 when the directors of the West India Company suggested to the States General that permission be obtained from officials of various provinces and cities to transport about three or four hundred boys and girls there from the country's poorhouses and orphan asylums. According to the plan, after the children had fulfilled their contractual obligations in America, they would be free to choose their own future, i.e., continue to work for their former masters on whatever terms they could obtain, or be given some free land and thereby become farmers. The proposal won official approval, and in 1654 Governor Stuyvesant was informed that about fifty boys and girls from the almshouses of Amsterdam were being sent to New Netherland on a trial basis. In 1655, seventeen orphans, seven boys and ten girls, twelve to twenty-three years of age, were sent to New Amsterdam, followed by another group in 1659. Children from orphanages and poorhouses were also sent to the Dutch settlements on the Delaware River.

Perhaps more children would have been sent, but the officials in New Netherland had reservations about the plan. In 1658, for example, Jacob Alrichs, an important official among the Delaware settlements, wrote his superiors in Amsterdam, "If possible, none ought to come less than 15 years of age or somewhat strong, as little profit is to be expected here without labor." Similarly, Governor Stuyvesant on April 21, 1660, informed the directors that "most of the children from the Orphan Asylums [were] accustomed and more inclined to carry a beggar's gripsack than to labor."[24]

Strange as it may seem, some Dutch settlers also came to America through the auspices of Sweden, which during the seventeenth century was determined to obtain a greater share of the world's trade. It was with this goal in mind that the New Sweden Company was founded in 1637 to trade and establish colonies on the North American coast. About half the capital invested in the New Sweden Company, however, was Dutch, and many important Hollanders were involved in its organization.

The promoters of the Swedish company selected the Delaware Valley as the site for their American colony, even though this territory was claimed by the Netherlands. Because Hollanders were deeply involved in organizing the venture and because it was difficult to get Swedes to emigrate, more Dutchmen than Swedes initially came to New Sweden, as the colony was called. The first settlers, for example, consisted of twenty-two Dutchmen who arrived in March, 1638, accompanied by Pieter Minuit, former governor of New Netherland. They located themselves on the right bank of the Delaware River near the present site of Wilmington. Here they founded Fort Christina, named after the Swedish queen. Two years later, about fifty Dutch colonists from Utrecht were settled under Swedish auspices a few miles above Fort Christina.

In 1641–42, the Dutch members of the New Sweden Company were bought out for eighteen thousand guilders, and the Company was reorganized under greater control by the Swedish crown. The original Dutch atmosphere of the colony was further changed under the dynamic leadership of Johan Bjornsson Printz, who served as governor of New Sweden from 1643 to 1653. In his report of 1647 to his superiors in Stockholm, Governor Printz stated, "It is of the utmost necessity for us to see how we can get rid of the Dutch from the [Delaware] river, for they oppose us on every side."[25] During his administration, a number of Swedish, Finnish, and English immigrants were brought in and a series of blockhouses and trading posts were erected.

Although the Swedish colony constituted a challenge to New Netherland, the Dutch were at first hesitant about taking firm counteraction. They had not located themselves at the most favored places for defense, and their garrison at Fort Nassau across the river from Fort Christina consisted of only twenty men. Holland also hesitated to take strong measures because Sweden and the Netherlands were allies in the Thirty Years' War raging in Europe at this time. The end of this war in 1648, and the replacement of the bungling Willem Kieft by the energetic and militant Pieter Stuyvesant as governor of New Netherland, changed matters.

In April, 1648, Stuyvesant ordered the construction of Fort

Beversreede, located within the limits of present-day Philadelphia, in the hope of diverting some of the fur trade that
was going to Fort Christina. Three years later, the Dutch governor, with a hundred twenty soldiers, marched to Fort Nassau
where he and his army were joined by a fleet of eleven ships.
He hoped this show of force would discourage Sweden from
further intrusion into Dutch territory. Before returning to New
Amsterdam, Stuyvesant personally supervised the building of
a fort strategically located for controlling the approaches to New
Sweden. It was named Fort Casimir, which is today the site
of New Castle. Stuyvesant also strengthened the Dutch position
in the south by encouraging persons from Manhattan Island
to move there.

These actions, instead of restraining the Swedes, spurred them
to take countermeasures of their own. Beginning in 1653, Swedish reinforcements and supplies were sent to the Delaware. On
May 21, 1655, the Swedes captured Fort Casimir and naturalized
the Dutch citizens who resided there. Stuyvesant thereupon
fitted out a fleet of seven ships and an army of between six and
seven hundred men, the largest military force to be organized
up to that time in the North American colonies. In September,
1655, the Dutch governor and his army retook Fort Casimir,
forced the surrender of Fort Christina, and brought about the
complete capitulation of New Sweden. Not only was the Swedish
threat to the Delaware Valley removed by these actions, but
New Netherland acquired a few hundred more colonists.[26]

One of the most energetic plans for colonizing New Netherland came not from the West India Company but from the
city of Amsterdam. Its interest in this matter resulted in part
from the fact that many of its citizens had invested heavily in
the Company and were anxious to protect their financial investments. Unstable conditions in the Baltic also influenced the
government of Amsterdam to consider establishing its own colony
in America. The city received much of its naval stores, including
masts and tar, from the Baltic, and looked upon New Netherland
as a substitute source for such supplies. In view of these considerations and knowing that the West India Company was
hard pressed for funds, the burgomasters of Amsterdam, in 1656,
offered to purchase a large section of land on the west bank of

the lower Delaware River. The Company accepted the offer.

The government of Amsterdam immediately took steps to develop its colony, which was called New Amstel. An elaborate prospectus, known as the "Conditions," describing the terms by which qualified individuals could take up land and settle there, was published and widely circulated. The city of Amsterdam promised to lend passage money to qualified settlers and to transport all tools and farm implements free of charge. Settlers had to agree to stay in the colony four years, but were guaranteed as much free land as was needed for "the plough as well as for pasture and meadow" and also free seed and provisions for the first year. A town was to be laid out with streets, a market, a schoolhouse, and a church, and provisions were made for furnishing New Amstel with a blacksmith, a wheelwright, a carpenter, and a schoolmaster. The latter was to serve also as a lay minister until there were two hundred families in the colony, at which time "a preacher and consistory" would be installed. A store where necessities could be purchased at reasonable cost was also promised. According to the "Conditions," settlers would be permitted to participate in the colony's government and, under certain limitations, to ship their agricultural and other products to Amsterdam.[27]

On December 21, 1656, the city of Amsterdam sent the *Prins Maurits* with one hundred thirteen settlers to begin the development of New Amstel. Because of storms and shipwreck, the settlers did not arrive at their destination until April 21, 1657. They took up land just south of Fort Casimir. Interest in the new colony continued to grow, so that by March, 1657, three hundred more people were ready to leave for New Amstel. Most of the later arrivals were Hollanders, but some were Waldensian Protestant refugees who had been driven out of the Piedmont Plain in the western Alps by the Catholic duke of Savoy and had fled to the Netherlands.[28] By 1658, there were about six hundred colonists in New Amstel.

Despite its auspicious beginnings, several mistakes were made which brought New Amstel to near ruin by 1660. Over half the colonists were women and children, and scant attention was paid to the recruitment of agriculturalists. Vice-director Jacob Alrichs declared that "scarcely three good farmers were to be found among the whole lot" of settlers who arrived on the three ships that followed the *Prins Maurits* to New Amstel.[29] The shortage of farmers meant that the colony could not even supply itself with the necessary food, let alone export agricultural products as had been planned. Heavy rains in 1658 also contributed to poor harvests. Disease, too, took its toll; in a single year of operation, about one hundred settlers died. There was also a shortage of skilled labor, especially carpenters, and various tools and implements vital to the colony's success were in short supply.

As a result of these developments, many colonists departed from New Amstel for the Dutch settlements on the Hudson and Long Island. Some even left for the English communities in adjoining Virginia and Maryland. A report of August, 1657, stated that there was "a great deal of murmuring" among the colonists because of the short rations, and that news of the discontent was causing many Hollanders to change their mind about emigrating there.[30] A ship captain visiting New Amstel in December, 1659, stated that it was "painful to behold how the people here complain," adding it was likely that "almost all of the people will leave that place."[31]

Fearful of what might happen to New Amstel if it did not attract more settlers, the city of Amsterdam tried several times during the early 1660's to revitalize the colony. On March 9, 1661, the Common Council of Amsterdam resolved that "a goodly number of free people be gratuitously conveyed over, with their necessary baggage, by the city." In 1663, the city magistrates purchased more land on the Delaware from the West India Company, and the "Conditions" for settlement were liberalized. An attempt was also made to encourage Swedes and Finns to migrate to the Delaware. As a consequence of these efforts, the population of New Amstel slowly increased after 1661.[32]

One of the most unusual plans for increasing the number of Dutch settlers in the Delaware Valley involved the establishment of a socialist community. The author of this proposal was a Dutch Mennonite named Pieter Cornelis Plockhoy, who for many years had been preaching universal brotherhood based on the ideals of popular government, religious freedom, and social and economic justice for everyone. In particular, he advocated the establishment of small, nearly self-sufficient communities in which "Husbandmen, Masters of Arts and Sciences, and Useful Handy Craft-People" would live together as one "Familie or Household-government." Because he was in sympathy with many of the religious and political views held by Oliver Cromwell, Plockhoy journeyed to England in 1658 to get permission to establish several utopian communities in that country. Cromwell showed some interest in the plan and met twice with Plockhoy, but the Lord Protector's death in September, 1658, prevented the plan from being pursued very far.

Shortly after his return to Holland, Plockhoy began negotiating with the burgomasters of Amsterdam for permission to establish a cooperative community in the Delaware Valley. The discussions resulted in an agreement signed on June 9, 1662, permitting Plockhoy to establish a settlement on Delaware Bay in the vicinity of the old patroonship of Swanendael. To help the new settlement get started, the city council agreed to lend one hundred guilders to each family who joined Plockhoy's venture and to pay for the passage of women and children.

Elated by this turn of events, Plockhoy made a concerted effort to ensure the success of his American utopia. As he had done several times in the past, he took up the pen to explain his views. A pamphlet, fourteen pages in length and known by its shortened title as *Kort en Klaer Ontwerp*, was published at Amsterdam in 1662. It specified that the community would be "composed of a peaceful, unified, and selected people who will assist each other . . . in agriculture, fishing, handicrafts, etc., to arrive at their desired goal." Members would work a fixed number of hours each week for the common profit of the entire community, and the money derived therefrom would be divided equally according to the size of a person's family. Plockhoy, however, did not envision a purely communistic society. Private ownership of property would be permitted, and settlers would be allowed to use their free time in whatever way they wished, even for their own private gain in agriculture and industry.

Plockhoy's plans called for complete separation of church and state, as well as freedom of religion. Communal living in central houses would be encouraged but not made mandatory. Although he preached the equality of all men, Plockhoy recognized that not everyone was equally skilled. He therefore promised special concessions for master workmen. He also acknowledged that without some kind of government in his settlement, chaos and anarchy would result; the *Kort en Klaer Ontwerp* therefore provided for various public officials to be elected annually. Provisions were also made for the defense of the colony, but anyone "who for conscientious reasons" was opposed to carrying military weapons would be excused by paying an annual tax which would be used to support the local militia.

Plockhoy succeeded in interesting only twenty-four families in his scheme; he had hoped to interest a hundred. For various reasons, especially the problem of getting enough colonists, the departure to America was delayed several months. Although the facts are not entirely known, the colonists apparently sailed from Amsterdam on the *St. Jacob* in early May, 1663, and arrived at New Amstel in late July. Shortly after their arrival, they located themselves, as planned, at the mouth of Delaware Bay on the site of the old patroonship of Swanendael. Here, Plockhoy and his followers proceeded to erect the first socialist community to be established in North America.[33]

While these developments were occurring in the Delaware Valley, colonization was also taking place in the northern part of New Netherland. Several Dutch settlements arose on western Long Island in addition to New Amersfoort and Brueckelen which had been founded earlier. Such new villages included Midwout (later called Flatbush) founded in 1651, New Utrecht in 1657, and Boswyck (Bushwick) in 1660. Meanwhile, English settlers, mostly from New England, had received patents from the Dutch governor at New Amsterdam to found towns in the midst of these Dutch settlements. The first of these so-called English towns was Hempstead, founded in 1643, followed by Gravesend and Vlissingen (Flushing) in 1645, Rustdorp (Jamaica) in 1655, and Middleburg (Newton) in 1656. According to the patents for these English towns, the inhabitants had to take an oath of allegiance to the Dutch authorities.[34]

Additional settlements also arose along the Hudson River, the most important of which were at Esopus and Schenectady. Esopus, named after the Esopus Indians, was located about fifty miles below Fort Orange. Its rich soil attracted some Dutch settlers from Rensselaerswyck as early as 1652. In August 1657, the reverends Johannes Megapolensis and Samuel Drisius of New Amsterdam wrote that the region around Esopus was "exceeding fine country," and that the "Dutch families settled there . . . are doing very well. They hold Sunday meetings and then one or the other of them reads from the Postilla [Book of Homilies]."[35] By 1660, Esopus had grown to such an extent that it received its own minister, Dominie Hermanus Blom. In the following year, Governor Stuyvesant gave the settlement a municipal charter and named it Wiltwyck, which was changed to Kingston shortly after the English occupied New Netherland in 1664.[36]

Schenectady's origin was very similar to that of the Dutch settlement at Esopus. In 1661, Arent Van Curler, who had served as Kiliaen Van Rensselaer's capable agent for many years, and several residents of the area around Fort Orange received permission from Stuyvesant to purchase some nearby land from the Indians for the purpose of founding a new settlement. The land, which was known as the "Great Mohawk Flat" or the "Great Mohawk Plain," was located about fifteen miles northwest of Fort Orange. Like the area around Esopus, the rich soil of this region appealed to the farmers of Rensselaerswyck. In 1662, Van Curler led a small band of settlers into the region and laid out farms and a town which became known as Schenectady.[37]

As might be expected, the influx of new settlers led to the further colonization of Manhattan Island. On March 4, 1658, Stuyvesant and his council gave notice that "for the further promotion of agriculture, for the security of this Island and the cattle pasturing thereon, as well as for the further relief and expansion of this City Amsterdam, in New Netherland, they have resolved to form a new village or Settlement." The new settlement was to be located at the north end of the island, and was to be called Nieuw Haarlem, after the city of Haarlem in Holland. Terms for settlement included a promise that each villager would receive from eighteen to twenty-four morgens of arable land and six to eight morgens of meadow on condition that he pay within three years eight guilders for each morgen of tillable land received.

Additional promises to the residents of Nieuw Haarlem included a degree of self-government, a garrison of twelve to fifteen soldiers when needed, and half the cost of maintaining "a good, pious, orthodox Minister" when the village had grown to twenty families. Provisions were also made for a good road, to be built with the Company's Negroes, "so that people can travel hither and thither on horseback and with a wagon," and a "Ferry and a suitable Scow" for "neighborly correspondence" with the mainland.[38] The terms were apparently satisfactory, because there were soon about thirty adult male residents, mostly heads of families, living in the new village. A few adventurous souls soon crossed the Harlem River and settled in the region today known as the Bronx and Yonkers.

❊　❊　❊　❊

By 1664, when New Netherland fell to England, the Dutch had established numerous settlements in North America, but only one was of moderate size. This was New Amsterdam, which had a population of about fifteen hundred. Next in importance was Fort Orange, but it was still a tiny wilderness community with a population of only a few hundred people. There were also small Dutch settlements scattered up and down the Hudson River as well as several on western Long Island. In addition, there were two settlements to the south on the Delaware River, namely, New Amstel and Plockhoy's community. The total white population of New Netherland in 1664 has been estimated at between eight and ten thousand, about two-thirds of whom were Hollanders.

CHAPTER III

# From Dutch to English Rule

ON AUGUST 28, 1664, FOUR BRITISH MEN-OF-WAR WITH SOLDIERS aboard appeared off New Amsterdam; a few days later, the colony surrendered to the English. The reasons for the loss of New Netherland were many, but the colony's failure to attract and to retain Dutch settlers was the primary cause. By contrast, the English went to America in much greater numbers and were more inclined to remain there. Without a reversal of this situation, it became only a matter of time before New Netherland would be "swallowed up" by the English. As a result of immigration and natural increase, New England had grown to nearly twenty thousand people in 1640 and to over fifty thousand in 1664. In addition, there were several thousand more English colonists to the south in Virginia and Maryland. New Netherland, on the other hand, had fewer than ten thousand white inhabitants in 1664.[1]

The failure of New Netherland to attract settlers poses several questions for the historian. Were there factors present in New Netherland which tended to keep the Dutch from American shores? Did specific circumstances in the mother country tend to discourage them from emigrating? Why did such elaborate plans as the patroon system, the utopian scheme of Plockhoy, and the city of Amsterdam's colony of New Amstel bring so few settlers to New Netherland? As is generally true of complex historical problems, there are no simple answers to these questions.

Various economic policies practiced in New Netherland by the West India Company made it difficult to attract colonists, particularly before 1640, and to keep them there after arrival. The first permanent settlers in New Netherland had to subscribe to a set of twenty-one articles known as the Provisional Regula-

[ 28 ]

tions. Although some of these articles contained guarantees designed to encourage emigration, several provisions had the opposite effect. Each settler, for example, was told where he had to reside and what crops he could cultivate. Trade *within* the colony was permitted but exportable goods could only be sold to the Company. There also were restrictions placed on establishing industries that might compete with similar enterprises in the mother country. The monopoly that the West India Company at first enjoyed over the fur trade also discouraged emigration to New Netherland during the colony's formative years. So, too, did various duties levied on imports and exports.[2]

There were also various features present in the patroon system inaugurated in 1629 that were not conducive to attracting new settlers. As was noted in the previous chapter, the patroons were given privileges which limited even such activities as fishing, hunting, and milling by the people who settled on their estates. In addition, the patroons received extensive judicial rights over their colonists. In view of such restrictions, it is understandable why a Dutch historian of a half century ago stated that Hollanders did not go in great numbers to New Netherland to settle on the patroonships because "they wanted to remain free, and not be serfs."[3]

The narrow base on which the government rested, like the economic restrictions, also prevented New Netherland from attracting and retaining large numbers of settlers. In October, 1644, a committee of leading men in the colony wrote several of the Company officials in Amsterdam that "it is impossible ever to settle this country until a different system be introduced here."[4] A remonstrance of 1649 to the States General was just as bold when it stated, "To describe it in one word . . . it is *bad government,* with its attendants and consequences, that is, to the best of our knowledge, the true and only foundation stone of the decay and ruin of New Netherland."[5]

The emphasis the West India Company placed on trade, particularly before 1640, also restricted the population growth of New Netherland. Although settlement was a more certain way of maintaining control of a colony, profits from colonization accrued slowly. The first years of colonization were expensive because of the need to transport settlers as well as cattle and agricultural implements. Maintenance of troops for the protection of widely scattered colonists was also costly. Trade, on the other hand, involved a minimum of expense and held out the promise of immediate profits. For several years, therefore, the Company brought in only enough farmers to satisfy the agricultural needs of the traders and officials, and a few artisans to take care of special needs, such as the repair of ships. "All other ends were incidental or superfluous."[6]

The fact that the claims of the Dutch West India Company ranged over such a large part of the globe—West Africa and Angola, the Caribbean, and the Americas—was also unfortunate for New Netherland. As one writer recently pointed out, "the West India Company had half of the world for its oyster."[7] The expenditures involved in Dutch efforts to take and hold Brazil between 1623 and 1654 far exceeded the profit that Holland derived from the region. Considerable time and money were also wasted in attempts to settle Guiana and some of the smaller islands in the Caribbean where Dutch entrepreneurs hoped to reap fortunes from sugar plantations and the slave trade.[8]

Given a choice of interests and a variety of places to practice those interests, the Company looked upon New Netherland as one of its least desirable holdings. The name West India Company indicates where the trade interests of the Dutch lay, namely, in the tropical regions. This was clearly shown in a report of June, 1645, which gave the number of ships required annually for some of the Company holdings as follows: Guinea, 4; Angola, 12; Brazil, 24; New Netherland and Curaçao, 2.[9] In fairness to the directors of the Company, it must be pointed out that with the exception of furs, most products available in New Netherland were also available in the mother country, or could be more easily acquired nearer home. A recent study has shown, for example, that even lumber and lumber products could be imported more cheaply from the Baltic region than from New Netherland, although such items were occasionally sent from America to Holland.[10]

In addition to its failure to attract immigrants, New Netherland also had the problem of remigration. As early as August, 1628, a report came out of the colony that a number of Walloons were returning "to the Fatherland" either because they had fulfilled the terms of their contract or because they were no longer of service to the Company. Similarly, of the eighty-two known settlers who went to Rensselaerswyck between 1630 and 1639, nearly half either returned home or settled elsewhere in the colony.[11] In February, 1643, the directors complained that opening up the trade in New Netherland "produces no true effect . . . inasmuch as many will go thither to trade without acquiring a domicile there; and therefore, population scarcely increases there."[12] The turnover among Company officials, including the clergy, was also high. One of the complaints included in the "Remonstrance of New Netherland," sent by some of Stuyvesant's critics to the States General in 1649, stated that the Company "from the first . . . sought to stock this land with their own employees, which was a great mistake, for when their time was out they returned home, taking nothing with them except a little in their purses and a bad name for the country."[13]

Periodic problems with the Indians also hindered the development of the colony. News about the massacre at Swanendael about 1631, Kieft's Indian War of 1640–45, and the two Indian uprisings on the lower Hudson during Stuyvesant's administration discouraged emigration from Holland. Such incidents also had a demoralizing effect on the settlers and caused some of them to return to the fatherland. Roger Williams, who was in New Amsterdam at the height of some Indian troubles in the fall of 1643, recorded that "mine Eyes saw . . . ye Flights & Hurries of Men, Women & Children, the present Remoovall of all yt Could for Holland."[14]

There are no figures available that show the total number of colonists who returned to Holland. Some idea of the remigration movement can be ascertained, however, by noting that the ship *Princesse*, sailing from New Amsterdam for Holland on August 16, 1647, carried about a hundred persons, and if one allows for a crew of twenty-five it means that seventy-five people were leaving the colony. This is a significant figure, considering the small size of New Netherland's population. Because Kieft's Indian War had already ended in 1645, this particular departure could not be ascribed to the Indian menace.[15]

In view of the need for more settlers, and under pressure from the States General as well as from colonists of New Netherland, the directors of the West India Company gradually loosened some of the restrictions on trade and colonization. The Company monopoly on the fur trade was abolished in 1639, and trade between the colony and the mother country was opened to private individuals in 1645. By 1650, colonists were also allowed to export agricultural products to Brazil and other places within the jurisdiction of the West India Company. In 1652, they were permitted to import slaves directly from Angola, Africa, in their own ships. The colonial population was also increased by developments noted previously, including a new charter for patroonships in 1640, the influx of refugees from Brazil, and the arrival of children from the orphanages and poorhouses of the Netherlands.

Although economic reforms and other developments helped increase the population of New Netherland, Dutch emigration to the colony continued to lag far behind the hopes of the officials of the West India Company. In explaining why the Dutch never went to America in greater numbers during the seventeenth century, several writers on New Netherland history have stated that the people of Holland were too content with living conditions at home to seek a new life elsewhere. As one historian put it, "The failure of New Netherland is a testimony to the successful organization of life in the old Netherlands."[16] Another writer placed so much stress on this that he entitled a chapter on the fall of New Netherland "The Comfortable Do Not Emigrate."[17]

There is no doubt that the flourishing trade and industry of the Netherlands made it difficult to convince large numbers of Hollanders to seek a new life for themselves in a wilderness three thousand miles across the ocean. Generally speaking, however, American historians have painted too rosy a picture of conditions in the mother country. Many people in Holland during the seventeenth century lived on the borderline of poverty. The increasing number of laws and ordinances issued during this period against begging, not only in the cities but also in the countryside, indicates that not everyone shared in Holland's "Golden Age." One of the best recent histories of the

Netherlands states that against the rather large group of citizens of substantial and moderate means

stood a much more numerous class of humble people, who continuously lived on the edge of famine. It is amazing . . . how it was possible that at the same time that the national wealth showed a strong growth through the expansion of trade and industry, especially in Holland and Zeeland, during the first half of the seventeenth century, that on the other hand poverty among large groups of the population increased rather than decreased.[18]

In view of the fact that poor economic conditions in the Netherlands prompted tens of thousands to emigrate to America during the nineteenth century, why did not the same thing happen during the seventeenth century when conditions were every bit as bad and perhaps worse? Some answers to this question are obvious. Economic and political conditions in America were more inviting during the nineteenth century than they were two centuries earlier. The Hollanders who came over later did not come to an untamed wilderness like New Netherland, but to a more developed country. Even the Dutch immigrants of the nineteenth century who came to the timbered regions of Michigan or to the virgin prairie lands of Iowa did not experience the dangers and uncertainties met by their countrymen two hundred years earlier. Obviously, many Hollanders of the seventeenth century, no matter how difficult their situation in the homeland, could see no reason to exchange it for a life that was just as difficult three thousand miles across the ocean.

There was, however, another reason why Hollanders were averse to emigrating to New Netherland during the seventeenth century. Because of the reputation that the Dutch had for industriousness, ability as farmers, knowledge about draining marshlands, and skills in certain trades, European governments vied with one another in efforts to attract Dutch emigrants. With opportunities nearer home and under more civilized conditions, why should Hollanders who were interested in bettering themselves make the dangerous crossing of the Atlantic and live in the wilderness on some river bank in America?

The Dutch were particularly encouraged to settle in England, but fairly large settlements of Hollanders could also be found in Sweden, Denmark, Holstein, Prussia, and France during the seventeenth century. According to one authority, so many Hollanders settled in other European countries that even today there are more traces of these immigrants in Europe than in America.[19] They were of various backgrounds, including farmers, laborers, businessmen, skilled tradesmen, and seamen. It was unfortunate for New Netherland, which was in desperate need of colonists, that more of them did not settle there.

Religious toleration as practiced in the Netherlands also tended to discourage emigration. Although there were some restrictions on public worship in the Netherlands during the seventeenth century, considerable freedom in private worship was permitted, even for Catholics and Jews. Such toleration tended to discourage Dutch religious groups from going to the New World in large numbers, as happened with the Puritans and Catholics of England.[20]

The only serious period of religious intolerance in the Netherlands during the seventeenth century occurred after the great Synod of Dordrecht in 1618–19. This ecclesiastical assembly had been convened to hear charges against the followers of Jacobus Arminius, who had favored a moderate view on predestination. When the Synod decided against the Arminians, the latter experienced the wrath of the orthodox Calvinist dominies. The period of religious intolerance, however, was of short duration, lasting only about a decade. Furthermore, Arminianism appealed primarily to intellectuals, like Hugo Grotius, who preferred exile at the courts of other European countries such as Sweden "to a trek into the wilderness."[21] Those few members of the lower classes who were attracted to Arminianism also preferred living in a neighboring country to migrating overseas.

Because of the reluctance of the Dutch to emigrate to America, the West India Company had to rely on foreign settlers to help populate New Netherland. The heterogeneous makeup of the settlers further weakened the colony and made it more vulnerable to invasion. It was this fear that prompted the directors in Amsterdam to send the following instructions to Stuyvesant concerning the English in November, 1653: "We cannot trust any of that nation residing under our jurisdiction. Their immigrating and having favors granted to them must therefore be restricted henceforth, that we may not nourish serpents in our bosom, who finally might devour our hearts."[22]

According to one writer, about 30 percent of New Netherland's population was non-Dutch in 1664.[23] In some regions, of course, the percentage was higher. Of the eighty-two known immigrants who went to Rensselaerswyck between the years 1630 and 1639, about thirty of them, or nearly 40 percent, were non-Dutch, including Englishmen, Scandinavians, and Germans.[24] The Jesuit missionary Isaac Jogues wrote in 1646, after a visit to New Amsterdam, that on "the island Manhate, and its environs, there may well be four or five hundred men of different sects and nations: the Director General told me that there were men of eighteen different languages."[25]

As New Netherland continued to fail in its efforts to attract more settlers, its position became increasingly precarious. Although the rate of immigration began increasing after 1650, it would have taken a long time for the population of New Netherland to equal that of the neighboring English colonies. Unfortunately for the Dutch, time was on the side of the English.

The first major loss for the colony was the Connecticut Valley, where the Dutch, because of lack of colonists, had to satisfy themselves with merely establishing one or two trading posts. Their weakness made it easy for the English to begin settling there in large numbers during the 1630's. Dutch protests against this "invasion" were ignored by the English, who in 1635 went so far as to found Hartford almost next door to the Dutch post known as Fort Good Hope. The movement into the Connecticut Valley was followed by the founding of several English settlements on eastern Long Island, which was also claimed by New Netherland. Powerless to resist these encroachments, the Dutch in 1650, by a settlement known as the Treaty of Hartford, gave up all effective claim to the Connecticut Valley and much of Long Island. The treaty was not honored by the English, who continued to settle to the west of the Hartford demarcation line.[26]

During the Cromwellian period of the 1650's, the English began pursuing a more active mercantile policy overseas. Through the Navigation Acts and by strengthening the navy, Oliver

Cromwell was determined to force the Dutch to share the seas with the English. It is therefore not surprising that when monarchy was restored in England, the directors of the West India Company were hopeful that commercial and diplomatic relations with England would improve. On September 20, 1660, they wrote Governor Stuyvesant: "Our reason for having a better opinion of our English neighbors is the change in government, which has taken place by the restoration of King Charles II; better things may be expected from his honesty and righteousness, than from the former unlawful government."[27]

The hopes of the directors, which were shared by Stuyvesant, were doomed to disappointment. On March 22, 1664, King Charles II granted the territory between the Connecticut and Delaware rivers—thus, all of New Netherland—to his brother James, Duke of York and Albany. Determined to make good his claim to this territory and anxious to humble the Dutch, whose commercial empire he had long envied, the Duke of York dispatched a fleet of four frigates carrying a military force of about four hundred men to American waters in order to take possession of New Netherland. The British fleet appeared off New Amsterdam on August 28, 1664, and was soon joined by additional forces from New England and eastern Long Island.

Defense against the English was hopeless: the walls of Fort Amsterdam were weak from lack of upkeep, less than a third of the gunpowder was serviceable, the soldiers in the fort numbered only about one hundred fifty, and not more than two hundred fifty civilians were capable of bearing arms. In addition, because of a shortage of foodstuffs, the settlement could withstand a siege of only a few days. The arrival of the West India Company slave ship *Gideon* with two hundred ninety slaves a few days before the appearance of the British fleet added to the food problem of New Amsterdam. Furthermore, Fort Amsterdam had been built primarily to withstand attacks from the Indians rather than from a British naval squadron.

Despite these weaknesses, Stuyvesant wanted to fight. Fortunately, cooler heads prevailed and New Amsterdam surrendered on September 5. The town was thereupon renamed New York—a name that was also extended to the colony—in honor of the new proprietor, the Duke of York. A few weeks later, the settlement at Fort Orange was renamed Albany in honor of another of the proprietor's titles.[28]

Although New Amsterdam and its neighboring settlements fell without use of force, such was not the case in the south on the Delaware River. Meeting with some resistance from the Dutch at New Amstel, Sir Robert Carr, the commander in charge of the operation there, resorted to strong measures and permitted his soldiers to plunder the Dutch settlement. Plockhoy's community suffered a similar fate. Despite its having been founded on the principle of brotherly love, the utopian settlement was destroyed "to a very naile" and many of its inhabitants scattered.[29]

Generally speaking, the Dutch colonists accepted British sovereignty gracefully in 1664. They had not been particularly happy under the rule of the West India Company, and were therefore not too averse to a change in government. The trade advantages that could be enjoyed under the British Navigation Acts undoubtedly made the transfer of allegiance more acceptable to Dutch mercantile interests in the colony than otherwise would have been the case. The leniency of the surrender terms also made the Dutch less hostile about accepting English rule. The Hollanders were given freedom to leave the colony and dispose of their property as they saw fit, while those who wished to stay were given the same citizenship rights as the English. Freedom of religion was promised and the Dutch were permitted to maintain the same close relations with the Reformed Church in the Netherlands that existed before 1664. Furthermore, inhabitants of the Netherlands were free to emigrate to the former Dutch colony if they wished.[30]

Even the doughty Peter Stuyvesant reconciled himself to living under the English. In May, 1665, he left for Holland to explain to the officials of the West India Company the reasons for the loss of New Netherland, but he returned to New York in 1668 and lived out the rest of his days on Manhattan Island. He died in 1672, and was buried beneath the chapel on his farm.

The Netherlands retook and briefly held a part of their former colony during the Third Anglo-Dutch War (1672–74). A Dutch fleet, carrying sixteen hundred men, under the command of Cornelis Evertsen, Jr., sailed into New York bay on

August 7, 1673. After a brief exchange of fire, New York surrendered to a Dutch landing party of six hundred men led by
Captain Anthony Colve. About a week after the fall of New
York, Albany was also occupied by the Dutch, as were other
towns on the Hudson and on western Long Island. Once more
there was a change of names: the colony again became known
as New Netherland, New York was renamed New Orange, and
Albany was called Willemstadt. A provisional government was
established with Captain Colve as governor.[31]

The Dutch magistrates of New Orange were very optimistic
about the future of New Netherland. On September 8, 1673,
they wrote as follows to the States General:

The reduction and recovery of this Province will, in time, be able to
confer, exclusive of the reputation and respect, great profit and
considerable advantage on the state of our beloved Fatherland . . .
this Province, which almost wants for nothing but people to promote
agriculture and farming, would be so advanced as in time to become,
for Fatherland, a granary and magazine of many necessaries which
are ordinarily imported.[32]

The communication pointed out numerous other advantages
of New Netherland: furnishing the Dutch colonies of Curaçao
and Surinam with certain necessities, serving as a strategic
location in time of war, trading in furs and tobacco, and providing a refuge where Hollanders who had been ruined by
the recent French invasion of the Netherlands could begin a
new life. The Dutch spokesmen of New Orange informed the
States General, however, that the latter would have to give the
colony "a helping hand" to achieve these ends, and warned
that if this were not forthcoming, the inhabitants of New
Netherland would have "nothing else to expect than total ruin
and destruction."[33]

Unfortunately for the magistrates of New Orange and other
like-minded colonists, the reoccupation of New Netherland lasted
only about six months—too brief to be of any real significance
for the future of the Dutch in America. By the Treaty of
Westminster (February 19, 1674), the province was restored
to England, although the formal transfer did not occur until
a few months later. The transfer took place quite peacefully, caus-

ing little more difficulty in 1674 than it had a decade earlier.

The majority of Dutch colonists stayed in their former place of residence after the arrival of the English, but some of them left after the two transfers of sovereignty in 1664 and 1674. A number of soldiers and a few settlers returned to the Netherlands, and others went to the Dutch colony of Surinam. Two shiploads of Hollanders left New York for South Carolina in 1674, while other Hollanders moved across the bay from New York and Long Island to northern New Jersey. Although both South Carolina and New Jersey were also under English rule, the migrants apparently thought that English authority in these regions would be less direct than in the province of New York.

Dutch emigration to America after the fall of New Netherland was small, but no figures are available to give even an estimate of the number of people involved. Although it is sometimes possible to calculate how many nationals emigrated from a given country to America during a specific time period by examining the passenger lists of ships leaving the country's ports, this method cannot be applied to the Netherlands. This is because many of the emigrants who departed from Dutch ports came from other countries. For example, of the 319 immigrant ships that arrived at Philadelphia between 1727 and 1775, 253 came by way of Rotterdam. So numerous at times were the foreign immigrants who embarked for America from Dutch ports that the States General had to take special measures to regulate the traffic.[34]

The steady stream of non-Dutch emigrants who departed for America from ports in the Netherlands undoubtedly caused some Hollanders to join in the exodus to the "promised land." Governor Thomas Dongan of New York reported on February 22, 1687, that during the past years "from Holland are come several Dutch Familys."[35] Many of those who emigrated from the Netherlands between 1664 and the American Revolution did so as individual persons and families. Most of them became ordinary laborers or tillers of the soil. They included, however, a few professional people, such as Dr. Johannes Van Beuren, who came to America in 1702 and was made director of New York City's first hospital, as well as a few dozen ministers who came to serve the Dutch Reformed churches, of which there

were about a hundred at the time of the American Revolution.
There were also a number of Dutch businessmen who estab-
lished themselves at such colonial ports as New York, Boston,
Baltimore, and Charleston.

In addition to the single persons and families who made their
way from the Netherlands to North America on a more or
less individual basis after the fall of New Netherland, two
organized groups of Dutch settlers reached American shores.
One of these was a mixture of Quakers and Mennonites who
settled near Philadelphia at the invitation of William Penn. The
latter was anxious to populate his colony of Pennsylvania, and
therefore made a concerted effort to recruit colonists on the
European continent, especially in the Netherlands and Germany.

*Een Kort Bericht ... van de Provintie ofte Landschap Penn-
Sylvania Genaemt, Leggende in America* (Some Brief Information on the Province or Region Called Pennsylvania Located
in America), published in 1681, was typical of the promotional
literature distributed in the Netherlands. It described such matters as the economic advantages of Pennsylvania, the spiritual
and social ideals on which the colony would be founded, and
the type of settlers that Penn hoped to procure for its development. According to the *Kort Bericht,* Hollanders could obtain
land in Pennsylvania at a cost of one hundred pounds per five
thousand acres, plus an English shilling quitrent for each
hundred acres purchased, but immigrants of limited economic
means could rent up to two hundred acres for one English
penny per acre.[36]

In addition to distributing literature such as the *Kort Bericht,*
several Dutch friends of William Penn spread the news in the
Netherlands about Pennsylvania. Benjamin Furley, an English
Quaker who had a mercantile business at Rotterdam and was
married to a Dutch woman, also acted as a kind of land agent
for the Quaker leader.

The idea of emigrating from the Netherlands to Pennsylvania
appealed to only two elements of the Dutch population—the
Quakers and the Mennonites. Dutch sympathy for William
Penn's socioreligious ideas dated back several years. Numerous
Quaker tracts had been translated into Dutch, and Quaker
missionaries began visiting Holland in 1655. Penn himself made

a missionary tour there in 1671 and again in 1677. On the latter occasion, he visited about twenty towns, preaching to the people about Quakerism and encouraging the formation of Quaker Meetings.[37] Dutch Mennonites were attracted to Quakerism because of similarity of beliefs, including pacificism, separation of church and state, freedom of conscience, aversion to dogma and ritual, and simplicity of dress and daily living.

In 1684–85, several letters written by Hollanders who had recently settled in Pennsylvania were published and circulated in the Netherlands in the hope of encouraging Dutch emigration to Penn's colony. Included among this correspondence was an interesting letter by Cornelius Bom, who originally came from Haarlem, the Netherlands, where he worked as a baker—the same vocation he followed in Pennsylvania. Bom had nothing but praise for his new home:

The country is healthful and fruitful, and the conditions are all favorable for its becoming through the blessing of the Lord and the diligence of men a good land—better than Holland. It is not so good now but daily grows better and better. The increase here is so great that, I believe, nowhere in history can be found such an instance of growth in a new country. It is as if the doors had opened for its progress. . . . I am above many, in good shape, and do not consider that I have less of my own than when I left Holland, and am in all respects very well-to-do.[38]

Despite the appeal that William Penn's religious and social ideas had for many Hollanders, and despite the promotional campaign for obtaining settlers, the number of Quakers and Mennonites who left their homes in the Netherlands for Pennsylvania was small. Penn achieved greater success in getting Hollanders living in the German Rhineland to become a part of his "Holy Experiment" in America.

As was noted earlier, although the Dutch never showed much interest in emigrating to colonial America, it was not unusual for them to settle in other parts of Europe. The German Rhineland especially appealed to Dutch emigrants. This region at various times in the past had been very close to the Netherlands culturally and economically, and, in some instances, even politically. The County of Meurs (Mörs), for example, had for many years been a personal possession of the House of Orange, and numerous Hollanders had settled there—particularly in the vicinity of the town of Krefeld, located a few miles from the Dutch border. Even after 1702, when, after the death of William III of Orange, Meurs reverted to the elector of Prussia, Dutch influence continued to be strong in the area; indeed, according to one authority, the Dutch language was still spoken in parts of Meurs as late as 1870. Numerous Hollanders also migrated farther up the Rhine to the Palatinate region. Many of the inhabitants of Kriesheim (Kriegsheim), near Worms, for example, were of Dutch descent, and Dutch influence among the Mennonite congregations of northwestern Germany remained strong until the close of the nineteenth century.[39]

Penn used the same methods to encourage the Quakers and Mennonites of the Rhineland to emigrate to Pennsylvania as he employed in the Netherlands. Promotional literature was circulated among the people, and visits were made by such agents as Furley of Rotterdam. There were two reasons why these efforts met with greater success in the Rhineland than in Holland. First, because many of these people or their immediate ancestors had emigrated once before, i.e., from the Netherlands to the Rhineland, they were more footloose and adventurous than most Hollanders and thus more willing to risk a journey across the Atlantic to begin a new life. Second, and of greater significance, the inhabitants of the Rhineland were restless because of social and religious problems that still lingered there following the devastating Thirty Years' War of 1618–48 and other conflicts.

A small group of immigrants from the Netherlands and the German Rhineland arrived in Pennsylvania in August, 1683, followed by another party of thirty-four settlers from Krefeld a few months later. On October 12, 1683, William Penn issued a warrant for six thousand acres of land about ten miles from Philadelphia to the Krefelders and to a German named Francis Daniel Pastorius. The latter had arrived in Pennsylvania a short time earlier to locate a site for establishing a religious haven for German Pietists. The tract was divided equally between Pastorius and the immigrants from Krefeld. In this way, the settlement that became known as Germantown got started. Additional settlers arrived during the years that followed.

Geographically, most of the early arrivals were of German origin, but ethnically and culturally many of them were Dutch. Consequently, despite references to Germantown being the first permanent German settlement in America, the atmosphere of the settlement was more Dutch than German at first. Most of the names of its first inhabitants were Dutch, as were those of many of the immigrants who followed. Of the one hundred seventy-five residents living there in 1690, all but eight or ten of them came from the Netherlands or from the towns of Krefeld and Kriesheim. Those coming from Krefeld were nearly all of Dutch descent, while those who hailed from Kriesheim were a mixture of Dutch and German-speaking Swiss. Several of the early documents of the colony and many of the religious books used by its residents were written in the Dutch language. Similarly, many of the Mennonites of Germantown and elsewhere in Pennsylvania looked to the Netherlands for assistance and guidance until late in the eighteenth century.[40] These facts prompted one authority to state that the name Dutchtown, or Hollandtown, or Netherlandtown, or New Krefeld would have been more correct than Germantown.[41]

The question must therefore be raised as to why, until recent years there has been so little mention of the role that the Dutch played in the founding of Germantown. The explanation, according to one writer, is that the German residents had a spokesman, Francis Daniel Pastorius, and the Dutch did not.

The Dutch founders of German town had no literary chronicler of their own to sound their praises and preserve their story, their character, and their fame to posterity. [Instead], a gifted German writer, Pastorius, who was the only university-trained and legal and literary man among them, wrote of them naturally from the German point of view.[42]

Pastorius, who came from Frankfort, Germany, was not particularly impressed by the Dutch, and therefore, in his writings, was likely to overlook the role they played in the founding of Germantown. In a letter of March 7, 1684, he wrote to acquaintances in Germany, "send only Germans, for the Hollanders (as sad experience has taught me) are not so easily satisfied, which in this new land is a very necessary quality."[43] Germantown remained primarily Dutch until about 1710, when, as a result of greatly increased German migration and intermarriage, the Dutch atmosphere began to disappear rapidly.[44]

At about the same time that Dutch Quakers and Mennonites were emigrating to Pennsylvania in the latter part of the seventeenth century, an organized group of Dutch Labadists were attempting to create a utopian settlement in nearby Maryland. The Labadists were adherents of a Dutch quietist sect founded by Jean de Labadie. De Labadie, who was born in 1610 in southern France, had prepared himself for the priesthood, but as a result of Jansenist influence and the study of John Calvin's writings, later joined the French Reformed church in 1650. About 1660, he went to Holland, where he served a Walloon Reformed congregation at Middleburg, in the province of Zeeland. De Labadie's theological and social ideas soon got him in trouble with the religious authorities, and he was suspended as a schismatic. Ostracized by Dutch society for their religious beliefs and unusual social customs, most of De Labadie's followers eventually isolated themselves at Wieuwerd, in the province of Friesland. Here they worshiped in an austere Calvinist manner and practiced communistic living. Small Labadist groups were also located at The Hague, Rotterdam, and elsewhere in the Netherlands.[45]

The Labadists soon gave consideration to establishing daughter communities overseas. They were motivated in this partly by the poverty of their members and the discrimination they experienced in the Netherlands, but also by a desire to convert the natives of the New World to the evangelical Christian faith. Their first attempt at colonization occurred in the Dutch colony of Surinam on the northwest coast of South America, but in June, 1679, two prominent Labadists, Jasper Danckaerts and Pieter Sluyter, were sent from Wieuwerd to investigate the prospects for founding a settlement somewhere in the English colonies of North America. Ten months were spent traveling through the middle colonies before they selected a site in what is today Cecil County, Maryland.[46]

After a brief visit in the Netherlands, Danckaerts and Sluyter returned to America in 1683, bringing with them the nucleus for a Labadist colony. The settlement, sometimes known as the "Labadie Tract," comprised about four thousand acres. It was also frequently called "Bohemia Manor" because it had been part of a larger plantation belonging to a well-to-do Bohemian named Augustine Herrman. The original band of settlers was joined from time to time by other Labadists from the Netherlands as well as by a few converts from among the Dutch population of New York.[47]

The Dutch Labadists of Bohemia Manor, like their co-religionists in the Netherlands, lived in a very simple manner and followed several communist practices. When the English Quaker minister Samuel Bownas visited them in the late summer of 1702, he recorded that they held

all things in common, respecting their household affairs, so that none could claim any more right than another to any part of their stock, whether in trade or husbandry; and if any had a mind to join with them, whether rich or poor, they must put what they had in the common stock, and if they afterwards had a mind to leave the society, they must likewise leave what they brought, and go out empty handed.

Bownas added that the Labadists "carried on something of the manufactory of linen, and had a very large plantation of corn, tobacco, flax and hemp, together with cattle of several kinds."[48]

Divine worship among the Labadists in America was also very simple, being led by what were called "speakers." The Labadists considered themselves God's elect, even to the point of claiming that their children were free from original sin. The latter belief was especially a major departure from orthodox Dutch Reformed theology. The Labadists also placed greater emphasis on the role of the Holy Spirit in men's lives than did the strict Reformed theologians. Furthermore, the Labadists made no distinction among the days of the week, considering all days equally holy in God's sight. Believing themselves to be members of God's elect, they hoped to keep themselves pure by separating from the world.[49]

The utopian colony that the Labadists established in America had little chance of success. Their austere living habits and cloistered way of life made it difficult to win converts and thereby increase the size of the settlement. Consequently, at its height, Bohemia Manor never had more than about a hundred people, including women and children. The failure of the Labadists to practice what they preached also caused internal dissension. Their avowed purpose of Christianizing the Indians was never pursued very diligently. Furthermore, although they criticized slavery, they bought slaves and used them to cultivate their plantations; and although they officially opposed the use of tobacco, they did not hesitate to grow it and sell it to others for profit. Meanwhile, the decline of the Mother Church at Wieuwerd, Friesland, also had a disheartening effect on the inhabitants of Bohemia Manor.

Eventually, their communist views on property holding were revised. When the Labadie Tract was broken up in 1698 into privately owned parcels of land, the leader of the community, Pieter Sluyter, ended up as a wealthy property holder with about one-fourth of the land, causing still further friction. Dominie Selyns of the Dutch Reformed church at New York City shortly thereafter reported to the Classis of Amsterdam that the Labadists of New Bohemia "are divided among themselves" and predicted that "in a few years they will have turned to nothing."[50] His prediction proved correct. When Bownas made another visit to the settlement in 1728, he wrote in his journal that the "people were all scattered and gone, and nothing of them remaining of a religious community in that shape."[51]

✳    ✳    ✳    ✳

The fall of New Netherland in 1664 was due to several causes, but the lack of settlers was a fundamental weakness. As a consequence, it became only a matter of time before the more numerous English annexed the colony. The transfer of sovereignty did not bring an end to Dutch influence; indeed, despite their small numbers in 1664 and despite the arrival of few new immigrants from Holland before the Revolution, Dutch culture not only survived but made its greatest impression on New York and New Jersey *after* the English occupation. Moreover, as will be explained in the following chapter, persons of Dutch descent spread outward in significant numbers from the various nuclei of settlements that had been established during the New Netherland period.

# CHAPTER IV

## Voortrekkers and Boeren

MANY DUTCHMEN IN THE AMERICAN COLONIES, ALTHOUGH basically conservative and opposed to change, found it necessary to leave their place of birth and seek new domiciles. Generally, such moves did not involve a great distance. Young men and newly established families merely moved outward from the settlements that had been established during the New Netherland period and advanced along the valleys and into the adjoining forests. Some Dutchmen, however, became true American pioneers, or *voortrekkers*, whose migrations of several hundred miles placed them on the outer perimeter of the frontier. Most of the migrants had been farmers, or *boeren*, in their former locations and continued this occupation in their new homes.

There were several reasons why Dutch colonists sometimes shifted their place of residence after 1664. Those living on Manhattan Island and western Long Island were frequently uneasy in English society, and moved to more isolated areas in hopes that conditions would be different. Others moved because of apprehension concerning the growing strength of the Anglican Church. Some of this fear was allayed when the Dutch Reformed congregation on Manhattan Island received its own charter in 1696, but apprehension continued to exist among the Dutch Reformed element elsewhere. The Leisler Troubles of 1689–91 also caused some migration, particularly from Long Island, where pro-Leisler feelings were strong.

An examination of the genealogical history of Dutch-American families indicates that a kind of insatiable wanderlust caused some individuals to push continually out toward the frontier. Hendrik Banta and his family, for example, made several moves: first from Bergen County to Somerset County, New Jersey, in the 1750's; then to York County, Pennsylvania, in the 1760's; and finally to Kentucky about 1780. Similarly, Joris Brinckerhoff moved with his family from Hackensack, New Jersey, to York County, Pennsylvania, in 1770. Later, in the 1790's, four of Joris's sons with most of their families moved to Cayuga County, New York. So, too, the descendants of Joannes Nevius of Long Island scattered themselves during the eighteenth century by settling in northern New York, northeastern New Jersey, central Kentucky, and various parts of Pennsylvania.[1]

The primary reason, however, why some Hollanders moved about in the American colonies was a desire to obtain cheap, fertile land. A decline in soil fertility resulting from "an exhausting cropping system without adequate fertilization" along with a rise in land values in the older settlements was always a factor in causing farmers to look for new lands,[2] but the demand was especially great among the Dutch. Although the common agricultural unit was from one to two hundred acres in size, Dutch farmers—often utilizing slave labor—sometimes brought several hundred acres under cultivation on a single farm. The large size of Dutch families also increased the need for more land as sons reached adulthood and required farms of their own.

Several procedures were open to a person wishing to obtain land. If open territory existed in the region where he planned to move, he could patent land for himself, as several Hollanders from Long Island did in the Hudson Valley between Fishkill and Albany. Another method was to purchase land from speculators who patented thousands of acres with the intention of reselling them at a profit to Dutch and other farmers. A third means was leasing in return for rent in kind, i.e., giving annually to the landlord a certain amount of livestock, poultry, or grain depending on the terms of the leasehold.

A memorandum of 1650 from the Secretary of New Netherland to the directors of the West India Company gives considerable information about the manner in which wilderness land was transformed into farm land during the colonial period. The procedure outlined in the memorandum is especially interesting because it held true for Dutch pioneers moving into frontier regions long after the fall of New Netherland. In fact, the procedures suggested in 1650 were similar to those followed nearly two centuries later when thousands of Dutch immigrants began settling in the forests of Wisconsin and Michigan.

According to the memorandum, the best time for a farmer to arrive at his new location was in the spring, enabling him to plant some vegetables for food as well as some grain for making flour and for feeding his livestock. After spending the summer and autumn building temporary shelters and caring for crops, the winter was devoted to cutting and clearing timber. The latter, after being felled, was usually burned in the field, except choice logs which were used for buildings and fences. In this manner, at a rate of from five to ten acres annually, the farmer gradually cleared more land and sowed more grain. Temporary shelters were soon replaced by more satisfactory dwellings. The memorandum recommended that a farmer begin with only a few cattle the first year because of the shortage of hay and barns. The raising of hogs was especially encouraged because of the ease with which they could be kept and the ready market for pork.[3]

Because neighbors were following the same procedure outlined above, the countryside, which a few years earlier had been wilderness, gradually became dotted with farms and farm buildings. Now and then, a cluster of dwellings would take on the appearance of a village, which hopefully had a few facilities to make pioneer life more bearable—a general store, a blacksmith, a tavern, a market, a school, and a place of worship.

As families grew in size and sons reached adulthood, and as new settlers arrived, it became increasingly difficult to obtain good land in the new settlement at reasonable prices. The "hive" would then begin to swarm; individuals, and sometimes large groups, would leave the community to find land elsewhere. On arrival at the new location, the pattern of development as outlined above would be repeated. New land generally would be found nearby, so that Dutch farms and villages steadily fanned out in an ever-expanding circle, as happened in the Hudson Valley and in northeastern New Jersey.

As early as the New Netherland period, Dutch settlers had crossed the Harlem River from Manhattan Island as well as the East River from Long Island to begin the settlement of what today is called the Bronx and the county of Westchester. In 1639, the Dutch West India Company acquired a tract of land known as the Keskeskeck Purchase from the Indians in this area. A Dane by the name of Jonas Bronck, after whom the present borough of the Bronx is named, was one of the first settlers to move into the new territory. In 1646, the title to a major portion of the Keskeskeck Purchase passed to Adriaen Van der Donck, one of Peter Stuyvesant's severest critics. Van der Donck encouraged farmers to settle on his lands, and in 1649 built a sawmill for them. Because he was of gentlemanly birth and was therefore addressed by the title "jonkheer," his settlement soon became known as "De Jonkheers Landt," or "De Jonkheer"—meaning the estate of the gentleman—and afterward simply as Yonkers.

As the lands along the lower Hudson River were gradually settled, several large estates were created that were reminiscent of those of the wealthy landed aristocracy in Europe. Philipsburgh manor can be cited as an example. Its founder was Frederick Philipse, who came to New Netherland from Holland in 1647, and began making his fortune as an official carpenter of the West India Company, and then by trading with the Indians. He later entered the West Indian trade as well as the African slave trade. By the time of his death in 1702, he had become one of the richest New Yorkers. A considerable portion of his wealth was in land. By purchases, royal grants, and marriages to wealthy Dutch widows, Philipse gradually added to his holdings along the Hudson until they totaled about 250,000 acres.[4]

At a point on Philipsburgh manor where the Pocantico River emptied into the Hudson, Philipse built a mill and shipping docks for the use of his tenants, as well as a manor house for himself and his family. The settlement that grew here became known as Tarrytown, a name whose origin has been the subject of some interesting conjecture. Washington Irving, the storyteller who became famous by lampooning the Dutch and who lived in the vicinity of Tarrytown, said it was so named because irate Dutch women complained that their husbands tended to tarry unnecessarily long at the village tavern whenever they visited the settlement. A more likely explanation is that the name was derived from the *tarwe* (the Dutch word for wheat) that the farmers brought to the village to be ground at Philipse's mill or to be shipped from his wharves. With the passage of time, "Tarwe town" became Tarrytown.

By 1697, there were enough settlers to form a congregation at Tarrytown. Frederick Philipse himself designed and helped construct a stone church for their accommodation. From the name of a ravine located near the church, it became known as the Sleepy Hollow Dutch Reformed Church, which was to be immortalized later in Irving's *Legend of Sleepy Hollow*. Except for a few Huguenot and English families, the congregation was made up of Dutchmen. As late as 1785, the latter were still so strongly Netherlandish in their customs that they stoutly resisted Dominie Stephen Van Vorhis when he had "the temerity to use the English language at a baptismal service."[5]

Despite the formation of Dutch Reformed congregations at Philipsburgh manor and other estates, their owners found it difficult to attract Dutch tenants. This was due in part to resentment of the feudalistic privileges enjoyed by the manorial lords, but also to the availability of land elsewhere that could be purchased at reasonable prices. Land speculators, of course, encouraged farmers to purchase their own land.

Helen Wilkinson Reynolds, in her excellent study of pre-Revolutionary Dutch houses in the Hudson Valley, states that "no better gauge exists by which to measure the extent of Dutch influence in a locality than the presence or absence of an organized congregation of the Reformed Dutch Church."[6] If we apply that yardstick, a number of villages along the Hudson had a distinctively Dutch atmosphere by 1750. These included, together with the dates when each organized a Dutch Reformed church, Kingston, 1659; Kinderhoek, 1712; Claverack, 1716; Poughkeepsie, 1716; Fishkill, 1716; Rhinebeck, 1731; Catskill, 1732; and Coxsackie, 1732.[7] By the time of the Revolution, several additional Dutch Reformed congregations had been organized along the Hudson. Generally speaking, the lower Hudson tended to attract Dutchmen from Manhattan and Long Island, whereas those who settled above Poughkeepsie came primarily from Kingston and Albany. Very few Dutch inhabitants of these communities came directly from Holland.

Most of the Dutch colonists living along the Hudson stayed close to the river bank, a practice that had been followed already in the settlement of Westchester County. There was, however, some movement inland along certain tributary streams, including the Esopus, Rondout, and Wallkill in Ulster County, all of which flow into the Hudson near Kingston, and the Mohawk River, which enters the Hudson about ten miles north of Albany.

As noted previously, Wiltwyck (later renamed Kingston by the British) had been founded as a Dutch town during the New Netherland period by several families from Rensselaerswyck who purchased farm sites in 1652 two-thirds of the way up the Hudson from New Amsterdam to Fort Orange. Before the fall of New Netherland, another Dutch town, called Nieuw Dorp (New Village), arose near Wiltwyck; it was later renamed Hurley. From the time of the first permanent settlement in this area until about 1700, there was a steady flow of settlers into what today is Ulster County. Although other national groups, including Huguenots, Walloons, Palatines, and English, were found among the settlers, Dutch influence remained dominant until the time of the American Revolution. One writer described this influence as follows:

> The mixed elements that formed the original group of settlers soon became a harmonious whole, one in the use of Dutch as the common language and one in Dutch feeling, a condition which was largely contributed to by the ministrations of the Reformed Dutch Church, into which communion all families were gathered and held in close association with each other under the guidance of Dutch pastors.[8]

By 1750, Dutch churches had been organized at Kingston, Hurley, Accord, Montgomery, Marbletown, Shawangunk, and Wawarsing. Most of the ministers serving these places received their theological training in the Netherlands, and preached in the Dutch language. Even the New Paltz church, which had been founded by French Reformed elements about 1683, substituted Dutch for French in the services in 1733, and did not switch to English until 1800.[9]

The Albany Dutch, who began expanding during the New

Netherland period by founding Kingston and Schenectady, continued to push outward after 1664. Peter Kalm, a Swedish traveler and an acute observer of the American scene, reported in 1749 that "the whole region about the Hudson River above Albany is inhabited by the Dutch: this is true of Saratoga as well as other places."[10] Cohoes, located at the point where the Mohawk River flows into the Hudson, was established by some Dutch settlers about 1700. Shortly thereafter, a few Dutch families also took up land across the river from Cohoes at Troy. Others pushed northward up the Hudson as far as Schuylerville.

There was an especially heavy migration westward up the Mohawk Valley, so that by 1750, Dutch Reformed churches had been organized at Niskayuna, Schenectady, Canajoharie, Stone Arabia, St. Johnsville, and Herkimer. As the Dutch proceeded westward, they came in contact with Palatines who, after 1700, began settling in large numbers in the western half of the valley, thereby causing some mixture of Dutch Reformed and German Reformed elements in the central area of the Mohawk region at St. Johnsville and Herkimer.

There was also a mixture of these two groups on the Schoharie River, a tributary of the Mohawk. The Palatines were the first to move into this area, followed soon after by the Dutch. The arrival of the latter was resented by the Palatines, and at times there was considerable friction between the two groups. The Dutch remained, however, and by the close of the eighteenth century, their farms were spread throughout a broad belt of territory south of and parallel to the Mohawk River. Dutch Reformed churches were soon organized at Sharon Center, Schoharie, Middleburg, Beaverdam, and Guilderland.[11]

In addition to settling on wilderness lands along the Hudson River and some of its tributaries, a considerable number of New York Dutch migrated to New Jersey after 1664. Several river systems, including the Hackensack, the Passaic, and the Raritan, made penetration into the interior of New Jersey relatively easy, particularly for the Dutch farmers living on Manhattan Island and western Long Island. It has been estimated that the Dutch living in New Jersey constituted about one-sixth of the total population of that state at the close of the American Revolution, a remarkable figure considering that only a small number of Dutchmen were living there when New Netherland fell to the English in 1664.[12]

Because of its proximity to Manhattan Island and western Long Island, and the presence of a few Dutch settlers already in the area, the Hackensack Valley was one of the first regions of New Jersey to attract Dutch farmers after 1664. Bergen, which had been founded during the New Netherland period, steadily grew in size, as did such nearby settlements as Communipaw and Paulus Hoek. Other settlers pushed farther up the valley. The Dutch Reformed church founded at Bergen in 1660 soon had nearly one hundred fifty communicant members. In 1686, a congregation was organized at Hackensack, and others were established nearby at Tappan, New York, in 1694, and at Schraalenburg, about five miles above Hackensack, in 1724. The records of these churches were written in Dutch until the time of the American Revolution, and preaching in that language was continued, at least to a degree, even later. In 1792, for example, Dutch was still popular enough with the Bergen congregation that when a call was sent to the Reverend John Cornelisen, it was stipulated that he should conduct half his services in the Holland language.[13]

Although not everyone who lived in the Hackensack Valley at the close of the colonial period was Dutch, a glance at the church records reveals a profusion of Netherlandish names.[14] In addition, there were many with non-Dutch names who had considerable Dutch blood or at least followed Dutch customs. In commenting on the composition of the Hackensack Valley on the eve of the American Revolution, one authority stated:

The men and women who made the Bergen County countryside the admiration of its neighbors spoke Jersey Dutch most of the time and English when they had to, just as many New Yorkers did. They listened to Dutch sermons on Sunday and gave their children Dutch names, and the women and children wore clothes having more than a hint of Holland in their style. Certainly no one could have confused the Dutch country in and around Hackensack with English settlements in middle Jersey or the Pennsylvania German settlements in the neighboring province to the south.[15]

Dutch colonists also settled along the Passaic River which, like the Hackensack, flowed into Newark Bay and was thus easily accessible to Hollanders from Manhattan Island and western Long Island. Bergen and Hackensack also served as jumping-off places for Dutch penetration of the Passaic Valley. Dutch Reformed churches were rapidly organized in this region, too, including congregations at Acquackanonck (later called Passaic) in 1693, Ponds in 1710, Fairfield in 1720, Totowa (later renamed Paterson) in 1726, and Pompton Plains in 1736. As was true in the Hackensack Valley, use of the Dutch language continued in these churches until the end of the eighteenth century. Thus, when the Reverend Henricus Schoonmaker found it difficult to accede to demands for more English sermons at Poughkeepsie and Fishkill, New York, he took charge, in 1774, of the church at Aquackanonck where Dutch preaching was still the order of the day. According to one authority, "he was, in his time, the most eloquent and impressive speaker in the Dutch language in this country."[16]

Dutch settlers were also attracted to the Raritan Valley, which had captured their fancy already during the New Netherland period. Cornelius Van Tienhoven, secretary of the colony of New Netherland, wrote as early as 1650 that "the district inhabited by a nation called the Raritangs is...the handsomest and pleasantest country that man can behold."[17] Although no settlements arose in the Raritan Valley during the New Netherland period, by 1699 a sufficient number of Dutch pioneers had congregated at a point about twenty miles up the river to form a settlement known as Raritan, and to organize a Dutch Reformed church.

By 1727, five more such congregations had been organized in the Raritan Valley—at Three Mile Run in 1703, Six Mile Run (today called Franklin Park) in 1710, New Brunswick in 1717, North Branch in 1719, and Harlingen in 1727. Several more congregations were organized in this area by the time of the Revolution, including churches at Neshanic (New Shannock) in 1752, Bedminster in 1758, and Hillsborough (Millstone) in 1766. The existence of such a large number of congregations in the Raritan Valley explains why the region was known for a long time as the "Garden of the Dutch Reformed Church." All these churches were still using the Dutch language at the time of the Revolution.[18]

Beginning in 1672, Dutchmen also began settling in nearby Monmouth County, New Jersey, and by 1709 were numerous enough there to organize a congregation of their own. Because of difficulty in getting a resident pastor, arrangements were made with the Reverend Joseph Morgan, a local Presbyterian minister who was able to preach in Dutch. According to the agreement, Morgan was expected to give three-fourths of his time to the Dutch Reformed congregation, and one-fourth to the Scottish Presbyterian—an arrangement that indicates the relative importance of the Dutch settlers in the region at this time. A second congregation was organized about 1721. The Dutch atmosphere was less strong in Monmouth County than among the other settlements of northeastern New Jersey, as is shown by the replacement of Dutch by English in the church services a generation or two earlier there than elsewhere.[19]

In addition to the Dutch settlers in northeastern New Jersey, a number of Dutchmen with a very different background located in the northwest corner of the colony along what was known as the Old Mine Road. This road, slightly more than a hundred miles long and probably the first of any great length to be constructed in the American colonies, was apparently built about 1660 for the use of wagons to move copper ore from the Minisink region of northwestern New Jersey to a point on the Hudson River for transshipment to Holland. Documents of the 1640's and 1650's contain several hints that the Dutch were engaged in open pit mining in this area by the close of the New Netherland period.[20]

Although the mines had become largely inactive by 1700, Dutch settlers were still found there at the opening of the eighteenth century, and others continued to move into the area. Eventually, a chain of small settlements arose along the Old Mine Road. In 1730, when the provincial government at Philadelphia became curious about the region and sent two surveyors with Indian guides to investigate reports about "Meenesink and the Mine Holes," they found numerous Hollanders living there. They also discovered groves of apple trees larger than those at Philadelphia, which gives some indication of the age of the Minisink settlement. The white inhabitants of the region spoke Dutch, and because the English surveyors knew no Dutch, both parties had to converse in the Indian language in order to understand one another.[21] At first, Dutch Reformed clergymen from Kingston, traveling by horseback, made periodic pastoral visits to the region, but by 1742, four Dutch Reformed congregations had been organized along the Old Mine Road.

Dutchmen, mostly from Long Island, began migrating in 1689 to Bucks County, Pennsylvania, just across the New Jersey boundary. This movement increased rapidly after 1700, and continued for about twenty-five years. By 1725, there were numerous families in this area with such Dutch-sounding names as Groesbeck, Hogeland, Vanartsdalen, Vandegrift, Van Deusen, Vandeveer, Vandeventer, Van Dyke, Van Horne, Van Vlecq, Van Zandt, and Wynkoop. At the close of the nineteenth century, their descendants still occupied the major portion of Southampton and Northampton townships of Bucks County, and were also numerous in adjoining Bensalem township. Most of them traced their Dutch-American lineage back to the New Netherland period.[22]

Despite the presence of other national groups such as the Welsh and the Scots, the Dutch of Bucks County clung to their national identity for a long time. The first Dutch Reformed church to be organized among them dates from 1710, with Dominie Paulus Van Vlecq serving as pastor. For a few years after he left in 1713, the congregation journeyed to nearby Abington to worship with the Scottish Presbyterians. Of the thirty weddings performed in the Abington church during those years, twenty-three were Dutch, and of the one hundred eight baptisms, fifty-eight were Dutch. Anxious to obtain a minister of their own faith, money was finally sent to Holland to pay for the theological studies of a ministerial candidate and for his passage to America. By the time of the American Revolution, there were two large Dutch Reformed churches in Bucks County, as well as a few "preaching stations," all of which were still using the Dutch language.[23]

Bucks County was not the only region in Pennsylvania that attracted Dutchmen from other parts of the American colonies. A considerable number of Dutch families also established themselves in York and Adams counties in southern Pennsylvania. There were several differences, however, between the two

Pennsylvania groups. The Dutch who went to York and Adams counties were of a later generation than those who settled in Bucks County, as there was more than a fifty-year span between the founding of the two settlements. Also, the families who settled in southern Pennsylvania came from Bergen and Somerset counties in New Jersey; the earlier group, on the other hand, came largely from Long Island. Furthermore, the Dutch settlers who went to Bucks County remained and many of their descendants still reside there today, whereas most of those who went to southern Pennsylvania stayed only a short time and then left to seek their fortunes elsewhere.

Dutchmen from New Jersey began to settle in York and Adams counties about 1765, and continued to arrive there for the next ten years. It took courage to make this move; not only did the migrants have to travel a long distance, but the site they selected was located along the outer limits of the frontier. The availability of land in southern Pennsylvania, however, was too tempting to ignore. Most of the Dutchmen were farmers with large families who, unable to get sufficient land in New Jersey for their growing sons, were attracted by the cheap, virgin soil of southern Pennsylvania. In 1770, for example, Joris Brinckerhoff (1719–1810), whose great-grandfather came to New Netherland from Holland about 1638, moved from Hackensack to southern Pennsylvania. He had seven children, all sons, and obtaining farms for them was of primary importance. Arriving in Pennsylvania, he settled on a farm of 520 acres about four miles from Gettysburg. He worked the land with the help of slaves he brought with him from New Jersey. Joris also purchased farms for his married sons, including one of 236 acres and another of 244 acres.[24]

Despite the presence of Presbyterian meeting houses in this area, the newcomers were determined to have their own church. By 1768, Dutch Reformed congregations were established at Conewago in York County, and at nearby Hanover in Adams County. Because the Conewago church, so named because of its nearness to Conewago Creek, was the more important of the two, the entire Dutch community in southern Pennsylvania was often called the Conewago settlement. The membership of the two churches soon totaled one hundred fifty families, indicating that the number of Dutchmen residing there was substantial.[25]

The land selected in southern Pennsylvania was of rather poor quality for farming. Consequently, the news about cheap, fertile land elsewhere caused most of them to leave the region beginning about 1781. Some left for central New York, but most of them migrated to Kentucky. Departures increased rapidly after 1793, with the result that the two Dutch Reformed congregations were soon so depleted that it became difficult to hold services. In 1817, when only five Dutch Reformed families remained, the congregations were dissolved and the members joined the Presbyterian church of nearby Hunters-town.

The group that left southern Pennsylvania for central New York was encouraged to do so because of the recent pacification of the Indians residing there and the opening up of new lands for settlement. The first contingent of Conewago Dutch, con- sisting of ten families, left for this region in 1793. It took slightly longer than two months to make the journey. They, along with a few families who had arrived earlier from New Jersey, formed the nuclei for several Dutch communities in Cayuga County, the most important being Owasco. In succeed- ing years, additional settlers arrived from Pennsylvania and New Jersey as well as other parts of New York. In 1796, a Dutch Reformed church was organized among them, and in the following year a small meetinghouse was built of hewn logs. By 1810, the congregation had already increased to the point that they needed a larger edifice.[26]

The Dutch pioneers from southern Pennsylvania who mi- grated to Kentucky were greater in number than the group that moved to central New York.[27] The first large contingent left for Kentucky about 1781, although a few individual fam- ilies may have left earlier. The journey from southern Penn- sylvania to Kentucky was a hazardous one involving a trek of nearly six hundred miles across unbroken wilderness. After arriving in Kentucky, the Conewago Dutch were undecided on where to locate, but finally selected some land near Boones- borough. Here they purchased several thousand acres which became known as the "Low Dutch Tract."[28]

An even larger body of settlers left the Conewago area for Kentucky in 1793. They made the difficult journey across the mountains by transporting their household goods and families in heavy, springless wagons, driving their cattle in front of them, and resting on the Sabbath to hold divine services. After reaching the upper course of the Ohio, they descended the river in flatboats until they arrived at Limestone, now Maysville, Kentucky. At this point, they again used the heavy wagons for transportation and finally reached their destination —the upper Salt River near the present town of Harrodsburg in Mercer County, central Kentucky.

Forty-four tracts of land were purchased by the Dutch in Mercer County by 1802. Among the purchasers were four families with the name Banta, three with the name Vanarsdall, and three with the name Vorhees. Other family names indicating the "Dutchness" of the settlement included De Mott, Leydt, Smock, Vanaylin, Vandervier, Van Dyke, Van Meter, Van Nuys, and Verbryke.[29] Although most of the settlers came from southern Pennsylvania, a few arrived directly from Bergen and Somerset counties, New Jersey. Some of the colonists who had settled near Boonesborough about a decade earlier also relocated in Mercer County. Nearly all the newcomers began farming, but some operated flatboats, distilleries, and saltworks.

It is interesting to note that despite their having been away from the mainstream of Dutch culture for many years, they were still strongly attached to the heritage of their forebears. Not only were they determined to continue the religious tradition of their fathers by establishing a Dutch Reformed church in their midst, but they still conversed in the Dutch language. A petition of 1795 for a minister, for example, specified a preference for a dominie who could preach in both Dutch and English. Organization of a church was delayed until 1796, and a resident pastor did not arrive until 1804. When he left in 1816, the church struggled on its own for a time before finally merging with a local Presbyterian congregation.

Difficulty in obtaining and holding a minister was only one of the problems that the settlers had to face. They also had difficulty in keeping the people together. They seemed to be afflicted with an insatiable desire to migrate, having moved in a period of less than thirty years from New Jersey to southern Pennsylvania, and then to Kentucky. If they needed an excuse to move once more, one was easy to find—the land on which they had settled proved to be poor for farming. This was perhaps the reason why some young Dutchmen who volunteered for service in the War of 1812 never returned to Kentucky.

Beginning about 1825, the Mercer County Dutch began leaving in significant numbers, although not as an organized body. A few went to Henry and Shelby counties, Kentucky, where some of the Conewago Dutch had gone earlier in 1781. Some went to Dark County, Ohio, and to Johnson and Switzerland counties, Indiana. Still others moved to points north and west in the territories of Michigan and Illinois. Those who remained behind gradually became English in their language and Presbyterian in their faith. According to one authority, in 1847 about three-fourths of the members of the Bethel Presbyterian church, near Harrodsburg, had Dutch or Huguenot names.[30]

From what has been stated, it is obvious that farming was a major vocation of the Dutch under English rule. It is ironical that although New Netherland had been handicapped by a shortage of farmers, the Dutch colonists after 1664 became particularly distinguished for their work in agriculture. In a sense, however, this is not surprising because agriculture had long been important in the economy of the Netherlands. Fruit and vegetable gardens flourished around the towns of Holland, and improvements in farming were frequently adopted there long before they were introduced in other countries.[31]

Wheat was one of the main crops grown by the Dutch farmers, while other popular grains included corn, oats, rye, and barley. Because of the availability of cheap land, the soil was not cultivated as intensively as in Holland, nor were crops rotated on a regular basis. In fact, it was not unusual to grow the same crop on a given piece of ground for several seasons in a row. Despite such shortcomings, the Dutch, along with the Germans, were "among the best farmers and gardeners in America."[32]

Although much of the field work during the colonial period

was done by hand, using hoes, shovels, hand sickles, and wooden flails, Dutch farmers were among the first to use ox- and horse-drawn implements. In 1662, for example, twelve plowshares and one hundred iron teeth for making harrows were sent to New Amstel from Holland.[33] The Frenchman St. John de Crèvecoeur, who settled in New York in 1765 and wrote about American agriculture, made several references to unique Dutch farm implements. These included a two-horse conveyance that doubled as a farm wagon on work days and as a family coach on Sundays; a special, heavy-duty plow; and a heavy, square-shaped harrow which, he said, "We call the Dutch one." Crèvecoeur also made reference to a "convenience" for preserving vegetables and roots in the winter "which we commonly call a Dutch cellar."[34]

Dutchmen were important producers of livestock. As early as 1625, according to the chronicler Wassenaer, the directors of the West India Company sent to New Netherland "one hundred and three head of livestock—stallions, mares, bulls and cows—for breeding and multiplying" as well as a quantity of hogs and sheep.[35] Farms on Long Island in 1675 averaged about eight dairy cows and beef cattle per farm. Hog raising was also popular, as it later was with the Dutch immigrants who settled in the Middle West during the nineteenth century. Although Dutch farmers also raised sheep, they did not show as much interest in them as the English. Similarly, the Dutch of New York and New Jersey, in contrast to the settlers of New England, seemed to prefer horses to oxen as draft animals.[36]

The large size of Dutch families was an asset in working the farms. During busy periods such as sowing or harvesting it was not unusual for all members of the family, including the women, to help in the field work. Dutch farmers also relied heavily upon slave labor, and as a result were often able "to bring several hundred acres under cultivation on a single farm."[37] According to one authority,

There seems to have been a high correlation between Dutch farmers and the number of slaves. Ulster County, [New York,] almost entirely rural and strongly Dutch in blood, listed over 10 percent of its inhabitants as Negro slaves [in 1790]. In the Albany area practically every Dutch farmer purchased one or more slaves if he were financially able.[38]

Travelers and other writers made frequent reference to the excellent quality of the Dutch farms found in colonial New York and New Jersey. Governor Dongan of New York wrote in 1687 that "the Dutch are great improvers of Land."[39] A visitor to the towns of Paramus and Aquackanonck, New Jersey, during the American Revolution reported that "these towns are inhabited chiefly by Dutch people. . . . The land is remarkably level, and the soil is fertile; and being generally advantageously cultivated, the people appear to enjoy happy competency."[40] The Frenchman Crèvecoeur about 1782 declared that the farm of the average Dutchman of New York was "the neatest in all the country; and you will judge by his waggon and fat horses, that he thinks more of the affairs of this world than those of the next." He also stated on another occasion that the size of a farmer's barn was a good criterion for judging his prosperity.[41] If true, the Dutch farmers were indeed prosperous, because their barns tended to be extremely large; the Swedish traveler Peter Kalm said they were "almost the size of a small church."[42] According to one authority, "the Dutch farmer spent large sums for his barn, whereas the Yankee laid out his money on his house."[43]

Because of the importance of trade in Holland, and considering that New Netherland had been founded primarily for reasons of commerce, it was to be expected that the Dutch in the American colonies would show an interest in this sector of the economy. Many of the agricultural products grown by the farmers of New York and New Jersey found their way into the coastal and export trade and were frequently handled by Dutch merchants. A visitor to New York City in 1759 reported that more than half its inhabitants were Dutch and almost all of them were traders.[44]

Some of the merchants carried on extensive trade relations. The Cromelins, who founded the Holland Trading Company in 1720, carried on a lucrative business between New York and Amsterdam for many years. Other merchants were active in the trade between New York and the West Indies, including the Dutch possessions of Curaçao and Surinam. Wheat, flour, horses, and pork were major export items to the Caribbean area. One of the largest Dutch trading firms was that of the Beekmans, which had business interests on four continents. As was true of many colonial merchants, the Dutch frequently ignored moral considerations when profits were to be made from such activities as smuggling, illicit trading with the Indians, and trading in slaves.[45]

Dutch merchants of Albany became particularly noted for the considerable trade they carried on with the Indians. Sixty of the seventy-two signatures of Albany citizens that were attached to a petition concerning the Indian trade in 1764 were Dutch.[46] Kalm reported in 1749 that "there is not a place in all the British colonies, the Hudson's Bay settlement excepted, where such quantities of furs and skins are bought of the Indians as at Albany."[47]

Some of the merchants, such as the Van Rensselaers, Van Cortlandts, and Schuylers, were also great landowners. Kalm reported in the mid-eighteenth century that "the greater part of the merchants at Albany have extensive estates in the country and large property in forests."[48] Other merchants often combined trade with industrial pursuits, including sugar refining, lumbering, milling, brewing, distilling, and ironworking.

The custom in the Netherlands of retaining business firms in the same family for several generations was also practiced by the Dutch in America. The effect of this practice and how it differed from the English and French has been well summarized in a recent study concerning a Dutch patrician family of Albany:

Dutch families were particularly noted for singleminded dedication to the family business by all their members including women, and for their custom of keeping the family fortune invested in the same business for generations, as a result of which the capital resources available to Dutch patrician merchants were greater than those of individual English and French merchants. . . . Dutch merchants handed over their valuable but intangible network of credit and commercial contacts intact to their sons. The roster of patrician families in Dutch cities and in Albany, therefore remained stable for generations while in English cities and English colonial towns the turnover of families in the merchant oligarchy was rapid.[49]

❀     ❀     ❀     ❀

Dutch farmers in the American colonies, although generally conservative by nature, oftentimes left their homes in order to begin a new life along the American frontier. They did not distinguish themselves as pioneers to the same degree as some other ethnic groups, but they nevertheless played an important role in opening up new lands in parts of New York, New Jersey, and Pennsylvania. Participation in the movement farther west was more limited, but those who did wend their way to Kentucky, Ohio, Illinois, and Michigan served as an inspiration for the wave of Dutch immigrants who began settling in the Middle West during the middle of the nineteenth century. As will be seen in the following two chapters, colonial Dutchmen, although sometimes widely scattered and having few contacts with their ancestral homeland, retained many of their Old World traditions until the American Revolution.

CHAPTER V

# Social and Cultural Life
# among the Dutch Colonists

It is rather astonishing in light of the brevity of New
Netherland history and the smallness of its population that
one can speak of a Dutch society and culture in the American
colonies. Nevertheless, Dutch influence was clearly discernible
in various parts of America even after the Revolution. The
Swedish botanist and traveler Peter Kalm wrote in 1749 that
"the inhabitants both of the town [of New York] and of the
province belonging to it are still for the greatest part Dutch,
who still, and especially the old people, speak their mother
tongue."[1] Similar observations were made by others during the
eighteenth and early nineteenth centuries with respect not only
to New York but also to northeastern New Jersey.[2]

Several factors explain the persistence of Dutch customs in
colonial America, but the influence of the Dutch Reformed
churches was one of the most significant. By reason of the
important role they played in setting the tone of a community's
social life and standards of conduct, and because of the close
ties existing between Dutch churches in the colonies and those
in Holland, it was only natural that Dutch influence would
remain strong. The Classis of Amsterdam, one of the most
influential ecclesiastical bodies in the Netherlands, exercised
considerable jurisdiction over the colonial churches until 1772,
and most dominies were born in Holland or at least received
their theological training there. As a consequence, there was a
continual "transfusion" of Old World ideas and practices into
the colonial ministry. Furthermore, the Dutch language continued as the language of the pulpit in most Dutch Reformed
churches until the early nineteenth century.

Compact communities and poor communications also made

[ 67 ]

Dutch influence more lasting than would have otherwise been the case. Non-Hollanders who settled in one of the ethnic "islands" of Dutchmen found in New York and New Jersey were frequently absorbed into the Dutch population. This was true of many Scandinavians who settled among them during the New Netherland period, and of the descendants of English soldiers who were garrisoned at places like Albany. Assimilation into Dutch society was also often the fate of Walloons, Huguenots, and German Palatines settling in predominantly Dutch regions. Some of them lost their national identity fairly soon because they or their immediate forebears had spent a generation or two in Holland before going to the New World. On the other hand, in places where the Dutch were in a definite minority, as in Delaware and parts of Pennsylvania, they were soon absorbed by the more numerous English or Germans.

Intermarriage among Dutch families also helped perpetuate Dutch customs and culture. This practice was quite common and was followed not only by the lower classes but also by families of wealth and influence. As a consequence, members of many prominent New York families were cousins, including the Schuylers, Van Cortlandts, Van Rensselaers, Verplancks, Beekmans, Cuylers, and Roosevelts. Sometimes such ethnic intermarriages extended through several generations. President Martin Van Buren, for example, whose Dutch ancestors settled in New Netherland, stated in his autobiography that his eldest son was the first Van Buren in six generations of Dutch-Americans to marry outside the Dutch line.[3]

In explaining the persistence of Dutch culture after the fall of New Netherland, it must be noted that although the number of Hollanders in the colonies was small in 1664, and although few emigrated there after that date, natural increase steadily raised their number. Dutch families were large, and some were very large—Hendrik Banta, whose ancestors came to New Netherland from Holland in 1659, had twenty-one children. The family of Joris Brinckerhoff was typical with seven sons, six of whom married and among them had forty-nine children. Dominie Henricus Selyns, pastor of the Dutch Reformed church in New York City, wrote in October, 1682, that children "multiply more rapidly here than anywhere else in the world."[4]

William Penn, in a letter written in 1683, following a visit to his lands in America, reported that the Dutch residing on the Delaware River "have fine Children, and almost every house full; rare to find one of them without three or four Boys, and as many Girls; some six, seven and eight Sons."⁵

The home was a central point in the life of Dutch colonists, and family ties were generally close. There was considerable equality between husband and wife, and women frequently participated in business affairs.⁶ Children were loved and warmly treated. An English woman who spent ten years as a child among the Dutch in Albany from 1758 to 1768 noted considerable difference between the rearing of Dutch and English children. She wrote that one never entered a Dutch home without meeting youngsters and that they were

indulged to a degree that, in our vitiated state of society, would have rendered them good for nothing. But [at Albany] . . . affection restrained parents from keeping their children at a distance, and inflicting harsh punishments. . . . They were tenderly cherished, and early taught that they owed all their enjoyments to the Divine Source of beneficence, to whom they were finally accountable for their actions. . . . The children returned the fondness of their parents with such tender affection, that they feared giving them pain as much as ours do punishment, and very rarely wounded their feelings by neglect, or rude answers.⁷

In view of the austerity and strictness that is traditionally associated with followers of Calvinism, one would assume the Dutch of colonial America thought of little else than going to church on Sunday and practicing piety in their daily living. Nothing could be further from the truth. Although puritanical sabbaths were the ideal sought by dominies, the frequency with which governmental regulations were issued on this matter during the New Netherland period indicates that the ideal was far from being a reality.⁸

A decree of October 26, 1656, is particularly interesting. It shows that the Dutch were not a solemn people to whom life was always a serious matter, but that they enjoyed a great variety of amusements. This decree, in addition to prohibiting on Sunday "any ordinary labor, such as Ploughing, Sowing,

Mowing, Building, Woodsawing, Smithing, Bleaching, Hunting, [and] Fishing" also prohibited the people from "frequenting Taverns or Tippling houses, Dancing, playing Ball, Cards, Tricktrack, Tennis, Cricket or Ninepins, [and] going on pleasure parties in a Boat, Cart or Wagon before, between or during Divine Service." On September 10, 1663, several items were added to the list of prohibited Sunday activities. These included "roving in search of Nuts and Strawberries and...too unrestrained and excessive Playing, Shouting and Screaming of children in the Streets and Highways."[9]

Horse racing was as popular with the Dutch in colonial America as it was in Holland, and sometimes called for regulatory laws. An edict of 1657 decreed that "no person shall race with carts and wagons, in the streets within the villages, but the driver while passing through villages must walk by the side of his horse or vehicle."[10] Golf, too, was a favorite sport and likewise had to be regulated by the authorities. In 1660, for example, the "worshipful magistrates" of Fort Orange ordered all persons to refrain from playing golf in the streets because of "diverse complaints from the burghers of this place against playing golf along the streets, which causes great damage to windows of the houses and exposes people to the danger of being wounded."[11]

In the wintertime, skating and sleighing were very popular among the Dutch. Mrs. Grant noted that at Albany about 1760:

They used in great parties to visit their friends at a great distance, and having an excellent and hardy breed of horses, flew from place to place over the snow or ice in these sledges with incredible rapidity, stopping a little while at every house they came to, where they were always well received, whether acquainted with the owners or not. The night never impeded the travellers, for the atmosphere was so pure and serene, and the snow so reflected the moon and starlight, that the nights exceeded the days in beauty.[12]

A visitor to New York City in December, 1704, reported that on a sleigh ride into the countryside, "I Believe we mett 50 or 60 slays that day—they fly with great swiftness and some are so furious that they'le turn out of the path for none except a Loaden Cart."[13]

Nor did the supposedly strict Calvinism of the Dutchmen make them prohibitionists; in fact, "it was a sad breach of politeness not to furnish the dominies when they made their pastoral visits with the choicest brew."[14] In an ordinance of March 10, 1648, Governor Stuyvesant and his council expressed alarm at the excessive drinking in New Amsterdam and at the profusion of taverns which, according to the ordinance, made up about one-fourth of the businesses of that town.[15]

Funerals were always occasions for considerable drinking, a practice that the Dutch Reformed Church condoned. When Pieter Jacob Marius, one of the wealthiest New Yorkers of his time and a member of the Consistory, died in 1703, twenty-nine gallons of wine and a half vat of beer were consumed at his burial. Interment of the poor was accompanied by similar libations. When Claes Janse, who was of the "poorer sort," died in 1695, the church at Albany paid the funeral expense of one hundred fifty-nine guilders, about two-thirds of which were payment for two half vats of beer, six bottles of rum, and five gallons of Madeira wine. Similarly, when Marritje Lievertse, a pauper, died in Albany in 1700, the church saw to her proper burial. Over half the expense was for beer, wine, and rum.[16]

Smoking, like drinking, was also popular among the Dutch, and even the women apparently smoked freely. According to a visitor to New York in the mid-eighteenth century,

Nearly all women who had passed their fortieth year smoked tobacco; even those who were considered as belonging to the foremost families. I frequently saw about a dozen old ladies sitting about the fire smoking. Once in a while I discovered newly-married wives of twenty and some years sitting there with pipes in their mouths.[17]

The Dutch tended to be aloof toward other ethnic groups. Thus, Kalm reported that those residing in New Brunswick, New Jersey, "keep company only with themselves, and seldom or never go amongst the other inhabitants, living as it were quite separate from them."[18] Although they were not very convivial toward outsiders, Mrs. Grant reported that at dusk the inhabitants of Albany would visit one another on their porches, "grouped according to similarity of years and inclinations. At one door were young matrons, at another the elders of the people, at a third the youths and maidens, gayly chatting or singing together, while the children played round the trees."[19] In addition to assembling on porches in the immediate neighborhood, the Dutch often journeyed to neighboring settlements to visit relatives and friends. New Year's day was especially devoted to the exchange of visits. The more well-to-do also went to New York City at least once a year, and sent their children there occasionally for a brief stay to learn more polished manners.

The particular type and style of homes of Dutch colonists varied as to time and place, as well as the availability of building materials. Some of the first dwellings were naturally very crude. Cornelius Van Tienhoven, the secretary of New Netherland, reported in 1650 that many of the earliest settlers, not having the means to build permanent dwellings, would

dig a square pit in the ground, cellar fashion, six or seven feet deep, as long and as broad as they think proper, case the earth inside all round the wall with timber, which they line with bark of trees or something else to prevent the caving in of the earth; floor this cellar with plank and wainscot it overhead for a ceiling, raise a roof of spars clear up and cover the spars with bark or green sods, so that they can live dry and warm in these houses with their entire families for two, three and four years, it being understood that partitions are run through these cellars which are adapted to the size of the family.[20]

Later, the crude houses were replaced by more substantial structures. Secretary Van Tienhoven noted that in about three or four years after their arrival, some of the first settlers "built themselves handsome houses, spending on them several thousands." It cannot be determined for certain whether the Dutch built log houses in the Hudson Valley during the New Netherland period, but they apparently did so to a limited extent in the Delaware Valley under Swedish and Finnish influence. Because of the abundant supply of timber and the early appearance of sawmills, considerable use was soon made of planks and clapboard in house construction. The Jesuit missionary Isaac Jogues described the houses of the patroon's colony of Rensselaerswyck in 1643 as follows: "All their houses are merely of boards and thatched, with no mason work except the chimneys. The forest furnishing many pines, they make boards by means of their mills, which they have here for the purpose."[21]

Although bricks were the traditional building material in the mother country, the shortage of kilns and bricklayers in America confined their use largely to chimneys, fireplaces, and ovens until after the New Netherland period. When bricks were in greater abundance, their usage in house construction became very popular in Albany and New York City. According to Wertenbaker, "Before the end of the [seventeenth] century New Amsterdam was almost as solidly built of brick as the cities of Holland itself."[22] Other areas showed a preference for different building materials. The Ulster County Dutch, for example, continued to use stone long after its usage declined elsewhere. Those residing in Dutchess County, on the other hand, often built frame houses. Wood was also used extensively on Long Island.

Houses generally were rectangular, although some were T- or L-shaped. As a family grew in numbers and wealth, additions were made to the original structure. A few farmhouses were built on the order of the Dutch peasant farmhouse with the barn and house under one roof. Thus, the carpenter Jan Cornelissen of Rensselaerswyck agreed in 1643 to build a farmhouse one hundred twenty feet long, forty feet of which would lodge the farmer and his family with the remaining eighty feet housing the laborers, cattle, and horses. Generally speaking, however, the combination house and barn arrangement, although popular in Holland, was not used a great deal among the Dutch colonists and practically disappeared after the close of the New Netherland period. In explaining this, Wertenbaker conjectures that

perhaps the labor of hewing out the huge beams for the framework was too great, [or] perhaps the heat from the cattle and horses was uncomfortable in the scorching American summers, [or] perhaps it was deemed unwise to have the thatched roof of the barn too near the roaring fire in the residence necessitated by the bitter cold of winter.[23]

Dutch houses of the colonial period had several distinguishing characteristics. Perhaps because of the pleasure Dutchmen derived from assembling on warm evenings outside their homes for family and neighborly conversation, porches were a common feature of their houses. They were floored like a room and had either a wooden roof or were covered with latticework overspread with wild vines. The porches were open on the sides, and frequently had seats all around. Distinctive gable ends, popular already during the New Netherland period, also became a unique feature of many Dutch houses. These took various forms, with each locality apparently showing a preference for a particular style. In Albany, the gable ends were usually stepped, whereas in the region outside the town, the straight-line gable was more popular. Some of the Dutch living elsewhere preferred curved gable ends, which along with the frequent use of clay pantiles—sometimes imported from Holland, but usually locally made—frequently gave their communities a close resemblance to towns in the Netherlands.

The gambrel style roof became popular with some colonists. It had two slopes between the ridgepole and eaves instead of the lengthy, single slant, and provided additional room in the attic. The gambrel roof, although known in Europe as well as New England and Virginia, was modified by the Dutch colonists so that the lower slope was longer and less steep, and also had a wide, curving bottom along the eaves. According to one authority, this departure from the norm made the Dutch style "the most beautiful gambrel known."[24]

During the eighteenth century, a few members of the great patrician families began building elegant dwellings in the Georgian style. Examples of such homes belonging to the Dutch elite of New York colony included Philipse Manor Hall in Yonkers, Van Cortlandt Mansion in Cortlandt Park, Schuyler House at Albany, and the second Van Rensselaer Manor Hall at Albany.

Travelers in the colonies were unanimous in describing the neatness of Dutch homes. A visitor to the Albany area in 1744 reported, "The Dutch here keep their houses very neat and clean, both without and within. . . . Their chambers and rooms are large and handsome. . . . Their kitchens are likewise very clean."[25] A Hessian general wrote after his first visit to Long Island during the American Revolution:

The prosperity of the inhabitants, whose forbears were all Dutch, must have been very great indeed. Everywhere one sees real quality and abundance. One sees nothing useless or old, certainly nothing dilapidated. . . . The houses are beautiful and are furnished in better taste than any we are accustomed to in Germany. At the same time everything is so clean and neat that no description can do it justice.[26]

Interiors of Dutch houses were frequently wainscoted or whitewashed. Kalm reported seeing very little wallpaper during his travels in New York and New Jersey, and stated that the people "seem in general to be little acquainted with it."[27] Planks made smooth by repeated scrubbings were used for flooring, as carpets were rare before the Revolution. Beds were frequently built into the walls, and could be closeted off by doors or draw drapes, so that it was possible to "go thro all the rooms of a great house and never see a bed."[28] For heat and cooking, there were stone fireplaces or ovens. According to Kalm, "The fireplaces among the Dutch were always built in, so that nothing projected out, and it looked as though they made a fire against the wall itself."[29] The fireplaces were sometimes framed with glazed blue tiles imported from Holland.

Education at the elementary level was quite widespread in the Netherlands during the seventeenth century, but was slow in developing in New Netherland. Although the charter establishing the patroon system in 1629 stated that the patroonships shall be provided with schoolmasters "as quickly as possible," the implementation of such pronouncements was slow. There is no evidence of a schoolmaster residing in New Amsterdam before 1638 or in Rensselaerswyck before 1648. As late as 1657, the reverends Megapolensis and Drisius of New Amsterdam informed the Classis of Amsterdam that unless more was done for education, one could "expect nothing else than young men of foolish and undisciplined minds."[30] By 1664, however, all but two of the eleven chartered towns of New Netherland had common schools, and New Amsterdam also had a Latin school.

The close ties existing in Holland between religion and education were transplanted to New Netherland. Morning and afternoon school sessions were opened and closed with prayer. Twice a week the schoolmaster instructed his pupils in the common prayers and in the Heidelberg Catechism, while the Bible, the

Book of Psalms, and the Proverbs of Solomon served as basic textbooks. The schoolmaster was frequently expected to perform various religious duties for the general laity, a custom carried over from Holland. According to one set of instructions, for example, the schoolmaster of New Netherland was obliged not only to teach "reading, writing and ciphering" to the youth but was also expected

to promote Religious Worship, to read a portion of the Word of God to the people, to endeavor as much as possible to bring them up in the ways of the Lord, to console them in their Sickness and to conduct himself with all diligence and fidelity in his calling, so as to give others a good example, as becometh a devout, pious and worthy Consoler of the Sick, Church Clerk, Precentor and Schoolmaster, in which capacities all persons, without distinction, were commanded to acknowledge him.[31]

Education during the New Netherland period was conducted under rather primitive conditions. Accommodations were poor, with teaching generally being carried on in the teacher's home or in a rented room. Teachers were often poorly qualified and poorly paid. Because of the latter, it was customary for them to take odd jobs during their off-hours to supplement their salary; such "moonlighting" included washing, barbering, furniture repair, mending shoes, looking after cattle, and hoeing gardens. Furnishings in the school were meager, consisting of little more than a desk and chair for the teacher and backless benches and writing tables for the pupils.

Some idea of the primitiveness of pedagogy during the early colonial period can be derived from this description of a teacher's desk in New Amsterdam:

Raise the lid of the early Dutch schoolmaster's desk and what do we find?—a pen knife, a small sand-box blotter, a bundle of goose quills, a glass full of black ink, an ink pot, a blue tile on which to mix inks, parchments, a few books of white, hand-made paper, an ink horn to hang by his side when he went out; on top of the desk— a candlestick with two lights, an arithmetic board on which to lay out counters, a rule, a rollbook of the names of students, a Bible, a prayer book, a psalm book, a testament, a reading desk for the Bible, and an oil can for the clockwork.[32]

The Dutch elementary school system underwent little change after 1664. Its purpose remained as before: educate the children in the three R's, but also make them into God-fearing Christians. Instruction in the Dutch language was continued in most communities until at least the middle of the eighteenth century. The consistories of the Dutch Reformed churches continued to play a significant role in administering the schools and appointing teachers. The latter were expected to be members of the Church, and to subscribe to its doctrinal standards. At Bergen, New Jersey, the consistory of the local Dutch church continued to appoint the schoolmaster until 1790.[33]

The semi-ecclesiastical nature of the office of schoolmaster also continued to prevail long after 1664. For example, when Anthony Welp was appointed schoolmaster in 1773 by the Dutch Reformed citizens of Flatbush, Long Island, he was expected to devote one afternoon each week to catechizing the children as well as "attend to the church services, such as reading and singing," and to assist at burials.[34] In the more remote settlements, where there was a shortage of ministers, the schoolmaster often substituted for the pastor on Sundays by reading a few passages from Scripture, leading the congregation in the singing of the favorite Dutch psalms, and reading a sermon.

Education of Dutch girls during the colonial period received less attention than that of boys. The former had to content themselves with domestic training in the home and only rudimentary training in reading and writing. According to one observer of the Dutch at Albany about the mid-eighteenth century, "Female education, of consequence, was conducted on a very limited scale; girls learned needlework (in which they were indeed skillful and ingenious) from their mothers and aunts; they were taught ... to read, in Dutch, the Bible, and a few Calvinist tracts of the devotional kind."[35] Despite not receiving the same educational opportunities as males, responsibility for carrying on religious instruction in the home generally devolved on the women.

For young Dutchmen interested in education beyond the common school, there was the College of New Jersey (now Princeton), founded in 1746, and King's College (now Columbia), founded in 1754. Some young men also continued their education at Boston or Philadelphia. As early as 1653, a son of Dominie Megapolensis of New Amsterdam went to Harvard College to study. Those who went into law or medicine often secured their training by hiring out as apprentices to practicing attorneys or physicians. In addition, a few prominent merchant families sent their sons to Holland for special business schooling.

Toward the close of the colonial period, Dutch colonists began showing an interest in founding a college of their own. They were especially motivated by a desire to establish an institution for the training of a qualified ministry. Because of their insistence on being served by well-educated, orthodox clergymen, the congregations, with few exceptions, either called their ministers from Holland or sent ministerial candidates there to complete their education. This dependence on foreign universities naturally created a shortage of pastors in the colonies. At the time of the Revolution, there were about a hundred Dutch Reformed churches in the American colonies but fewer than forty ministers.

Beginning in the middle of the eighteenth century, a few dominies established "private academies" in their homes in order to train young men for the ministry, but these attempts met with only limited success. Continued efforts by the Dutch Reformed clergy to promote higher education finally culminated in their receiving a royal charter in 1766 to found Queen's College. This school, to be located at New Brunswick, New Jersey, became the eighth college in the American colonies, and was the forerunner of present-day Rutgers University. Its purpose, as set forth in a revised charter of 1770, was "the education of youth in the learned languages, liberal and useful arts and sciences, and especially in divinity; preparing them for the ministry, and other good offices."[36]

Several difficulties prevented Queen's College from making much progress at first, and classes even had to be suspended on a few occasions. A schism of long standing among the Dutch Reformed congregations—revolving primarily around the question of greater independence from the religious authorities in Holland—was a major impediment to the school's growth. Although the schism gradually came to an end after 1772, church members wanting to retain close ties with the mother denomination in Holland were slow in giving their support to the school. The American Revolution also had an adverse effect on the school's growth. The countryside around New Brunswick was ravaged periodically by British troops and the town itself was occupied for a time. After the war, severe financial difficulties further retarded the college's development for many years. The new school also disappointed its founders because of the slowness with which a theological faculty was added to its staff.

As might be expected, the clergy were the most highly educated people among the Dutch during the colonial period. Typical of the early ministers was the Reverend Jonas Michaelius, who studied for six years at the University of Leiden. He arrived in 1628 as the first ordained minister in New Netherland. His biographer says of him:

We may . . . conclude that Michaelius was a man of culture and learning. He not only speaks and writes his mother-tongue well . . . but he administers the Lord's Supper to the Walloons in the French language, he also uses Greek words, and he also is able to write a long letter in praisworthy Latin. Michaelius had read St. Chrysostom, from whom he quotes, and also Horace.[37]

Space permits mention of only a few of the more distinguished dominies of the post-1664 period. Henricus Selyns, who served the Dutch church at New York City from 1682 to 1701, was a graduate of the University of Leiden. As a poet he versified in both Dutch and Latin. One of his longest Latin poems, written in 1697, was seventy-six lines in length and was prefixed to some of the published works of Cotton Mather, with whom he carried on correspondence. Cornelis Van Santvoord, who served at Staten Island from 1718 to 1742, and at Schenectady from 1742 to 1752, was also a graduate of Leiden. He was a supporter of the Great Awakening, and wrote a penetrating treatise in its defense. Van Santvoord preached in both French and Dutch, and also translated some Dutch works into English. Eilardus Westerlo, who served the Dutch church at Albany from 1760 to 1790, was a graduate of the University of Groningen. He was a classical scholar who could write ably in Greek and

Latin as well as Hebrew. Dr. Ezra Stiles, president of Yale College and a well-known classical scholar, said that Dominie Westerlo wrote Latin of a greater purity than any man he had ever known.[38]

A few laymen of New Netherland also showed considerable sophistication. Jacob Steendam, who migrated in 1650 and prospered as a trader and dealer in real estate, wrote poetry as a pastime. He had at least one book of poems published before he left Holland for New Netherland. One of his later poems, a eulogy of the beauties of primeval New Netherland and the glorious opportunities to be found there, was affixed to the *Kort en Klaer Ontwerp* of Cornelius Plockhoy, the Dutch Mennonite who led a group of settlers to the Delaware Valley in 1663. Steendam's poetry was generally of a lyrical nature, and dealt with various themes—love, religion, simple pastoral scenes, nature—and showed that he had more than a passing acquaintance with history and classical mythology.

Other New Netherlanders who merit mention because of their literary activity include Nicasius De Sille and Adriaen Van der Donck. The former served for a time as second in command of the colony under Stuyvesant. As an amateur poet, he showed a love for simple pastoral subjects and an unquestioning trust in divine providence. Van der Donck, a member of Stuyvesant's council and the leading spirit among the governor's critics, had a law degree from the University of Leiden. The very lengthy "Representation of New Netherland," which he wrote in 1649 as spokesman for Stuyvesant's critics, and his *Description of New Netherland*, published in 1655, are two of the best contemporary accounts of the colony.

There were also a few Hollanders of the post–New Netherland period, besides the clergy, who had distinguished careers. Johannes Van Beuren (ca. 1680–1755) was a physician from Amsterdam who came to New York in 1702. As a student at Leiden University, he studied under the world-renowned physician and professor Hermannus Boerhaave. Van Beuren established an extensive practice in New York and was one of the city's best-trained medical doctors. In 1736, he was appointed medical director of a newly constructed hospital which was the forerunner of present-day Bellevue Hospital. Five of his sons also became doctors. David Rittenhouse (1732–96) won a worldwide reputation for his work in astronomy and mathematics. His ancestors came from Arnhem, and his great-grandfather, William Rittenhouse, was the chief founder of the first paper mill erected in America in 1690. Simeon De Witt, a graduate of the class of 1776 at Queen's College, distinguished himself as a geographer and surveyor, becoming Chief Geographer of the United States Army from 1780 until 1783, and Surveyor General of New York State from 1784 until 1834. He was the author of numerous scientific papers. Several Hollanders of the colonial period also had distinguished careers as public officials—mayors, officers in the militia, members of provincial assembles, and delegates to constitutional conventions.[39]

Although there were no Dutch painters of the colonial period whose work compared to that of their kinsmen in the Netherlands, a few of them exhibited considerable talent. Unfortunately, the artists of some of the early works are not known for certain. Because of the limited demand for their paintings, the artists frequently had to engage in other occupations, including glass making, house painting, trade, and farming.

One of the most distinguished of the early Dutch artists of colonial America was Jacobus Gerritsen Strycker, who emigrated to New Netherland with his wife and two children in 1651. Although little is known of his early life, he obviously had received excellent art training in Holland, but never pursued painting as a profession. In New Netherland, Strycker earned his livelihood by trading and farming, and also frequently served as a public official in New Amsterdam. He continued, however, to paint as an avocation. Concerning his painting of Adriaen Van der Donck—one of New Netherland's leading citizens—Strycker's biographer says: "One marvels that such a portrait could have been painted in this country at that early period, and one realizes that Jacobus Strycker, before he left Holland, must certainly have been in touch with the best of the great Dutch school."[40]

The Duyckincks were a remarkable family of Dutch artists that lived in the colonies. Evert Duyckinck, a contemporary of Strycker, came to New Amsterdam in 1638, where he practiced the crafts of glaziery and glass making, but also did some portrait painting. A son, two grandsons, and a great-grandson continued for about a hundred fifty years the artistic tradition begun by Evert Duyckinck; the last of the quintet, Gerardus II, died in 1797. Other Dutch painters of ability included Hendrik Couturier, who was listed as a member of the Leiden guild of painters before his arrival at New Amsterdam in 1661, and Pieter Vanderlyn, who, on his arrival from Holland about 1718, settled first at Albany and later at Kingston. Vanderlyn's son, Nicholas, was also an artist and his grandson, John, became a famous portrait, historical, and landscape painter of the nineteenth century.

Generally speaking, Dutch painters of the seventeenth century did not try to idealize their subjects, but simply depicted them as they saw them: sober, stiff, and plain looking. Backgrounds were usually dark and most of the figures sat with their face to the front. In the eighteenth century, the subjects appear more natural on canvas, and greater use was made of color as well as background. Some of the paintings, particularly those of the upper Hudson Valley, depict a kind of Dutch folk culture.

In both numbers and quality of workmanship, Dutch gold- and silversmiths were more significant than the Dutch painters. According to one authority, "The Dutch tradition determined the forms and decorations of much of the silver produced in New York before the Revolution."[41] Another writer has stated that their skill was about equal to that of the best European competitors.[42] Although their workmanship was influenced by styles followed by their forebears in Holland, they nevertheless produced work that was uniquely American, and excelled in producing tankards, porringers, teapots, and casters as well as ecclesiastical plate. Their products were frequently decorated in an elaborate manner with engraving and applied ornamentation, with a preference shown for fruit, flowers, leaves, and birds.

Space permits mention of only a few gold and silver craftsmen. One of the greatest was Cornelius Kierstede (1675–1757), who began his career in New York but later moved to Connecticut, where, according to one authority, he was "without doubt that Colony's unsurpassed craftsman."[43] Another was Jacobus Van der Spiegel (1668–1708), whose tankard now in the possession of Yale University has been described as having "no rival in its intricacy of engraving."[44] In Albany, Koenraet Ten Eyck and his two sons, Jacob and Barent, displayed excellent workmanship. Others of importance were Gerrit Onckelberg, Peter Van Dyck, and Jesse Kip.

If one excludes the clergy and takes note of such exceptions as Steendam, Strycker, Van Beuren, Kierstede, and a few others, it must be said that Dutchmen of the colonial period were not great patrons of culture. At first glance, this is somewhat surprising in view of the fact that the colonial period in American history coincided with the *Gouden Eeuw*, or "Golden Age," of Holland—a time in which the Dutch were admired throughout Europe for their achievements in art and science. Upon closer examination, however, the failure of the Dutch in America to imitate the cultural life of their contemporaries in Holland is not too strange.

It must be borne in mind that even the largest American communities inhabited by Dutchmen were very small when compared to such cities as Leiden and Amsterdam and could not have been much of a cultural inspiration to their inhabitants. New York City had only about 5,000 people in 1700, and at the outbreak of the Revolution, not many more than 21,000. A census taken in 1697 shows that there were only 1,452 people living in Albany, and a visitor there in 1744 reported that it had "about 4,000 inhabitants, mostly Dutch or of Dutch extract."[45]

In explaining the dearth of cultural activity among the Dutch during the early colonial period, it must also be noted that the immigrants of the New Netherland period were not of a sort from whom one would expect great artistic or literary achievements. Of the forty-four men who attached their "signatures" to a document in 1643, nineteen were unable to write their names and instead had to make a mark. In addition to rather widespread illiteracy, the early settlers tended to be a quarrelsome and rowdy lot. This is indicated by the biographical sketches of the residents of Rensselaerswyck between the years 1630 and 1658, a large number of whom were fined or reprimanded for stealing, brawling, excessive drinking, or failure to pay debts. The behavior of the people at New Amsterdam was no better, and perhaps was worse. One authority states that during the period April 22, 1638, to April 28, 1639, approximately fifty civil suits and forty-three criminal cases, including twenty-eight on complaints of slander, were heard by the director general and his council.[46]

Although cultural life among the Dutch colonies improved after 1664,, the transformation was not universal. In 1732, for example, Dominie Cornelius Van Schie, a graduate of the University of Leiden, described his parishioners at Poughkeepsie and Fishkill, New York, to friends in the Netherlands as follows: "Many people here were born, and grew up, in the woods, and know little of anything else except what belongs to farming. . . . Most of these people can neither read nor write."[47] Conditions were very similar among the inhabitants of the Raritan Valley in central New Jersey, and could hardly have been any better among those living in such frontier regions as York and Adams counties, Pennsylvania, Cayuga County, New York, and Mercer County, Kentucky.

A thirst for learning was often lacking even among the upper classes. The wealthier people of Albany, for example, bought little reading material other than religious manuals and school books. Nor did they contribute any writing among themselves, "in contrast to the Pennsylvania Germans, who by the 1740's were supporting two German newspapers and a thriving market in other printed materials."[48] The few Dutch books published in the American colonies were almost all on religious subjects, although the publication of American almanacs in Dutch began in 1741.

Doctor Alexander Hamilton, who traveled extensively in New York and New Jersey during the middle of the eighteenth century, stated that the Dutch were "at best rustic and unpolished" and had "little desire . . . for conversation and society, their whole thoughts being turned upon profit and gain."[49] Peter Kalm also considered the Dutch colonists rather boorish, and made an interesting comparison between their manners and those of the French and English:

When one spoke of refinement as the word is now used, and in applying it to the French and the Dutch, it was just as if one had lived a long time at court while the other, a peasant, had scarcely ever visited the city. The difference between the English and the Dutch was like that of a refined merchant in the city and a rather crude farmer in the country.[50]

Kalm noted, however, that there were exceptions, and added that although the Dutch were not as polite and well-bred as the French and English, "their intentions were good and they showed their kindly spirit in all they did."[51]

Hamilton's characterization of the Dutch as being primarily concerned with "profit and gain" is interesting because it addresses itself to certain traits that are today frequently ascribed to the Dutch, namely, that they are hard-working and dependable but shrewd in matters of money, and are thrifty to the point of being parsimonious. These latter concepts are inherent in such currently used phrases as "Dutch treat" and "Dutch auction." What evidence is there that would support similar remarks about the Dutch of colonial times? The answer depends on the period of history under scrutiny.

Sources indicate that the inhabitants of New Netherland were often shiftless and indolent, rather than thrifty and industrious. As early as September, 1626, Isaac De Rasiere, the chief commercial agent in the colony, declared that many people showed a "lazy unconcern" about bettering themselves.[52] Dominie Jonas Michaelius wrote in August, 1628, that "many among the common people would have liked to make a living, and even get rich, in idleness, rather than by hard work, saying, they had not come to work, that as far as working is concerned, they might as well have staid home."[53] Similarly, in 1660, Stuyvesant complained that too many of the newly arriving colonists were unaccustomed to labor, and asked the directors of the West India Company not to "take up and engage whomever chance may throw your way."[54] Complaints were also voiced by officials on the Delaware. Thus, Vice-Director Alrichs in October, 1658, wrote his superiors in Amsterdam, "Many who come hither are as poor as worms, and lazy withal, and will not work, unless compelled by necessity."[55] Although some of these complaints were made by Company officials and thus may be biased, the court records of New Netherland indicate that its residents were far from being model citizens.

The character of the Dutch colonists of a later date apparently changed for the better. Later generations seemed to possess more of the proverbial Dutch capacity for hard work and thriftiness than did their forebears—at least so it would appear from the accounts written by travelers who visited them during the English period. William Penn, in 1683, said of the Dutch residing in the Delaware Valley that he saw "few Young men more sober and laborious."[56] A New England physician reported in 1697, "I cannot say I saw any of ye Dutch that were tollerably well drest, though rich enough to weare what they pleased, they are a parcimonious people, & expend Little on theyr livelyhood, which makes them usually well moneyed, & good paymasters."[57] An English traveler reported about the middle of the eighteenth century that the Dutch of New York were "habitually frugal, industrious, and parsimonious."[58]

❅     ❅     ❅     ❅

Generally speaking, the Dutch in the colonial period did not distinguish themselves in the arts and learning, although there were a few men of repute among them who resembled their confreres in the Netherlands. Lack of interest in these matters, however, must not be construed to mean that Dutchmen led a dull or humdrum existence. They enjoyed the pleasures of this life as much as members of other ethnic stocks. In addition to appreciating the simple joys of home and family life, they indulged in a variety of amusements and derived satisfaction from their success as farmers and businessmen. Furthermore, they took considerable interest in church life, as will be seen in the following chapter.

CHAPTER VI

# The Tie that Binds: Church and Language

THE PEOPLE OF THE NETHERLANDS THROUGHOUT MOST OF THEIR history have shown considerable interest in religious matters, and this was particularly true during the early modern period. A semimonastic order of laymen, known as the Brothers of the Common Life, for example, enjoyed great popularity in the Low Countries during the fifteenth century, and many Dutch people reacted vigorously against the religious policies of their overlord, Philip II of Spain, during the Protestant Reformation. That this religious fervor did not abate later is shown by the attention given to the spiritual needs of Dutch settlers and traders living abroad during the seventeenth and eighteenth centuries.

The various groups and individuals that had economic interests in New Netherland, such as the West India Company and the patroons, assumed responsibility for providing the colonists with ministers and lay preachers. Thus, when the city of Amsterdam founded New Amstel on the Delaware in 1656, it promised to install a "Preacher and Consistory" as soon as the colony had two hundred families, and, in the meantime, to send a schoolmaster there who, in addition to his pedagogic duties, would "read the Holy Scriptures and set the Psalms."[1] Generally speaking, however, groups and individuals who had an economic interest in New Netherland confined their religious activities to paying the salaries of the ministers and to settling disputes between the latter and the secular authorities. Supervision of most other religious matters was left in the hands of church officials in Holland. By 1636, the Classis of Amsterdam had assumed almost full responsibility for sending ministers to New Netherland and for supervising congregations in matters of faith and church discipline. It continued to direct the affairs of the Dutch Reformed churches in America even after New Netherland

[ 87 ]

fell to England in 1664, and persisted in this until shortly before the American Revolution.

The first men who were sent out to look after the religious needs of the colonists were lay workers. They were Bastiaen Jansz Krol, who arrived in March, 1624, and Jan Huygens, who arrived in May, 1626. The official title of these men was *ziekentrooster* or *krankenbezoeker*, a loose translation of which is "comforter of the sick." In addition to visiting and consoling the sick, a *ziekentrooster* read prayers on appropriate occasions as well as a few chapters from the Bible and sometimes a sermon from an approved book of sermons. He was also frequently asked to assist in the catechetical instruction of the youth. Although not permitted to administer the sacrament of the Lord's Supper, he was allowed by special permission to baptize and to perform marriages. In time, the title *voorlezer*, meaning literally "forereader," was customarily substituted for *ziekentrooster*. During the eighteenth century, the *voorlezer* frequently served as a general "utility man," whose religious duties were combined with those of church janitor, bell ringer, grave digger, schoolmaster, and town clerk.[2]

Although the *ziekentroosters* helped satisfy the religious requirements of the settlers of New Netherland, an ordained minister was sorely needed. It was in response to this necessity that the Reverend Jonas Michaelius, who had previously served Dutch outposts in Africa and Brazil, arrived in the colony in April, 1628. He soon organized a church at New Amsterdam, with approximately fifty communicant members, and remained in charge of it until his return to Holland about 1632. The (Dutch) Reformed Church in America dates its formal beginnings from the founding of this church in 1628.[3] By the time New Netherland fell to the English in 1664, thirteen additional congregations had been organized in the colony.

An examination of the life of the Reverend Johannes Megapolensis illustrates the status of religion among the early Dutch colonists and the manifold problems confronting the ministers. This venerable man of God, who came from the vicinity of Alkmaar, the Netherlands, spent the first seven years (1643–49) of his ministry in America at Rensselaerswyck in the service of the patroon, Kiliaen Van Rensselaer. By mutual agreement,

Dominie Megapolensis promised to serve the patroon's colonists for an annual salary of one thousand guilders plus an allowance for food and housing. As was true of pastorates elsewhere in New Netherland, his life at Rensselaerswyck was anything but easy. Public worship services were conducted in his home until a storehouse was finally remodeled to serve as a church. The church had only nine pews, indicating the smallness of the congregation. In addition to preaching to the colonists and catechizing the children, the dominie was expected to carry out a miscellany of mundane duties for the patroon. Despite his numerous responsibilities, Megapolensis found time to study and to write about the customs and language of the Mohawk Indians and to carry on missionary work among them. On at least two occasions, he assisted in obtaining the release of Jesuit missionaries held captive by the Indians.

In 1649, Megapolensis took charge of the church at New Amsterdam, a position he retained until his death in 1670. The new pastorate was more enviable than that at Rensselaerswyck. It had an authentic-looking church building made of stone, and the congregation of one hundred seventy members was much larger than his previous charge. The frequent drunkenness and brawling among the people, however, did not make the minister's work any easier. At New Amsterdam, Megapolensis continued his efforts to convert the Indians, but with only very limited success. He also concerned himself with furthering the education of the youth and worked hard at organizing new Dutch Reformed congregations.[4]

Various decrees were issued during the New Netherland period that were designed to ensure a privileged position for the Dutch Reformed Church over competing denominations. A regulation of March 28, 1624, for example, declared that the colonists "shall within their territory hold no other services than those of the true Reformed Religion, in the manner in which they are at present conducted in this country."[5] Similarly, the first article of Stuyvesant's commission, taken under oath, specified that he was "not to permit any other than the Reformed doctrine."[6]

Such pronouncements, however, were not always well observed. In part this was because the directors of the West India Company feared that a strict interpretation would discourage some persons from emigrating to New Netherland. Thus it happened that the Jesuit missionary, Isaac Jogues, made the following observation about New Amsterdam in 1646: "No religion is publicly exercised but the Calvinist, and orders are to admit none but Calvinists, but this is not observed, for besides the Calvinists there are in the colony Catholics, English Puritans, Lutherans, Anabaptists, . . . etc."[7]

Several perplexing questions were raised concerning the status of the Dutch Reformed Church after the English takeover of the colony. What, for example, was to be its relationship to the Classis of Amsterdam? Could its members, especially the ministers, be subjects of the British government yet owe ecclesiastical obedience to a church body in Holland? In the absence of the West India Company, who was to pay the salaries of the ministers? Should the Dutch Reformed people of New York and New Jersey contribute to the financial support of an established English church?

Although there were occasional difficulties with the secular authorities during the years immediately after the English conquest, the major problems of the Dutch Reformed churches were at first internal. The shortage of pastors was of special concern. At the opening of the eighteenth century, there were only six Dutch Reformed ministers in the American colonies, although the number of churches had increased to twenty-three. Because of this shortage, a minister frequently had to serve two or more churches. In other instances, congregations had to rely almost exclusively on a *voorlezer*, with an occasional visit from an ordained pastor to administer the sacraments.

Difficulty in collecting ministerial salaries constituted another problem. During the New Netherland period, Dutch pastors generally received most, if not all, of their pay from the West India Company. Although the latter had frequently been lax in paying salaries, the ministers were nevertheless better off in this respect under Dutch rule than they were during the early years under the English. Shortly after the English takeover, laws were passed providing for compulsory support of a church in each parish, but such statutes were not always observed. As one writer stated, "the governors were loath to press non-Dutch to pay taxes for the Dutch Reformed church."[8] Nor were free-will offerings among the congregations helpful. The Reverend Megapolensis reported in April, 1669: "On Sundays we have many hearers. People crowd into the church, and apparently like the sermon; but most of the listeners are not inclined to contribute to the support and salary of the preacher. They seem to desire, that we should live upon air and not upon produce."[9] When he spoke with the English governor about the matter, he was told that "if the Dutch will have divine service their own way, then let them also take care of and support their own preachers."[10]

Except for a few isolated incidents, the English governors for many years after the conquest made no determined effort to establish the Anglican Church among the Dutch colonists. Beginning in 1692 with Governor Benjamin Fletcher, however, the governors, on orders of the English crown, tried not only to impose the Anglican Church on New York, but also to acquire the right to approve or to disapprove the appointment of *all* ministers. To deal with this problem, the New York provincial assembly, whose membership included many persons of the Dutch Reformed faith, passed the "Ministry Act" in 1693, which was intended to give local congregations greater privileges. The strength of the Dutch Reformed Church was demonstrated even more clearly in 1696 when the congregation in New York City was given its own charter, making it less vulnerable to the whims of the secular authorities.[11]

The agreement of 1696 became the model for charters that were later given to Dutch Reformed congregations elsewhere. Its significance was explained in a letter from Dominie Selyns to the Classis of Amsterdam written in September, 1696:

Its contents are in respect to the power of calling one or more ministers; of choosing elders, deacons, chorister, sexton, etc.; and of keeping Dutch-schools, all in conformity to the Church-Order of the Synod of Dort, Anno, 1619; also, the right to possess a church, a parsonage and other church property as our own, and to hold them in our corporate capacity, without alienation. Also the right to receive legacies of either real or personal property, and other donations, for the benefit of the church, etc. This is a circumstance which promises much advantage to God's church, and quiets the formerly existing uneasiness.[12]

The Dutch Reformed Church also showed its influence in a test of strength over a similar matter with Lord Cornbury, governor from 1701 to 1710.[13]

Despite such problems as a shortage of ministers, inadequate funds, and occasional trouble with royal governors, the Dutch Reformed churches continued to grow after the fall of New Netherland. At the opening of the eighteenth century, there were twenty-three Dutch congregations in the American colonies, an increase of ten over the number existing in 1664. By 1740, the number had grown to sixty-five, and at the outbreak of the American Revolution it stood at slightly over a hundred.

Much of this growth resulted from the natural increase of the Dutch population that had settled in the American colonies before 1664, because emigration from Holland practically ceased after the English conquest. Growth of the churches can also be attributed to the arrival of Huguenot refugees from France and Palatine immigrants from Germany. Both of these groups were Calvinist oriented, and not only frequently associated with the Dutch Reformed denomination, but sometimes were almost totally assimilated by the Dutch. In referring to the Palatines, for example, particularly those on the upper Hudson and in the Schoharie Valley of New York, one writer states that they

intermarried with the surrounding Dutch, worshipped at the same church, sent their children to the same school. It was in vain that they appealed for preachers and teachers who could speak both German and Dutch. Eventually they were absorbed into the Dutch population and so lost their identity.[14]

The Dutch Reformed Church, as a Calvinist denomination, placed considerable emphasis on creeds and doctrines. Attention was especially given to the decrees of the Synod of Dort of 1618–19, at which time an uncompromising stand was taken in favor of strict predestination, and against Arminianism. The Heidelberg Catechism was also looked upon as a statement *par excellence* of orthodox Calvinism. Children were taught its tenets at an early age, and a good understanding of it was required before a person could become a communicant member of the Church. Every dominie was expected to preach one of his Sunday sermons on the Catechism, and in order that he could get through it once a year, the Catechism was divided into fifty-two "Lord's Days."

Worship services consisted of Scripture reading, prayers, and congregational singing, but the sermon was the most important part. It was usually doctrinal and always lengthy. The Consistory of New York City on January 29, 1747, recommended that the ministers limit their sermons to not more than one hour "so as to remove the complaints about the long sermons, to increase the audiences and hold the people together, and so enlarge the alms and other revenues of the church."[15] The dominies expressed agreement with the proposal, but it was not well observed. When the Swedish traveler Peter Kalm attended two Dutch services in a single Sunday in New York City in 1749, he reported that the morning sermon lasted two hours, and that of the afternoon, two and a half hours. He stated it was impossible to remember a sermon that lasted so long, and began the entry in his diary for that date, November 9, as follows: *"Hunc diem perdidi"* (This day I have spent uselessly).[16] In some congregations, the layman who had charge of turning the hourglass was obliged to inform the dominie when it had run out for a second time.

It is open to question whether or not the Dutch colonists were greatly inspired by the lengthy sermons and the excessive doctrinal preaching to which they were exposed—literally from the cradle to the grave. Judging from the quarrelsome nature of many New Netherlanders, it would appear that the early dominies had only limited success in improving the social behavior of the colonists. The frequency with which decrees had to be issued on the subject of sabbath observance also indicates that Dutch preaching was not always effective.[17] A remark made by a New England physician during a visit to New York City in 1697 further illustrates that the Dutch were far from puritanical in their behavior on Sundays: "The Dutch seeme not very strict in Keepeing the Sabbath, you should see some shelling peas at theyr doors children playing at theyr usuall games in the streetes & ye taverns filled."[18] Similarly, a visitor to New York in 1704 noted that the people there were not as "strict in keeping the Sabbath as in Boston and other places where I have been."[19]

The impressions that the religious life of the Dutch of the

Albany area made on an English girl who lived there about the middle of the eighteenth century are particularly interesting. She wrote that

their religion, . . . like their original national character, had in it little of fervor or enthusiasm; their manner of performing religious duties was regular and decent, but calm, and to more ardent imaginations might appear mechanical. None ever doubted of the great truths of revelations, yet few seemed to dwell on the result with that lively delight which devotion produces in minds of keener sensibility.[20]

Traditionally, the Dutch Reformed ministers were opposed to any kind of revivalist-type preaching. In 1657, the reverends Megapolensis and Drisius of New Amsterdam wrote in reference to the Quakers and Anabaptists: "We trust that our God will baffle the designs of the devil, and preserve us in the truth, and bring to nothing these machinations."[21] These same two ministers in discussing Rhode Island as a haven for religious refugees declared that it was "the receptacle of all sorts of riff-raff people, and . . . nothing else than the sewer of New England. All the cranks of New England retire thither."[22] Dominie Selyns, in 1685, complained to the Classis of Amsterdam about tailors, cobblers, and others who were coming from Holland and endeavoring to be appointed as *voorlezers* and schoolmasters. "They speak against the church, public prayers and the liturgy of the church. . . . True believers are grieved at these things and look forward to very great troubles therefrom to the church of God."[23]

In view of the above, it is understandable why the evangelistic preaching of William Bartholf, one of the precursors of the Great Awakening, was criticized in some Dutch circles.[24] Born in Holland of humble background, Bartholf came to America with his wife and family about 1683, settling eventually at Hackensack, New Jersey. He soon began serving the church there and at neighboring Acquackanonck as *voorlezer*. His hearers were so impressed by his labors that they persuaded him to go to Holland in order to be examined and ordained as their regular pastor. Upon returning to America in 1693, Bartholf plunged zealously into his work, serving not only the churches of Hackensack and Aquackanonck but also neighboring Dutch communities in northern New Jersey as well as a few in southern New York.

Through forest and stream, over rugged hills and broad plains, up quiet valleys, wherever a group of Dutchmen had cleared for themselves homes in the wilderness, he went comforting the sick and troubled, baptizing children, bringing into the hard and lonely lives of the settlers the cheer of his kindly presence and longed-for news of distant relatives and friends.[25]

Bartholf's success in northern New Jersey was repeated a short time later in the central part of the province by the Reverend Theodorus Jacobus Frelinghuysen, one of the leaders of the Great Awakening in the Middle Colonies. Although of German descent, his homeland of East Friesland was on the Dutch border and many of its inhabitants were members of the Dutch Reformed Church. After an excellent theological education and a brief pastorate at Emden, he decided to go to the American colonies, where, from 1720 to 1747, he served the Dutch Reformed congregations in central New Jersey.

His task was not an easy one. Most of the time he was responsible for looking after six churches. The long absence of any settled minister among his parishioners had made them unconcerned about religious matters. One writer has stated that their morals resembled the physical appearance of the countryside—wild and uncultivated.[26] Frelinghuysen seemed to appreciate the challenge, however, and plunged with boundless energy into his work, a pace he maintained for over a quarter of a century.

As was true of other pastors of the Great Awakening, Frelinghuysen's preaching was evangelical in nature. He was critical of dogmatic, stale orthodoxy and formalized religion, and tried to make religion a more personal experience. Considerable stress was placed on the need of the people to be reborn spiritually. Unfortunately, his direct and outspoken manner of preaching antagonized many of his hearers, who wanted "to keep things in the Dutch way."[27] His strict ecclesiastical discipline, which was not always administered according to official church order, also made it difficult for some persons, including other ministers, to accept him.

Despite considerable criticism, Frelinghuysen was very successful as an evangelical preacher. Nineteen of his sermons were published in the colonies, in Dutch, between 1721 and 1745, as well as several English translations. When the eminent George Whitefield preached in the Dutch sections of New Jersey in the fall of 1739 and again in the spring of 1740, he attributed his success there in part to Frelinghuysen, who, he said, was "the beginning of the great work ... in these parts."[28]

The dissension that Frelinghuysen and the Great Awakening caused in some Dutch Reformed circles was accentuated by an attempt to make the colonial congregations less dependent on the Classis of Amsterdam. A significant number of ministers, including revival-oriented preachers like Frelinghuysen, became convinced that too heavy a reliance on ecclesiastical officials in Holland was hampering the growth of the churches. Debate over this question disturbed the peace of the colonial churches for almost a half century, and even led to a temporary schism among them.

There is no doubt that the subordination of the churches in America to the religious authorities in Holland created numerous difficulties. All important matters had to be handled by the Classis of Amsterdam, located three thousand miles across the ocean. Although permission was granted occasionally for a small conclave of ministers in America to deal with a particular problem, such instances were rare. The Classis delayed months and sometimes years before making decisions. It had to rely on written reports that were nearly always tardily received and were often biased and incomplete.

Dependence of the colonial churches on the Classis of Amsterdam for their ministers was especially a point of weakness. The procedure for calling and sending ministers from Holland took considerable time, and resulted in a chronic shortage of pastors. During most of the colonial period, there were about three times as many churches as ministers. Choices made by the reverend brothers of Amsterdam were often unwise. Sometimes they selected persons of mediocre ability who were unable to obtain pastorates in Holland. In 1725, mutterings were heard in some of the colonial congregations that the Classis made decisions on the basis of nepotism and "family influence," with no consideration given to the candidate's fitness.[29] Furthermore, most candidates had little or no acquaintance with conditions in America and were often young and inexperienced.

Suggestions were made from time to time that an organization be established which could deal with disciplinary problems, solve internal disputes, and examine and ordain young men for the ministry—all without recourse to Holland. As early as 1662, for example, the Reverend Johannes Polhemus of Long Island proposed that an association of ministers and churches be formed in New Netherland because "we stand in need of communication with one another in the form of a Classis, after the manner of the Fatherland."[30] Similar requests were made in 1706 and 1732.[31]

Such suggestions, however, fell on deaf ears. In 1709, the Classis of Amsterdam replied to the request of 1706 as follows: "The formation of a Classis among you, to correspond to ours at home, is yet far in the future, and we hardly dare to think of it."[32] In the following year, the Classis added that "such a Classis would be the ruin of the churches of New York. This is so obvious that it needs no proof."[33]

Something, however, had to be done. By 1740, it had been over seventy-five years since New Netherland had been lost, and it could not be expected that the American churches would remain dependent on authorities in Holland forever. Although some kind of an ecclesiastical vassalage to the Classis of Amsterdam was undoubtedly needed during the New Netherland period, the Dutch Reformed Church in the colonies had grown considerably since 1664. The congregations in the provinces of New York and New Jersey were fast becoming more numerous than even the strongest classis in Holland.[34] The subordination of the colonial churches to the Classis of Amsterdam was also part of the larger question of whether they would always be confined to one ethnic group or whether they would be expanded to include others. Some idea of the non-American nature of the churches is indicated by the fact that all but seven of the sixty ministers who had served in the colonies to 1737 came from Europe.[35]

Because of these considerations, several Dutch Reformed ministers and elders met at New York City in September, 1737, and

again in April of the following year, to discuss the formation
of an ecclesiastical union. At the latter meeting, a constitution
was drafted for a Coetus[36] consisting of a minister (or, in his
absence, a *voorlezer*) and an elder from each church to meet
annually on the first Monday in September. The Coetus was
empowered to "consider, determine, give sentence upon, and
settle all matters and dissensions that occur, or which are
brought before us for action; for being on the ground, we are
in the best possible position to judge of them, and to check and
smother them in their very beginnings." The Classis of Amsterdam
was assured that the Coetus would conform "to the Churches
of the Fatherland" and would correspond with them regularly.
Anyone who felt himself aggrieved by its decisions could appeal
to the Classis.[37]

It soon became apparent, however, that there was a variety
of views among the colonial dominies. The more conservative
element wished to retain all the old ties with the Classis of
Amsterdam, and merely limit the role of the Coetus to corresponding with the Classis. Others wished it to investigate disputes
and pass recommendations to the Classis. Still others wished
to authorize the group to make decisions, but with the right
to appeal the decisions to Amsterdam. There were also a few
who wished to end all connections with Amsterdam, and give
the Coetus the same rights and privileges enjoyed by any
Classis in Holland.[38]

Such divergent views prevented the Coetus from accomplish-
ing much until, by majority vote, its powers were broadened in
1754. From that date forward, stated meetings were regularly
held and minutes were kept. The reorganized Coetus ordained
ministers and refereed disputes. In 1766, it played an important
role in obtaining a royal charter from George III permitting the
Dutch Reformed Church to establish a college—Queen's College—
in New Jersey. The Coetus ministers hoped that by offering
theological studies the new school would make the colonial
churches less dependent on Holland for its ministers.

Meanwhile, a minority group, headed by Dominie Ritzema
of New York City, refused to accept the actions of the reorganized Coetus, favoring instead continued subordination to
the Classis of Amsterdam. Ritzema's followers were apprehen-

sive that the actions might lead to other changes affecting such matters as doctrine, mode of worship, church government, and perhaps even the name of the church. They were especially worried that the ordination of ministers in America might result in a less learned and less respected ministry, a fear that was particularly great before the plans for establishing Queen's College had been made.[39] As a consequence, the opponents of the reorganized Coetus soon created an ecclesiastical body of their own. It became popularly known as the Conferentie, and held firmly to the idea of subordination to the Classis of Amsterdam.

The schism, which lasted almost twenty years, was tragic for the colonial churches. Many Dutch Reformed people became discouraged and joined other denominations. Vehement language was frequently exchanged between the two groups. Minister was pitted against minister and congregation against congregation. Sometimes congregations had serious divisions within their own midst. At Hackensack, New Jersey, for example, there were two ministers, two sets of consistories, and two congregations which took turns using the church edifice. At times, there was even violence, with ministers being assaulted and some groups being forcibly prevented from using a church building for worship services.[40]

Meanwhile, the ranks of the Coetus group steadily increased. Ministers who were ordained in the colonies had no strong attachment for the Classis of Amsterdam, nor did churches that experienced long delays in acquiring a minister from Holland. Also, by 1765, the idea of political independence was germinating among the American people, and this kind of thinking began affecting the arguments of some of the Dutch colonial church leaders. Thus, the Coetus informed the Classis on one occasion that it would not argue on the basis of past history as to whether the colonial churches should be subordinate to the Classis of Amsterdam, but would argue instead from "inherent rights."[41] It also declared that "as a free people" it was a matter of their choice whether or not the ministers wished to correspond with the Amsterdam body.[42] Gradually, too, the Classis of Amsterdam, which in the past had often either sided with the Conferentie group or followed an ambiguous policy, showed a greater willingness to compromise with the Coetus faction.[43]

As a consequence of these developments and the efforts of the Reverend John H. Livingston, the schism finally came to an end. Livingston, a member of one of New York's most prestigious families, had discussed the problem with various church leaders in Holland while studying there at the University of Utrecht during the 1760's. Later, as pastor of the Dutch Reformed congregation in New York City, he succeeded in bringing the contending parties together for discussions.[44]

A plan was finally drafted based on the ideas Livingston had helped formulate in Holland. It was known as the Articles of Union, and embraced the following basic points: (1) the churches would adhere to the doctrine and policy of the Reformed Church in Holland; (2) the churches would be divided into five circles, in which ministers and elders would meet together three or four times a year in special bodies known as Particular Assemblies; (3) each of these in turn would send delegates once a year to a larger body, known as the General Assembly, representing the entire colonial church; (4) the General Assembly would have the right to examine and ordain young men for the ministry; (5) the college at New Brunswick would be placed under the control of the General Assembly and provided with a professor of theology; and (6) close correspondence, including a yearly report, would be maintained with the Classis of Amsterdam. In June, 1772, the delegates assembled again, and formally approved the Articles of Union.[45] Thus, the Dutch Reformed Church in America was once again united— although a few ministers and churches remained aloof from the union for several more years.

The ecclesiastical independence that was achieved in 1772 did not signify a complete break with the past. At first, the new denomination was known as the Dutch Reformed Church in North America and as the Reformed Dutch Church in the United States of America, but in 1819, it was incorporated as the Reformed Protestant Dutch Church in North America. These names indicate that an attachment to things Dutch lingered for many years. About 1840, an attempt was made to drop the term "Dutch" from the official title but the proposal was voted down by a large majority. It was not until 1867, almost a century after achieving ecclesiastical independence from Holland, that the present name of Reformed Church in America came into use. To avoid the confusion of using several different names, the shortened title of Reformed Church is used henceforth to designate what before 1772 had been the American branch of the Dutch Reformed Church of the Netherlands.

It was particularly in matters of doctrine that the Reformed Church continued to resemble the mother church in Holland. The authoritative Calvinist doctrinal standards that had been accepted there during the Protestant Reformation, including the Belgic Confession, the Heidelberg Catechism, and the Canons of Dort, were retained by the new American denomination. Thus it happened that a recently arrived immigrant from the Netherlands could report with a degree of amazement in 1848 that the New Jersey church in which he worshipped was still remaining "faithful to the ancient rules and confessions."[46]

The new American denomination also retained much of the polity of the Netherlands church, with its hierarchy of representative bodies. The consistory was the smallest judicatory, consisting of a minister and several laymen, known as elders and deacons, elected from the congregation. The elders concerned themselves primarily with the spiritual interests of the congregation, while the deacons looked after poor relief and various mundane affairs. A classis consisted of the ministers together with one elder from each consistory within a specific geographical area. It was responsible for the general supervision of the churches within its bounds, including the examining and licensing of ministers. Several classes formed a particular synod, composed of four ministers and four elders from each classis. The entire system culminated in the General Synod, consisting of delegates from each particular synod.

Although the Reformed Church borrowed its doctrine and polity from the Netherlands, it gradually became more Americanized after 1772. Its judicatories, while similar to those of Holland, were better able than before to adjust ecclesiastical policies to suit conditions unique to America. These conditions included sparse population, poor communications, a shortage of funds, and a miscellany of religious denominations and ethnic groups.

Increasingly, too, more and more of the ministers received their education in America rather than the Netherlands. Rutgers College, formerly called Queen's College, became particularly important for training young men for the ministry. Its special appeal to persons of Dutch descent and its Reformed Church orientation continued for many years. Until the Civil War, for example, its student body was drawn primarily from the old Dutch families of New York and New Jersey, with an increasing number coming from the new Dutch immigrant settlements in the Middle West. In 1840, four of the six teachers in the college were ordained ministers and three of them also taught in New Brunswick Seminary, as the theological division of the school became known. Furthermore, until 1909, two-thirds of the trustees had to be members of the Reformed Church. The abolition of this requirement and the continued secularization of its curriculum and faculty finally led to the school's becoming a state institution in 1917. In the meantime, Rutgers College and New Brunswick Seminary had drifted away from each other, a separation that was virtually complete by the time of the Civil War. The Seminary, however, remained on the Rutgers campus, where it still is today, and continued to be sponsored by the Reformed Church.[47]

The Americanization of the Reformed Church during the closing decades of the eighteenth century was particularly manifested in the substitution of English for Dutch in the worship services. This came about primarily because of the declining usage of Dutch in everyday life. In addition, the language was becoming more and more perverted from its original conditions of sound and vocabulary, and was being combined with an abundance of English words. On a boat trip from New York to Albany in 1744, for example, a traveler observed that everyone except himself and his servant could speak Dutch and seemed to prefer it to English, but added it was not a pure Dutch but a "medley of Dutch and English as would have tired a horse."[48] Similarly, when the Reverend Herman Boelen arrived from Holland in 1776 to take charge of the Queens County churches on Long Island, "his language was so pure that the parishioners, accustomed to corrupted

Dutch mixed with English words, had difficulty in understanding him."[49]

The declining use of Dutch by the colonists had long been a source of concern to the leaders of the Reformed Church. As early as 1726, the consistory of New York City had expressed alarm about this matter. Although the reverend body acknowledged the need for Dutchmen to learn English "in order properly to carry on one's temporal calling," it declared that parents should not neglect any opportunity for teaching the ancestral language to their children because "the true doctrine of comfort in life and in death is preached in the clearest and most powerful manner, in the Dutch tongue."[50]

Holding divine services in the Dutch language gave the colonists who were of Netherlands descent a cohesiveness that was helpful in maintaining their separate identity in the face of increasing numbers of Englishmen. The use of the ancestral language, however, was protracted beyond the time needed. A report in the *Independent Reflector* of January, 1754, noted that "the Dutch tongue, which though once the common dialect of this province [of New York], is now scarcely understood, except by its more ancient inhabitants," and added that the next generation very probably would be able to furnish no one except the clergy who were "well acquainted with the tongue."[51] In January, 1763, the consistory of New York City reported to the Classis of Amsterdam that the "mother tongue" had become so undermined that there was "scarce a principal family in this city and even in our own church, whose children clearly understand the Dutch language," and as a result their youth were so swelling the ranks of the English congregations that they "for the greatest part, consist of persons who are descendents of parents who were formerly communicants of our church."[52]

In response to several petitions by church members, the consistory in July, 1763, asked the Classis to obtain a properly ordained minister for New York City who could preach in English. The man selected was the Reverend Archibald Laidlie, a Scot, who had been serving an English congregation at Vlissingen in the southern part of the Netherlands. According to his instructions, English services were to be limited to two per week, "either both times on Sunday, or once on Sunday and once in the week, according to the pleasure of the Consistory."[53] Upon his arrival in 1764, Laidlie was assigned to the New Dutch Church on Nassau Street, later called the Middle Dutch Church.

Not all Dutchmen in New York City, however, were prepared to accept English preaching in one of their churches. Protests were sent to the Classis of Amsterdam, but they were answered with the reply that the "Everlasting Gospel" could be preached as well in English as in Dutch. The pro-Dutch party also appealed to the public authorities, including the provincial governor and the courts. The protestors claimed that the congregation as a whole and not the consistory should have the final decision on introducing English into the services. These attempts failed; English preaching had come to stay. This was clearly demonstrated by the steady growth of Laidlie's congregation, and in 1769, a call was sent to Amsterdam for a second minister qualified to preach in English.

Not long after New York City began introducing English preaching, other churches started following suit. In 1787, for example, the six collegiate churches of Kings County, Long Island, called a second minister, the Reverend Peter Lowe, to preach in English, while the Reverend Martinus Schoonmaker continued to deliver his sermons in Dutch until his death in 1824. In communities which had only one church or which were too small to support two ministers, a special kind of rotation plan was followed. Thus, the pastoral call of 1776 by the Reformed congregations of Bucks County, Pennsylvania, stipulated that the minister deliver half his sermons during the summertime in English, as well as a third of them during the winter months. Similarly, an agreement of 1795 with the pastor at Second River (now Belleville), New Jersey, stipulated that "to gratify the aged, who love to hear the word in their mother tongue," the morning sermon on the first sabbath of every month would continue to be preached in the Dutch language.[54] The switch from Dutch to English preaching was slower in coming to some places than others. At Paramus, New Jersey, for example, English services were not introduced until

1811, and some Dutch continued to be used there long after that date.

Steps to introduce English into the Reformed Church took other forms besides using it in the sermons. As early as 1763, the consistory of the New York City churches approved a plan for translating some of the psalms into English, but using Dutch musical scores. By 1782, approval had been given for a special translation of the Heidelberg Catechism into English to be used as a textbook for children. Shortly after the Revolution, the ruling body of the denomination appointed a special committee to supervise publication of a manual in the English language containing the creeds and liturgy as well as the rules of church order as these existed in the mother church in Holland. The committee's report was published in 1793 under the title of "The Constitution of the Reformed Dutch Church in the United States of America." The translators omitted whatever was unsuitable for the situation in America and inserted explanatory articles when needed. In 1794, the General Synod, the denomination's highest judicatory body, began keeping its minutes in English, at which time it may be said that English replaced Dutch as the official language of the Church.[55]

Although the substitution of English in the Church services continued unabated, the declining usage of Dutch in everyday language must not be exaggerated. In 1788, for example, to help win acceptance of the proposed United States Constitution, the Federalist Committee at Albany, New York, published a translation of it in Dutch. Similarly, when the Reformed Church at Hackensack, New Jersey, was rebuilt in 1791, the consistory decided to finance it by subscriptions. Two copies of the plan were circulated, one in English and the other in Dutch. The former received eighty-three signatures while forty-nine persons, more than a third of the total, signed their names to the Dutch version.[56]

Even with the virtual disappearance of Dutch preaching, the language continued to be used for a long time in parts of New York and New Jersey. According to one historian, some of the children living in Ulster County, New York, in 1850 spoke nothing but Dutch, learning English only after they started school.[57] As late as 1866, the wife of John Rutger Planten, consul-general from the Netherlands to the Port of New York, wrote her sister in Amsterdam:

The Dutch language has been handed down from parents to children and sometimes as far as the fifth generation. . . . I personally have observed the above very often in New Jersey where my brother was settled. A great many descendants of the Dutch live in that neighborhood. And it is a fact that one out of ten people will be able to understand you although it is not our civilized Dutch that they speak.[58]

The prolonged use of the Dutch language in New York and New Jersey during the colonial period naturally resulted in many Dutch words being adopted into the American vocabulary. Although some of them gradually became extinct through disuse, many others survived. In view of the small number of Holland-born who came to the colonies, this influence cannot be considered anything but spectacular. According to one authority, "More words per capita have been borrowed into American English from [the] early Hollanders than from any other sort of non-English speakers."[59]

Although the origin of words is often difficult to determine, those frequently mentioned by etymologists as likely being of Dutch origin include, among others: boss (*baas*, master), clove (*kloof*, ravine or crevice), coleslaw (*kool*, cabbage, plus *slaa*, salad), cooky (*koekje*, small cake), dope (*doop*, thick liquid, sauce, or gravy), dumb (*dom*, stupid or dull), golf (*kolf*, club or bat), hook (*hoek*, point of land or cape), kill (*kil*, creek or channel), patroon (*patroon*, proprietor of a manor), pit (*pit*, kernel or pith), scow (*schouw*, flat-bottomed boat), skate (*schaats*, skate), sleigh (*slede*, vehicle on runners), snoop (*snoepen*, to eat sweets in secret), spook (*spook*, ghost or spirit), stoop (*stoep*, small, covered porch), waffle (*wafel*, batter cake).[60]

"Santa Claus," the name by which the legendary character most loved by American children is commonly known, is a corruption of the Dutch *Sinter Klaas*, and was introduced to America during the New Netherland period. "Saint Nicholas," another popular name for Santa Claus, is also of Dutch origin. His makeup and appearance in America, however, has changed from that of his counterpart in Holland, where he appears in the colorful regalia of a medieval bishop. The traditional date for his giving gifts has also been changed—from December 6 in Holland to Christmas Eve in America. Even the word "Yankee" was perhaps introduced by the Dutch, being derived, according to some authorities, from Jan Kaas or Jan Keese, the name of a Dutch freebooter that was later applied as a term of contempt for Connecticut traders "whose business ethics stirred something less than admiration among Hollanders."[61]

Several derisive phrases having reference to the Dutch also found their way into American speech. Many of them were coined by the English because of the long-standing naval and commercial rivalry between the two nations, and perhaps would have entered the American vocabulary even if there had never been a New Netherland. Such opprobious expressions and their meanings include, among others: "double Dutch"—to talk in a gibberish manner; "Dutch auction"—a sale in which prices are marked deliberately high with the foreknowledge they will be lowered; "Dutch concert" or "Dutch medley"—a babel of noises; "Dutch courage"—false courage induced by intoxicating drink; "Dutch treat" or "go Dutch"—to pay for one's own entertainment or refreshments at a party; "to get in Dutch"— to incur the wrath or dislike of someone; "Dutch uncle"—someone who talks to another in a severe manner; "Dutch bargain"— a one-sided sale, but it can also mean a business transaction sealed with a drink.[62]

Finally, it can be noted that numerous geographical place-names serve as reminders of the important role the Dutch once played in the history of the eastern United States. Names in the New York metropolitan area dating back to the New Netherland period, although not always with the same spelling, include Manhattan Island, Staten Island, Broadway, Wall Street, Yonkers, Harlem, Brooklyn, and the Bowery. Similar survivals in the Delaware Valley include Cape Henlopen, Bombay Hook, Middleburgh, Schuylkill River, and Maurice River. The names of Dutch sea captains who visited American waters during the early seventeenth century have been preserved in such landmarks as Cape May (after Cornelis May) and Block Island (after Adriaen Block). Several communities have also been named after prominent colonial families of Dutch descent, including Schuylerville, Hasbrouck Heights, and Voorhees, New York, and Verplanck and Voorheesville, New Jersey.

*    *    *    *

The Dutch Reformed Church became the most important institution established by the Hollanders of the New Netherland period. From humble beginnings in the early seventeenth century, it grew to nearly a hundred congregations by the time of the Revolution. This growth occurred despite its general lack of an evangelistic spirit and despite its subservience to the absentee divines at Amsterdam. It retained the ancestral language intact in the church services for nearly a hundred fifty years, enabling it to serve as a binding force among persons of Dutch descent and to absorb many people of other ethnic backgrounds into the Dutch way of life. For the continued success of the Church, however, the traditional ways could not be continued indefinitely. As a consequence, the Dutch Reformed Church gradually underwent a degree of Americanization after about 1750. Fortunately, much of the popular agitation caused by these changes had been moderated in time for it to meet a new problem, namely, the American Revolution.

CHAPTER VII

# The Revolutionary War and Its Aftermath

THE HISTORIAN WHO DISCUSSES THE ROLE OF THE DUTCH COLONISTS in the American Revolution is confronted with several important questions. Did they tend to side primarily with the Patriots or were their sympathies with the Loyalists? Or did they not have any strong feelings on the issues of the Revolution but merely wanted to be left alone to work their farms or take care of their shops? Did the attitude of the Dutch vary according to their particular economic and social standing in the colonies? Were there differences between one locality and another? What was the attitude of the Reformed Church and her ministers toward the Revolution?

Writers attempting to answer these questions have generally confined themselves to a particular geographical area or to a special aspect of the problem. Past studies have also sometimes been too chauvinistic to be classified as good history, stressing the idea that the Dutch supported the Revolution almost to a man, and did so primarily for two reasons: a tradition of liberty which they inherited from their forebears in Holland and a lingering resentment toward England because of her "treacherous attack" on New Netherland in 1664. The truth of the matter is that the Dutch, like other colonists, reacted to the Revolution in a variety of ways. Some sided with the Patriots, others joined the Loyalists, and still others attempted to remain neutral. Furthermore, the reasons for their actions stemmed from a medley of motives.

Contemporary views about the attitude of the colonists toward the Revolution frequently indicate that many Dutchmen preferred remaining neutral in the conflict. Samuel Curwen, a Loyalist writer from Massachusetts, wrote on May 4, 1775, shortly after the battles of Concord and Lexington, that the

"Quakers and Dutchmen ... from their former experience, have too great a regard for ease and property to sacrifice either, at this time of doubtful disputation, on the altar of an unknown goddess, of rather doubtful divinity."[1] A French aristocrat, the Marquis de Chastellux, who served with the French forces in America for two and a half years, stated in 1782 that the Dutch of the Albany area were inclined toward neutrality but the Indian menace and the plundering raids carried out by British troops made such a policy difficult. The Marquis added that the Dutch "concern themselves much more with domestic economy than with public government," and that "their interests and their efforts are, so to speak, individual; their views are centered on their families, and it is only from necessity that these families form a state."[2]

An historian who has done considerable research on the Dutch of colonial New York supports the thesis that their thoughts and traditions centered more on private concerns, such as the family and religion, than on politics. According to this writer, participation in government never seemed as important to the Dutch, either in Holland or in America, as it did to the English, and therefore they did not get too excited about the political rhetoric of the American revolutionaries.

'Liberty' to them was far less the power to govern themselves than freedom to trade, to own land, to practice a craft, and to worship without restrictions. ... When they finally did take sides it was not because of appeals to their public conscience, but because one side or the other infringed or protected their private liberties by force of arms.[3]

Neutrality, even when desired, was not an easy policy for many Dutchmen to follow because their homes were often located in the thick of the fighting. The province of New York, for example, which had a heavy concentration of persons of Dutch descent, was the arena for innumerable battles and skirmishes. "Armies marched and countermarched through its principal river valleys, strewing death and destruction behind them. Nearly one-third of the engagements of the war were fought on New York soil."[4] A similar situation prevailed in northern New Jersey, where Dutchmen were also very numerous. A writer recently described the situation in the Hackensack Valley during the Revolution as follows: "Both British and American forces moved into it often, seldom in such strength as to risk a major battle, but never so quietly that Jersey Dutchmen could forget they lived in a frontier open from all sides."[5] Persons of Dutch descent living along the frontier were also frequently caught up in the fighting through no personal choice of their own, but because they feared attack from the Indian allies of the British.

Some Dutchmen who remained neutral or who joined the Loyalists undoubtedly thought they were being realists in refusing to take up arms against the British. As one historian recently stated, many colonists must have wondered "how could two and a half million people, nearly 20 per cent of whom were slaves, fight a nation of eight million people, a nation which only a few years earlier had achieved the pinnacle of world power in the Seven Years' War?"[6] Similarly, the occupation of New York City and Long Island by the British during most of the war must have influenced the thinking of many Dutchmen residing in those places. It was only natural in regions occupied by the British that "motivations of personal safety, and the preservation of their property, would necessarily induce many either to remain inactive, or join the ranks of the [occupying force]."[7]

Various other explanations have been given as to why some Dutchmen sided with the British. One of the most interesting is that Toryism had a natural appeal for ethnic minorities. According to a proponent of this view, if one excludes British-born Tories, whose allegiance to England tended to be habitual and natural,

the Tories more commonly drew their recruits from the non-English than from the English parts of the community. The two most purely English provinces, Virginia and Massachusetts, were the strongholds of the Revolution. It was in the patchwork societies of Pennsylvania and New York that the Tories were strongest. Among almost all cultural minorities, the proportion of Tories seems to have been clearly higher than among the population at large.[8]

The basis for this argument is that minority groups believed that a purely Anglo-American majority would constitute a threat to the existence of their old ethnic mores, whereas continued dependence on England would protect them from "cultural aggression." The writer of the above further stated that the less Anglicized the non-English were, the more prone they were to support the Loyalist cause.[9]

Although the assertion that ethnic minorities tended to support the British may be true as a general statement, it cannot be applied as a hard and fast rule to the Dutch. Those residing in Albany, for example, were far from being Anglicized in 1775, yet they tended to support the Patriot cause. A similar situation prevailed in northern New Jersey, where often "Dutchmen who were most deeply committed to plain Dutch ways were Whigs ... [and] the Dutchmen who had in greater or less degree abandoned his Dutch ways ... became a Tory."[10]

For the Dutch, local issues and considerations played an important part in their decisions to join one side or the other. In the case of Albany, for example, the bold espousal of the principles of the Revolution by the popular dominie of the Reformed church, the Reverend Eilardus Westerlo, undoubtedly caused some of the colonists there to join the Patriots. Furthermore, some of the great Dutch merchants of Albany had a special resentment toward the Britishers who, during the French and Indian War, began establishing rival businesses in the area and receiving plush military contracts that had formerly gone to Dutch firms.[11] The hostile attitude of the mercantile class of Albany toward the English was shared by the common people. Peter Kalm reported in 1749 that "the hatred which the English bear against the people at Albany is very great, but that of the Albanians against the English is carried to a ten times higher degree. This hatred has subsisted ever since the time when the English conquered this section."[12]

Other Dutchmen living in the upper Hudson Valley also often joined one side or the other in the conflict for reasons that were purely local and had little to do with revolutionary principles or with their being of Dutch descent. Those living in the Schenectady area north of Albany, for example, tended to favor the Patriots in part because of their long-standing hatred of the late Sir William Johnson and his Scottish tenants, a hatred that was passed on to the Loyalist heirs of Johnson. The Schenectady Dutch also leaned toward the Patriot cause because their nearness to the frontier exposed them to Indian raids.[13] Many Dutchmen in the Kinderhoek region to the south of Albany, on the other hand, had no strong leanings toward the Patriots, a sentiment that also resulted primarily from local conditions. As one writer expressed it,

> Kinderhoek, unlike Schenectady, represented a district very well sheltered from invasion. . . . To its population of farmers and rivermen the burning issues of the Revolution must have seemed very far away. Battle never threatened them. They owned their own land and so had no community of interest with tenant agitators. They did not engage in foreign trade and so had no direct concern with the problems which aroused merchants.[14]

It is possible that the presence of the Reverend Johannes Ritzema at Kinderhoek after 1778 also helped keep pro-Patriot feelings to a minimum. For almost thirty-five years prior to his arrival at Kinderhoek, he served the Dutch churches of New York City, and was for many years the leader of the reactionary Conferentie party of the Reformed Church. It is difficult to state positively that Ritzema was a Tory sympathizer, but generally speaking, the adherents of the old Conferentie group tended to sympathize more with the Loyalists than the Patriots. Thomas Jones, the Tory historian from Long Island, referred to Ritzema as "a worthy, honest, good, loyal, and religious man."[15] Rudolph Ritzema, the dominie's son, after serving for a time in the Patriot army, switched sides and became a colonel in the Loyalist army.

Political "cronyism" also influenced the decisions of certain distinguished Dutch colonists. For many years prior to 1775, there had been two major political groups in the colony of New York: the De Lancey faction and the Livingston faction. The former was pro-Anglican and only moderately critical of England; the latter was identified with the non-Anglicans and became increasingly outspoken against British imperial policies. When the Revolution broke out, many persons continued to support the group with whom they had been associated during the previous years. As a consequence, some prominent persons of Dutch descent, such as Nicholas and Peter Stuyvesant and Nicholas Van Cortlandt, who had traditionally supported the De Lancey faction, became Loyalists, while others, such as Henry Rutgers and Isaac Roosevelt, who had supported the Livingston faction, became Patriots.[16] Persons of lesser social and economic standing were undoubtedly also prone to support the one group or the other depending on which, in the past, had given the most patronage in the way of government contracts or minor political positions.

The disposition toward neutrality or Toryism that was exhibited by a segment of the Dutch colonists must not be construed to mean they never entertained any ill-will toward the English. To be critical of British imperial policies, however, was one thing; to take up arms against the king was something else, and to talk about independence was complete anathema to some Dutchmen. New Jersey, whose population was about one-sixth Dutch at the time of the Revolution, was not inclined toward political radicalism, although it had its share of critics of imperial policies. "Left to its own resources and inclinations, it is unlikely that New Jersey would have opted for independence in 1776 or at any time in the foreseeable future."[17] Many colonists, although resentful of British policies, were fearful that lawlessness would result if radical Patriot leaders were given power. This dilemma explains why some moderate Dutchmen who opposed such measures as the Stamp Act and Townshend Acts and even participated for a time in extralegal committees and congresses later became neutral or joined the Loyalists when the Revolution broke out.

In addition to becoming disenchanted with the radical trend of anti-British criticism, the idea of independence raised some special fears among merchants engaged in transoceanic shipping. Not only did they stand to lose the protection given them by the mightiest navy in the world but their old trading pattern of carrying on commerce with British West Indian ports and working through London mercantile houses would be disrupted. There were exceptions to this, however, among Dutchmen. Some of the Beekmans, Schuylers, and Gansevoorts, of New York and

Albany, for example, who were heavily engaged in trade, sided with the Patriots. Nor does an examination of comparative wealth among the Jersey Dutch indicate that the more wealthy among them tended to support the Loyalists more than the Patriots.[18]

One of the most interesting metamorphoses of a Dutchman who changed from a critic of British policy to being a Loyalist, and who after living as an exile in England changed his views about America once more, was Peter Van Schaak, a prominent attorney. Before the Revolution, he was a moderate critic of British policy and served on several extralegal committees, including the Committee of Correspondence, in the province of New York. When the "day of reckoning" arrived, however, Van Schaak, like many other colonists, refused to take up arms against England and even opposed the Declaration of Independence.

Van Schaak was a highly educated man, having graduated first in his class at King's College. He was one of the few Loyalists to base his opinions of the Revolution on political theory and to put his views in writing. According to one authority,

His own political speculations were unhurried and cool, and with deliberation he turned his back on the rush of events in order to consult his reason and his conscience. . . . During the winter of 1775–6, when friends like Gouverneur Morris and John Jay had put aside thought and were busy with war, Van Schaack shut himself up at his farm [near Kinderhoek] with his books. He went through and annotated Locke, Vattel, Montesquieu, Grotius, Beccaria, and Puffendorf, and then wrote out his opinions on the Revolution.[19]

Failing in his effort to remain neutral in the Revolution, Van Schaak went to live in England in 1778. While in exile, his views on the Revolution and on Anglo-American relations changed and he evinced a desire to return to America. Because of the moderate position he had taken on the conflict and through the influence of friends, especially his very close friend John Jay, he was permitted to return in 1785, and his property that had been confiscated was returned. A man of considerable legal training, he reopened his law office in Kinderhoek and again took students as he had before the Revolution, training almost a hundred young lawyers in forty years. In 1826, six years before his death, Columbia University awarded him an honorary Doctor's degree.[20]

Peter Van Schaak has been termed "one of the thoughtful and scrupulous" Loyalists,[21] a remark that cannot always be made about Dutch colonists who sided with the opposition. William Bayard, for example, a wealthy merchant and landowner of Dutch and Huguenot descent, was undoubtedly inspired by self-interest to join the Loyalists. He had long been closely associated with the British government and during the French and Indian War was awarded plush contracts for supplying the British army. As was true of many Loyalists, he lost his property by confiscation, and moved to England after the war. Abraham C. Cuyler, mayor of Albany, also sided with the Tories and eventually became a major in a Loyalist regiment. His decision, too, was influenced by various favors he had received in the past from the British government. His property was confiscated and after the war he settled in Canada.

In a sense, the presence of a significant number of Tories among the Dutch is not surprising considering that both New York and New Jersey were Tory strongholds. Although New York ranked seventh out of thirteen in total population, it had three or four times more Loyalists than any other state; New Jersey ranked fourth in this respect, and ahead of any New England state.[22] When one realizes that on the eve of the Revolution about one-fifth of the population of New York and about one-sixth of the population of New Jersey were of Dutch descent, the possibility is strong that, given the strength of Toryism in those two states, its incidence among Dutchmen would be high.

Fortunately for the pride of today's Dutch-Americans, the presence of Loyalists among the Dutch colonists was counterbalanced by a large number of Dutchmen who supported the Revolution wholeheartedly. The Albany area alone contributed three generals to the Patriot cause: Peter Gansevoort, Philip John Schuyler, and Abraham Ten Broeck, all of whom were descendants of Hollanders who came to America during the New Netherland period. Gansevoort won the official praise of Congress for his heroic defense in 1777, at the age of twenty-eight, of Fort Stanwix (later Fort Schuyler) against an over-whelming force of Tories and Indians. Schuyler, a landed mag-nate in the true sense of the word, had won his spurs in the French and Indian War. During the Revolution, he participated in several engagements and for a time was placed in command of the department of northern New York with headquarters at Albany. Ten Broeck, who had been active in public affairs since the 1750's, played a role in the defeat of Burgoyne in 1777.

Unfortunately, as is often true in war, unless a soldier of the Revolution was of high rank or was socially prominent, his name and personal participation in the conflict often escaped notice by later historians. Exceptions to this were those humble foot soldiers who, frequently by chance, had a brief encounter with fame and as a result have had their names recorded in to-day's history books. One such person was John Paulding, a descendant of Joost Paulding who emigrated from the Nether-lands to New York about 1688. It was Paulding who with two fellow soldiers captured the noted British spy Major John André near Tarrytown, New York—an act that led to the discovery of Benedict Arnold's treachery.[23]

Yet there were thousands of other persons of Dutch descent who fought valiantly in the Revolution—and sometimes made the supreme sacrifice—whose names today are of interest only to genealogists. For example, six of the seven sons of Joris Brinckerhoff, a Dutch farmer living in southern Pennsylvania, served in the Revolutionary War.[24] Histories of localities that had a strong concentration of Dutchmen abound with Dutch-sounding names of persons who served honorably in the Con-tinental Army or militia.[25] An examination of the genealogical records also indicates that many Dutchmen living in New York, New Jersey, and elsewhere were strong supporters of the Revolu-tion. Eighty soldiers with the name Voorhees, for example, served with the Patriot troops from New Jersey.[26]

Not all Dutchmen who became serious supporters of the Patriot cause made their contribution as battlefield soldiers. Richard Varick (1753–1831), great-grandson of Jan Van Varick who came to New York from the Netherlands about 1687, joined the army as a captain in 1775. General Washington displayed great confidence in Varick and selected him in 1781 as his confidential secretary to head a staff charged with the task of arranging, classifying, and copying all the correspondence and records of the Continental Army. The task was completed in 1783 and totaled over forty volumes. In a personal and warm letter of January 1, 1784, Washington thanked Varick for "the fidelity, skill and indefatigable industry" that he manifested in the performance of his public duties.[27] Also important on Washington's staff was Simeon De Witt, who after serving for a time as an army surveyor became Chief Geographer for the army in 1780.

Nearly all Dutch colonists, no matter whether they were Patriots, Loyalists, or neutrals, suffered extensively from the war. In fact, perhaps no other ethnic group, taken as a whole, endured more from the conflict. The extent to which Dutch communities suffered at the hands of the British during the Revolution is clearly shown in the treatment often accorded their churches in New York and New Jersey. Several of the Dutch churches on British-occupied Long Island were used as storage sheds, powder magazines, or barracks. Frequently, the seats and floors were removed and used as building material or firewood. In New York City, the South Dutch Church, also called the Garden Street Church, was the only one that did not need extensive repairs after the Revolution. Several Dutch churches elsewhere were burned, including those at Staten Island, Kingston, Raritan, and Millstone.

A description of the suffering experienced by the Dutch-Americans during the Revolution was sent to the Classis of Amsterdam by two dominies in October, 1778. Although an exaggerated account (understandably so, in view of the British desecration of Dutch churches), it reveals the heated and bitter feelings of many Dutch patriots.

We are from time to time increasingly strengthened and confirmed, among other things, by the unrighteous acts and unheard of cruelties committed by the English army everywhere; the inhuman maltreatment of so many thousands of our prisoners, in noisome prisons and ships, suffering from hunger, cold, nakedness and other never-heard-of barbarities; the wanton burning of our houses, villages, towns and cities; . . . the incessant robbing and plundering wherever they gain the upperhand; the instigation of the savage barbarians against our peaceful inhabitants, and the murdering of men, women and children; above all, the malicious and God-provoking destruction of our churches, both in New York and in the country; and a thousand other cruelties which have been and are still daily being committed with inconceivable bitterness and fury.[28]

Not all the misfortunes suffered by Dutchmen, however, can be blamed on the British. Considerable hardships were inflicted on them by their own neighbors. Thus, some of the inhabitants of Long Island,

not inconsiderable in number, were desirous for the opportunity of rioting upon the property of their neighbors, thereby benefitting themselves, without the liability to punishment. And it so happened that more frequent and daring outrages, upon persons and property, were practiced by our own citizens, than by many who had come three thousand miles to force our submission to the tyranny of a foreign master.[29]

Because of the presence of several factions—Patriots, Loyalists, and neutrals, with various shades in between—northern New Jersey, too, witnessed considerable fighting among its inhabitants. Dutchmen of both Tory and Patriot sympathies participated in this "war of neighbors" and in turn were frequently victimized by it, depending upon whose side they were on and which side at the moment seemed to be winning. Sometimes members of the same family were pitted against one another. Among the Dutch of Bergen County, for example, "division of loyalty within families was not uncommon. Several of a family served the King and others the patriot cause."[30]

Some conception of the hardships suffered at the hands of foraging parties trying to find supplies for American troops can be derived from an account written in December, 1778, about the Dutch and other farmers living in the "no man's land" of northern New Jersey:

Before the war they must have been in an affluent and happy state . . . but now they sow and plant, and know not who will reap the fruits of their labor, for their grain and other produce are taken for the use of the continental army, and in lieu certificates are given to be paid at the Treasury at Philadelphia; to many of them, especially those they imagine are inimical to their cause, they have barely left sufficient for the support of their families and the stock on the farms for the ensuing Winter.[31]

Among the Dutch colonists, the strongest support for the Patriot cause came from leaders of the Reformed Church. As early as six months before the Declaration of Independence, the consistory of the church at Millstone, New Jersey, referred to the struggle as "an unhappy and unnatural dispute between the ill disposed ministry of Great Britain and the oppressed colo- nies."[32] George Washington, after a visit to Albany, wrote the consistory there on June 28, 1782, stating that "while I consider the approbation of the Wise and the Virtuous as the highest possible reward for my services, I beg you will be assured, Gentlemen, that I now experience the most sensible pleasure from the favorable sentiments you are pleased to express of my Conduct."[33] Similar letters of gratitude were written from time to time to other Dutch church leaders.[34] William Living- ston, governor of New Jersey, wrote Henry Laurens, president of the Continental Congress, that "the Low Dutch clergy, both in this and the state of New York, are almost universally firm friends of these United States."[35] The General Synod, the high- est judicatory body in the Reformed Church, never once ques- tioned the righteousness of the American cause; in fact, its min- utes indicate a strong fidelity to the principles of the Revolution. In 1780, for example, the General Synod specifically declared that the war was "just and necessary."[36]

The Reverend Jacobus Rutsen Hardenbergh, pastor at Raritan and neighboring Dutch congregations during most of the war, can be cited as an example of a determined champion of the Revolution. His preaching aroused considerable enthusiasm for the revolutionary cause and led to the burning of the Raritan church by a Tory raiding party in 1779. A newspaper report of 1778 lists the following donations as having been recently re- ceived by the hospital at Princeton:

From the Rev. Mr. Hardenbergh's congregation at Raritan, 180 pairs of stockings, 62 good shirts, 43 ditto jackets, 11 shirts, 50 woolen jackets, 25 ditto pairs of breeches, 17 coats, 4 blankets, 5 pairs of shoes, besides a quantity of old linen and wollen for hospital use.[37]

Governor Livingston of New Jersey, in his praise of the Reformed clergy, specifically singled out Hardenbergh as one "who had been exceedingly instrumental in promoting the cause of America."[38] Washington's armies were camped for two winters within the bounds of Hardenbergh's pastoral charge, during which time he and Mrs. Washington often visited the dominie's home. The Reverend Hardenbergh also participated actively in helping form the state government of New Jersey. He was a delegate to several sessions of the General Assembly of the state and served on various governmental committees.

Of the more than forty ministers who were serving the Dutch churches when the Revolution broke out, not more than a half dozen became Loyalists. The most important was Dominie Garret Lydekker, who before the Revolution served the church at English Neighborhood, New Jersey, a community that, despite its name, was inhabited primarily by Dutchmen. Lydekker was a man of means, having inherited a four-hundred-acre farm from his father, and was an accomplished linguist in Dutch and English. He soon became an ardent Tory, refusing to omit from his church services the prayers for the English king. In November, 1776, he was forced to seek refuge in New York City, where he remained until the end of the war. It is possible that his marriage in 1770 to an English woman who had just emigrated from London influenced his Tory sympathies. With the exception of a younger brother, all the collateral members of the Lydekker family sided with the Patriots.

Lydekker became the acknowledged leader of the pro-English Dutch people living in New York City, and served as pastor of the Reformed Church inhabitants of the city. Because the British had requisitioned all the Dutch churches for use as barracks, hospitals, and prisons, Lydekker's congregation was given permission to use St. George's chapel during those Sunday hours when the Anglicans were not using it. In late 1782, when negotiations for peace were going on, he helped draft a petition, later sent to England, arguing against independence for the colonies. At the close of the war, Dominie Lydekker went to England, where he died in exile in 1794.[39]

In typical Calvinist fashion, the church leaders attributed the tragic events of the war to the sins of the people. The General Synod, therefore, recommended in 1775 and again in 1778 that the Reformed churches set aside a specific "day of solemn humiliation, with fasting and prayer, for the forgiveness of sins and the averting of deserved miseries."[40] In the dark days of 1780, with the defeat of the American army in the South as well as the treachery of Benedict Arnold and the emptiness of the treasury, clergymen called for a strengthening of the moral fiber of the people. At its October meeting in New Paltz, New York, the General Synod sent a resolution to the governor and members of the legislature of New York urging them to use their powers to strengthen and enforce the laws against immorality and crime as a means to curry God's favor in the conflict.[41]

Several reasons may be advanced as to why the Reformed ministers supported the Patriot cause so enthusiastically. Like many ministers of other denominations, they viewed with alarm the growth of the Anglican church in the colonies and were fearful that it would become even more of an established church than it already was.[42] Furthermore, the Coetus-Conferentie schism had made many of the ministers more conscious of liberty and independence. The support given the cause of American independence by the Coetus ministers was thus an indication of their desire to continue the Americanization of the Dutch Reformed Church. It is significant in this respect that not one minister whose sympathies lay with the Coetus group joined the Loyalist side, whereas those who did so had been sympathetic with the Conferentie faction.[43]

A discussion of the Dutch colonists and the American Revolution would be incomplete without mention of the attitude of their ancestral homeland toward the conflict. There is little doubt that the great majority of the inhabitants of the Netherlands was indifferent to the Revolution. The masses of the people were too busy with the everyday problems of earning a living to concern themselves with events taking place three thousand miles across the ocean. There were two groups of Netherlanders, however, who took a great interest in the Revolution: the so-called *patriotten* and certain businessmen. Among both groups, this interest later had a bearing on Dutch emigration to the new American nation.

The *patriotten* were political reformers who, infatuated by the rationalism of the Enlightenment period, were sympathetic to the political ideas of the American revolutionaries. When the conflict broke out, they showed an immediate readiness to support it as best they could by speeches and pamphlets. Their leader was an energetic Dutch aristocrat named Johan Derk Van der Capellen, who declared it was not only an honor to support the Revolution but that it was the cause of all mankind. The debt owed him by the American revolutionary leaders for his public support is shown in the many letters of gratitude he received from such notables as George Washington, Benjamin Franklin, and John Adams.[44] In 1787, four years after the American Revolution ended, the Dutch *patriotten* attempted a revolution of their own. It was aimed at limiting the power of the stadtholders and the patrician families, and at instituting a form of government that would be more sympathetic to the interests of the middle class. When it failed, hundreds of *patriotten* fled to France, but a few of them emigrated to the United States.

One of the most noteworthy of these émigrés was Francis Adriaen Van der Kemp, who arrived in New York with his family in 1788. For six years, he tried being a gentleman farmer at Kingston, New York, and later in the central part of the state near New Rotterdam (now called Constantia), which consisted of about a dozen crude log cabins. In 1797, he moved to Olden Barneveld (now called Barneveld), a small Dutch community where a few political exiles like himself were residing. He died there in 1829.

Van der Kemp, who had received a university education in Holland and had a personal library of over a thousand volumes, did considerable writing in America on a variety of subjects, including religion, politics, law, geography, history, and agriculture. Governor De Witt Clinton, a close personal friend, engaged him to translate the Dutch colonial records of New York. He worked at this task from 1818 to 1822, but unfortunately the twenty-four manuscript volumes resulting from this effort were destroyed in the fire that swept through the state capitol in 1911. An indication of Van der Kemp's standing with the great men of America is shown in the following communication about him from John Adams to Thomas Jefferson in 1816: "His head is deeply learned and his heart is pure. I scarcely know a more amiable character.... Had he been as great a master of our language as he was of his own, he would at this day have been one of the most conspicuous characters in the United States."[45] His reputation as a scholar earned him an honorary Doctor of Laws degree from Harvard College.

The interest of Netherlands businessmen in the American Revolution stemmed from motives very different from those of the *patriotten*—namely, profits. In a letter of August 4, 1779, John Adams, who became minister to the Netherlands, evinced the hope that a close association would be formed between "the Hollanders and us." He wrote: "The similitude of manners, of religion, and, in some respects, of constitution, the analogy between the means by which the two republics arrived at independency, but, above all, the attractions of commercial interest, will infallibly draw them together."[46] A year later, however, Adams was less optimistic, and wrote from Amsterdam on December 10, 1780, to the president of the Congress, that "almost all the professions of friendship to America which have been made, turn out, upon trial, to have been nothing more than little adulations to procure a share in our trade."[47] Nevertheless, he succeeded in negotiating a loan of five million guilders from several Amsterdam banking houses for the new republic. This was the first of several such loans, which by 1794 totaled thirty million guilders.

In addition to loans, businessmen in Holland were interested in selling military supplies to the rebels. This was done as early as 1775 and against the objections of the British government as well as the pro-English stadtholderate family and those Hollanders who were fearful of being drawn into a war with England. Profits from the contraband trade were high; according to one authority, merchants in the Netherlands could lose two cargoes out of three and still make a considerable profit.[48] Most of the contraband trade in arms and ammunition was channeled through the Dutch colonies in the Caribbean, especially the small island of St. Eustatius. Sir Joseph Yorke, British ambassador at The Hague, declared in 1776 that it was "the rendezvous of everything and everybody meant to be clandestinely conveyed to America."[49] It therefore was not surprising that England occupied St. Eustatius in 1778.

The interest shown in America during the Revolution by businessmen from the Netherlands continued after the conflict ended. The Netherlands had once been the leading commercial nation of Europe, but the economic rise of other countries together with protective tariffs weakened the Dutch. They hoped therefore to recoup some of these losses after the Revolution by entering the American market. In particular, they desired to export manufactured goods, especially textiles and certain products dealt in by the Dutch East India Company, such as tea and spices, in return for American agricultural products like wheat, tobacco, rice, and indigo.

Netherlands businessmen were disappointed in the amount of trade that developed between them and the United States, and with the rapidity with which England regained the commercial primacy she enjoyed there before the Revolution. There were several reasons for this disappointment. The products of Dutch industry, with a few exceptions, did not suit the tastes of the Americans. The language problem as well as the difference in the system of weights and measures were also factors. Furthermore, Dutch merchants were not as inclined to grant long-term credit to American buyers as were the English. Finally, the Industrial Revolution had given English merchants a competitive edge in both quality and price over Dutch merchants.

Despite these disappointments and problems, there was greater economic involvement in the United States by Netherlanders after the Revolution than before. Several Dutch banking firms in the late 1780's began to speculate in American securities—both state and federal—and in other business ventures. In 1789, four Dutch banking houses dispatched a special agent, Théophile Cazenove of Amsterdam, to look after their interests. For ten years, Cazenove remained in the United States advising various Netherlands firms on possible American investments, including securities, manufacturing schemes, canal companies, and especially land.

Fearful that the Netherlands would soon be involved in a general European war, especially after the outbreak of the French Revolution in 1789, Dutch bankers were desirous of investing their money in a "safe" area of the world. In 1791–92, several Amsterdam and Rotterdam financial houses sent Gerrit Boon and Jan Lincklaen to the United States to purchase land for a maple sugar industry. Thirty-six thousand acres were acquired for this purpose in central New York north of Fort Stanwix. Unfortunately, the project failed after only two years of operation.

The most extensive economic venture undertaken in the United States by Netherlanders during the early national period centered on the activities of the Holland Land Company. This organization was created in late 1792 by six Amsterdam banking houses for the purpose of acquiring extensive lands in the United States. Through the sale of Holland Land Company stock on the Amsterdam exchange, ordinary citizens of the Netherlands along with wealthy bankers became involved in the project. Within a few years, the Holland Land Company had acquired title to almost five and a half million acres in central and western New York and in northern and western Pennsylvania. It remained in operation until about 1850, and although it experienced some reverses from time to time, especially in Pennsylvania, in the long run it showed a good profit from the sale of its lands.

The various economic ventures undertaken by Netherlanders, including some of the businesses that failed, had permanent consequences. New communities were established along the frontier regions as new land was opened for settlement. The Boon-Lincklaen maple sugar project, for example, hastened the settlement of lands north of Utica, New York, and also led to the founding of the town of Olden Barneveld, named after one of Holland's greatest statesmen. Other communities whose founding was encouraged by Dutch economic projects included Cazenovia, Boonville, Lincklaen, Batavia, and New Amsterdam. The latter village was laid out in 1803, and its name was changed to Buffalo in 1810. To ensure the success of these communities, the Dutch agents in charge of development would sometimes, as in the case of Olden Barneveld, erect sawmills, gristmills, stores, taverns, stables, and even a few family dwellings in order to attract settlers. An offer to extend credit to potential settlers was also sometimes practiced in this paternalistic system.[50]

The growing economic interest shown by some Netherlanders in America led to a small increase in Dutch emigration to the United States during the early national period. As might be expected, the largest number of arrivals were businessmen who, either for themselves or as agents of Dutch firms, were looking for new opportunities for investment. Some of them settled in the major cities, including New York, Boston, Philadelphia, Baltimore, Charleston, and New Orleans. The new immigrants also included a number of tradesmen, such as distillers, blacksmiths, millwrights, gardeners, and glassblowers, as well as a few farmers. Strangely enough, not many of the latter settled on the lands of the Holland Land Company, but instead were scattered throughout several states.

Although Dutch emigration to the new American nation was small during the immediate decades after the Revolution and most of the arrivals were ordinary people, there were a few among them who distinguished themselves in a special way. One of these, the *patriot* Francis Van der Kemp, has already been discussed. Two others were André Everard Van Braam Houckgeest and Gerard Troost.

Van Braam Houckgeest became especially noted for his collection of Chinese objects gathered during two lengthy stays in China covering a period of more than twenty years. An admirer of the principles of the American Revolution, he wrote Benjamin Franklin in 1777, "I must tell you Monsieur, ... that I am wholly devoted to the Americans and to their cause, and so I learn of all their advantages with joy as if all that were my own good fortune."[51] After the Revolution, he emigrated to America and later built a magnificent mansion, called "Chinese Retreat," on the Delaware River not far from Philadelphia. Here he surrounded himself with his Chinese collection and entertained such distinguished guests as Washington, Lafayette, and Talleyrand.

Gerard Troost, who had a medical degree from the University of Leiden and also studied for a time in Paris, became one of America's first great geologists. On arrival in this country in 1810, he lived in Philadelphia for several years. After a brief stay at the utopian Owenite community at New Harmony, Indiana, he became professor of geology, natural history, and chemistry at the University of Nashville, Tennessee, in 1828. As a result of his own travels and through careful exchanges with scientists in America and Europe, Troost accumulated an extensive natural history collection that included, among many other things, fourteen thousand mineral specimens and three thousand specimens of fossils.[52]

&ast;   &ast;   &ast;   &ast;

It was thus frequently from a welter of causes that Dutchmen became Loyalists or Patriots or, if possible, remained neutral during the Revolution. Until more studies are made, however, the historian can only generalize as to these motives. The Revolution itself marks a kind of watershed in the history of the Dutch in America. Dutch culture that was popular in colonial times was being altered by 1776 as American life in general changed and as the usage of the ancestral language declined among descendants of the New Netherlanders. In other ways, too, as explained in the following chapters, the Dutch impact on America entered a new phase as Netherlands immigration, which had been dormant for nearly one hundred fifty years, surged steadily upward.

## CHAPTER VIII

# The Beginning of the Great Migration, 1840–61

ALTHOUGH THE DUTCH HAD NOT SHOWN MUCH INTEREST IN migration to America during the colonial and early national period, this attitude began changing about 1840. From that date until the outbreak of the Civil War in 1861, about twenty thousand Netherlanders went to the United States to find a new home, compared to fewer than twenty-five hundred during the previous twenty years. This interest increased after the Civil War, reaching a peak during the decade of the eighties, when nearly fifty-five thousand Dutch immigrants reached American shores.[1]

The origins of the Great Migration have been the subject of considerable debate, with the problem centering on the question of whether it was "the hunger of the souls of the Dutch folk or the necessities of their bodies that chiefly motivated their mass migration to America."[2] An objective examination of the facts seems to indicate that both "souls and bodies" must be taken into consideration, but that religious causes, which were very important at first, were soon superseded by economic motives.

The religious factor stemmed primarily from the determination of King William I to force conformity on a group of his subjects who refused to abide by certain royal decrees concerning the state church, especially the Church Reorganization Law of January 7, 1816. By this law, the name of the state church was changed, in Dutch terminology, from the *Gereformeerde Kerk* to the *Hervormde Kerk*. Both terms can be translated to mean Reformed Church, but in the minds of critics, Hervormde meant "reorganized" rather than "reformed"— reorganized, that is, to suit the wishes of the king. Under the new

[ 129 ]

law, ecclesiastical bodies such as synods, classes, and consistories were left as before, but were supervised more closely by the state. The training and examining of ministers were also placed under stricter governmental control.

The criticism that arose among some orthodox Calvinists over state interference in church matters was accentuated by several other developments. Some churchgoers resented the introduction of evangelical songs as a supplement to the Old Testament psalms customarily sung during the church services. Dissenters showed their displeasure with such substitutions by wearing their hats during the singing of the obnoxious hymns, or by waiting outside the church until the singing had ended. Some critics also claimed the government was trying to keep the Bible out of the public schools, thereby making religious education a "mere general moral one, offensive to neither Jew nor Roman Catholic."[3] Finally, a religious awakening, known as the *réveil* and participated in primarily by intellectuals, was highly critical of ministers for being too rationalistic in their preachng. Supporters of the *réveil* advocated a return to the strict ideas of the early Dutch Reformed fathers and upbraided the national church for becoming too formalistic and complacent.

At the University of Leiden, a small group of theological students, influenced by these religious developments, frequently met to worship together and to exchange views. The group became known as "Scholte's Club," after the name of its most ardent member, Hendrik Pieter Scholte. Following their ordination into the ministry, several of its members became determined opponents of the Church Reorganization Law of 1816. They included, besides Scholte, the reverends Albertus Christiaan Van Raalte and Anthony Brummelkamp. Later, Scholte and Van Raalte were each responsible for leading several hundred Dutch immigrants to Iowa and Michigan, respectively.

The controversy over church reorganization and other religious problems finally culminated in the so-called Secession of 1834, when the Reverend Hendrick De Cock publicly seceded from the *Hervormde Kerk*, along with his entire congregation at Ulrum, in the province of Groningen. De Cock's action served as an example for other ministers, including the Reverend Scholte, who was serving a church at Doeveren in North Brabant, and the Reverend Van Raalte, who was ministering to two small congregations in Overijssel. By 1835, sixteen congregations had seceded from the state church.[4]

The determination of the government to force Seceders back into the fold must be viewed in the light of the political temper prevailing at this time among the ruling classes of Europe. Their mood was one of apprehension, following the excesses of the French Revolution in the late eighteenth century and the rioting and revolutions that continued to plague Europe during the first half of the nineteenth century. Unfortunately, in dealing with popular unrest during this period, governments invariably resorted to repression rather than the introduction of needed political and social reforms. As a consequence, although the Seceders certainly were not liberal in their political views, the authorities thought that in "seceding from the state church . . . [they] were in effect seceding from a branch of their government."[5]

In deciding to enforce religious conformity, the government argued that the clause in the Constitution of 1814 guaranteeing religious freedom referred only to existing churches, and not to new groups, such as the Seceders. Articles 291 and 294 of the Napoleonic Code, which had been retained from the Napoleonic era, were consequently invoked. These articles prohibited the gathering of twenty or more persons for the purpose of political, cultural, or *religious* meetings without permission from the public authorities.

The government attempted to break up meetings of the Seceders by arresting persons attending them, especially the ministers. Fines were imposed, and refusal or inability to pay sometimes resulted in imprisonment. Dominie Scholte claimed that during a period of about a decade, he had paid thirty-two hundred dollars in fines. To break the morale of the dissenters, hardened and obnoxious soldiers were billeted in the homes of Seceders. The latter also frequently found themselves discriminated against by nondissenting employers and ostracized at social gatherings.

Persecution failed to break the spirit of the Seceders, and it was partly for this reason that the government later showed itself willing to compromise. The change in official attitude was also part of a liberalizing trend taking place among governments throughout Europe during the 1840's. In the Netherlands, religious persecution gradually declined after the abdication of William I in 1840, and practically disappeared when a new liberal constitution was adopted in 1848.

The relaxation of laws against the Seceders came too late for many who, in the meantime, had decided to "become the salt of the earth in some new settlement in America."[6] By the time persecution had diminished, a kind of emigration psychosis had taken such a firm hold on the minds of many Hollanders that it would have been difficult to reverse the trend. Shortly before Van Raalte left for America in 1846 with a large number of emigrants, for example, he told a fellow secessionist minister: "You will not be able to stop this emigration any more than you can stop the Rhine in its course."[7] In several instances, almost entire congregations of Seceders, with their ministers, decided to find a new home in America where they could worship as they pleased.

Religious problems, however, represented only one set of causes leading to the Great Migration. Poor economic conditions were also significant, and eventually became very important. Indeed, Seceders never constituted a majority among the Hollanders emigrating to America during the 1840's; even Roman Catholic emigration exceeded that of the secessionist group. Furthermore, because Dutch emigration continued in significant numbers after persecution had practically ceased in 1848, it is obvious that religion was not the only factor influencing the Great Migration.[8]

The adverse economic situation stemmed from many causes. Because it was a small mercantile nation, the Netherlands suffered more than most countries from the wars of the French Revolution and the Napoleonic Era. Although the Netherlands was by no means lacking in capital during the first half of the nineteenth century, frustration and a defeatist state of mind made the great merchants and bankers—long the leading elements in Dutch society—hesitate to invest in industrialization. Yet, this was needed to combat pauperism and unemployment, which during the 1840's rose to a higher level than at any time since 1813. According to one estimate, 27 percent of the Dutch population was on relief in 1850. Furthermore, taxes were very high, falling heavily on those least able to bear them. High rents, small farms, and a limit to how much land could be reclaimed from the sea also brought on an agricultural crisis.[9]

The economic difficulties were aggravated by several other problems. Periodic floods ruined farmlands that had been patiently rescued from the sea, and diseases among the livestock added to the hardships of the rural people. A cholera outbreak in 1832 carried off thousands of townsmen and farmers alike. The winter of 1844–45 was one of the most severe in Holland's history. Finally, a potato disease, that reached its height in 1845–46, caused a serious shortage in the basic source of food for all Hollanders—city and rural alike—resulting in famine conditions in parts of the country.

Hollanders who considered emigration a solution to their problems did not decide immediately upon the United States as the site for their new home. Suggestions were made for state-sponsored emigration to the Dutch colonies as a means of combating poverty. The government showed itself in sympathy with such plans, and in 1846 four ships carrying three hundred eighty-four settlers were dispatched to Surinam, on the northern coast of South America. Within six months after their arrival, nearly half the settlers had died, and so many others left for other locations that the new settlement was abandoned in 1853. The failure of the project was attributed to poor management, the unfavorable climate, and the inability of farmers to market their products.

Consideration was also given to the Dutch East Indies (present-day Indonesia) as a possible site for immigrant settlements, but the idea never took firm root. The arbitrary expulsion of several Roman Catholic clergymen from Java in 1846 made some of the Separatist ministers apprehensive that they might experience the same repressive acts in the East Indies that they were encountering at home. The difficulties experienced in Surinam also raised serious questions about the feasibility of white emigration to the tropics. Finally, the cost of transportation halfway around the world would have been prohibitive for many Hollanders.

The presence of numerous persons of Dutch descent in South

Africa also made that region a potential outlet for Hollanders wanting to emigrate, but it, too, had several drawbacks. These were summarized by Dominie Scholte as follows:

In the first place one would have to deal with the English government and although on promising not to conspire with the exiled boors [i.e., Dutch farmers in South Africa], a colonization of Natal might perhaps be permitted, yet the manner of living over there is too different from our customary way of life for us to dare advise the multitude to proceed thither. Moreover, one is still exposed there to the attacks of the heathen Kaffirs. Among the exiled boors one might find adherence to ancient [religious] forms, but not so much living faith, while in addition slavery is permitted by them. Furthermore, the cost of transportation and settlement would be a hardship for a great many, and would probably exceed the means of our Christians.[10]

As emigration continued to be discussed in the Netherlands, attention turned more and more to the United States. In looking upon it as the Promised Land, many Hollanders were influenced by the thousands of European emigrants, especially Germans, who were embarking for America from Dutch ports. Many of these foreign emigrants spent three or four weeks in the Netherlands before sailing. Translations of American literary works at this time also heightened interest in the United States. Thirteen of James Fenimore Cooper's novels, for example, were translated into Dutch between 1826 and 1840, as well as Washington Irving's books about the Dutch in the Hudson Valley.[11] Guidebooks for emigrants particularly helped create an interest in America, especially among the common people. These described the geography of various regions of the United States, including topography, climate, soil conditions, types of crops, growing seasons, and so on. Various procedures for acquiring cheap land were explained, as were also the means by which an emigrant acquired American citizenship.

Even more influential than the guidebooks were the letters written by relatives and friends who had emigrated to the United States, and who had the warmest praise for their newly adopted country. As an emigrant of 1846 declared: "These reports roused many of us who earned our bread with hard toil but who could not possibly dream of owning farms [in the Netherlands]."[12] The Reverend Cornelius Van der Meulen, who led a large number of Hollanders to Michigan in 1847, later recalled how his followers viewed the United States: "Rumor spread that on the other side of the ocean there was room for all in which to find a more ample existence. Those who had gone to America sent such glowing reports to us that we thought free America could be compared almost with our promised Canaan."[13]

Most of the emigrants, cognizant of the problems they would meet en route to America and the difficulties they would face on arrival, were convinced that their undertaking should be a joint effort. Unity would give them strength and a greater chance of success. The ministers also strongly urged group migration. As Dominie Scholte expressed it, "Through colonization, those who leave will be able to hear the Gospel in their native tongue during the first few years at least, and may thus receive that spiritual sustenance which will confirm them in the faith, kindle them in love, warn them against the cravings of the flesh that militate against the spirit."[14] Associations were therefore frequently established which chartered one or more ships for the specific purpose of transporting members en masse across the ocean. On arrival in the United States, they not only continued to travel as a unit, but settled near one another to form distinctively Dutch communities.

Of the many immigrant associations created in the Netherlands, three became particularly important. They were known as the Utrecht, Arnhem, and Zeeland associations, and were headed respectively by the reverends Scholte, Van Raalte, and Van der Meulen, all of whom were secessionist ministers. The charters of the associations contained detailed regulations pertaining to such matters as membership, financial obligations, conduct aboard ship, method of choosing a settlement site, and the manner in which a new settlement would be administered during the formative years. As might be expected, nonbelievers and Catholics could not become members of the Seceder-oriented associations, but their charters were quite liberal in accepting nonseceding Protestants. Provisions were frequently made for transporting emigrants who had limited economic means, with the understanding that repayment would occur at a later date on terms agreeable to all parties. Governing boards were established for solving problems that might arise before the emigrants left the Netherlands, and to supervise affairs en route and at the settlement site. A small, advance group was generally sent to prepare the way for the main party. It made inquiries and obtained information that would be helpful when the main body arrived.[15]

Persons of Dutch descent, some of whose American lineage dated back to the New Netherland period, were of assistance to the new arrivals. The Protestant Evangelical Holland Emigrant Society, organized at Albany, New York, by the Reverend Isaac Wyckhoff, pastor of one of the Reformed churches of the city, was especially helpful. There were also two Dutch immigrant aid societies in New York City, where the Reverend Thomas De Witt, also a Reformed minister, took a charitable interest in assisting newly arrived immigrants. The *Christian Intelligencer*, an official magazine of the Reformed Church, was another important means by which immigrants received help. It carried numerous articles urging readers to assist newly arrived immigrants with money, food, and housing, as well as employment.[16]

The first advance group of the Arnhem Association sailed for Baltimore in late May, 1846, followed shortly by another group destined for Boston. A third party, including Dominie Van Raalte, the leader of the Arnhem Association, arrived in New York City on November 17. Van Raalte, accompanied by a large number of immigrants, immediately set out for Wisconsin. The selection of this site was influenced by information received from one of the vanguard parties that had settled there, and by favorable reports from some German immigrants. Unfortunately, by the time Van Raalte and his party reached Detroit, winter had set in and boat service on Lake Michigan had been suspended. The group therefore decided to remain in the Detroit area, finding whatever work they could, and continue the journey in the spring.

In the meantime, various civic and religious leaders from Detroit and Kalamazoo persuaded Van Raalte to look into western Michigan rather than Wisconsin as a settlement site.

A reconnaissance trip to the former region convinced him their advice was good, and on January 26, 1847, he purchased about a thousand acres of wooded land from the government as well as from private speculators.

Upon being informed that land had been purchased, some of Van Raalte's followers immediately left Detroit by rail for Kalamazoo, and then by sleigh for Allegan, located about twenty miles southeast of the site. The remainder of the journey was made by sleigh and by foot, the final destination being reached in mid-February, 1847. In the spring, the rest of the party that had stayed at Detroit arrived, as well as some who had remained in the East. A group of Dutch immigrants who had debarked at New Orleans but were uncertain about a final destination also came to Van Raalte's colony.

Farming constituted the major occupation of the Michigan immigrants, but there were blacksmiths, weavers, tailors, shoe-makers, and other craftsmen among them. Consequently, shops of various kinds soon appeared, marking the beginning of what is today the thriving community of Holland, Michigan. A visitor described this settlement in July, 1848, as follows:

Holland City is pleasantly situated, high, dry and level, the streets partly cleared out. I should think there were about 200 houses of all descriptions, from the rude hut covered with bark, to the well finished and painted frame house, every lot occupied having a fine garden and yard, in front of the house a gate, and at every window on the street the neat white curtain. Here are already several stores . . . where goods are sold as cheap as in any county or village in Michigan.[17]

Additional immigrants, many of whom were members of other associations, continued to arrive and more settlements were founded. Not long after the arrival of Van Raalte's main party, for example, a large group from the Zeeland Emigration Association settled about six miles east of Holland, where they purchased fifteen hundred acres. Their community was appropriately named Zeeland. Other communities, too, frequently bore Dutch names, including Vriesland, Groningen, Overisel, Drente, Zutphen, Nordeloos, and Harderwyk. Because they were near one another, the settlements were often referred to collectivly as *De Kolonie* (The Colony). A journalist from New York who visited *De Kolonie* in the autumn of 1853 reported it had about four thousand inhabitants.[18] As more artisans and men of enterprise arrived, Holland and the surrounding communities began branching out into activities other than farming and crafts. Factories gradually appeared, including lumber mills, flour mills, and brick kilns.

Life among the early Michigan settlers was anything but easy. The first need of an immigrant on arrival was to obtain temporary shelter. Sometimes several families lived together for months in a small two-room cabin, or had to make do with storage sheds. Others resorted to makeshift shelters. The remark made by an immigrant who arrived at Zeeland in 1848 was typical of many: "Our first task was to place sticks in the ground, cover them with the bark of trees, and gather leaves for our bed—and our house was ready."[19] The task of clearing the forest by hand was monumental and completely unfamiliar to the immigrants. Until the settlers developed skills, the trees seldom fell in the direction intended. Even after the trees were cut down, the stumps and roots made planting and cultivating grain difficult. Being unacquainted with log construction also made the building of permanent houses and barns a formidable task.

Because the great majority of Hollanders in Michigan were poor, and because supplies at first had to be hauled long distances by ox-team or backpack, food was frequently scarce and the diet was nearly always monotonous. Potatoes, corn meal, and soup made of corn and turnips were common fare. In view of their diet and in the absence of adequate medical facilities, sickness and death were commonplace. As reported by one who arrived with the first settlers,

Many became ill, and, what made matters worse . . . they lacked everything sick people needed. The beds were poor, food was bad, and care of the sick was inadequate. If ever a people were poor and miserable, we were the one during the first summer. . . . Many people died, so many that funerals sometimes could not be conducted decently. There were parents who had to bury their children with their own hands.[20]

Although conditions improved after a few years, as late as 1858, when a severe sickness hit *De Kolonie,* forty-five of one hundred twenty-three youngsters died in a single school district.[21]

At the same time that Van Raalte's colony was developing in the woods of Michigan, another Dutch colony was being established on the prairie in southeastern Iowa. Its founders were members of the Utrecht Association led by Dominie Scholte. As in the case of Van Raalte's group, a "scouting party" of eight families from the Utrecht Association departed before the main body. It left Rotterdam on October 2, 1846, arriving at New Orleans on November 19—just two days after Van Raalte arrived in New York. A steamboat brought them up the Mississippi River as far as St. Louis, where they went into winter quarters, finding whatever work they could.

The main body of the Utrecht Association departed in the following spring in four sailing vessels expressly chartered for the purpose. Carrying about eight hundred emigrants and loaded with household goods and farm machinery, these vessels arrived in Baltimore in late May and early June. Commenting on the arrival of the first of these ships, the *Baltimore Sun* of May 27, 1847, reported as follows:

We have seen many emigrant ships, but we never saw one more cleanly in its appearance than this, and we have never yet seen in any ship so fine a body of emigrants. They number one hundred and eighty, all Hollanders, and they have been remarked as beyond comparison superior to any ship load which has reached port.[22]

Scholte, who, with his family, made the crossing by steamship, arrived a few weeks before the main body of immigrants. While awaiting their appearance, he visited New York, Albany, and Washington to secure information on possible settlement sites. Upon hearing of the arrival of his followers, he immediately went to Baltimore and soon had them on their way west. After three weeks of travel by rail, canal boat, "mountain car," and steamboat, the main body joined the vanguard group at St. Louis. Here they remained while a committee of five land-seekers, headed by Scholte, searched for a settlement site.

Scholte's visits with various individuals in the East had convinced him that his group should locate on the prairies of the Middle West, a view that had already found considerable sympathy among members of the Utrecht Association before they left the Netherlands. Most of them favored Iowa, although there was some discussion of Wisconsin and Texas. From the standpoint of unity and finding strength in numbers, it would have been wise for Scholte to join his followers with those of the Michigan colony, a merger that Van Raalte tried to bring about. Later, in explaining why he refused to do this, Scholte declared that the Michigan colony was too far north, lacked good roads, and was too distant from other white settlements. He especially criticized it for being forested, declaring that

to the farmer who had already spent a part of his life in the level hay lands and fields of Holland, the unusual battle with trees and the constant view of stumps in the midst of meadows and cultivated fields could not be agreeable. Not to detract from Michigan's fertility, nor from the value of many kinds of wood, nor from the pleasure of hearing the warble of birds in the cool shade of virgin forest, I had, however, experienced enough of real life to know that stumps of trees are disagreeable obstacles to farmers, and that the value of wood decreases very much when everything is wood. Besides, I was too well convinced that the Hollanders who were coming to North America were more prosaic than poetic, and consequently they thought not so much of pleasing their eyes and ears as of buying soil suitable for farms, the easier to cultivate the better.[23]

A recent biography of Scholte suggests other reasons, besides economic considerations, for not locating his followers next to Van Raalte's colony. Scholte was above all else an individualist and would have found it difficult to play a role that was subsidiary to another person, which might have been the case had he located in Michigan. He also opposed the idea of "transporting a 'Dutch' church to the new land," whereas Van Raalte envisioned a church that would adhere strongly to the religious traditions and practices of the Netherlands. Furthermore, Van Raalte was interested in establishing a kind of theocratic society in which the church would play an important role in the government—an idea that Scholte abhorred.[24]

In looking for a settlement site, Scholte learned about some desirable land, only slightly inhabited, in Marion County, in southeastern Iowa. After investigating this region on July 29, 1847, he and his committee decided the location and soil were good, and proceeded to purchase over eighteen thousand acres of government land and partially developed farms. Shortly thereafter, most of the immigrants who had been waiting at St. Louis departed for their new home, taking the steamboat as far as Keokuk—a two-day journey—and traveling the rest of the way by wagon or by foot. Others remained at St. Louis until the following spring.

Although the Iowa Hollanders were faced with numerous problems and disappointments, their difficulties did not compare with those experienced by the Michigan settlers. In the first place, the Iowa colonists had available for immediate occupancy a few houses that had belonged to the farmers Scholte's committee bought out. Immigrants unable to obtain immediate housing, which included the majority, made temporary shelters from canvas or from slabs of prairie sod, which were more satisfactory than the makeshift homes of the Michigan Hollanders. Having some crops already growing that had been sown by the former tenants of the land was also an advantage the Iowa Dutch had over their Michigan brethren. Furthermore, Scholte's pioneers did not have to contend with the tremendous task of clearing a forest before they could cultivate the soil. Breaking virgin prairie land, although no easy task, was easier than felling trees and clearing stumps. Finally, the Iowa group was, on the whole, wealthier than those who had settled in Michigan.

The main town of Scholte's colony was named Pella, signifying "refuge," after the town to which some of the Christians had fled when Jerusalem was destroyed by the Romans in 70 A.D. Scholte viewed his settlement in exactly that light—a place where poor people from the Netherlands could begin a new life. A reporter for an Iowa newspaper gave this account of the town and its inhabitants about a month after the arrival of the first Hollanders:

I discovered a new race of beings . . . a broadshouldered race in velvet jackets and wooden shoes. . . . Most of the inhabitants live in camps, the tops covered with tent cloth, some with grass bushes. The sides barricaded with countless numbers of trunks, boxes and chests of the oldest and most grotesque description that Yankees . . . ever beheld. . . . Their present population numbers something like 700 to 800 souls with the expectation of a numerous accession of numbers the ensuing spring. They appear to be intelligent and respectable, quite above the average class of European immigrants that have ever landed upon our shores.[25]

In the same way that Van Raalte was the dominant personality among the Michigan Hollanders, Scholte was the driving force behind the Iowa settlers. He was at one and the same time a minister, farmer, land agent, notary, attorney, banker, broker, dealer in farm implements, publisher, school-board member, and postmaster as well as the owner of a sawmill, stone quarry, and lime kiln. It is no wonder that a writer has referred to him as "the Atlas on whose shoulders rested the world of the Iowa colony."[26] Later, he also became active in state and national politics.

A visitor from the Netherlands to the Pella area reported in 1853 that "though the men who have settled here thus far have not yet become capitalists, [nevertheless] with industry, thrift, and perseverance nearly all have achieved a fairly large measure of prosperity, and their own appearance as well as that of their houses supports this contention."[27] News about the prosperity of the Iowa Hollanders brought in settlers from other Dutch communities in the United States as well as directly from the Netherlands. On the eve of the First World War, it was estimated that there were about twenty thousand Hollanders, by birth and descent, living within a radius of fifteen or twenty miles of Pella.[28] Long before this, however, the Pella colony had begun to "swarm," as will be explained in the next chapter, and Hollanders from there began founding daughter colonies in northwest Iowa, Nebraska, and Kansas.

In addition to Michigan and Iowa, a significant number of Hollanders settled in Wisconsin during the early decades of the Great Migration. In fact, in 1860, there were more Holland-born living within its borders than in Iowa—4,906 as compared to 2,615.[29] Wisconsin, however, never became as significant in the minds of the Dutch-Americans as Iowa or Michigan, and emigration to it later declined. In part, this was because many of the Hollanders residing there before the Civil War were Roman Catholics, who, without an "ethnic" church of their own lost their Old World identity more quickly than did the Dutch Reformed. Furthermore, the Wisconsin Hollanders were more scattered throughout the state. Finally, they never had a spokesman comparable to Dominie Van Raalte or Dominie Scholte, especially after the early death of Father Van den Broek, the man who led the first contingent of Dutch Catholics to Wisconsin.

Some Hollanders settled in Wisconsin before 1846, and for a time it appeared that it rather than Michigan would become the chief attraction for newcomers from the Netherlands. A few of Van Raalte's advance group settled there, and he himself initially planned to do the same. Some of the first arrivals settled in Milwaukee, and in time a Dutch community known as *Hollandsche Berg* (Dutch Hill) arose there. By 1851, the Dutch population of Milwaukee numbered nearly eight hundred out of a total of about six thousand inhabitants.[30] Franklin Prairie and Town Eight, both located near Milwaukee, also had a few Dutch inhabitants.

In 1847, the Reverend Pieter Zonne brought a group of Dutch farmers as well as some laborers to Sheboygan County, about fifty miles north of Milwaukee. Here they established a settlement called Holland, later renamed Cedar Grove, and another named Oostburg. In the following year, an even larger group of immigrants arrived under the leadership of the Reverend Gerrit Baay. They settled a little farther west, principally in the towns of Alto and Waupun. In the meantime, the town of Amsterdam was founded on Lake Michigan about twelve miles from Sheboygan. Its inhabitants were engaged primarily in cutting cordwood, which was shipped down the coast to Milwaukee. The success of the Dutch settlements of Sheboygan County is indicated by the appearance of *De Sheboygan Nieuwsbode* (The Sheboygan Messenger) in 1851, the first Dutch-language newspaper to be published in the United States.[31] Other small Dutch settlements established in Wisconsin before the Civil War included New Amsterdam, about fifteen miles north of La Crosse on the western border of the state, and Friesland, about twenty miles southwest of Alto.

The largest single group of Hollanders to settle in Wisconsin during the 1840's were Roman Catholic. Although Dutch Catholics did not show much interest in emigration before the twentieth century, some of them were sufficiently dissatisfied with economic conditions and religious discrimination at home to consider moving to the United States.[32] In late 1846, a Catholic emigration association was created at Nijmegen, one of the strongholds of Catholicism in the Netherlands, and plans were made for establishing a Dutch Catholic colony somewhere in the United States, perhaps in Missouri or Wisconsin.

The first large group of Catholic emigrants left for New Orleans under the auspices of the Nijmegen organization in late February, 1847. The interest shown in their departure was described in one of the Catholic newspapers as follows:

Just now we have witnessed here for the first time a scene of large-scale emigration. After Mr. C. Verwayen with his 120 Catholic fellow-travelers early in the morning had attended Holy Mass, and the majority had fortified themselves with the Holy Communion for the last time on their native soil, he mounted the steamer while thousands of spectators, who at an early hour jammed the quay and the adjoining streets, cheered and waved. It is unbelievable, how this scene stirred the crowd; all around one could hear conversations in which people approved of the plan, complained bitterly of the decline of the national welfare, and expressed the desire to flee the sinking fatherland.[33]

Unfortunately, these immigrants dispersed into small groups after reaching New Orleans, and the second group of Catholics that was supposed to follow the first party never set sail.

A Roman Catholic group that settled in Wisconsin under the direction of the Reverend Theodore J. Van den Broek was more successful. Born and educated in the Netherlands, Van den Broek, after taking his priestly vows, went to America in 1832 as a missionary. He soon began work among the Indians at Little Chute, near Green Bay, Wisconsin. In the late summer of 1847, while on leave of absence in the land of his birth, Father Van den Broek tried to persuade some of his coreligionists to accompany him back to Wisconsin to establish a Dutch Catholic colony like that of the Protestants in Michigan or Iowa.

The response to his appeal far exceeded his expectations; instead of having to charter one ship, three vessels had to be hired.

The first group left the Netherlands on March 19, 1848, arriving in Wisconsin on June 10 after a journey of eighty-three days. They were soon joined by those who had boarded the other two ships. Most of the Dutch Catholics located at Little Chute, but others founded a new settlement about fifteen miles to the east, which became known as Hollandtown. Despite numerous problems, including inadequate housing and a lack of funds, and despite the early death of Father Van den Broek in 1851, the Dutch Catholic communities managed to survive.

The prosperity of the Wisconsin Hollanders, Protestant and Catholic alike, varied. Laborers and skilled artisans found work in the towns, although their pay was generally low. So many of the workers in the *Hollandsche Berg* district of Milwaukee lived near the poverty level that one Hollander was prompted to declare that "in Scripture parlance, they were the hewers of wood and drawers of water for the well-to-do Yankees."[34] Although a few Dutch immigrants in Wisconsin had sufficient wealth to purchase farms that were already under cultivation, like some of the Hollanders who settled in Iowa, most of them were as poverty-stricken as Van Raalte's followers in Michigan. Their problems were also similar, but perseverance and hard work eventually paid off, as explained in a letter written by a Hollander who emigrated there in 1847:

First, five to ten acres of stumpy and rooty land, a small log house with wooden chimney and floor made of hewn logs or rough boards, a small stable for the cattle, a pigpen, and a henhouse—such were the rude beginnings of farm life in those days. However, things gradually began to change for the better. Frame house and barn took the place of the old log buildings; horses replaced the slow, patient oxen; the roads became more fit for travel; board fences replaced those made of rails.[35]

In addition to the organized groups of immigrants who settled in Michigan, Iowa, and Wisconsin, several Dutch settlements were established in Illinois during the years just prior to the Civil War. The most important were Lage Prairie (Low Priarie), founded in 1847, and Hooge Prairie (High Prairie), established in 1849.[36] They were located six miles apart and about twenty miles south of the center of present-day Chicago. This area is now part of Metropolitan Chicago, and the communities are known respectively as South Holland and Roseland. At the time they were founded, the region was largely uninhabited, consisting of woods, prairie, and marshes. The land sold for seventy-five cents to five dollars per acre, and because some of the Hollanders who first settled there were quite well off financially, several of them bought sizeable amounts of land. By draining the marshes, a task for which the Hollanders had a good reputation extending back many centuries, the value of their land was greatly increased.

Cattle raising became profitable because of the abundance of hay, and the coming of the railroad in 1852 facilitated the marketing of garden products and dairy produce in Chicago. As news of the prosperity of the Illinois settlements spread, additional Hollanders arrived, some coming from Michigan and Wisconsin, and others directly from the Netherlands. The rapid growth of the Dutch communities is shown in the need to enlarge periodically the Reformed church at Roseland. First constructed in 1850, it had to be rebuilt in 1856, 1867, and again in 1887. On the last occasion, a fine brick and stone structure was built to accommodate twelve hundred people; it proved none too large.

Although truck gardening and dairying continued to be important occupations for the Illinois Hollanders, increasing numbers of the second and third generations found employment in the growing industrial city of Chicago itself. In this way and by locating near one another, new Dutch enclaves were formed. For example, so many Hollanders settled in Englewood that a Dutch church was organized there in 1886 and another in the following year. Other Dutch communities were soon established in Oak Park and Cicero. By 1900, there were nine Dutch churches in the Chicago area.

Not all Dutch immigrants arriving in the United States during the early years of the Great Migration moved to the Middle West. Some remained in the East, settling near relatives or friends who had emigrated earlier. Rising industrial cities such as Albany, Rochester, and Buffalo in New York, and Paterson and Passaic in New Jersey, attracted many of the new arrivals. The presence of Dutch communities and churches in these regions, some dating back as far as two hundred years, was also an incentive for some immigrants to remain in the East. In a few instances, large numbers of Hollanders settled at a particular place. Thus, nearly one hundred fifty Dutch immigrants had located in Rochester by 1845, attracted by the town's rapid economic growth and by the presence of a small Dutch community existing there since the town was established in the early nineteenth century. By 1850, the Hollanders of Rochester had their own Protestant and Catholic churches.[37] Needless to say, the immigrants who stayed in the East were of great assistance in advising the tens of thousands of Hollanders who came to American shores after the Civil War.

Many of the immigrants remained in the eastern states only long enough to acquire sufficient money to continue their journey westward. They had been poor farmers or farm laborers in the Netherlands and had emigrated in order to own their own farms in places like Michigan, Iowa, and Wisconsin. A large group of immigrants under the leadership of Dominie Seine Bolks, for example, spent a year at Syracuse, New York, before moving to Michigan in 1849. Others stayed behind temporarily because of illness in the family—a not infrequent occurrence in view of living conditions aboard immigrant ships.

Frequently, what was intended to be a brief stopover in an eastern city became a permanent one. Thus, a Hollander by the name of Donner, who arrived with his family in New York City in 1851 with thirty-five other Dutch immigrants, all of whom intended to push on to Chicago, was obliged to remain behind when his wife became sick in Albany. This halt in his journey was supposed to be temporary, but he explained in his memoirs in 1897 that when his wife became well enough to resume the trip to Chicago, an economic depression "made me apprehensive about finding a job in the West and now 40 years later, here I still am in Albany with 7 married children and 24 grandchildren."[38]

Smaller communities in the East also attracted Dutch immigrants before the Civil War. In the late 1830's, two Hollanders, Jan Cappon and Jacob Pynbrook, became so enthusiastic over the possibilities of Wayne County, New York, as a farming region, that they wrote several letters to relatives and friends in the Netherlands encouraging them to emigrate. These letters, along with poor economic conditions in the Netherlands, led to the emigration of a significant number of Dutch families to Pultneyville and East Williamson during the years 1841–45. Other small communities in New York that held the attention of Dutch immigrants during the 1840's included Sayville, on Long Island, and Clymer and Lancaster, near Buffalo. These smaller communities frequently consisted of Hollanders who came from a particular region of the Netherlands, such as Zeelanders at Sayville, Gelderlanders at Clymer, and Frisians at Lancaster. Each group sometimes distinguished itself in a particular way. Thus, the Sayville Hollanders prospered in the oyster business, while the Lancaster group specialized in dairying. Many of those residing at Rochester went into truck gardening.[39]

*   *   *   *

As a result of religious and economic factors, the number of Hollanders emigrating to the United States rose sharply during the two decades prior to the Civil War. Although some of the new arrivals settled in the eastern states, most pushed farther west, particularly to Michigan, Wisconsin, and Iowa. Other than the Indian threat, the new Dutch-Americans experienced about the same problems as other pioneers of the mid-nineteenth century who settled near the frontier. These difficulties included poverty, primitive housing, back-breaking work, and isolation. Despite these problems, the settlements prospered, and within a short time became overflowing. As a result of this and the continued arrival of new immigrants, many of their inhabitants set out to found daughter colonies in states and territories farther west.

## CHAPTER IX

# Daughter Colonies and Other Settlements, 1861–1914

DURING THE PERIOD FROM THE CIVIL WAR TO WORLD WAR I, numerous new Dutch communities appeared in the United States, particularly in the Middle West. Because many of these were offshoots of settlements established during the 1840's in Wisconsin, Michigan, and Iowa, it is not inappropriate to term them "daughter colonies." A few, however, were the result of immigrant groups coming directly from the Netherlands, and several were founded as profit-making ventures.

Economic conditions in the Netherlands after the American Civil War did not improve sufficiently to discourage emigration to the United States. The rapid growth in population after 1870 and the lack of industrialization resulted in low wages and unemployment. Jobs were often handed down from father to son, and in the event of a vacancy there were frequently dozens of applications. Economic conditions were also difficult in agricultural areas, where young men of rural background found it increasingly difficult to obtain farms on reasonable terms. Children of poor families had to go to work at an early age, with little prospect for advancement.

In view of these conditions, it is no wonder that the rapidly expanding economy of the United States acted like a magnet in attracting discontented Hollanders to her shores. Factories and handicraft industries in the United States grew from about 150,000 in 1860 to over half a million by 1900, and the value of manufactured goods rose from $1 billion to $13 billion. Industrial growth was accompanied by increasing urbanization, resulting in the population of communities over 2,500 doubling between the Civil War and 1900.[1] The liberal land policy of the United

States government, as exemplified in the Homestead Act of 1862, and the sale of millions of acres of land by the railroad companies proved particularly attractive to Dutch immigrants. As a result of these developments, about 175,000 Hollanders entered the United States during the period 1860–1910, with a peak of nearly 10,000 in 1882.[2]

Information about economic opportunities in the United States after the Civil War reached the Netherlands in a variety of ways, but personal correspondence was one of the most important. The number of letters sent by immigrants to relatives and friends must have been enormous. The postmaster of Orange City, Iowa (a Dutch settlement founded in 1870), for example, reported in 1882 that twenty letters left his office daily for the Netherlands.[3] Such letters were often passed around among the inhabitants of a community in the Netherlands for others to read, and were sometimes published in the local newspaper. The influence of such correspondence is shown by the large number of immigrants who, upon arrival in America, stated they were joining relatives or friends.[4] Various projects undertaken by state governments also helped attract Hollanders. Thus, the government of Iowa sent Henry Hospers, a Dutchman from the Pella community, to the Netherlands to recruit immigrants, while other states distributed promotional material in the Netherlands outlining the economic opportunities of particular regions. Railroad companies desirous of selling land to immigrants, and anxious to increase the number of farmers who would use the railroads for shipping grain and livestock, also published literature in Dutch aimed at convincing Hollanders that the American West was the "Promised Land."[5]

Typical of the information circulated in the Netherlands by persons and agencies trying to get Hollanders to emigrate to newly opened lands in the United States was a thirty-six-page pamphlet published at Rotterdam in 1883, praising Minnesota and the Dakotas as a place for settlers.[6] It gave detailed instructions on how to obtain government and railroad lands, as well as information about agricultural machinery, draft animals, cattle, seed grain, and farm buildings. The pamphlet strongly emphasized that lack of capital should not discourage a poor Hollander from emigrating. "Some persons assert," stated its author, "that there is no chance for the poor to get ahead, but I must strongly object to that assertion. There are hundreds, no thousands, who began with nothing but are now independent. The idea that the far west is a haven of refuge for the poor is not an exaggeration." Not much was needed to start: twenty acres would do—planting nineteen of them with wheat and the remaining acre with "potatoes, beans, onions, and other vegetables." More important than money were "good health, a pair of strong arms, temperance, thrift, and a firm will to get ahead."

Immigrants who came directly from the Netherlands made up only a segment of the Dutchmen who settled in the trans-Mississippi West after the Civil War. Indeed, in many instances, the majority of the inhabitants of a newly founded Dutch community was made up of descendants of Hollanders who had emigrated during the 1840's and 1850's. Reasons varied as to why they moved from the older Dutch communities in Michigan, Wisconsin, Iowa, and elsewhere to locate farther west. Some who lived in urban areas moved because they were unable to find the type of employment desired, while others were dissatisfied with the growing strength of labor unions, or considered the cities a poor place for raising children. Many businessmen and artisans of Dutch descent joined the trek westward in the expectation of finding greater economic opportunities.

The primary reason why many Dutch-Americans decided to move farther west, however, was their desire for cheap, fertile land. Natural increase of the population and the continued arrival of new immigrants from the Netherlands led to overcrowding in the older settlements, causing an increase in land values and rent, and making it difficult for sons and grandsons of earlier immigrants to start farming. For them, the enactment of laws like the Homestead Act of 1862 and the sale of railroad lands were a godsend. G. W. Rensker, who accompanied a group of Dutch homesteaders from Michigan to the central part of Dakota Territory in 1885, declared, "Nine-tenths of the people wanted land—lots of it and with the idea of building up a colony and getting rich in a short time."[7] Although Rensker was referring particularly to Hollanders moving into the Dakotas, his remarks are applicable to those moving into other regions as well. The interest of Netherlanders in land is clearly shown in the census report of 1910, which lists over two-thirds of the 120,053 Holland-born then living in the United States as being located in the middlewestern and western states.

Dutchmen already living in the United States frequently learned about the availability of land in the same manner as Hollanders who came directly from the Netherlands. Many were influenced by letters written by relatives and friends, and by pamphlets published by railroad companies, real estate agents, and state and territorial governments. Dutch-language newspapers published in the United States, of which there were over twenty by the late nineteenth century, were a particularly important means for informing Dutch-Americans about new lands being opened for settlement. Influential newspapers included *De Grondwet* of Holland, Michigan, *De Weekblad* of Pella, Iowa, and *De Volksvriend* of Orange City, Iowa. Magazines published by the Reformed and Christian Reformed churches, both of which were predominantly Dutch-American in membership, also carried considerable information about new settlements.

One of the most important daughter colonies was located in Sioux County in northwest Iowa, where, in 1870, three wagon trains of Dutch families and single men from Pella, three hundred miles to the southeast, took possession of thirty-eight sections (24,320 acres) of land.[8] They also plotted a town which they named Orange City, after the royal family of the Netherlands. The excellent quality of the soil together with the Dutch talent for farming caused the settlement to prosper. As glowing reports of its success were circulated by letters and Dutch-language newspapers, hundreds of additional settlers arrived not only from the Pella region but also from Dutch communities in Michigan, Wisconsin, and elsewhere. A significant number of immigrants also arrived directly from the Netherlands.

The arrival of additional settlers resulted in more prairie land being broken up for farms, and in the founding of more towns with such Dutch names as East Orange, Maurice (for Prince Maurice, the son of William the Silent), Middleburg, and Newkirk. Several new towns with non-Dutch names were also settled primarily by persons of Dutch descent, and are still very Dutch to this day. Sioux Center, a name of Indian origin and located about ten miles from Orange City, can be cited as an example. Of the approximately eighteen hundred names listed in its 1973 telephone directory, almost two hundred seventy-five begin with the prefix "Van" (Van Beek, Van Bruggen, Vande Berg, and so forth) and almost one hundred fifty with the prefix "De" (De Boer, De Groot, De Jong, and so forth).

Just as the Michigan colony had excellent leaders in men like Van Raalte and Van der Meulen, and the Pella community had Scholte, the Sioux County Hollanders were fortunate in having Henry Hospers and the Reverend Seine Bolks to guide them during the critical years. Henry Hospers, who was born in the Netherlands in 1830 and emigrated with his parents to Pella, Iowa, in 1847, was among the committee of locators that chose Sioux County as the site for a new colony. From the outset, he played a commanding role in Orange City's development, including that of banker, storekeeper, notary, attorney, newspaperman, member of the county board of supervisors, insurance agent, and promoter of education. Dominie Bolks, as spiritual leader of the colony, stood ready to comfort the people during their frequent periods of adversity and sorrow. He, too, was born in the Netherlands, and led a large group of immigrants to Michigan before moving to northwest Iowa. Several of the early Sioux County Hollanders later recalled that if it had not been for the encouraging words of this saintly man, many settlers would have become downhearted and sought new homes elsewhere.

By 1880, the Dutch population of northwest Iowa was over five thousand and still growing.[9] Soon no more land was available for homesteading, and land already occupied could be obtained only at high prices. Many of the Hollanders consequently had no choice but to look elsewhere for farms, which sometimes resulted in the founding of more daughter colonies. Some went to adjoining Minnesota and South Dakota, others went to Nebraska and Kansas, and a few went as far as Montana and Washington.

The first major Dutch settlement founded in Minnesota after the Civil War was established by two Holland-born businessmen—Theodore Koch and Martin Prins—who in 1885 purchased thirty-four thousand acres of railroad land about seventy-five miles west of Minneapolis.[10] They undertook an extensive advertising campaign to encourage Hollanders from the Middle West and the Netherlands to settle there. Land was offered at prices averaging about eight dollars per acre, and promises were made to assist in building churches and towns. The chief town, Prinsburg, was named after one of the colony's founders. Other towns were named Clara City, in honor of Koch's wife Clara, and Roseland, after a Dutch community near Chicago. By 1900, the colony encompassed about twenty square miles, and its Dutch-speaking population totaled about fifteen hundred.

In the meantime, a Dutch community of significant size was gradually developing on the prairie in southwestern Minnesota, particularly around the towns of Holland, Leota, and Edgerton. Railroad companies and real estate agents strove mightily to promote Dutch settlement of this area. Expense-paid excursion tours from northwest Iowa, for example, were conducted to the region, and land was advertised in *De Volksvriend* of Orange City at seven to nine dollars per acre, with liberal terms of payment. In view of the rising cost of land in northwest Iowa and the proximity of the area, it is no wonder that a number of Hollanders moved to southwestern Minnesota. The United States census report for 1920 listed nearly eighteen hundred Holland-born residing there.

Small Dutch settlements were also established elsewhere in Minnesota at the close of the nineteenth century. These included a group of four—Pease, Ogilivie, Friesland, and Groningen—located about eighty miles north of Minneapolis. Theodore Koch, the land promoter who played a decisive role in bringing Dutch settlers to the central part of the state at Prinsburg, sold about twenty-five thousand acres in this area to Hollanders beginning in 1895. By 1900, there were about seventy-five families living at Friesland and Groningen and one hundred twenty at Pease. The poor soil, cold climate, and burned-over timber land kept them from prospering with the result that many of the settlers began moving away after the First World War.

Contemporary with these developments in Minnesota, Dutch settlers were also moving into the Dakotas, attracted there by reports about vast stretches of unoccupied grassland and fertile soil.[11] As expressed by a Hollander who moved there in 1883, "This was the poor man's land, his fairy dream. Some people . . . seeing this opportunity for gaining wealth, sold out and bought large tracts of land in the territory of the Dakotas. . . . They came with few exceptions from the older Dutch colonies in Michigan, Wisconsin, and Iowa."[12]

The first Dutch communities in the Dakotas were established by families who simply moved across the border from Sioux County, Iowa, and southwestern Minnesota, followed soon after by a movement farther westward. In the mid-1880's large numbers of Dutch-Americans from Michigan began settling in Emmons County, in south-central North Dakota. News about the success of these communities continued to attract persons from other parts of the United States, but also directly from the Netherlands. Thus, in 1892, several immigrant families from the province of Friesland settled at Springfield, near Yankton, South Dakota, where a small group of farmers from Orange City, Iowa, had established themselves as early as 1874. Similarly, in 1906, a number of Hollanders who arrived directly from the province of Overijssel settled in the Litchville-Marion area of North Dakota, where a group of Dutch-Americans, also from Orange City, had relocated a few years earlier.

In addition to several small Dutch communities like those described above, most of which still exist today, two large colonies were established in the southern part of South Dakota. One was located in Douglas County, and the other in adjoining Charles Mix County. The former was founded in 1882 by settlers who came primarily from northwest Iowa, where land values were high and the prospect of free land in the Dakotas was very alluring. The colony in Charles Mix County, on the other hand, was founded by immigrants who came directly from the Netherlands. Its chief promoter was an interesting person named Albert Kuipers, a self-made but prosperous farmer from Friesland. Motivated by personal ambition and a concern for his country's poor farmers, Kuipers led a band of Dutch immigrants to Charles Mix County in 1882. The new colonies were soon joined by other immigrants and persons from older communities in the United States. Thus, as early as February, 1883, a Dutch pastor, after a visit to Charles Mix and Douglas counties, reported that "anyone who intends to move there and to live among the Hollanders should not hesitate because the land in both counties is being rapidly taken up."[13] By 1920, the two counties boasted ten Dutch churches, with a total membership of nearly three thousand.

Hollanders who settled in the trans-Mississippi West faced several special problems. The difficulties encountered by those who moved to the Dakotas can be cited as examples, because their experiences were similar to those undergone by Hollanders who moved into other thinly settled regions during the latter part of the nineteenth century.[14]

Most Hollanders lacked capital upon arrival in the Dakotas, although there were a few who were quite well off, especially if they had lived elsewhere in the United States first. William Cleveringa, for example, who left the Netherlands for Michigan in 1881 and moved to Iowa in 1884 and to Emmons County, North Dakota, in 1887, started farming in the latter area equipped with three horses, two mules, and a good plow. The family of Maurits Van Soest was less fortunate, for they arrived in the Dakotas about 1885 with only a wagon of furniture and a horse and cow hitched together for pulling the wagon. The family of Hendrikeus Van der Pol, who arrived from the Netherlands in 1883, was even worse off, having only a yoke of oxen and five dollars. The plight of the Van der Pols was typical of many Dutch immigrants who came to the United States during the 1880's and 1890's. As late as 1903, over half the immigrants arriving in the United States from the Netherlands had less than thirty dollars in their possession.[15]

Because of lack of money, improvisation was often the order of the day. One early Dutch resident recalled her mother making mittens and everyday shoes from old grain sacks, real shoes being worn only to church and to the post office. Another recalled field corn being roasted and ground for coffee, and dried sunflower leaves being used for tobacco. Lard was used in a variety of ways. It was frequently mixed with lye to make soap, and sometimes a rag in a flat dish of lard was used for lighting the home if the family could not afford candles. Lard was also used for "buttering" bread, so that real butter could be sold for cash to be used for other needs. A variety of home remedies were resorted to in the event of illness.

In other ways, too, farming on the Great Plains was difficult. Preparing the virgin soil for crops was often back-breaking work. In summer, drought and severe hailstorms, as well as prairie fires and grasshoppers, frequently discouraged the settlers, while the long, cold winters, interspersed with blizzards, added to their melancholy life. Housing conditions were generally primitive. Settlers who could afford it used lumber for their first buildings, but these were often crude and makeshift because good building material was either too costly or unavailable. Poorer families, of which there were many, frequently made their first houses of slabs of sod, or "Dakota bricks," as they were sometimes called. One of the early Dutch residents of the "Sod House Frontier" described the building of these shanties as follows:

The first thing that had to be done when my folks arrived at their homestead was to get out the breakplow and find a patch of tough sod for building the sod house. The sod was cut into the lengths desired and then loaded on a make-shift stoneboat or wagon. Then the slabs of sod were placed criss-cross on top of each other until the desired wall-height was reached. The roof was made of rough lumber and covered with a thick layer of tar paper with dirt piled over that. The houses were cool in summer and warmer in winter than many frame houses, but the windows were small and few. My parents lived in that twelve-by-sixteen foot sod house [with their four children] without a board floor for two and one-half years.[16]

The prairie could at times be an awesome and lonesome experience for the early Hollanders of Dakota, especially during the cold winter months. J. Van Erve reported in 1897 that during his first winter in Campbell County, South Dakota, his wife did not see anyone she knew for seven months. Far from neighbors and having to work from dawn until sunset, it was easy to lose track of time. "So, for example," according to Van Erve, "our friend P. Droog who after having worked on Sunday, on the next day dressed himself for church and, with his Bible under his arm, arrived at K. Scholten's house where they convinced him with great difficulty that it really was Monday."[17]

Despite its vastness and its dangers, the prairie could nevertheless be beautiful beyond comprehension. Albert Hasper, a Hollander who settled in Emmons County in 1885, declared, "When we first came here, we thought it was just like a big ocean of grass."[18] Prairie sunsets were particularly beautiful spectacles, as is borne out in the memoirs of early Dutch travelers and settlers. Nothing, however, could rival the beauty of the unspoiled prairie in the spring. Wild flowers were numerous and of various colors, such as white buttercups, blue violets, and purple sweet williams. Meadowlarks and plovers were in abundance, as well as blackbirds, robins, wild canaries, bobolinks, and a variety of owls. There were also numerous game birds, including prairie chickens, ducks, and geese.[19] Even getting lost on the prairie on a summer night was not without its pleasant experiences. The clear, starlit skies and the stillness of the prairie seemed to bring man closer to his Maker. An early settler in North Dakota recorded how, when he was lost at night, he would contentedly pass away the time by singing Dutch psalms.[20]

In light of the above remarks, it is interesting to note a comment by a university professor from the Netherlands who spent considerable time in the United States in the late 1920's doing research on the history of the Dutch in America. He considered the Hollanders in the Middle West more conservative than those residing in the eastern part of the United States, and attributed this in part to the influence of prairie living. The Dutch historian took his cue from a South Dakota author, Haydn Carruth, whom he quoted as follows: "The Prairie is the world in its calm, serene, beautiful old age, meditative, unhurried, unafraid; approaching Nirvana. . . . The Prairie is but the desert watered, and as hath been said, 'The desert is of God, and in the desert no man may deny Him.'" According to the Netherlands professor, the calmness and the endlessness of the prairie were conducive to fostering a "meditative and contemplative life" among the settlers and therefore "orthodoxy and all that pertained thereto" flourished longer among the Hollanders residing on the Great Plains than among those living in the eastern states.[21]

Several communities similar to those in Iowa, Minnesota,

and the Dakotas were founded in the southern Great Plains in Nebraska and Kansas. One of the earliest was located about fifteen miles south of Lincoln, Nebraska, in Lancaster County, where a small number of Dutchmen, mostly from Wisconsin, founded the town of Holland in 1868.[22] Later arrivals settled in the neighboring towns of Pella (named after Pella, Iowa) and Firth. Like other Dutch colonies on the prairie, the Lancaster settlement had its economic cycles, depending primarily on weather conditions. Thus, in 1875, as a result of a severe drought, farmers lost half their wheat harvest and the entire corn and vegetable crop. In the following year, however, when nature was kinder, excellent crops were grown. Although some settlers left the Nebraska colony each year, thinking that the problems and discomforts of prairie living were too much to endure, other Hollanders always arrived to take their place. As a result, the settlement continued to grow. By 1920, it had three Reformed churches, with a combined membership of about two hundred fifty families.

To the south, in the neighboring state of Kansas, three distinctively Dutch communities were established. Two were named after cities in the Netherlands. Zutphen, founded near Salina, had only a brief existence. Founded in 1867, it failed after two years because of drought, and its founders returned to Pella, Iowa, whence they had come. Rotterdam, in Jewell County near the Nebraska border, was founded in 1870 also by Hollanders coming from Pella, Iowa. It managed to survive and still exists, although its name has been changed to Dispatch. In 1920, its two Dutch churches had a combined membership of about seventy-five families.

The third settlement, called Luctor (derived from one of the words on the emblem of the Dutch province of Zeeland, *Luctor et Emergo*, meaning "I Struggle and I Succeed"), was the most important of the Dutch communities in Kansas. Located near the town of Prairie View, about sixty-five miles west of Rotterdam, it was started in 1877 as a daughter colony of Holland, Nebraska, in much the same manner that Orange City was founded by former residents of Pella, Iowa. It also attracted settlers from other Dutch communities throughout the Middle West, and a few came directly from the Netherlands.

By 1900, the Luctor settlement was spread over an area twelve by twenty miles, and had about one hundred fifty families. Conditions were still primitive, however, as described by one of its residents in 1896:

> The earliest settlers . . . were isolated so to speak, from the rest of the world—to shift for themselves as best they could. Money usually was scarce, and so they were forced to seek a chance to labor in the adjoining state of Colorado. Each year they trekked to that state to provide themselves and their families with necessaries while their loved ones in the meanwhile remained on their homesteads. As the climate was not severe in winter, they erected rude sod houses and so solved the problem of shelter cheaply. Many of these houses are occupied even at the present time; and whenever the lack of money today prevents the erection of more imposing buildings this material is still used to make comfortable, if rude, dwellings.[23]

Montana eventually surpassed Nebraska and Kansas in the number of Dutch-American inhabitants, although at first they were slow in settling there.[24] The Reverend Andreas Wormser, a Reformed minister born in the Netherlands but educated in the United States, was responsible for founding the first important Dutch colony in Montana. As a result of an excursion to the Far West, Dominie Wormser became interested in Montana as a possible site for a Dutch agricultural colony. Although his plans were not intended as a moneymaking scheme for himself, he received strong backing from real estate interests. The proposed colony was widely advertised in Dutch-language newspapers in the United States, and Wormser even made a trip to the Netherlands, where his display of maps and photographs as well as samples of Montana products awakened considerable interest. The site chosen for the new colony was located near the town of Manhattan, in the southwestern part of the state. The first settlers arrived in 1891, and despite occasional setbacks, the colony prospered. Crop failures in other Dutch communities, especially in the Dakotas, brought new settlers, and promotion of the colony continued unabated. By 1920, its two Dutch churches had over six hundred members.

The success of the Manhattan colony encouraged the formation of other Dutch settlements in Montana. These were located at Wormser City, about sixty miles west of Manhattan; Huntley and Columbus, in the vicinity of Billings; Conrad, Farmington, and Choteau, northwest of Great Falls; and several near the Canadian border. In contrast to similar settlements founded in other states, a few of these were occupied by Dutch Catholics. Unfortunately, none of the later communities were as successful as the one at Manhattan. The problems they frequently faced are well described in a report of 1926. It was carried in *The Banner*, an official magazine of the Christian Reformed Church, which was primarily Dutch in membership,[25] and was written in order to solicit aid for some of the Montana congregations.

Conrad and vicinity has suffered much by drought and grasshoppers. . . . It makes a saddening impression to see so many houses and stores empty in neighboring villages, and also to see a good many farmhouses deserted in the country. Even good size houses that bear witness of the good opinion the builders once had of this country are empty. The original inhabitants have left for the more settled East or for the mild and green Western coast.[26]

In the long run, the state of Washington proved more attractive to Hollanders than Montana, Nebraska, Kansas, or even the Dakotas. This is demonstrated in the steady increase of Holland-born settlers living in Washington: from 227 in 1890 to 632 in 1900, 2,157 in 1910, and 3,097 in 1920. The figure for 1920 was nearly twice that of Montana and ranked tenth in the nation. Actually, the number of Dutch-Americans living in Washington was considerably higher than these census figures indicate because they do not include the numerous American-born descendants of Dutch immigrants residing there.

A few businessmen from the Netherlands began emigrating to Washington as early as the 1880's. The shortage of capital and the consequent high interest rates on the west coast of the United States appealed to several financial firms in the Netherlands, where there was a surplus of capital and relatively low interest rates. By 1918, there were five Dutch lending institutions in Spokane, three in Seattle, and one in nearby Portland.[27] Beginning in the 1890's, Dutch farmers also began settling in Washington. As elsewhere, railroad companies and real estate agents did considerable advertising in Dutch-language newspapers in both the United States and the Netherlands, pointing out the state's advantages.

W. E. Werkman, a Netherlands-born real estate agent, was particularly active in promoting Washington as a mecca for discontented Dutchmen. In 1894, he persuaded a Netherlands banking firm, S. Ellens and Company, to purchase eighteen thousand acres on Whitbey Island, near the entrance to Puget Sound. As an agent of this firm, Werkman and a close associate, Hein Te Roller, who also was Holland-born, traveled throughout the midwest to entice Dutchmen into moving to Whitbey Island. They were so successful that within two years there were about two hundred Hollanders living there. In 1920, a visitor to Whitbey Island described the settlement as having about eight hundred Hollanders, most of whom were engaged in vegetable gardening, dairying, and poultry farming. About a third of them were Holland-born.[28]

Periodic bad harvests in parts of the Middle West during the 1890's and overcrowding in several Dutch settlements, together with extensive advertising and the general success of the Whitbey Island settlement, led to the founding of additional Dutch colonies in Washington. The Yakima Valley, in the south-central part of the state, soon began attracting Dutch settlers, especially from northwest Iowa, as did also the area around Everett. The land in the latter region proved to be excellent for truck gardening, a vocation in which the Dutch have particularly excelled. By World War I, several cities in Washington, particularly Seattle, were also attracting Dutchmen.

Lynden, in the extreme northwest corner of Washington, held the greatest attraction, and for a time was the largest Dutch settlement on the Pacific Coast. It had been a thriving lumber town until the depression of 1893, after which it was virtually abandoned. Three Hollanders, Gerrit Veleke, Hermann Oordt, and Douwe Zijlstra, saw possibilities in revitalizing its lumber industry, especially the production of shingles. They also noted that Lynden was readily accessible to markets, and that the soil surrounding the town was of excellent quality. Through the efforts of these men, numerous Hollanders began moving into the region in 1900. They came from various parts of the United States as well as Canada and the Netherlands. Some new arrivals went into lumbering, but most of them became farmers. Later, many became eminently successful as dairymen and fruit growers. In 1920, there were six hundred eighty-six Holland-born living in the Lynden area, which was nearly one-fourth of the total found in the state.

A significant number of Hollanders also settled in Utah after the Civil War.[29] This came about because of the attraction Mormonism held for some inhabitants of the Netherlands, especially the so-called Zwijndrecht Brothers, so named after the town of Zwijndrecht, near Rotterdam, where many of them lived. Shortly after 1850, when dissension broke out among them, a few of the Zwijndrecht Brothers went to America to live among the Mormons, whose religious beliefs were somewhat similar to theirs.

In 1861, two Dutch Mormon elders, A. W. Van der Woude and P. A. Schettler, who had emigrated to Utah earlier, returned to the Netherlands to do missionary work. Through preaching and the distribution of Mormon tracts they won a significant number of converts, particularly in the northern province of Friesland. Convinced that God was about to wreak his vengeance on a sinful Europe, they strongly urged emigration to Utah, the new Canaan. Given the Mormon's predilection for missionary work, Van der Woude and Schettler were the first of a series of Mormon proselytizers to visit the Netherlands. As a result, the number of Holland-born in Utah steadily increased from 12 in 1860 to 523 in 1900, and to 1,980 in 1920. In contrast to the general pattern of Dutch settlement in the West, only a few Dutch Mormons located in rural areas. In 1920, for example, nearly all of Utah's Holland-born were living in two cities—874 in Salt Lake City and 749 in Ogden. Their Dutch ways were not immediately lost, as is shown by the publication of their own newspaper, *De Utah Nederlander.*

Although California has today become one of the favorite states for Dutch-Americans, the number who resided there before 1900 was rather small. From time to time, however, it appealed to small groups having a special interest. The gold strike of 1849, for example, brought a few Hollanders directly from the Netherlands as well as from Dutch communities in the United States, but their number was not large. Even Hollanders from

Pella, Iowa, which lay on one of the main routes to California, did not catch the "gold fever" to any great degree. A few Dutchmen also came to California at an early date to invest capital, just as they did in the state of Washington. It was a Hollander, James De Fremery, for example, who founded the San Francisco Savings Union.

By the close of the nineteenth century, at least five large-scale projects had been undertaken in California for the express purpose of founding Dutch agricultural settlements. They were scattered throughout the state, and had their origins both in the Netherlands and among Dutch-American residents of the state. A few of the promoters were inspired by philanthropic ideas, but generally the profit motive was paramount. Unfortunately, none of the settlements was successful, despite such appealing names as Hollandia and Queen Whilhelmina Colony.[30]

An examination of the Holland-California Land Company illustrates the kind of problems these settlements faced and their reasons for failure. In 1889, this company purchased four thousand acres of land in Merced County in the lower San Joaquin Valley. After setting two hundred acres aside for a town, which was given the name of Rotterdam, the tract was divided into holdings of about twenty acres each to be devoted primarily to fruit and vegetable farming. Although most of the promoters were Dutch-Americans residing in California, efforts to recruit colonists were centered primarily in the Netherlands. The climate was described as excellent and the scenery as beautiful. California products were displayed in various cities and the people were informed these could be easily grown and readily marketed. Despite the high cost of land—one hundred sixty to two hundred dollars per acre—plus the need for about two thousand dollars for equipment to start farming, about fifty tracts were quickly sold in the Netherlands, sight unseen, and by May, 1890, four separate groups had left for the *nieuwe kolonie*. A few Hollanders also arrived from Michigan. Another town, to be called Amsterdam, was projected for the colony, and some stately homes were built by the well-to-do.

High hopes were quickly replaced by disillusionment. Inadequate water and the hard subsoil made it difficult—given the state of agricultural science at this time—to grow the products planned. The land proved to be worth only a fraction of its selling price, and the temperature, which sometimes reached one hundred ten degrees in the summer, was considered unbearable by many of the new arrivals. Worst of all, most of the colonists, having been recruited from among the well-to-do, were woefully ignorant of farming. Henri Albert Van Coenen Torchiana, a member of an old and distinguished family of the Netherlands and one of the first to settle in the colony, later summed up the reasons for the failure of the Merced County experiment: "The wrong people were brought to the wrong land at the wrong prices. Therefore the Colony had from its very inception, within its bosom, all the elements of failure."[31] Within five years, the Dutch colony in Merced County practically faded into oblivion as its settlers scattered to places that offered a better future.

It is no wonder, therefore, that the various colonization schemes brought few Holland immigrants *permanently* to California before 1900. Between 1880 and 1900, the number of Holland-born in the state increased from only about seven hundred to one thousand. In the end, the founding of successful Dutch communities was carried out primarily by Dutch-Americans rather than immigrants coming directly from the Netherlands. Numerous distinctively Dutch enclaves appeared in the San Francisco, Los Angeles, and Long Beach areas. The towns of Chino, Compton, Artesia, Bellflower, and Hynes in southern California had especially heavy concentrations of Hollanders. According to a report of 1927, for example, Hynes was sometimes referred to as *kleine Nederland* (Little Netherlands), and Dutch was heard as much as English on main street.[32] Dairying became a major occupation of these Hollanders, and when farm work was lax in the Middle West during the winter months, hundreds of Dutch farm boys went to southern California during the 1920's and 1930's to work as milkers, many of them settling there permanently.

A grandiose colonization scheme similar to those attempted in California was also tried in Colorado.[33] It began with the founding in 1892 of the Holland American Land and Immigration Company, with headquarters in Utrecht, the Netherlands. Its promoters claimed they had title to fifteen thousand acres of

land in the San Luis Valley near Alamosa in the southern part
of Colorado, where they planned a colony to be known as
Utrecht. Considerable propaganda in praise of the region was
distributed in the Netherlands. Its soil was described as being
so fertile that a farmer with only eighty acres of land would
be able to support his family and meet his financial obligations
and still have about six thousand guilders left over each year.

On October 15, 1892, about two hundred adults and a large
number of children from all over the Netherlands left for the
"promised land," arriving at their destination on the last day
of November. A newspaper correspondent reported their arrival
at Alamosa as follows:

The biggest thing in the way of a colonization scheme that has
ever been undertaken in Colorado has just had its beginning here.
Tonight at six o'clock a special train bearing three hundred and
fifty Holland immigrants arrived in town. . . . This is but the vanguard of over two thousand Holland farmers and their families who
will settle in the sunny San Luis valley before another year rolls
around. . . . After the [welcoming] supper, speeches were made by
several of the leading citizens and translated into the Dutch language, so the strangers could understand, as they responded by
singing their national anthem, and giving three hearty cheers for
Alamosa and her citizens.[34]

Unfortunately, most of the promoters were unprincipled men
who, interested only in quick profits, had grossly misrepresented
the project. The land was unable to support worthwhile vegetation without extensive irrigation, and they did not even have
clear title to it. Furthermore, the new arrivals were crowded
into very inadequate housing and a shortage of food developed.
When diphtheria and scarlet fever broke out, thirteen children
died within a few days. Most of the immigrants quickly became
discouraged and left for other places in Colorado and the
Middle West or returned to the Netherlands. Those who remained established a small settlement near Alamosa called
Rilland, after a town in the southern part of the Netherlands.
With help from Dutch communities elsewhere in the United
States, it managed a precarious existence. A Dutch church,
organized there in 1904, had eleven families in 1920, which

had expanded to only thirty-one by the time of the Second World War.

In contrast to the Middle West and West, the number of Hollanders who settled permanently in the southern states was never very large. Several explanations can be given for this. The presence of slavery before the Civil War was a factor, as was low wages for farm laborers after that conflict ended. The fact that New York, Boston, and Baltimore, rather than southern ports, were the favored terminal points of immigrant ships plying between the Netherlands and the United States also tended to favor settlement in the northern tier of states. Climatic conditions likewise discouraged Hollanders from settling in the south, as did unfamiliarity with cultivating such southern crops as cotton, peanuts, and rice. Finally, many Hollanders preferred the northern states after the Civil War because of the presence there of relatives who had accompanied men like Van Raalte and Scholte during the 1840's.

This does not mean that the Dutch never showed any interest in the South. As was true of Washington and California, the need for capital in the New South attracted the interest of several financial firms in the Netherlands. Dutch capital and entrepreneurship, for example, were heavily involved in the construction of the Kansas City Southern Railroad running from Kansas City to Port Arthur, Texas, which got under way in 1895. Several Dutch names were given to stations along the line, including Amsterdam, Zwolle, De Ridder, Vandervoort, Bloomburg, and Mena.[35] Limited Dutch interest in the South was also created by favorable newspaper and other accounts. Thus, in 1881, Charles Boissevain, a well-known journalist from the Netherlands, reported after a visit to the United States that the climate, contour of the land, and products of the Southeast reminded him of France and Italy. In like manner, he described the Chesapeake Bay as "the Marseille and the Liverpool of the United States, which may someday replace New York as America's shipping center." Boissevain also had high praise for the climate and fertile soil of Missouri.[36]

The most serious attempt to found a large Dutch colony in the South occurred in 1867 in Amelia County, Virginia, about twenty-five miles southwest of Richmond.[37] None other than

Dominie Albertus Van Raalte, founder of the famous community of Holland, Michigan, played a significant role in the creation of this settlement, which soon had over fifty families. Some of the Hollanders who settled there came from Michigan, but many came directly from the Netherlands, attracted in part by the favorable letters written by Van Raalte. The 1870 census report listed one hundred sixty-nine Holland-born living in Amelia County, but by 1875, the colony had virtually disappeared. Lack of skills on the part of the immigrants, low wages, high land values, and reports of cheap, fertile land in the Middle West contributed to the failure.[38]

From an early date, consideration was also given to establishing Dutch colonies in Texas. Hollanders from Pella, Iowa, once seriously thought of settling there, but their interest declined when a daughter colony was established in Sioux County, Iowa, in 1870. The most ambitious scheme for settling Hollanders in Texas was undertaken by the Kansas City Southern Railroad and the Port Arthur Land Company, both of which were heavily financed by Netherlands bankers. In 1896, these firms acquired a large tract of land a few miles north of Port Arthur, Texas. The land was divided into twenty-acre plots to be sold at twenty to forty dollars per acre to persons who would derive their living primarily from rice culture. A town, appropriately named Nederland, was also plotted.[39]

An extensive advertising campaign was undertaken to entice Hollanders to settle at Nederland. A fifty-five-page pamphlet was distributed in the United States and the Netherlands, describing the soil as good for growing all kinds of crops as well as vegetables and fruit trees. The site was also advertised as suitable for dairying and commercial fishing.[40] Extensive promotional activities, together with poor harvests elsewhere in the United States, caused some Hollanders from older settlements to relocate at Nederland. A significant number of immigrants also arrived from the Netherlands. In a short time, the Texas colony had six hundred inhabitants and even published its own Dutch-language newspaper.

By 1900, however, the colony began declining. Unfamiliarity with rice culture and a misunderstanding with the irrigation company that was supposed to supply the farmers with water caused many to leave. Others found the climate unsuitable. Today, only the town's name and a few family names are all that remain of a one-time promising Dutch community in southeastern Texas. This was unfortunate, because, as later events demonstrated, the region around Nederland was ideally suited for cultivation as well as for dairying and truck gardening. Attempts to found other Dutch colonies in Texas, such as at Winnie and Hamshire, near Port Arthur, about 1909, and at Paris, in the northeastern part of the state, in 1915, were no more successful than that at Nederland. In 1920, there were only five hundred fifty-four Holland-born living in Texas, making it twenty-second in the nation in terms of Dutch-American inhabitants.

One of the most prosperous and wholly unplanned Dutch communities to be established in the late nineteenth century was located not in the Middle West, where so many Hollanders settled, but in the East. During the 1880's, several inhabitants of Whitinsville, Massachusetts (located about fifteen miles southeast of Worcester), ordered a shipment of Frisian-Holstein dairy cattle from the Netherlands. A few young Dutch immigrants who were brought over to take care of the cattle were so pleased with their new home that they urged relatives and friends to join them. These arrivals in turn influenced other Hollanders to settle in the Whitinsville area, often sending money for their passage. At first, most of the new immigrants went into farming, but an increasing number found employment in nearby factories.

The snowball-like increase in Whitinsville's Dutch population is shown in the growth of the Christian Reformed church that was organized by the first arrivals—from 13 families in 1895 to 70 in 1907. In 1926, when its membership stood at 700, half the services in this church were still being conducted in the Dutch language. According to the census of 1920, there were 2,071 Holland-born living in Massachusetts, and about a third of them were located in the Whitinsville area.[41]

One of the last Dutch settlements established in the United States between the Civil War and World War I was a small utopian colony. Its founder was Frederick Willem Van Eeden (1860–1932), a Netherlands literary figure and social reformer. After the failure of an agricultural cooperative, appropriately called Walden, that he had founded near Amsterdam, he acquired in 1909, with the help of a land development company, seventy-five hundred acres near Wilmington, North Carolina. Here he founded "Van Eeden Kolonie," which stressed social equality and rustic living. Although Van Eeden himself never took up permanent residence at the North Carolina retreat, he visited it on several occasions and also traveled throughout the eastern states. His socialist ideas and his fame as a writer brought him in contact with several prominent Americans, including Upton Sinclair, with whom he corresponded for many years. He also had an audience with President Theodore Roosevelt.[42] Although "Van Eeden Kolonie" never prospered, Hollanders from the Netherlands and places in the United States became a part of the experiment, and its last vestiges did not disappear until 1939.[43]

A few words of caution are needed to conclude this description of daughter colonies and other settlements. The appearance of new communities did not spell the end of those that had been founded before the Civil War. Indeed, most of the latter continued to thrive and to grow in numbers. Many Dutch-Americans who had arrived before 1861 or were descendants of earlier immigrants were untouched by the fever of adventure or by the desire for cheap land, preferring instead to remain in their old abodes. Furthermore, thousands of Hollanders who emigrated during the decades before World War I continued to locate in the older settlements.

As was true during the pre–Civil War period, many of the later immigrants never made the trek westward to become farmers, at least not immediately. Instead, they helped supply the labor force required in America's growing industries, such as the textile mills and machine shops of Paterson and Passaic, New Jersey, the Pullman plants of Chicago, or the furniture factories of Grand Rapids, Michigan. Others served the growing population of the cities by working as dairymen or truck gardeners. As in the rural areas, these immigrants frequently congregated together, a practice which, together with their Dutch-language churches and their ethnic press, served as a magnet in attracting new arrivals from the Netherlands. In 1920, for example, according to the census report, 60 percent of the 12,737 Holland-born living in New Jersey resided in Passaic County.

Cognizance must also be taken of the fact that although tens of thousands of Hollanders lived in distinctively Dutch communities on the eve of World War I, there were many others who were virtually isolated from contacts with the ancestral language and the customs of the fatherland. According to the census of 1920, for example, about 30 percent of the eight hundred forty-six Holland-born living in Nebraska resided in the Dutch communities of Lancaster County, but the remaining 70 percent were scattered in sixty-nine counties. In the absence of what the Dutch call *samenleving* (i.e., having close social and cultural ties with people of their own kind), Hollanders such as these soon lost whatever Old World traditions they once had. Today, there is little left to indicate their Dutch ancestry except their family names.

Finally, the total number of Hollanders who emigrated to America between the Civil War and World War I must not be exaggerated. There was no mass exodus from the Netherlands. The 175,000 immigrants who arrived, although considerably more numerous than those who came in previous decades, represented only a fraction of the total population of the Netherlands. Moreover, when compared to the 25,000,000 Europeans who emigrated to the United States during this same period of time, the number of Dutch immigrants appears rather miniscule.

❋     ❋     ❋     ❋

During the period between the Civil War and World War I, numerous Dutch communities arose in the trans-Mississippi West as well as a few elsewhere. Generally speaking, Hollanders were attracted to these regions by reports of cheap land. In contrast to the settlements founded before the Civil War, many of the later colonies were established, not by immigrants, but by second and third generation Dutch-Americans, although immigrants soon came to live in them. Some of the new colonies, such as those in Sioux County, Iowa, southwestern Minnesota, and Lynden, Washington, became vigorous communities whose present population includes thousands of persons of Dutch descent. Other new colonies had only limited success, such as Luctor, Kansas; New Holland, South Dakota; and Conrad, Montana. Of them, it may be said that the elements of nature were too unfavorable to permit the extensive growth anticipated by their founders. There were also a few settlements, generally those in which the profit motive was the primary reason for their appearance, that ended up as almost complete failures.

# CHAPTER X
## Recent Dutch Immigration

DESPITE THE VARIED ACTIVITIES OF THE NETHERLANDS IN WORLD trade and its possession of considerable colonial territory, its nationals traditionally showed little inclination to emigrate. Before the First World War, the United States held by far the greatest attraction among overseas countries for Dutch immigrants,[1] yet that interest was comparatively small. The high point of Dutch emigration to the United States occurred during the decade of the 1880's when 53,701 Hollanders went there to find a new home. This figure represented only slightly more than 1 percent of the 1880 population of the Netherlands and was behind that of most European nations.[2] After the Second World War, however, the tide of Dutch emigration moved significantly upward. About a half million Hollanders have left the Netherlands since 1945 to find a new home in some other country. Nearly 20 percent of them located in the United States.

What was the cause of the postwar exodus, and why was there a sudden change in the thinking of the Dutch on the matter of emigration? The explanation is simple: a series of unsettling experiences—the economic depression of the 1930's, the rise of Nazism, and the Second World War—together with a concern about the future helped create a psychological climate conducive to extensive emigration. The war, in particular, was a shocking experience. Five years of systematic plundering by the occupying forces, inundation of much farm land by salt water, deterioration of industrial equipment, deportation of about a half million workers to Germany, and famine conditions in the cities not only left many Hollanders disillusioned, but made them receptive to the idea of beginning a new life in another country.[3]

Pessimism about the future of the Netherlands also made the

Hollanders more emigration-minded than they had been in the past. Their grim experiences in the Second World War made them especially apprehensive about a possible World War III and Russian occupation. The economic future, too, looked very bleak after 1945, and many Hollanders doubted that there could ever be a complete return to prewar conditions. Germany, which had been one of the Netherlands' best customers before the war, was in no position to buy Dutch exports. Shortage of machinery and lack of parts severely crippled Holland's industry. Fear of import restrictions by other countries on Dutch goods also contributed to the economic gloom. The eventual loss of the East Indies (present-day Indonesia) was a major blow to the Dutch economy; before the war, it supported directly or indirectly between 10 and 15 percent of the Netherlands' population.[4]

The pessimism shared by many Hollanders about their country's future was increased by the conviction that the Netherlands was rapidly becoming overpopulated. Statistics seemed to bear out this fear. The country's population increased 100 percent between 1830 and 1900, and doubled again between 1900 and 1950. No other country in western Europe had a comparable population increase, and by the mid-twentieth century the population density of the Netherlands was one of the highest in the world.

The Dutch government itself after 1945 followed a more active emigration policy than it had in the past. It looked upon emigration as a means for relieving population pressure, reducing unemployment, and solving the alarming housing shortage. It also hoped that emigration would broaden the base of the export trade, on the supposition that persons who left the Netherlands would continue their interest in buying Dutch products. As a result of these considerations, the government in 1949 began granting subsidies to persons wishing to emigrate. The money was intended primarily to defray costs of transportation, but the amount varied with the financial needs of the applicant. In addition, vocational training centers were established where aspiring emigrants could learn new skills to enhance their chances for admission into the country of their choice. The government also negotiated agreements with receiving countries in order to assure Dutch emigrants that they would be treated virtually the same as citizens of the countries to which they moved.

There were also several private organizations, some of which had existed since the 1920's, working on behalf of Netherlanders planning a new life in another country. These included trade unions, agricultural associations, and church societies. Both the Dutch government and the private organizations carried on extensive information programs for acquainting prospective emigrants with the cultural life, religion, customs, and so forth, of the country of their destination. They also offered language courses, and assisted in filling out necessary forms and translating documents such as diplomas and testimonial letters that might be helpful to an emigrant in finding work. From 1951 to 1961, the Netherlands Emigration Service in The Hague gave a weekly radio broadcast in which the human and practical aspects of emigration were amply discussed. In view of all this activity, it is not surprising that net government expenditures for sponsoring emigration totaled 218 million guilders between 1946 and 1966.[5]

The combination of these various factors created after the Second World War what some writers have called an emigration psychosis in the Netherlands. So pronounced was this emigration-mindedness that it was estimated in 1948 that about one out of three Hollanders seriously considered emigration.[6] In the final analysis, however, the half million people who have left the Netherlands since the war—a very high number in view of past unwillingness of Hollanders to emigrate—fall far short of one in three. Thus, it is meaningful to ask: What considerations influenced some of them to take the final step and leave their native land? Conversely, what factors caused other Hollanders, who had thought of emigrating, to change their minds and remain in the Netherlands?

Many of the answers to these questions can be found in a careful study made during the late 1950's under the auspices of the Netherlands Commissioner for Emigration.[7] The inquiry examined 1,000 "units of emigrants," i.e., single men and families, to determine their motives for leaving the Netherlands during the years 1955 and 1956. Their destination included Australia (407 units), Canada (327), South Africa (105), the United

States (89), and New Zealand (72). The study examined the traditional economic and demographic explanations of emigration, but also analyzed sociological and psychological factors. To shed light on the motives, the researchers also investigated reasons why nonemigrants preferred staying in the Netherlands.

The so-called followers emigration, which had played an important role in past emigration from the Netherlands, continued to be significant after the Second World War. According to this explanation, the decision to leave the Netherlands was encouraged by relatives and friends who had emigrated earlier and had achieved success in their newly adopted country. Such influence was noticeable as a motive among 70 percent of the persons examined in the study, and was a major factor for 25 percent of them. It is interesting to note, however, that this motive did not operate as an emotional thing, i.e., a longing to be with one's relatives; rather, it served as an example for a potential emigrant to imitate and as a source for obtaining assistance and information.

As might be expected, the 1955–56 survey, as well as several other recent Dutch studies, pointed out that persons who were dissatisfied with their particular socioeconomic environment or who were not closely identified with their peer group showed a greater tendency to leave the Netherlands than those who were satisfied with their lot. This does not mean that the postwar emigrants were made up of the poor and misfits among the Dutch. As one writer stated, "people who are in really serious economic, social or psychological difficulties rarely desire to emigrate."[8] Nor do the above remarks mean that persons who were unhappy with conditions in the Netherlands simply moved for the sake of moving. Most Hollanders who thought of emigrating had to believe that their socioeconomic aspirations could be better achieved elsewhere. Otherwise, they stayed where they were. In some instances, their decision to leave was influenced by a desire to obtain a more promising future for their children. A longing for better housing was also of considerable significance, with one person in four in the survey indicating that he was definitely dissatisfied with housing conditions in the Netherlands.

Personality factors must also be considered, because the manner in which the pros and cons of emigration were viewed by individual Hollanders and whether their views were translated into decisions to emigrate or to stay in the Netherlands ultimately depended on personal resolutions. Some individuals when faced with a socioeconomic problem would decide to emigrate, while others when faced with the same difficulty would resign themselves to the situation and try to make the best of it. Still others would decide to learn a new trade and in some instances migrate internally, i.e., from the country to the city or from one city to another. By comparing emigrants with nonemigrants, the 1955–56 study showed that the decision to emigrate often depended on a variety of personal factors, including age, marital status, family difficulties, personal problems of a somewhat permanent nature, presence of children, ownership of property, independence of spirit, and willingness to take risks.

A Hollander's decision to emigrate was also affected by various factors over which he had little or no control, especially during the years immediately after the war. Although the emigration policy of the Netherlands has always been based on the principle that its citizens should have freedom to emigrate, governmental subsidies were granted selectively at first, until liberalized in 1951, in the hopes that persons with critical skills would be induced to stay and help in the country's recovery. The amount of hard currency that a Hollander could take with him out of the country as well as the shortage of shipping because of war losses also restricted emigration for a time. Availability of jobs in the chosen country of destination was also important.

Immediately following the Second World War and for several years after, the United States was the favorite choice of Dutch emigrants.[9] The influence of thousands of relatives and friends who had moved there during the decades before the war partially explains why so many Dutch emigrants preferred it to other countries. The important role that the United States played in freeing the Netherlands from Nazi tyranny also helped endear it to the hearts of many Hollanders. Responses to a questionnaire distributed in the Netherlands after the war indicate that the United States was held in very high regard by the Dutch people. To the question: "For what great power do you have the greatest liking?" 48 percent of the replies showed a preference for the United States, 22 percent for England, and 9 percent for the Soviet Union. The remaining 21 percent named other countries or had no preference.[10]

The prosperity and economic opportunities of the United States made it especially appealing to Dutch emigrants. According to a wage and price comparison made in 1956 by the Netherlands Commissioner for Emigration,

If we put the average real income of the [Dutch] emigrant before his departure [from Holland] at 100, then the average income of a single group of people in Canada is 160, in the United States 240, in Australia 140 and in New Zealand 170. If in the receiving country an emigrant eventually occupies the same place in the income scale as he did in Holland, then his real income will on average increase by half.[11]

Although the United States was the country of destination favored by most Dutch emigrants immediately after the Second World War, the number of Hollanders who could move there was severely limited by the so-called quota system. This system, which became fully operative in 1929, restricted the number of arrivals from each country to an annual quota based on the ethnic composition of the American people as reflected in the population census of 1920. This meant that countries which in the past had contributed most to the ethnic stock of the United States were given the largest quotas.

The principle of national origins, on which the quota system was based, obviously favored the countries of northern and western Europe; they were given 82 percent of the total world quota of 150,000, whereas southern and eastern European countries received 14 percent and the rest of the world was assigned the remainder.[12] Not all countries of northern and western Europe, however, received advantageous quotas. Countries which had not sent large numbers of their people to American shores before the 1920's, and thus had no broad base upon which a high national origin quota could be set, also found themselves discriminated against in matters of future emigration to the United States. This was obviously the case for the Netherlands, as is shown in the following statistics:

|  | 1920 European Population | 1929 National Origins Quota |
|---|---|---|
| Great Britain | 42.8 million | 65,721 |
| Germany | 59.2 million | 25,957 |
| Ireland | 4.1 million | 17,853 |
| The Netherlands | 6.9 million | 3,136[13] |

Thus, Great Britain, for example, with a population about six times as great as that of the Netherlands was given a quota that was more than twenty times as great.

Although the national origins principle was of no great consequence to the Dutch during the depression years of the 1930's and during the war when little emigration occurred, it became very important during the postwar years when the desire to leave seemed to pervade the very air of the Netherlands. The waiting list in 1952, for example, was about forty thousand, which meant that even discounting inactive cases, new applicants had to wait about three to five years.

The immigration law based on national origins remained in effect until 1965, but substantial numbers of nonquota immigrants were occasionally permitted entry in order to help various countries solve special problems. Such exceptions to the quota restrictions had an important bearing on Dutch emigration to the United States. In 1953, for example, the Refugee Relief Act authorized an additional 17,000 visas for Dutch emigrants above the usual quota of 3,136. Persons eligible included individuals and families who had experienced great personal loss in World War II, refugees from the great flood that struck Holland in 1953, and repatriates who left the Dutch East Indies when it acquired independence from the Netherlands as the new state of Indonesia.

The mass repatriation to the Netherlands of over 300,000 Dutch-Indonesians constituted a unique problem for such a small country. Finding it difficult to assimilate them in a short period of time, the Netherlands government asked help from the United States in the form of a special quota for these refugees, above what was provided by the Refugee Relief Act of 1953. Congress responded with the Walter-Pastore Act of 1958 which allowed 8,900 Dutch subjects from Indonesia to emigrate to the United States during a four-year period. Because the assimilation of repatriates from Indonesia into Dutch society continued to be a problem, another special legislative act, commonly called Walter-Pastore II and identical to that of 1958, was passed in 1960.[14] After it expired in 1963, Dutch emigration to the United States was again determined by the old quota system of 3,136 persons annually.

In view of the importance of the Dutch-Indonesian immigrants, a brief description of their origins, their reasons for coming to the United States, and their assimilation into American society is appropriate.[15] Of the approximately 300,000 refugees who left Indonesia for the Netherlands, about 250,000 departed voluntarily, the remainder being deported. Some of them were of pure Dutch blood and others were of unmixed Indonesian ancestry, but "for the most part they were culturally and racially a blend of Dutch and Indonesian."[16] Persons of mixed parentage could consider themselves Dutch citizens because of a law of 1892 stating that a child of a father who possessed Netherlands' citizenship at the time of the child's birth was a Dutch citizen if such a paternal relationship was recognized by the father or could be definitely proven.

At the time of independence, the 170,000 "Eurasian" Dutch citizens were given two years in which to decide whether they wished to retain their old citizenship status or opt for Indonesian citizenship. The vast majority (over 85 percent) decided in favor of the former. In doing so and by reason of the strong anti-Dutch feeling that existed in Indonesia after independence, most of them, together with those of pure Dutch ancestry, resettled in the Netherlands. Some indigenous Indonesians, especially the Ambonese, also decided to make this move because of their dissatisfaction with the new regime.[17]

The problem of absorbing such a large number of refugees into a country that was already overpopulated caused the Netherlands government to render assistance to any Dutch-Indonesians willing to uproot themselves once more and settle in another country. This aid consisted primarily of financial help, language courses, and retraining programs for persons wishing to learn new skills. The Dutch government at the same time appealed to other countries to accept some of these "colonial castaways" for whom it felt responsible.

Although the integration of Dutch-Indonesians into the social and economic life of the Netherlands generally went smoothly, a significant number of the refugees were dissatisfied with their new surroundings. Some of them found the climate of Holland distasteful and others were displeased with the relocation centers in which they were housed, but economic conditions were the primary cause for dissatisfaction. The cost of living in the Netherlands was such that a higher pay scale was needed in order to live at a level equal to what they had formerly enjoyed in Indonesia. The possibilities for advancement in various occupations, and concern for their children's future, also caused disenchantment among the refugees. As a consequence, some of them accepted the government's offer of assistance in remigration.

The United States, to its credit, was the only country which agreed to accept a significant number of Dutch-Indonesian repatriates. About thirty-five thousand of them, half of whom had been born in the Netherlands, were admitted into the United States, mainly under the provisions of the special refugee acts noted above. American voluntary agencies played an important role in assisting them when they arrived in the United States. About 64 percent of them were sponsored by Protestant organizations associated with Church World Service and 19 percent by Catholic Relief Services. Nearly all the refugees came to the United States by the way of the Netherlands rather than directly from Indonesia.

The refugees, as a whole, adjusted to American life more easily than most immigrants. Many of them came from the middle-class level of society, but from a variety of backgrounds, including business, accounting, sales, mechanics, and crafts. Members of these groups upon arrival in the United States were able to pursue their former vocations or something similar, although not always at the level of responsibility they had before or for which they had been trained. Adjustment for persons who had been employed in the government or military was more difficult because many of them were basically unskilled.

Assimilation into American life was favorably influenced by several factors. Because the Dutch-Indonesians had been uprooted once before, they possessed valuable experience in solving problems associated with immigration. Adjustment was also made easier because most of the refugees had at least some knowledge of English when they arrived in the United States.[18] It is likely, too, that integration met with a high degree of success because they did not at first have the same opportunity as other immigrants to return to their original home (Indonesia) if they did not enjoy living in the United States. As a consequence, they were more determined to succeed in their new surroundings. By 1965, nearly half the adults had enrolled in adult education courses, an excellent indication that they wished to play a significant role in their new homeland. Similarly, nearly a third of them had taken steps to purchase their own homes.

Despite progress in assimilation, a strong bond of unity continues to exist among the generation born and raised in Indonesia. They still speak considerable Dutch among themselves, and use the words *mijnheer* and *mevrouw* rather than the American informal "you" when addressing strangers. Indonesian-style food continues to be popular—rice with *sambal* and *sojoer* being preferred to potatoes in their daily diet. Various personal habits practiced in Indonesia have been retained, and their ideas about family life tend to follow traditional lines. The woman's place is considered to be in the home, and permissiveness in rearing children is frowned upon.

The second generation of Dutch-Indonesians, however, has been developing along lines different from those of the older immigrants. With reference to those residing in California, where most of the Dutch-Indonesians located,

Their children, who were small when they arrived here, are now grown up, going to college, etc. They hardly speak Dutch anymore, mingle with and marry Americans, and don't understand their parents' behavior patterns. The generation gap, here, is perhaps greater than among the Americans. Also, many of them are aware that the Dutch-Indonesians will, not too far in the future, cease to exist. The older generation will have died and the younger ones, having married

Americans, will be absorbed in the American mainstream. This is quite different from the Mexican-Americans and the Chinese and Japanese.[19]

In choosing a place to live, the Dutch-Indonesians showed a preference for California over other states. Their reasons for this were the same as those of other Dutch immigrants, but in addition they considered the climate and vegetation of southern California as having the closest resemblance to that of tropical Indonesia. Hawaii was attractive for the same reason, but its limited job opportunities as compared to California restricted the number who went there to about a hundred families. They also located in sizeable numbers in Massachusetts, Michigan, Arizona, and Florida. Although relations between the Netherlands and her former colony have improved considerably during recent years, few Dutch-Indonesians have returned to Indonesia to live, but some have gone there on vacation.

The special refugee acts permitted the number of Dutch citizens who emigrated to the United States after the Second World War to be considerably larger than it would have been had the 1929 quota system been rigidly followed. Between 1945 and 1965, 79,650 Dutch nationals were given permission to enter the United States as immigrants. This represented 19 percent of the 425,565 Dutchmen who emigrated during those years. Despite this high percentage the United States ranked behind Canada, which received 151,931 Dutch immigrants, or 36 percent of the total, and Australia, which had 125,304, or 29 percent, but still ahead of South Africa with 33,557 (8 percent) and New Zealand, which received 23,941 (6 percent).

The new immigration law of 1965, which did not become fully operative until July 1, 1968, had no immediately noticeable effect on Dutch emigration to the United States. Although it drastically curtailed emigration from the north and west European countries,[20] it did not make that much difference to the Netherlands because of her low quota under the old system. Its effect was also of limited significance because Dutch interest in emigration had been steadily declining for several years before the new law became effective. The peak year in total Dutch emigration was reached in 1952, when nearly 49,000 persons left the Netherlands to find a new home for themselves. Decline was steady thereafter: 30,000 in 1955, 24,000 in 1960, and an annual average of 9,300 from 1965 to 1968. This overall decline was also manifested in Dutch emigration to the United States, where the average was less than 2,000 per year from 1963 to 1968.

Hollanders showed a declining interest in emigration during the sixties for several reasons. Many of the people who were most anxious to leave after World War II had done so by the end of the 1950's. The fear of a possible World War III and Russian occupation had also diminished. More important, the earlier pessimism about the economic future of the Netherlands had been superseded by optimism as a result of increasing prosperity and near full employment. Indeed, by 1960, the Dutch government began admitting large numbers of Greeks, Turks, Spaniards, and persons of other nationalities to relieve a serious labor shortage. Occasional economic recessions and lessening prospects in the major receiving countries, including the United States, also dampened the Hollander's enthusiasm for emigration.

The type of Dutch immigrants who came to the United States after World War II varied from time to time. As noted earlier, workers whose skills were deemed essential to the reconstruction of the Netherlands were initially encouraged to remain in the land of their birth. Farmers, on the other hand, were in surplus. Population growth caused a special hardship for them because it was nearly impossible to split Dutch farms into smaller holdings. Although considerable fertile land was reclaimed in the Zuiderzee and Wieringermeer projects, these gains were nullified by the construction of roads and by urban expansion.

The imbalance that had favored farmers and common laborers in the immigration statistics gradually shifted during the 1950's. This came about partly as a result of the lessening need for skilled workers to aid in the economic recovery of the Netherlands, which had the natural result of decreasing the proportion of agriculturalists and ordinary laborers among the immigration totals. Furthermore, the improved lot of the rural classes in Holland enabled them to give their children a better education than before, which in turn improved their chances for obtaining jobs in the cities.

Advancements in communications, especially by means of television, also made the rural people less parochial in their thinking and more willing to take positions in the cities. In the past, Dutch farmers and their sons were so strongly attached to the soil that they preferred continuing their occupation as immigrants in some other country rather than giving it up in exchange for a different type of work. This attitude began changing during the late 1950's. As one Dutch writer put it, the farmers began showing a greater willingness to exchange "their wooden shoes for a motor cycle, and their plow for a lathe."[21] As a result of this change of attitude, the number of Dutch farmers departing for the United States steadily declined from 48 percent of the total number of employed immigrants in 1948 to 21 percent in 1950, 10 percent in 1955, and 2 percent in 1960. During the period 1966–68, they constituted only 1 percent of the total.[22]

At the same time that the percentage of farmers and laborers among Dutch immigrants decreased, the percentage of those drawn from the professional and semiprofessional classes steadily increased. In fact, authorities in Holland were worried for a time about a "brain drain." During the period 1956–61, 15.1 percent of the annual output of science and engineering graduates in the Netherlands emigrated to the United States. For all of Europe, only Switzerland and Norway had higher percentages, with 17 and 16.2 respectively. This fear of a brain drain abated somewhat during the 1960's.[23]

Naturalization statistics of the United States indicate that recent Dutch immigrants have been unusually successful in their newly adopted country. Of the approximately 5,000 employed Hollanders who became American citizens during the period 1966–68, nearly 1,200, or about 25 percent, were classified as professional and technical workers. Another 931, or 19 percent, were classified as craftsmen, foremen, and kindred workers, and 390, or 8 percent, were listed as managers, officials, and proprietors. Only 202 were listed as ordinary laborers, 93 as farmers and farm workers, and 61 as private household workers. These last three categories combined made up only 7 percent of the total.[24]

Proportionately, the Orthodox Calvinists contributed the most immigrants during the early postwar years. Although they constituted only 9.7 percent of the total population of the Netherlands in 1947, they made up 20 percent of the Hollanders who went to the United States during the period 1948–52. Corresponding percentages for the Dutch Reformed were 31 and 20.5, and for the Roman Catholics, 38.5 and 10.5. The proportion of Roman Catholics who emigrated was nevertheless higher than it had been in the past, and continued to increase. During the period 1958–62, for example, they constituted 35 percent of all Dutch immigrants entering the United States, whereas the Orthodox Calvinists made up only 6 percent.[25] The increase in the number of Catholic immigrants came about primarily because the clergy encouraged emigration more than it had in the past. The creation of a special Episcopal Commissary for Emigration and the enhanced activities of the Catholic Emigration Foundation were outgrowths of that interest.[26]

In choosing places to live in the United States, Dutch immigrants of the post–World War II period differed markedly from those of earlier decades. This is shown in a comparison between the census reports of 1940 and those of 1970 with reference to the number of Holland-born persons residing in selected states.[27]

|  | 1940 | | 1970 | |
|---|---|---|---|---|
|  | Number | % | Number | % |
| United States (total) | 111,064 | 100.0 | 110,570 | 100.0 |
| Michigan | 24,722 | 22.3 | 15,095 | 13.7 |
| New York | 13,842 | 12.5 | 11,421 | 10.3 |
| New Jersey | 11,841 | 10.7 | 8,575 | 7.8 |
| Illinois | 11,634 | 10.5 | 5,825 | 5.3 |
| California | 9,754 | 8.8 | 27,993 | 25.3 |

The change in choice of domiciles on the part of Dutch immigrants since World War II is also shown in recent naturalization statistics. Of the 10,406 Netherlanders who became American citizens during the period 1966–71, 43 percent resided in California. New York was a distant second with 9 percent, and Michigan, which had been very popular with Dutch immigrants before World War II, ranked third with 5 percent of the total. According to recent immigrants, California was preferred over other states as their new home because it offered a better chance for work and a more promising future for their children. The style of living of Californians and the state's excellent climate also had great appeal.[28]

The agricultural states of the Middle West were not as popular with the Dutch immigrants as they once had been. In 1940, for example, there were almost eight thousand Holland-born residing in Iowa, yet during the five-year period 1966–71 the number of Hollanders residing in that state who became American citizens averaged fewer than thirteen per year. This change reflects the small number of farmers found among recent immigrants referred to earlier. The figures also demonstrate that the latest Dutch-Americans have been part of the trend taking place in the United States toward city and urban living. Of the six hundred thirty Hollanders in California who became naturalized citizens in 1971, only ten were classified as rural. Similarly, forty-six of the fifty-three naturalized in Illinois during that year lived in Chicago, while over half of the one hundred seventy-six new Dutch citizens in New York lived in New York City.[29]

Post–World War II emigration to the United States differed from that of a century ago in other ways besides those of occupation and location of the persons concerned.[30] As was noted, a quota system dating from the 1920's restricted to slightly more than three thousand the number of Hollanders who could enter each year. By contrast, the doors were nearly wide open to Dutch immigrants during the nineteenth century. Post–1945 emigration was also much more complicated than that of a century ago because of the governmental "red-tape" that had to be taken care of on both sides of the Atlantic before an immigrant could set foot on American soil. No longer was it possible, as happened in the case of one of the grandparents of this writer, for a young Dutchman to tell his parents on one day that he was going to America, go to Rotterdam on the following day to book passage, and leave the country of his birth on the third day.

On arrival in the United States, the post–1945 Dutch immigrant also witnessed a scene that was very different from that of the past. The nineteenth-century immigrant arrived in a country that was still very young and undeveloped; in fact, much of it was still uninhabited. New York, a favorite debarkation port for Dutch immigrants, had a population of about 700,000 in 1850; in 1950, it had almost eight million. On arrival at his final destination in America, the immigrant's new place of residence was also vastly different. If he planned to farm, he did not have to anticipate living in a log house or sod hut as did many of the immigrants who came with or followed Van Raalte and Scholte. Similarly, if he located in the city, the home of the new immigrant was equipped with conveniences that the Hollander of a hundred years ago would have considered beyond the realm of possibility.

Also different was the manner in which immigrants could develop a sense of identification with the basic ideas and customs of their newly adopted country and with those of the local community in which they located. In some respects, assimilation was easier for the earlier immigrants. Many of them settled in Dutch communities where the ancestral language and Netherlandish customs still prevailed. Those who did not locate among Hollanders frequently found themselves, by reason of the tremendous exodus of Europeans to the United States, rubbing shoulders with members of other national groups, such as Germans and Scandinavians, who were faced with the same problems of adjustment and who sometimes shared similar "Old World" points of view. By contrast, assimilation of later immigrants into even older Dutch communities presented problems that had not occurred before, because of the Americanization these "racial colonies" had undergone between World Wars I and II, and because of the increased tempo of American life.

Nevertheless, despite immigration having turned more complex after World War II, and despite the fact that American life has become more rigorous and animated, recent immigrants had several advantages not enjoyed by those of a century or even a half century ago. It will be recalled that recent immigrants received valuable advice and assistance from various public and private agencies before leaving the Netherlands. Furthermore, they did not have to undertake a harrowing ocean crossing of several weeks aboard uncomfortable and unsanitary ships on which the food was poor and serious ill-nesses were commonplace. Death en route from the Nether-lands and burial at sea were not unusual aboard nineteenth-century immigrant ships. By comparison, crossing the Atlantic aboard a surface vessel after World War II was a pleasure cruise.

Although the good-byes and farewells between the Hollan-ders who left their ancestral homeland and those who stayed behind never changed, recent immigrants never had the feeling they were "burning their bridges behind them" to the same extent as did those of the nineteenth century. Distance had lost its dread because of air transportation; the Atlantic crossing could be measured in terms of hours rather than miles, and it was possible to return quickly to the land of one's birth in the event of an emergency. The telephone and improvements in the postal system also enabled immigrants to keep in closer touch with relatives and friends left behind.

Recent Dutch immigration was also a less unpleasant experi-ence than it had been in the past because of the activities of various organizations in the United States. These included several that were religiously oriented, such as the Christian Reformed Resettlement Service and Church World Service, as well as many that were more secular in nature. The latter numbered more than fifty. During the heyday of Dutch immi-gration in the 1950's, these associations assisted newly arrived immigrants in obtaining housing and employment, gave advice on naturalization problems, arranged religious services in the Dutch language, and provided various forms of entertainment.

Dutch-American organizations in the United States were especially helpful in providing newly arrived immigrants with what the Dutch call *gezelligheid*, meaning conviviality or "chumminess." As explained recently by the secretary of one of these associations,

Upon arrival in the U.S.A. many immigrants felt the need to remain together, to hold on to each other, as it were. The main reasons for this attempt to associate with likeminded people were a lack of knowledge of the English language, a feeling of loneliness, and confrontation with a totally different and new situation. The hardships resulting from these inconveniences could conceivably lead to an immigrant's failure to adjust to his newly chosen country. In getting together and experiencing the sense of belonging to a group, the immigrants found that they all struggled with similar problems. Loneliness and isolation could lead to failure. Seeking the company of each other and showing solidarity in times of difficulty helped to make the immigration process a success for many.[31]

Two of the largest and most active Dutch-American organizations created since World War II are the Dutch Immigrant Society and Dutch Club AVIO. The former is primarily a Michigan-based body, and the latter is concentrated in California. The Dutch Immigrant Society, or DIS, as it is popularly known, was established at Grand Rapids, Michigan, in 1950. One of its prime purposes initially was to provide worship services in the Dutch language for newly arrived immigrants who had little knowledge of English. To this day, DIS has a strong religious base and draws its membership primarily from adherents of the Christian Reformed and Reformed churches.

Although the number of Dutch immigrants who settled in Michigan during recent years is considerably smaller than it was in the 1950's, there has been no decline in either the membership or activities of the Dutch Immigrant Society. Its membership in 1973 totaled nearly 11,000, but because about 10,000 of these are family groups its individual membership is much higher. In addition, a daughter organization in the Netherlands has nearly 3,500 members. Publication of a magazine, appropriately known as *DIS*, was started in 1970. A quarterly with 14,000 copies printed per issue, it contains information about activities of the organization, as well as numerous articles of a historical nature bearing on the Dutch in America (primarily the Middle West) during the nineteenth and twentieth centuries. About 75 percent of the material is polyglot, i.e., Dutch and English, with the remainder in English only.

Dutch Club AVIO[32] was organized in California in 1959, and in 1973 it had over 30,000 members. They were distributed as follows: California, 19,000; Utah, 1,450;[33] the Netherlands,

10,000; other states and countries, 300. AVIO's great variety of activities, some of which are unique, together with the fact that California attracted the largest number of postwar Dutch immigrants, help explain the club's tremendous success.

Dutch Club AVIO issues a monthly polyglot magazine with a circulation of eleven thousand and has its own radio program known as "The Holland Hour." The latter broadcasts six hours weekly, all in Dutch, from Los Angeles, as well as one hour from San Francisco, San Fernando, and Salt Lake City. Group hospitalization insurance is available for members, and the club has its own blood bank with the Red Cross in Los Angeles. Recently, the AVIO group began constructing a new community about midway between Los Angeles and San Diego. To be known as Holland, it will feature a "Dutch Retirement Village" for elderly persons and a tourist attraction called "Hans Brinker's Shopping Village." The latter will resemble a small Dutch village, complete with mill, canal, drawbridge, gabled houses, shops, and so on. It is expected to attract over a million visitors annually, thereby defraying costs for the retirement homes and providing work for semiretired people.

In addition to organizations that are broadly immigrant-oriented, there are many smaller associations in the United States that cater to a select clientele of Dutch-Americans. A few examples can serve to indicate their general nature. The distinctive Netherlands Club of New York, founded in 1903, is a private, gentlemen-only club with high membership fees and a luxurious lounge and dining room located in the heart of Manhattan. It caters primarily to business executives and professional people. Full membership, which totals about five hundred, is limited to persons who are citizens and former citizens, or sons of citizens and former citizens, of the Netherlands. The Netherlands-American Medical Society, established in 1965, functions as a kind of alumni group of doctors practicing in the United States who received their medical education in the Netherlands. The organization maintains close relations among members by means of a bimonthly newsletter and annual meetings. Its two hundred fifty members in 1972 resided in thirty-six states and Canada, but its largest following was in the eastern part of the United States. A Netherlands-American

University League also existed for many years. Its membership, as the name indicates, was drawn primarily from college and university teachers.

Homesickness and economic failure were the greatest fears facing post–World War II immigrants; to be forced to return to live in the Netherlands under such circumstances and face old friends and relatives would have been humiliating. Organizations such as the Dutch Immigrant Society and Dutch Club AVIO were very helpful in keeping such instances to a minimum. By the sixties, most of the new immigrants were comfortably settled, had steady jobs, were in the process of purchasing their own homes, and no longer had a serious language problem.

As immigrants became American citizens and gradually adjusted themselves to their new environment, and as fewer and fewer new immigrants arrived from the Netherlands, the Dutch-American organizations began expanding their activities. They are still as helpful today as they were in the past in assisting new immigrants, but many of their present activities are designed to maintain close ties of kinship among former immigrants as well as with the mother country. Low-cost charter flights for members wishing to visit the Netherlands have become an important part of their activities, as has the sponsoring of traveling vocalists, choirs, small ensembles, and organists as well as art exhibits from the Netherlands.

With a little more time and money and with the availability of charter flights, many of the post–World War II immigrants began visiting the Netherlands. For example, about five thousand members of the Dutch Immigrant Society took advantage of charter flights to the Netherlands in 1971, and six thousand did so in 1972. The results of such visits were sometimes surprising. As described by an immigrant who arrived in the United States with his wife in 1953 and who had visited the Netherlands four times between 1961 and 1972,

a new interest in the old country was brought back by thousands of travelers. They "rediscovered" their fatherland. They found it changed and moving at a different pace than they used to know it, but the old *gezelligheid* is still there. So is . . . the atmosphere and character of the cities, each one of them different; small towns where the ages still look down upon you. Immigrants visiting the Netherlands see things now they never gave a second look when they still lived there.[34]

❀   ❀   ❀   ❀

In view of the limited interest shown in Dutch emigration during the past, the large number of Hollanders who evinced a desire to emigrate after World War II is at first glance surprising. A careful examination of conditions in the Netherlands immediately after the war, however, explains why nearly a half million Dutch citizens sought new homes overseas after 1945. Most of the emigration occurred before 1960, after which time the inclination to leave the Netherlands declined considerably because of improved economic conditions. Nearly one-fifth of the Hollanders who left went to the United States, and the number would have been much higher if it had not been for the quota system. Recent arrivals to American shores differed from those of the past in many ways, chief of which were their economic background and their choice of location in the United States. Great care was also taken on both sides of the ocean in helping them adjust to their newly adopted country.

## CHAPTER XI

# Struggles over Church and Mother Tongue

AT THE TIME OF THE AMERICAN REVOLUTION, THE REFORMED Church[1] had about forty ministers serving nearly a hundred congregations. By 1820, it had expanded to about a hundred ministers and two hundred churches, and when the Civil War broke out, these figures had more than doubled. Much of the growth, however, was internal and took place in New York and New Jersey. Although the increasing use of English in the worship services made it easier for the Reformed Church to appeal to persons of non-Dutch background, it did not engage in much evangelism before the Civil War, especially when compared to such denominations as the Baptists and Methodists. As one writer put it,

The Dutch seemed content to labor with other Dutch, and with those who were already committed to the Reformed interpretation of the Scriptures. What was lacking was the daring to move out into the American population with the Gospel and with the confidence that Americans might be made Christians after the Reformed order.[2]

The Great Migration that began during the 1840's provided the Reformed Church with an important source for obtaining new members. Many of the mid-nineteenth-century immigrants were God-fearing people, and some of them left the Netherlands for religious reasons. New arrivals who settled in the eastern states frequently associated with long-established Reformed congregations, but those who located in the Middle West at first maintained a separate church life. As a consequence, the Michigan settlers created an ecclesiastical organization of their own known as the Holland Classis, consisting of seven congregations with a total of six hundred twenty-nine families.[3] In

1850, following a year of discussion, it became affiliated with the Reformed Church. Most of the immigrants who had located at Pella, Iowa, soon followed suit. There were thus joined two separate strains of Dutch-Americans—those located primarily in the East who traced their descent from the New Netherland period, and those located in the Middle West who had recently arrived from Holland.

Not all the new immigrants were satisfied with this union. When the newly arrived immigrants in Michigan joined the Reformed Church in 1850, they therefore did so with the understanding that "they would be most perfectly free at any time they found an ecclesiastical commitment opposed to their religious prosperity or enjoyment to bid [the Reformed Church] a brotherly farewell and be by themselves again."[4] After considerable friction, a number of members of the Michigan group together with two ministers withdrew from the Reformed Church on April 8, 1857, and in the following month established a separate organization with a membership of about seven hundred fifty. The new denomination, which became known as the Christian Reformed Church,[5] was similar in many respects to the Reformed Church. Both denominations adhered to the historic creeds of the Reformation period, i.e., the Belgic Confession, the Heidelberg Catechism, and the Cannons of Dordt. The polity of both was also presbyterian, with the usual Reformed trademarks of consistory, classis, and synod.

In view of these similarities, why was the religious unity that had been established in 1850 shattered within less than a decade? And why, during following years, did many persons continue to leave the Reformed Church and join the Christian Reformed body? The explanation is found in various miscellaneous practices in the older denomination. Some of these were reminiscent of the ecclesiastical situation immigrants had criticized in the Netherlands, including the use of hymns in the worship services instead of the Old Testament psalms and the neglect of catechetical preaching and teaching. Permitting non-Reformed Protestants to participate in Holy Communion without prior consent of the local consistory was also considered anathema by some of the new immigrants and their descendants. In time, considerable criticism was leveled at the Reformed

Church for permitting church members to join secret lodges, such as the Freemasons. Finally, the matter of parochial versus public schools became a bone of contention between the two religious groups.

For these reasons, the Christian Reformed Church continued to attract individual families and sometimes entire congregations from the Reformed Church. Thus, in 1882, six Michigan congregations, together with their ministers, switched their allegiance. Similarly, in 1890, a group of New Jersey Reformed churches, whose roots reached back to the colonial period, joined the new denomination. The New Jersey congregations had been maintaining a separate existence since 1822, when they withdrew from the Reformed Church because of its alleged departures from Calvinist teaching.[6] Most of the growth after the Civil War, however, resulted from the continued arrival of new immigrants from the Netherlands, a figure that reached nearly 175,000 by World War I. Because of the favorable attention the new denomination had received in the Netherlands, many immigrants upon arrival in America joined it rather than the Reformed Church. In 1914, the Christian Reformed Church had over 200 congregations and 70,000 members.

Generally speaking, the Christian Reformed Church remained more conservative in its outlook than the Reformed Church. The early opposition of the former to such matters as using hymns instead of Old Testament psalms, admitting lodge members to church membership, and permitting open Holy Communion has already been noted. It also tended to hold on to Dutch preaching longer, and even today a good reading knowledge of the language is recommended for its ministers so that they can read the works of noted Dutch theologians in the original language. Attitudes toward the ecumenical movement further illustrate the difference between the two denominations. Whereas the Reformed Church is today a charter member of both the National Council of Churches and the World Council of Churches, the Christian Reformed body does not participate in either of these organizations.[7] The Christian Reformed Church has, on the whole, also been less compromising in its attitudes toward worldly amusements and luxuries, and more severe in condemning divorce, mixed marriages, and abortion. Finally, participation of women in church affairs has likewise been less pronounced in the Christian Reformed Church than in the Reformed Church.[8]

The greater conservatism of the Christian Reformed Church stems from several causes. Paramount among them is its stricter adherence to Calvinist doctrines and ideas of church government. Having its own grade and secondary schools has also made it easier for the Christian Reformed Church to indoctrinate its young people in the beliefs and customs of the denomination. Its greater conservatism also stems from its being a younger denomination that has been exposed to only a century of Americanization as compared to 350 years for the Reformed Church. The numerical strength of the Christian Reformed Church being centered in the more conservative Middle West is likewise a factor. In 1971, only 39, or about 6 percent, of its 660 churches were located in New Jersey and New York, as compared to 417, or 44 percent, of the 939 congregations adhering to the Reformed church.

The degree of conservatism among even the Reformed churches varies, however, from region to region, and is least among the eastern congregations. This stems not only from the latter having been exposed to a longer period of Americanization, but also from their membership being increasingly drawn during recent decades from a more varied ethnic and religious background. As a consequence, there are today many Reformed churches in the East whose Dutch membership is in a decided minority. Most churches of the Middle West, on the other hand, are still made up primarily of members of Dutch descent who were born and reared in a Reformed tradition that is not far removed in time from what prevailed among nineteenth-century immigrants.[9]

What was the nature of this Reformed tradition that lingered on for several generations? A Dutchman who lived in Holland, Michigan, from its first days recounted the community's stern Calvinist morality and the influence of the churches as follows:

The spirit of the Massachusetts Pilgrim fathers ruled the settlement, and many felt the sting of discipline as severe as any inflicted by the Blue Laws. . . . The dominie and consistory exercised extensive ruling power, settling disputes, applying justice, rebuking people. Mrs. Fannie D. had gossiped about a neighbor woman who complained to the consistory. The penalty was public confession in church. ...An elder had noticed a young lady, Sesine S. who improperly exposed her neck. So a cloth was placed over the offending neck and thus modesty was restored....[When] the time came for Holy Communion [and] according to custom all sat near the table, an elder stood at each end to keep unworthy persons from sitting down and prevent infraction of the regulations.[10]

The ministers were held in high regard and had tremendous influence. Their eloquent preaching enabled the settlers to remain steadfast in the faith, even during adversity. In addition, they assumed various mundane tasks in looking after the needs of their parishioners. A Dutchman of Zeeland, Michigan, had this to say about Dominie Cornelius Van der Meulen, who served a church there from 1847 to 1859:

Poor as any other of the settlers with a family to support, he was at once minister, doctor, land-looker, and judge. When worn and tired and discouraged, the colonists came out of the woods from different directions on Sabbath mornings, the old saint of God would preach to them with a pathos and a fervid eloquence now seldom heard, and would send them back in the evening to their humble cabins with new courage, with firmer purpose and more unfaltering trust, to renew the struggle in the forest and hew out a home.[11]

Although Middle West conservatism has been breaking down in recent years, the process has been slow. Thus, in 1947, Sioux Center, Iowa, then a town of about twenty-five hundred of whom at least 95 percent were of Dutch descent, decided by popular referendum to prohibit the showing of movies in the town hall. The local Ministerial Association, which looked upon the theater as "Satan's tool," led the fight on behalf of the antimovie forces.[12] At nearby Orange City, a county seat of about thirty-six hundred and also very Dutch, all business places, including service stations, are closed on Sundays although the town is located on a major highway. Even a few Dutch communities that arose in the East during the Great Migration have retained this conservative outlook. Prospect Park, adjoining Paterson,

New Jersey, for example, continues to enforce several ordinances of the "blue law" variety, especially with respect to sabbath observances.[13]

In addition to the Reformed and Christian Reformed churches, which had a membership in 1973 of about 380,000 and 285,000 respectively,[14] two smaller Protestant denominations of primarily Dutch origin put in an appearance in the United States. They became known as the Netherlands Reformed Congregations and the Protestant Reformed Churches of America, and still exist at present.[15] The former traces its origins to small bands of immigrants who had seceded from the state church of the Netherlands beginning in the 1830's. Because of differing doctrinal views, they refused to associate in a religious union with the larger secessionist groups of immigrants led by men like the reverends Van Raalte, Vander Meulen, and Scholte. Instead, they organized their own congregations, including one at South Holland, Illinois, in 1865 and another at Grand Rapids, Michigan, in 1870.

These churches were at first independent of one another, and were referred to by such designations as "Nederduitsch Reformed" and "Old Reformed." In 1907, however, they were united, as were like-minded churches in Holland, under the name of Netherlands Reformed Congregations. In 1972, there were fourteen such churches in the United States, with 5,073 professing and baptized members scattered throughout nine states, but concentrated in New Jersey, Michigan, and Iowa. Half the congregations in 1972 were still conducting a part of their services in the Dutch language, indicating their Netherlandish origins. A bimonthly magazine, *The Banner of Truth,* which began publication in 1934, is issued partly in Dutch and partly in English. The Netherlands Reformed Congregations is an ultraconservative denomination that takes a very puritanical attitude toward such matters as sabbath observance and worldly amusements.

The Protestant Reformed Churches in America originated in 1924 after several consistories were suspended and three ministers were deposed from office by the Christian Reformed Church. At issue were opposing interpretations of the Calvinist doctrines of grace and election, concerning which the persons deposed took a restrictive view. The leader of the dissenters was the Reverend Herman Hoeksema (1886–1965). In 1973, the denomination consisted of nineteen congregations located in ten states, with a total membership (communicant and baptized) of about thirty-five hundred. The greatest concentration is in the Grand Rapids, Michigan, area.

This denomination still resembles the Christian Reformed Church, and in some respects is more conservative than the parent body. It has its own parent-controlled day schools, and does not permit women to vote at congregational meetings or serve in the consistory or ministry. It also takes a dim view of labor unions, movies, dancing, and lodge membership, and places considerable emphasis upon disciplining members who "walk contrary to Scripture." Although conservative in religious matters, the Protestant Reformed churches ceased using the Dutch language in their services about fifteen years ago. The denomination maintains a seminary at Grand Rapids, Michigan, and issues several publications, of which the semimonthly *Standard Bearer* is best known.

It will be recalled that Dutch Catholics who came to the United States during the Great Migration were considerably fewer than Dutch Protestants. Nevertheless, economic hardship and religious discrimination did bring some Catholic Hollanders to American shores.[16] Many of them settled in the cities. Thus, a parish in Chicago, appropriately named St. Willibrord after an Anglo-Saxon missionary of about the year 700 who spent considerable time in the Netherlands, was composed largely of Dutch immigrants. Dutch Catholics were also sufficiently numerous in the New Orleans area so that Holland-born priests were sent to minister to them. Most of the Dutch Catholics, however, were farmers who lived in small settlements that were thinly scattered throughout the Middle West and West.

In 1907, the Association of Belgian and Holland Priests was organized with headquarters at Chicago. Its two-fold purpose was to provide for the spiritual needs of neglected Dutch and Belgian Catholics and to assist them on their arrival in the United States. As an affiliate of the Church Extension Society, it helped establish several small Dutch Catholic rural communities, including one in Mille Lacs County, Minnesota, which was named New Netherland, and another in Dunclin County, Missouri, called Wilhelmina, after the beloved queen of the Netherlands.

With a few exceptions, Dutch Catholic settlements did not survive long as distinct ethnic communities. In large part, this was due to their small numbers, which made it difficult for them to develop an ethnic communal life of their own. Furthermore, the Roman Catholic Church was an international body that cut across national bounds, in contrast to the Dutch Protestant immigrant churches which were generally ethnic in their membership and maintained the ancestral language and mores of the mother country for a long time. The Catholic priests also frequently brought in other ethnic groups, such as French Canadians and Germans, to settle among the Hollanders and actively encouraged the Americanization of immigrants. When Dutch Catholics were numerous enough, however, as in the area around Little Chute and Hollandtown, Wisconsin, they retained their ancestral language and Dutch customs for an extended period of time. Thus, a Dutch Catholic newspaper, *De Volksstem* (The Voice of the People), published at De Pere, Wisconsin, still had a circulation of 1,250 in 1950, and did not cease publication until 1919.

The Dutch Catholics, like the Dutch Calvinists, were zealous in their faith. They were regular in church attendance and were strong supporters of parochial education for their children, as were their coreligionists in the Netherlands. So much preparation went into readying Little Chute, Wisconsin, for a visit from the bishop of Milwaukee in 1850 that one Hollander declared "it was like Our Lord coming to Jerusalem on Palm Sunday."[17] Several religious orders that were particularly strong in the Netherlands established branches in the United States. The Canons Regular of the Order of the Holy Cross, commonly known as the Crosier Fathers, was especially active among Dutch Catholics in Wisconsin and Minnesota. The Sisters of Our Lady, Mother of Mercy, came to America in 1874 from their motherhouse at Tilburg, the Netherlands. Most of their activity was centered in Connecticut. The Premonstratensian Fathers, also called the Norbertines, came to America in 1893 from their abbey at Heeswijk, the Netherlands. They ministered particularly to the needs of Catholics in Wisconsin, but were also found in other states.

These religious orders looked after the spiritual needs of Dutch and other Catholics through the founding of churches, elementary schools, and convents. Nor was higher education neglected. The Premonstratensians established St. Norbert's College at De Pere, Wisconsin, in 1898. Intended as a school for training young men for the priesthood, it is today a coeducational institution with an enrollment of about fifteen hundred students. Similarly, in 1922, the Crosiers founded a small seminary and monastery at Onamia, Minnesota, where they had helped locate some Dutch Catholic immigrants shortly before World War I. Dutch influence was reflected in the design of the monastery, which was reminiscent of architectural styles in the Netherlands.

In contrast to the puritanical manners of the Dutch Calvinist communities, in which dancing, card playing, and drinking were frowned upon, life among the Dutch Catholics was more lighthearted and easygoing. Among those of Wisconsin, for example, there was considerable carnival-like entertainment just before Lenten fast. The annual shooting match, which was patterned after those of the "old country," was also a special day of festivities. House raisings and marriages were occasions for feasting and merrymaking, and dancing was especially popular. Sundays were also observed differently among the genial Catholics than was the case among the staid Calvinists. A Dutchman who grew up in Hollandtown recounted how he and others would gather "on Sunday afternoon at the house of some neighbor, where the men played cards and took an occasional drink from a jug of liquor; the women, meantime, sipped their tea or coffee and chatted over household affairs and current news; while the boys found amusement in innocent games."[18]

Like the Roman Catholics, the Dutch Protestants showed an interest in religion-oriented education for their children. Parochial schools under the supervision of local consistories had been an important part of the educational scene in Dutch communities during the colonial period, but this practice rapidly fell into disuse after the Revolution. Many of the nineteenth-century Protestant immigrants, however, who were products of such schools in the Netherlands,[19] became convinced that American public education was not providing their children with sufficient religious training along with instruction in the three R's. As a consequence, particularly after 1880, they began establishing their own day schools. Because the ancestral language was used as a medium of instruction for several years, they were frequently referred to as Dutch or Holland schools, but later became known as Christian schools. Although most popular in the Middle West, they were also found in the East. A Christian school was established at Paterson, New Jersey, for example, as early as 1892.

The Christian Reformed Church was in the forefront of the Christian school movement, whereas many members, but not all, of the Reformed Church were satisfied with public education for their children. In time, nearly every community in the United States that had a sizeable Christian Reformed constituency also had a Christian school. In 1973, such institutions totaled over two hundred including about forty offering courses at the secondary level, scattered among twenty-eight states. Strictly speaking, they are not parochial—which implies church control—but are private, parent-operated schools.

Although there were differences of opinion between the Reformed and Christian Reformed churches on the matter of schools for children, Dutch immigrants belonging to both denominations urged that education for young men and women be given in the light of God's Word. They therefore established a number of preparatory schools, or academies, whose purpose was to prepare young people, in a Christian manner, for higher education as well as to give formal instruction of a terminal nature at the high school level. When public secondary education expanded and as the penchant for parochial education declined in the Reformed Church, most of the academies disappeared. A few of them, however, evolved into private junior colleges and later into senior institutions.

In 1851, Dominie Van Raalte and others established a school at Holland, Michigan, for the Dutch colonists there. It was first known as the "Pioneer School," but in 1855 was renamed "Holland Academy." Its stated purpose was "to prepare the sons of the colonists for Rutgers College, and also to educate their daughters."[20] In 1866, collegiate level courses were introduced and the school was chartered as "Hope College." It is presently recognized as an excellent liberal arts college, and had a student enrollment of 2,105 in 1973.

As Dutch settlers moved farther westward, the Reformed Church gave consideration to establishing a second divinity school, in addition to New Brunswick Seminary, which had been founded in New Jersey in the late eighteenth century. With approval of the General Synod, Hope College in 1866 began offering special courses in theology for the training of Reformed ministers. In 1884, the theological program was separated from Hope College, thereby creating an independent institution known today as Western Theological Seminary. At the beginning of the 1973–74 school term, it had a student body of 113.

In the same way that Hope College came to serve the interests of the Dutch in western Michigan, steps were taken to aid Hollanders west of the Mississippi River. In 1916, the Reformed Church took over the administration of Central University at Pella, Iowa, a Baptist school founded in 1853 that had fallen upon hard times. Under its new auspices, it became known as Central College. A general liberal arts school, it had a student body of 1,216 in 1973. In like manner, Northwestern Classical Academy was founded at Orange City, Iowa, in 1882 to serve the Reformed constituency in northwest Iowa. A two-year junior college program was added in 1928, and a senior college in 1959, at about which time the academy was terminated. Today known as Northwestern College, it had an enrollment of 701 at the beginning of the 1973 fall term.

The Christian Reformed Church, too, has established several schools of higher learning. At first, young men who wished to become ministers in the Christian Reformed Church were privately tutored. In 1876, however, a special school was founded at Grand Rapids, Michigan, with a six-year curriculum. The first years constituted an academy, and the last two a divinity school. Until 1894, only pre-theological students were admitted to the preparatory school. This marked the beginning of Calvin College and Seminary. In 1906, two years of college work were added to the preparatory school, as was a third year in 1910, and a fourth in 1920, thus making a four-year liberal arts college.

The preparatory department was discontinued in 1921. In the meantime, the theological school added a third year, and a master's program was instituted in 1932. At the beginning of the 1973–74 academic year, Calvin College had a student body of 3,253 while the Seminary had 159 students.

In 1955, members of the Christian Reformed churches of Iowa, Minnesota, and the Dakotas founded Midwest Christian Junior College at Sioux Center, Iowa. Its primary purpose was the training of young people for teachers in the Christian schools. The name was changed to Dordt College in 1956, and in 1963 it became a four-year school. Despite its nearness to Northwestern College, sponsored by the Reformed Church, the new school has shown phenomenal growth, having a student body of 895 in 1973. Trinity College, founded in 1959 at Palos Heights, Illinois, near Chicago, also has primarily a Christian Reformed constituency. In 1973, it had a student enrollment of 358.

As might be expected, the Great Migration led to a revival of Dutch preaching beginning in the 1840's—only a generation or two after it had practically disappeared from the American scene. At first, many of the new immigrants who settled in the eastern states met together on Sundays in one another's homes or in a rented hall to listen to a Dutch sermon read from an approved book of sermons and to sing their favorite psalms. In time, however, as happened at Albany, New York, in 1859, new churches were organized in which the Dutch language was used exclusively for the convenience of new immigrants. The problem of providing Dutch services for the early immigrants who settled in the Middle West was, of course, less acute because they had frequently been accompanied to America by their own ministers.

Preaching in the Dutch language was continued by the new congregations for several decades, and in some instances for nearly a century. When the Christian Reformed Church celebrated its fiftieth anniversary in 1907, there were only seven "American speaking churches in the West," six of which were in Michigan and one in Illinois.[21] Similarly, in 1910, only three of the nearly one hundred Reformed churches west of the Mississippi River used the English language exclusively in public worship.[22] Even among the eastern immigrant churches, Dutch preaching did not disappear until after the First World

War. Some of the Reformed churches in the Rochester, New York, area, for example, were still using the Dutch language during the 1930's, and a few in the Paterson, New Jersey, area still had occasional Dutch services in the early 1940's.[23]

When English preaching was introduced among the new congregations, it was done in much the same manner as occurred in the older churches in the East during the late eighteenth century, i.e., gradually and on a part-time basis. Thus, in 1924, the Luctor Christian Reformed congregation in Kansas, which then had a membership of seventy-three families, reported that "young as well as old seem to be quite familiar with the Dutch tongue," and that only the evening services in summer and the Sunday School classes were conducted in English.[24] Similarly, in 1926, the Christian Reformed church of Whitinsville, Massachusetts, reported that its congregation of one hundred sixty families regularly filled the church building, "the morning service being conducted in the Holland language and the afternoon services in English."[25]

The decline in usage of the Dutch language in the churches was hastened by the First World War. This came about partly because the use of a foreign tongue was looked upon as unpatriotic in some areas during time of war. In Iowa, for example, which ranked fifth in the nation in terms of Holland-born citizens, the governor issued a proclamation requiring the use of the English language at religious gatherings. Although this was not aimed specifically at the Dutch-speaking population, it caused considerable hardship among persons who were not bilingual. The proclamation was later modified, but not before a Reformed church had been set afire in the Pella area by some ultrapatriots.

The First World War was only the tip of the iceberg which in time virtually brought an end to Dutch preaching in the United States. Its disappearance must be considered in the light of the total Americanization movement taking place among the immigrants and their descendants, a process that was discernible in the cities quite soon. As early as 1881, for example, an immigrant pastor from the Netherlands stated in an informative, firsthand account written for the benefit of prospective immigrants:

In the cities one sees many children of Hollanders already drift-
ing away from the life of their parents in the American world; so
that they are soon almost ashamed of their background and no longer
speak the Dutch language. In the country our national character is
better preserved along with the Dutch language, and it will doubt-
less be some time before our Holland colony in Michigan is
Americanized.[26]

Several factors accelerated the pace of Americanization during
the period between World Wars I and II. The introduction of
the quota system during the 1920's brought on a decline of
Dutch immigration, thereby cutting off an important means by
which immigrant culture could be periodically replenished and
renewed. The widespread introduction of the automobile and
improvements in city transportation systems gave Hollanders
an opportunity to enjoy close social and religious ties with other
Hollanders without being compelled to locate in Dutch neigh-
borhoods. As Dutchmen came in contact with non-Dutchmen,
and as they began seeking wider opportunities outside the con-
fines of the ethnic community, new cultural patterns were frequently adopted. The acculturation process was also furthered
by such developments as public education and the radio.[27]

The Americanization of Dutch-Americans after World War I
particularly manifested itself in the disappearance of Dutch-
language newspapers. In contrast to the colonial period when
the Dutch press was limited to a few books and religious tracts
and an occasional almanac, nineteenth-century immigrants and
their descendants published a number of newspapers as well
as several religious magazines in the Dutch language. Most of
them lasted only a brief period, but a few continued publication
for a half century or longer. The first Dutch language newspaper, the *Sheboygan Nieuwsbode* (Sheboygan Messenger),
was published in 1849 in Wisconsin. It was joined during the
following year by *De Hollander*, a Michigan newspaper that
initially was bilingual, Dutch and English. The first Dutch-
language newspaper to appear in Iowa was *Pella's Weekblad*
(Pella's Weekly), which began publication in 1861.[28]

As might be expected, most of the Dutch newspapers appeared
in the Middle West. None was published in the West, but several appeared in the eastern states, including one at Rochester,

New York, and three at Paterson, New Jersey. The most important newspapers were *De Grondwet* (The Constitution), published at Holland, Michigan, from 1860 to 1938; *De Standaard*, which appeared at Grand Rapids, Michigan, from 1875 to ca. 1935; *Pella's Weekblad*, noted earlier, which lasted from 1860 to 1942; and *De Volksvriend* (The People's Friend), published at Orange City, Iowa, from 1874 to 1951. All four of the above were weeklies, except the biweekly *De Standaard*, and generally consisted of from twelve to sixteen pages.

Dutch newspapers served the Hollanders in many ways. Editors translated proclamations and messages of the President and governors, explained what legislators were doing, reported proceedings of the boards of supervisors, and so on. As one writer put it, "In the native tongue of the readers they introduced the immigrants to the ways and ideas of America, and served them as a training school in American politics."[29] International affairs were likewise reported, with special coverage given to events in the Netherlands. The newspapers also carried the traditional editorial page, in which most editors supported the Republican party. Because of the importance of religion in the life of the Hollanders, news about churches and denominational developments received considerable attention. Serialized fiction stories, usually with a Netherlands setting and often with moral lessons, were also featured.

Of great interest to readers was news about Dutch communities elsewhere in the United States. *De Volksvriend*, for example, had correspondents wherever there were important Dutch settlements, even in the distant states. News items about these communities dutifully appeared in print under their proper geographical heading. Because these newspapers were a main source of news and an important means for keeping in contact with friends and relatives who had settled in other parts of the United States, it is no wonder that subscribers eagerly awaited the arrival of each issue. The more popular newspapers, such as *De Grondwet* and *De Volksvriend*, had a circulation extending from coast to coast.

At the time of World War I, about twenty-five Dutch newspapers and periodicals were still being published in the United States. From one point of view, it was unfortunate this number was so large. Had there been less competition, perhaps one or two newspapers would have survived to serve the wave of immigrants who came from the Netherlands after World War II, and would still be in circulation today.[30] Unfortunately, the last Dutch-language newspaper in the United States, *De Volksvriend*, ceased publication in 1951. Periodicals suffered a similar fate, so that only one all-Dutch journal, *De Wachter* (The Sentinel), continues to be published. It is a biweekly religious magazine which began publication in 1868 as an official organ of the Christian Reformed Church. About half of *De Wachter*'s twenty-seven hundred subscribers live in the United States and the remainder in Canada. In addition, a few polyglot journals of a popular nature are still being published by Dutch-American organizations. The most important are *DIS*, issued by the Dutch Immigrant Society of Grand Rapids, Michigan, and *AVIO*, published by Dutch Club AVIO of La Habra, California. The former is a quarterly, and the latter appears monthly. They have a circulation of about fourteen thousand and eleven thousand respectively.

The change in attitude of later generations of Dutch-Americans toward the ideas held by their immediate forebears can be illustrated by comparing reactions to two events occurring about a half century apart, namely, the Boer War of 1899–1902 and the Nazi invasion of the Netherlands on May 10, 1940. During the former incident and the events leading to it, inhabitants of Dutch communities from Paterson, New Jersey, in the East to Lynden, Washington, in the West showed considerable sympathy for the "boers," or Dutch farmers, of South Africa who were engaged in armed conflict with English troops. Rallies were held at which the colors of the Boer republic were displayed and fiery speeches were delivered on their behalf. Considerable relief money was raised on these occasions—sometimes as much as four hundred dollars at a single meeting—and there were reports about determined young Dutch-Americans going to South Africa to join in the fight against the English. In South Dakota, a town was renamed Joubert, in honor of one of the Boer generals and statesmen, and some Middle West farmers even named their horses "Oom Paul," after Oom (meaning "uncle") Paul Kruger, another famous Boer leader.[31]

As a result of the Americanization process and the death of many of the older immigrants, pro-Dutch feeling had greatly dissipated among Holland-Americans by the time Nazi troops invaded the Netherlands in World War II. It is true that considerable sympathy was still shown at that time for the "fatherland" among the older and second-generation Dutch-Americans. They expressed their feelings in the press, in telegrams, and at religious gatherings, but in no way did their reaction compare to the excitement generated by the Boer War. Third- and fourth-generation Dutch-Americans were also disturbed by the treacherous attack, but their feelings stemmed primarily from moral outrage over the general injustice of the act rather than from its being carried out against their ancestral homeland. Taken as a whole, it is doubtful that the later generations showed much more resentment about it than they did about the German invasion of Norway and Denmark about a month earlier.[32]

In short, by World War II, the story of the Dutch-Americans who were products of the Great Migration was rapidly reaching the end of an epoch. Nineteenth-century immigrants, although desirous of becoming bona fide citizens of their adopted country, generally continued to think of the past in terms of William the Silent, the Dutch Revolt against Spain, the brothers De Witt, and the *Gouden Eeuw*, or Golden Age, of Rembrandt's time. Nostalgic ideas about the "fatherland" and about things Dutch were passed on to their children born in America. To a large extent, second-generation Dutch-Americans patterned their lives after their parents; they continued to converse in Dutch, attended Dutch church services, and read Dutch-language newspapers. By the time of World War II, however, many of the inhabitants of Dutch communities that had been established during the nineteenth century were third- and fourth- and even fifth-generation Holland-Americans. Most of them no longer understood the language of their forefathers,[33] and their feelings about Old World traditions were less strong. They identified themselves with New World mores and thought of history in terms of Daniel Boone, George Washington, the American Revolution, and Abraham Lincoln.

The rate of disappearance of the Dutch "racial frontier" that had been established during the nineteenth century was accelerated by several developments after World War II. Tens of thousands of Dutch-American G.I.'s who had spent time in other parts of the United States or overseas brought with them on their return home a new outlook on life and society. Increasingly, too, young Dutch people began selecting marriage partners from other ethnic backgrounds—a practice that had been strictly taboo in many communities before the war. Finally, as happened in the Netherlands itself, the popularity of television helped to end the cultural isolation of many persons residing in rural areas.

Despite the steady progress toward Americanization, several developments have occurred during recent decades aimed at recapturing some of the Old World heritage and preserving the story of the Dutch in America for posterity. Thus, three of the chief centers of Dutch concentration in the United States, namely, Holland, Michigan, and Pella and Orange City, Iowa, began holding annual spring celebrations to commemorate their Netherlands origins. These celebrations, called "tulip festivals," have become increasingly elaborate with the passage of time. The first Orange City festival held in 1936, for example, was a one-day affair attended by about 3,500 persons. It expanded to a two-day affair in 1938, and became a three-day festival in 1950. The 1973 event at Orange City attracted nearly 100,000 visitors, many of whom came from surrounding states.

In keeping with the name of the festival, the streets are lined with tens of thousands of colorful tulips. Each fall, new bulbs are planted along the curbs to ensure plenty of flowers for the following spring. Other thousands of tulips are planted in decorative beds in the parks and on private lawns of the townspeople. As part of the pageantry, hundreds of the local people, including children who can hardly walk, are dressed in traditional Old World costumes, with baggy breeches, multipetticoats, lace caps, and wooden shoes. The attire indicates the patchwork makeup of social and political life that existed in old Holland. Thus, there are costumes representative of Scheveningen fishermen, Frisian farmers, Gelderland aristocrats, Zeeland *huisvrouwen*, Amsterdam burgers, and so on.

Each day's festivities begin with an inspection of the main street over which the Tulip Queen, accompanied by her court, must travel to the coronation ceremony. As might be expected, the town mayor, dressed in the garb of a Dutch *burgemeester*, with broad hat, dark robes, and satin breeches, accompanied by his *gemeenteraad*, or town council, pronounces the street deplorably dirty and orders it cleaned. Dozens of men, women, and children, all dressed in costume, thereupon begin scrubbing the street, the men traveling to and fro carrying buckets of water suspended from wooden neck-yokes, while the women and children wield long-handled brushes and brooms.

Other highlights consist of folk dances by young people, all appropriately clad for the occasion, including *klompen*, or wooden shoes, and a parade of floats and marching bands. Many of the floats seek to recapture some of the charm of life in the "old country," while others depict scenes from the early history of the settlement. Because of the importance of religion in the life of Dutch communities, there are also several floats with religious themes. Throughout the day, guests may visit various historical exhibits, treat themselves to traditional Dutch dishes served in the town restaurants or in the special "stands" set up for the occasion by local church organizations, or shop for souvenirs, of which miniature wooden shoes and windmills are most popular.

In addition to activities such as tulip festivals, a variety of organizations have taken steps to preserve the heritage of the Dutch in America. One of the oldest and most prestigious of these is the Holland Society of New York, founded in 1885 by a group of prominent and historical-minded New Yorkers of Dutch descent. Its membership is primarily comprised of descendants in the direct paternal line of residents of the Dutch colonies in America prior to or during the year 1675.[34] Membership in the Society totals about a thousand, nearly two-thirds of whom live within two hundred miles of New York City. There are also twenty-one branches located throughout the United States for the benefit of persons unable, because of distance, to attend the meetings and gatherings held in New York.

The Holland Society maintains an extensive library at its headquarters in New York for the purpose of collecting and preserving information on the early history of the Dutch in America and encouraging research on that subject. It also publishes a quarterly magazine, appropriately named *De Halve Maen* (The Half Moon) after the famous ship of Henry Hudson, whose explorations gave the Netherlands a claim to New Netherland in 1609. It contains scholarly articles on the Dutch in the American colonies and also keeps members abreast of current actvities of the Society. Despite its Dutch title, the magazine's articles are all in English—a necessity because only a very small fraction of the members of the Holland Society are able to read Dutch.

Like the Holland Society, numerous museums and libraries have made a special effort to collect Dutch-Americana. The new Dutch Galleries of the Museum of the City of New York, for example, have several permanent exhibits illustrating various aspects of life among the Dutch of New Amsterdam. The Museum of the New York Historical Society in New York City also has several displays bearing on the Dutch, including folk art, silver, and portraits of notable Dutchmen. The Society's library contains considerable material among its archival holdings on the Dutch in colonial America, as does the Long Island Historical Library in Brooklyn. One of the best collections of manuscripts and printed materials on the early history of the Dutch churches is found in the Dutch Church Room of the Gardner Sage Library at New Brunswick Seminary, New Brunswick, New Jersey.

During recent years, several Dutch houses of the colonial period in the New York area have been restored and preserved as reminders of the important role the Dutch once played in the region's history. These include the Jan Martense Schenck house, built in 1675, which has been reconstructed in the Brooklyn Museum and equipped with authentic Dutch furnishings of the period, and the Voorlezer House of Richmond, Staten Island. The latter was built prior to 1696 for use as the church and school of the local Dutch congregation and as the home of the *voorlezer*, a kind of lay-preacher who often doubled as schoolmaster. Similar restorations have taken place throughout the Hudson Valley.

In the face of increasing Americanization, Dutch-Americans residing in the Middle West have also been taking steps to preserve their heritage. Thus, the Netherlands Museum was established in 1937 at Holland, Michigan. Its primary purpose has been the preservation and exhibition of artifacts of the early history of the Michigan *kolonie*, and the collection of pertinent letters, newspapers, pamphlets, books, and so forth. Similarly, Calvin College at Grand Rapids, Michigan, has been making a strenuous effort during recent years to collect memorabilia bearing on the Dutch in America, especially anything pertaining to the Christian Reformed Church. In 1963, an organization known as the Dutch-American Historical Association was created to coordinate the collection of Dutch-Americana among several Michigan institutions. Northwestern College in Orange City, Iowa—one of the three colleges sponsored by the Reformed Church—has been doing its part in these endeavors by constructing a special library room, known as the Dutch Heritage Room, for housing manuscripts and printed materials pertaining to the Dutch in northwest Iowa.

Perhaps because of the growing concern with ethnic studies, scholarly interest in the Dutch in America has increased during recent years. In the fall of 1971, for example, the Holland Society of New York together with the Institute on Man and Science sponsored three days of meetings at Rensselaerswyck, New York, on Dutch colonial contributions to the cultural and social evolution of the United States. Papers were read on such subjects as Dutch laws and politics, rural customs, and limners of the upper Hudson Valley. Similarly, in the fall of 1972, the New Jersey Historical Society at its twenty-second annual meeting at Nyack, New York, made "Hudson Valley History and Culture" its central theme. Seminar sessions were devoted to various aspects of Dutch culture including architecture, interior decoration, and the restoration of certain landmarks. National and local historical journals have also published numerous articles on the Dutch in America during recent years.

There has also been a growing interest in Dutch language and culture among college students. In the forefront of this movement were Columbia University and Calvin College. In 1913, the former established, with help from the Netherlands government, the Queen Wilhelmina Chair of the History, Language, and Literature of the Netherlands. Calvin College of Grand Rapids, Michigan, which has been offering extensive courses in Dutch language and culture since its founding in 1876, created a similar professorship in 1953, known as the Queen Juliana Chair of Dutch Language and Culture. In 1949, these were the only two schools of higher learning in the United States offering such courses, but their number has since increased to about twenty. One of the latest is the University of California at Berkeley, which in 1971, in cooperation with the Netherlands government, established the Princess Beatrix Lectureship in Dutch Language and Literature.[35]

❀   ❀   ❀   ❀

Most Hollanders who came to America were intensely religious, but for various reasons many of them refused to associate with the old Reformed Church, preferring instead to establish their own denominations. The new immigrant churches, as well as the Reformed Church in some regions, were a major means for binding together persons of Dutch descent and for perpetuating the customs of the "old country." The stern morality practiced by the Dutch Calvinists left its mark on many communities, as did also their views on education. Because of the New World environment, however, and the decline of emigration after World War I, it became only a matter of time before the new immigrant churches fell prey to the Americanization process. Simultaneously with these changes, there occurred an overall decline in the use of the ancestral language as Dutch communities began losing some of their ethnic identity. As a counterbalance to these developments, several attempts have been made in recent years to preserve for posterity the heritage of the Dutch in America.

Although intensely religious, the average Dutch-American was not an ascetic. His success in farming and in the business world is ample proof of this. Furthermore, although theological disputations interested him more than political argumentation, politics was not ignored, as will be seen in the following chapter.

CHAPTER XII

# The Dutch in American Politics

IT HAS BEEN SAID THAT "HOLLANDERS ARE NOT, LIKE THE IRISH, born politicians."[1] The statement is perhaps true, but it must not be interpreted to mean that persons of Dutch descent have no interest in politics. On the contrary, they have repeatedly shown themselves to be as ready as any ethnic group to oppose actions inimical to their welfare. Furthermore, individual Dutchmen have played important roles in government at the state and local levels, and a few have reached positions of national importance.

From an early date, the inhabitants of New Netherland manifested a determination to force changes in policies they considered unfair. Repeatedly the colonists demanded that the directors of the West India Company allow them to engage in business within the colony, to participate in the fur trade, and to receive better terms for land tenure. After winning some concessions in these matters, the citizens took the next step and asked for a greater voice in the colony's government.

The concern of New Netherlanders for political affairs was shown in their frequent criticism of their last governor, Peter Stuyvesant. Views expressed about him by his contemporaries included: "Whoever has him opposed, has as much as the sun and the moon against him"; "[He struts] like a peacock, with great state and pomp"; "Our great Muscovy Duke goes on as usual with something of the wolf; the older he gets the more inclined is he to bite"; "He likes to assert the maxim 'the Prince is above the law.' "[2] Despite his arbitrary manners, Stuyvesant, under pressure from the colonists and from his superiors in Holland, was obliged to widen the base upon which the government rested and adopt a more tolerant religious policy. Much still remained to be done in granting self-government to New Netherland when it fell to the English in 1664, but the Dutch colonists had repeatedly shown that their interests could not be ignored with impunity by those placed in authority over them.[3]

The so-called Leisler Troubles of 1688–91 also demonstrated that Dutchmen of the early colonial period were not indifferent to politics and sometimes took opposing sides on issues. This confusing episode in New York history began when news reached the colonists that the Catholic king, James II, had been deposed. On learning of this, the citizens of Boston arrested the governor of the newly created Dominion of New England, Edmund Andros, an appointee of James II. The province of New York was affected by the arrest because it was a part of the Dominion. To add to the confusion, Francis Nicholson, Andros' young and inexperienced lieutenant governor in New York, fled the country. There were also rumors about a French invasion and a Catholic plot to take over the English colonies in America. In the absence of an effective government, a citizen's committee appointed Jacob Leisler, a captain in the colonial militia, as a pro tem governor.

Not everyone acknowledged Leisler, and as a result, the province of New York became divided into two highly antagonistic factions. Although there were exceptions, the aristocratic and more wealthy element among the population opposed Leisler. So, too, did all the Dutch Reformed ministers. Some of the lower classes, especially in the New York City and Long Island areas, on the other hand, tended to support him. Despite opposition, Leisler managed to maintain himself in office, frequently by arbitrary means, for twenty months. When the government in England finally dispatched a new governor to New York in 1691, Leisler hesitated to relinquish his authority. He was therefore arrested, found guilty of treason, and executed on May 16, 1691.

Unfortunately, the death of Leisler did not quell the passions that had disturbed New York politics during the previous three years. In October, 1692, almost a year and a half after Leisler had been executed, the Dutch pastors sent the following communication to the Classis of Amsterdam:

Our ministers have been cast under suspicion through slanders against them; while the populace, ever ready for any change, were advised not to contribute for the support of religious services or for ministers' salaries. . . . Members of the Council (of former Governors), who were also mostly Elders of the church, have been saluted by the unheard of titles . . . of traitors and papists.[4]

In 1698, the relatives of Leisler and of his son-in-law, Jacob Milbourne, who had also been executed, were given permission to exhume the bodies, which had been buried near the gallows, and give them a Christian burial under the floor of one of the Dutch churches. This was carried out with considerable joy and fanfare among the people, but against the protests of the Dutch church officials and many of the well-to-do citizens.[5]

Generally speaking, after the Leisler Troubles simmered down, the common people among the Dutch were not overly concerned with politics until the American Revolution. On the other hand, members of the Dutch "aristocracy," i.e., the privileged families of wealth, both landed and commercial, did assert themselves in local and provincial politics by serving as mayors, justices, and assemblymen. Their political influence was strong in part because many of the electorate consisted of tenant farmers who, in the absence of the secret ballot, tended to vote in accordance with the wishes of the landlords. Furthermore, the upper classes regularly married among themselves, thereby creating a close personal bond that at times operated almost like a "political machine." Linked together through marriage were such prominent Dutch families as the Van Cortlandts, Van Rensselaers, Beekmans, Banckers, Rutgers, Van Hornes, Philipses, Schuylers, Van Dams, Stuyvesants, and Roosevelts.[6]

The attitude of the Dutch in the Revolution, as explained earlier, also demonstrated that they were not entirely passive in political matters and were not always of one mind in their views. Some of them merely wanted to be left alone, while others, among both the common people and the "aristocracy," held definite views on the conflict. The Albany Dutch, for reasons of their own, were frequently anti-British, whereas many of those living in the Kinderhoek region and in western Long Island showed Tory sympathies. Similarly, whereas some Dutchmen served on committees opposing British imperial policies

and later became members of Revolutionary tribunals when
hostilities broke out, others actively supported the Tory cause
and left the United States to live in England or Nova Scotia
after the conflict ended.

As might be expected, Dutchmen who were prominent before
the Revolution and who embraced the Patriot cause played a
role in the politics of the post-Revolutionary period. Although
none of them achieved the stature of a Washington or a Jefferson,
considerable evidence indicates that they were interested in
politics during the early national period. According to one
authority, "During the first two post-Revolutionary decades sixty
Dutch-Americans served in the United States Congress."⁷ Many
others held offices at other levels. To mention only a few, John
Lansing had a distinguished judicial career spanning a quarter
century, 1790–1814; Nicholas Van Dyke served as the first
president of Delaware, 1783–86; Pierre Van Cortlandt became
the first lieutenant governor of New York in 1777, serving in
that capacity for eighteen years; and Cornelius P. Van Ness
became governor of Vermont (1823–29) and minister to Spain
(1829–37).

Dutchmen holding public offices during the early national period were generally Federalist in their political thinking. Important Federalist leaders among them included Stephen Van
Rensselaer, Leonard Gansevoort, Gulian Crommelin Verplanck,
and Philip John Schuyler. But as was true during the Revolutionary period, not all persons of Dutch descent were of the same
mind politically. For example, through his letters and pamphlets,
Abraham Yates, a member of a long-established Dutch family,
became a leading publicist for the Antifederalists.⁸

It is interesting to note in this respect that some of the founding
fathers in America evinced considerable praise for the people
of the Netherlands and their customs. Thus, Benjamin Franklin
once wrote, "In love and liberty and in the defense of it, Holland
has been our example."⁹ When it came to the actual workings
of the Dutch government, however, a very different view was
sometimes expressed. Alexander Hamilton and James Madison
several times cited the decentralized character of the Dutch
governmental system and the problems this created for the
Netherlands as an argument for why the Articles of Con-

federation should be replaced by a document giving more power to the central government.[10]

Dutch-Americans from among the lower classes at times also asserted themselves politically during the post-Revolutionary period, as is shown by their participation in the antirent movement. The letter was directed against the great landed magnates, who, as a group, owned nearly two million acres of land in east-central New York at the opening of the nineteenth century. Some of their holdings were of tremendous size—the Van Rensselaer family, for example, possessed almost a half million acres, consisting of over three thousand farms, on both sides of the Hudson River below Albany. For about a century and a half, the tenants on these estates—many of whom were of Dutch descent—were burdened down with various rents and taxes, as well as mundane duties and services, some of which were survivals of the patroon system of the New Netherland period.

After the Revolution, with its discussion about inalienable rights, the Hudson Valley farmers found the provisions of their leaseholds increasingly galling, and refused to be treated any longer as semiserfs. Their agitation finally culminated in the so-called Anti-Rent War of 1839–46. In this "conflict," embattled Dutch farmers stood shoulder to shoulder with husbandmen of other ethnic backgrounds in order to obtain a redress of their grievances. Sometimes using violent means, but usually resorting to political measures, the farmers finally won out, and the terms of their leaseholds were liberalized.[11]

That it was possible for a Dutchman of humble background to go far in American politics during the first half of the nineteenth century is shown in the career of Martin Van Buren (1782–1862), the eighth President of the United States. Van Buren was born of pure Dutch stock at Kinderhoek, New York, where his father followed the combined occupations of farmer and tavern keeper. Young Martin, after admission to the bar in 1803, established his practice at Kinderhoek, but politics became his first love. After holding various political offices, including those of governor of New York and United States senator, he became Vice-President under Andrew Jackson in 1832. Four years later, his party nominated him to succeed Jackson, and he won the election easily. Unfortunately, the economic depression that began in 1837, along with other developments, hurt his popularity, and he was decisively defeated for reelection by the Whig candidate, William Henry Harrison, in 1840.

In his politics, Van Buren was a supporter of states rights, favoring local initiative and a limited role for the national government. Because of these convictions, he refused to take decisive federal action that might have alleviated the distress caused by the financial panic of 1837. At times, however, he showed a willingness to compromise, a trait that, together with his genius for political organization, gained him the reputation of being a shrewd politician. He has therefore been referred to as "The Red Fox of Kinderhoek" and "The Little Magician."

In describing Van Buren, his biographers have used expressions like "witty," "reserved," "a knack of presenting conclusions in a clear, concise manner," "cautious," "charming," and "not speaking his mind on an issue until after considerable study." In view of such remarks and the strict constructionist opinions that Van Buren held about the Constitution, the historian must perforce ask whether they were the result of his Dutch background. In answering this question, one of his biographers stated that

it would be mere fancy to find in the statesman particular traits brought from the dyked swamp lands whence . . . his ancestors came. Those who farmed the rich fields of Columbia county [in which Kinderhoek was located] were pretty thorough Americans; their characteristics were more immediately drawn from the soil they cultivated and from the necessary habits of their life than from the lands . . . from which their forefathers had emigrated.[12]

Van Buren was the first of three Presidents of Dutch background whose ancestors in the male line can be traced directly to the New Netherland period. The two Roosevelts, Theodore and Franklin, were descendants of a farmer named Claes Martenszen Van Rosenvelt, or Roosevelt, who emigrated from the Netherlands to New Amsterdam about 1649. Numerous United States senators and congressmen, as well as other public officials of recent years have also been able to trace their lineage to Dutch ancestors of the New Netherland period. Frederick

Van Nuys (1847–1944), for example, who had a distinguished career as a senator from Indiana, was a descendant of Auke Janse Van Nuys, who arrived in the New World from Holland about 1650. Similarly, Horace Jeremiah ("Jerry") Voorhis, who served five terms in Congress as a representative for the Twelfth California District before being defeated by Richard Milhous Nixon in 1946, can claim Steven Coerten Van Voorhees as his paternal ancestor. The latter emigrated to New Netherland in 1660.

In view of the many years that elapsed between the time these descendants of "old" Dutch families served in office and when their ancestors arrived from Holland, it is obvious that, as in the case of Van Buren, little, if any, of their political philosophy can be attributed to their Dutch background. In fact, because of generations of intermarrying, Dutch influence was likely to be even less potent among them than in the case of Van Buren. According to the latter's own memoirs, there was not "a single intermarriage with one of different extraction" from the time the first Van Buren arrived in New Netherland about 1633 until the marriage of his eldest son, a "period of over two centuries and including six generations."[13] Few, if any, politicians of the twentieth century whose Dutch-American ancestry dates from the New Netherland period could claim such a pedigree. Franklin D. Roosevelt, for example, on the maternal side was perhaps more Swedish than Dutch.

Although intermarriage and the lapse of time make it difficult to discern Dutch influence among politicians whose American ancestry goes back to the colonial period, several observations can be made about the later immigrants and their immediate descendants. Hollanders who arrived in the United States during the second half of the nineteenth century were grateful for the opportunities offered them by their adopted country, and seemed anxious to demonstrate their patriotism. Thus, in 1851, a Dutchman at Little Chute, Wisconsin, wrote his relatives in the Netherlands that although the Hollanders of his community were not numerous enough to stage a parade on the Fourth of July, they set fire to a large brush pile to light up the sky and show they were as patriotic as anyone.[14] Similarly, Dominie Scholte wrote, "Directing my words to Netherlanders, I can no longer speak as a Netherlander. I have severed myself from social position in the land of my birth. I have become bound to the American people."[15]

Second- and third-generation Dutch-Americans evinced a similar feeling. A minister of the Reformed congregation at Sayville, Long Island, in 1897 expressed the feelings of many Hollanders when he told the Dutch-Americans in his parish that they should be proud of their American citizenship, no matter whether it came to them by adoption or by birth.[16] Gerrit John Diekema (1859–1930), a congressman from Michigan, where his parents had emigrated, and a one-time ambassador to the Netherlands, had a highly developed sense of patriotism. His public speeches, frequently delivered in Dutch, were filled with references to the "founding fathers" and to America as the land of liberty.[17] When the United States entered World War I, the Synod of the Christian Reformed Church, which was predominantly Dutch in its makeup, unanimously resolved to send a message to President Wilson pledging the Church's wholehearted support in the conflict. This occurred despite the Netherlands itself being neutral in World War I.[18]

Hollanders of the Great Migration found it difficult to understand the American ideal of social equality. Dominie Scholte, after a visit to Washington to inquire about the availability of good land, expressed amazement at the willingness of government officials to help him in every way possible. "I did not experience any gruffness," he wrote, "nor did anyone exhibit any greed; instead, they answered all my questions in an unassuming manner, and furnished me with various kinds of printed information free of charge." He reported that the same courtesies were extended him during his stay in Albany, New York, and St. Louis, Missouri. All of this, said Scholte, was in sharp contrast to the type of official treatment a person received under similar circumstances in the Netherlands.[19]

Dutch immigrants throughout the nineteenth century continued to be amazed at the contrast between social life in the Netherlands and in the United States. The Reverend Roelof T. Kuiper, who in 1879 at the age of fifty-four emigrated to Michigan, made the following comment about American social life shortly after his arrival:

Here there are fewer restricting and oppressive laws, rules, regulations and orders. There are far fewer formalities and rules of conduct. Everyone associates on a more equal level. . . . One who is somewhat ahead of others, because of intelligence and education, possessions and income, profession or position, does not allow himself to be very prominent; and whoever is less endowed in one or in all of these respects does not need to stand back on that account. . . . Here there are not waiting rooms and coaches with first, second, and third class, as in the Netherlands; but the Yankee (American) and the immigrant, the boss and the workman get their tickets at the same window, remain in the same waiting room and sit in the coaches next to or immediately behind one another on similarly covered, and even upholstered seats.[20]

Despite a lack of experience, the new immigrants were determined to participate in politics. In the early summer of 1848, through Dominie Van Raalte's efforts, the clerk of the Ottawa County Circuit Court visited the Michigan colony and received applications for first naturalization papers from about three hundred Hollanders. A similar interest in citizenship was expressed by Scholte's followers in Iowa. As a result, the state legislature passed a special act in 1848 permitting the recently arrived Hollanders to vote immediately for local officials and even to run for such offices themselves. Under normal circumstances, according to the state constitution, the immigrants would have had to wait several years for such privileges.

Generally speaking, the new arrivals initially preferred the Democratic party. In the first election of the Michigan colony in March, 1851, for example, there were ten Democratic voters to every Whig.[21] Similarly, in the presidential election of 1856, the Hollanders in the Pella community cast 345 votes for the Democrat Buchanan compared to 136 for the Republican Fremont.[22] The reasons for this political preference were varied. The reputation of the Democratic party as the party of the little man appealed to Hollanders, most of whom were of humble background. They also believed it favored a more liberal policy in admitting immigrants and granting them quick citizenship.

Initially, Dutch-language newspapers appearing in the new settlements were nearly all sympathetic to the Democratic party. The first such newspaper was *De Sheboygan Nieuwsbode*, ap pearing in October, 1849. In the following year, *De Hollander,* also decidedly pro-Democratic, began publication at Holland, Michigan. Scholte, who at first refused to join any party, established the *Pella Gazette* in 1855. "Although it carried the motto 'Independent in Everything,' it began by supporting the Democrats, and ended up radically Republican."²³ It ceased publication in 1860.

Gradually, during the 1850's, many Hollanders began deserting the Democratic ranks, transferring their allegiance to the Whigs and later to the newly formed Republican party. This came about in part because of growing opposition to the Democratic view of slavery. The realignment of political affiliation also resulted from Republican promises of a liberal homestead law and repudiation of measures hostile to immigrants. Dutch newspapers with a Whig or Republican point of view also began appearing.

Although there was general agreement among the Hollanders that slavery was an evil institution, there was disagreement among them as to its abolition. Some were vehemently opposed to it and urged immediate abolition. A few Hollanders, such as Cornelius Kuyper and Jan Ton in the Chicago area, played an active role in the Underground Railroad, by which slaves were "smuggled" to freedom into Canada. Others urged moderation, thinking it would gradually pass out of existence of its own accord. Even the leaders of the Reformed Church were not in agreement on its abolition. As late as 1855, a prominent Dutch minister from New Brunswick, New Jersey, wrote a pamphlet defending slavery on biblical grounds.²⁴

Dominie Scholte of Iowa was opposed to slavery on principle, but at first declared it was a sectional issue and therefore should not be handled by the federal government. He feared that considering it in any other light might lead to civil war. Later, however, Scholte served as a delegate from Iowa to the national Republican convention in Chicago which nominated Abraham Lincoln, and wrote several newspaper articles and delivered numerous speeches on his behalf. Correspondence was exchanged occasionally between the two men, and later the President presented the Iowa Hollander with a cane as a gift and offered him a diplomatic post.²⁵

Although not everyone was in agreement on how to deal with the slavery issue, Hollanders throughout the northern states rallied to the support of the Union at the outbreak of the Civil War. Four hundred nineteen of them from Ottawa County, Michigan, served in the Union army, all of whom were volunteers except five or six, and all foreign-born except one.[26] Van Raalte's own sons volunteered for service, and one of them, Dirk, lost an arm during the siege of Atlanta in August, 1864. Hundreds of young Dutchmen from Wisconsin, Iowa, and the eastern states also served in the Union army. Dutch women volunteered their services in collecting necessities for sick and wounded soldiers, and prayers for the Union cause were a regular part of Dutch church services.[27]

Some of the views expressed about the Civil War make interesting reading because they show a determination of many Hollanders to be patriotic Americans. Thus, a Dutchman from Cedar Grove, Wisconsin, wrote:

The blood of their forefathers coursed yet through the veins of their offspring when they fought against oppression and tyranny; their sons who have made this their adopted country, responded nobly to the call when the country was in danger, they stood shoulder to shoulder with the American born citizen in defense of their common country.[28]

Persons of Dutch descent like to refer to their ancestral love for freedom, but the influence of geography cannot be ignored by the historian in explaining their support of the Union cause. If New Netherland had been founded a few hundred miles farther south, the descendants of the Van Rensselaers, Van Cortlandts, and others probably would have become southern plantation owners instead of Yankee gentleman farmers and merchants, and at the time of the Civil War would have viewed the slavery issue in a different light. This becomes very plausible considering that when slavery was abolished in New York and New Jersey about 1800, the strongest opposition to abolition came from Dutch and German farmers.[29] Americans of Dutch ancestry residing in the South were apparently as strongly pro-Confederate in their views as those living in the North were pro-Union. A study of the Van Deventer family shows that sixty-six persons with this surname (but with varied spellings) served in the Union army, as against seventy-six who fought on the Confederate side.[30]

As was true of many Northerners, not all Hollanders who supported the Union equated freeing the slaves with treating them as equals. No better example of this can be given than the case of Dominie Scholte. Campaigning for Lincoln in 1860, Scholte wrote several editorials condemning slavery. When the Civil War broke out, he promised a town lot in Pella to each Dutch soldier upon his return from service. These actions, however, must not be interpreted to mean he looked upon the Negroes as equals. In 1857, Scholte wrote:

> Intermarriages between the different white nationalities indicate that distinction on account of place of birth is unknown among us [Hollanders]; but we have not lost our self-respect so completely, as to open our family circles to amalgamation with the black race. . . . We do propose overwhelmingly to vote down the infamous principle of Negro Equality.[31]

Generally speaking, Dutch immigrants and their descendants have favored the Republican party since the time of the Civil War. The conflict itself was in part responsible for this. According to one report, inhabitants of the Netherlands considered Abraham Lincoln "one of the great emancipators of modern times and placed in the same category as William of Orange, the 'Father of their Country.' "[32] Hollanders who believed that and emigrated to this country quite naturally gave their allegiance to the Republicans—Lincoln's party.

After a brief period, most of the influential Dutch language newspapers became Republican, and were of great influence in molding Dutch political opinion. *De Grondwet,* published at Holland, Michigan, from 1860 to 1938, has been described as "a paper which for two generations was destined to mold Republican sentiment among the Dutch immigrant settlers."[33] The influence of these newspapers frequently extended over a wide area. *De Volksvriend,* for example, which began publication at Orange City, Iowa, in 1874 and continued until 1951, carried not only information of local interest, but state, national,

and international news as well. It became decidedly pro-
Republican, and was subscribed to by Hollanders scattered
throughout the United States. As a consequence, communities
that had no Dutch language newspaper of their own, such as
those in Washington and California, had their views shaped in
part by a paper published as much as two thousand miles away.

Michigan Hollanders have almost consistently favored the
Republicans since the Civil War, although there have been
occasional elections in which local issues or a well-run Democratic campaign made inroads into Republican ranks. An examination of Ottawa County gives a good indication of how
Hollanders voted, because it was one of the most "Dutchified"
counties in Michigan. According to the Census Report of 1930,
about two-thirds of its native white population who were born
of foreign or mixed parentage were of Netherlands ancestry.
During each of the four times that Franklin Roosevelt ran for
the presidency, Ottawa County went Republican, and sometimes
did so by a wide margin, viz., 3 to 2 in 1932 and 2 to 1 in 1944.
This happened despite Roosevelt's Dutch name, his carrying
the state as a whole in 1932 and 1936, and his losing the state
by only slim margins in 1940 and 1944.[34]

The popularity of Republicanism among the Hollanders of
Ottawa County cannot be attributed to its lack of urbanization.[35]
Neighboring Grand Rapids, Michigan's second largest city, is
also very Dutch and very Republican. Commenting on Michigan's
Fifth Congressional District, which is made up of Grand Rapids
and the surrounding area, a recent handbook on American
politics makes the following interesting observation:

The most salient fact about it politically is that a very large number
of the people who live here are of Dutch descent, the largest such
concentration in the United States. Almost 10% of the district's residents are first or second-generation Dutch, and many more are
descended from the Dutch immigrants who originally settled around
Grand Rapids. Politically, Dutch-Americans are very conservative—
a reflection of the stern Calvinism of their Christian Reformed
Church. Grand Rapids is, therefore, a thoroughly Republican city.[36]

Hollanders elsewhere in the Middle West have also generally
voted the Republican ticket. Several examples can be cited to

support this statement. In the election of 1896, according to one estimate, 80 percent of the Dutch in Chicago favored the Republican presidential candidate, William McKinley.[37] The support for Republicans changed very little during the next few decades; a study of 1926 stated that "the Dutch of Chicago are Republican almost to a man."[38] Several hundred miles to the west in rural Nebraska the same situation prevailed. There, among the Holland settlements of Lancaster County, Franklin Roosevelt in 1932 received the largest number of votes ever given a Democratic candidate for President since 1896, yet he received fewer votes than his opponent.[39] Sioux County, in northwestern Iowa, where the ethnic origin of the population is about 75 percent Dutch, became a stronghold for Republicanism, the Republican candidate for President having won there in every election since 1920, except 1932 and 1936. In the Democratic landslide of 1964, Sioux County was only one of six counties in the state, out of a total of ninety-nine, that cast a majority for the Republican candidate, Barry Goldwater.[40]

Although there have been exceptions, Dutch-Americans in the eastern states whose forebears came during the Great Migration have also tended to vote Republican. Two of the last Dutch communities to be founded in the East, Whitinsville, Massachusetts, and West Sayville, Long Island, are predominantly Republican. According to one inquiry, for example, the voting pattern of the Whitinsville area as a whole reveals that its residents have traditionally voted about two to one Democratic, but among residents of Dutch descent the ratio has been about two to one Republican.[41] In Paterson, New Jersey, nineteenth-century Dutch immigrants strongly favored the Republicans, and their descendants have continued to do so until the present day.

Turning from the East Coast to the western states, a similar situation is encountered. In Washington, for example, northern Whatcom County, which has a heavy concentration of Dutch-Americans, is strongly Republican. So, too, are the Dutch communities in California. Although registered Democrats are in a majority among California's population as a whole, Republican registrants are in a very decided majority among persons of Dutch descent. Dutch-Americans in Montana and

Colorado also tend to vote Republican, but to a lesser extent than in other regions.[42]

Various reasons may be given in explaining the popularity of the Republican party among Dutch immigrants and their descendants. Chief among these reasons has been typical Dutch conservatism, a trait that was already manifested in the colonial period. Most of the Hollanders who came to the United States during the Great Migration were drawn from the conservative rural classes. They not only retained their conservative views after arrival in this country, but frequently passed them on to their descendants due to the cohesiveness of Dutch families. The conservative religious life of many Dutchmen also helped perpetuate a kind of continuum in their outlook on politics.

Dutch views on economic matters also explain their past voting habits. These views were often a reflection of Dutch religious practice resulting from the Calvinist emphasis on hard work and frugality. The average Dutchman believes that by hard work and diligence he can compete above the norm in any business, whether it be farming, dairying, horticulture, baking, furniture making, or whatever. As a consequence, according to a Democratic party worker in southern California, "The conservative Republican philosophy, where the marketplace becomes the pricing agency for goods and services, without government control or subsidies, is the choice of the Holland-American."[43] A California Dutch-American working in the Republican party organization expressed a similar opinion when he declared that the average Dutchman "thinks that to be a good, progressive American citizen one should find his own way in life and not be dependent on government aid."[44]

These same views were expressed by Dutchmen in other parts of the United States. Thus, a clergyman serving the Dutch community of West Sayville, Long Island, stated:

The often-times fierce independence of the people here rebels against the socialistic-type programs promulgated by the Democrats of recent years, beginning with the New Deal, continuing through the Fair Deal, then the Great Society movement. Our people in this community do not favor government handouts in any form. The current status of welfare programs is not particularly appreciated by them. As a result, they have consistently voted Republican.[45]

Several miscellaneous reasons may also be offered in explaining the popularity of the Republican party with respect to specific regions. Among strict Calvinists in some eastern cities, the pro-Republican vote was, in part, a reaction to the prevailing Roman Catholic tone of the Democratic party. In some agricultural areas, it can be partially attributed to the Great Depression of the 1930's. Dutch farmers who managed to weather the depression on their own by hard work became resentful toward the Democratic administration for enabling others to make it the "easy" way by government handouts. Some of them still harbor that grudge, and have passed it on to their descendants. In the same manner, many Dutch immigrants argued that they came to this country under adverse conditions, but nevertheless prospered through sheer hard work; if they could do it, others could do the same. During the early history of a few settlements, such as Orange City, Iowa, an anti-Hollander campaign that was waged by "Americans" (who happened to be Democrats) helped build up, with the assistance of the local Dutch-language press, a Republican tradition.

Despite their proverbial individualism, some Dutchmen were no doubt influenced by the political climate of the region in which they happened to settle. Their neighbors voted Republican, and they merely followed suit. The extreme conservatism of Orange County, California, where some Hollanders settled—a few coming directly from the Netherlands and others being transplanted from the Middle West—undoubtedly helps explain why some Dutch-Americans residing there have consistently followed the Republican party standard. So, too, some newcomers to pro-Republican areas like Sioux County, Iowa, or parts of Passaic County, New Jersey, were undoubtedly encouraged to vote the way they did because of their neighbors. Due to the political apathy of people in general and the family cohesiveness of the Dutch in particular, the custom of voting Republican was no doubt frequently passed on from generation to generation.

There are, of course, exceptions to the tendency for Americans of recent Dutch descent to vote Republican. Some persons with a strong sense of the social needs of others less fortunate than themselves believe that the Democrats have a better reputation for dealing with such matters and vote accordingly. In the larger cities, trade unionism has influenced some Dutch-Americans to switch from the Republican to the Democratic party. Furthermore, some Hollanders have favored the Democrats, just as others have favored the Republicans, due to the political traditions of the area in which they lived; the people around them voted Democratic, and they simply followed suit. Finally, variations appear in the voting pattern from time to time because of special issues in a particular campaign or because of the unique qualifications (or lack of them) in a certain candidate for political office.

In addition to individual cases of voters departing from the norm, a few blocs of Dutch-Americans have tended to vote Democratic. The Dutch Catholics make up one of these blocs. In 1876, for example, Little Chute, Wisconsin, founded by Father Theodorus Van den Broek during the late 1840's, voted 94 percent Democratic. During the same election, the Dutch Protestant communities of Holland and Alto, also in Wisconsin, voted over 80 percent Republican.[46] Similarly, an examination of voting patterns in the Chicago area after World War I indicates that the Dutch Catholics residing there were not nearly as pro-Republican as the Dutch Protestants.[47]

Dutch Catholics have continued to vote contrary to the manner of Dutch Protestants. In 1956, for example, at Little Chute, Wisconsin, which was still a heavily Catholic community, the magic of the name Eisenhower enabled him to beat Stevenson by a vote of 1,167 to 521. They returned to the Democratic fold in 1960, however, influenced by the religious pull of the Catholic Kennedy, who received 1,467 votes to Nixon's 573. This represented a change of 41 percentage points, whereas in Wisconsin as a whole there was a change of only 10 percentage points.[48]

The Protestant Hollanders of southeastern Iowa have also been a major exception to the general pattern of Dutch voting habits. Lake Prairie Township, which includes Pella and the surrounding area, voted Democratic in every national election from 1860 to 1952. Various factors can be noted in trying to explain this aberration. The settlement's first Dutch-language newspaper, *Pella's Weekblad*, which appeared in 1861 and was Democratic in its political sentiments, was not without influence. Furthermore, Dutch immigration to the Pella area rapidly declined after the Civil War because cheap land was no longer available. As a consequence, it was less subject to any modifying views that might be brought in by new arrivals. Finally, the anti-Hollander sentiment expressed by Republican-Whigs in the area during the early history of Pella helped build up a Democratic tradition, just as a similar movement, but this one directed by Democrats, helped strengthen GOP sympathies among the Dutch in Sioux County, Iowa.[49]

The fact that residents of Dutch communities have frequently voted alike must not be construed to mean they were highly organized for political action or voted as political bosses told them to vote. Nothing could be further from the truth. Dutchmen traditionally vote their conscience, which happens to lean toward conservatism most of the time. Individualism is as much a trait of the Dutch as is conservatism, and this individualism militates against attempts to organize them into parties or blocs. A study undertaken after World War I of the Dutch communities of Chicago stated that in preparing a slate of candidates for city and county offices, attempts were made to satisfy every racial group except the Dutch, who were "usually ignored because they were so unorganized politically."[50]

Several instances can be cited showing Dutchmen pitted against Dutchmen. The Leisler Troubles and the "Great Schism" in the Reformed Church are examples from the colonial period, and many Dutchmen were on opposite sides in the Revolution. Similarly, Martin Van Buren's background never made it any easier for him to get along with others of Dutch blood if they did not belong to his political faction. This was exemplified in his disagreements with two other prominent politicians of Dutch descent, Peter Van Schaack and Stephen Van Rensselaer.

Hollanders who were products of the Great Migration also generally put political philosophy and individual conscience before ethnic loyalty. Dominie Henry Scholte of Iowa and Jacob Quintus of Wisconsin, both newspaper editors, carried on a bitter feud during the 1850's. Dutch voters of western Michigan showed an independence of mind in their occasional opposition to Gerrit Diekema, who held both state and national elective offices. Such opposition occurred despite his being a son of immigrant parents, a resident of Holland, Michigan, and very active in the Dutch church. That Hollanders put political philosophy before ethnic loyalty was also demonstrated several times in their refusal to support the Roosevelts in presidential elections. On the other hand, Gerald Ford's non-Dutch name obviously was no handicap in his serving as congressman from Michigan's heavily Dutch Fifth Congressional District, centered in Grand Rapids, for a quarter of a century before his appointment as Vice-President in late 1973.[51]

As might be expected, in view of the religious convictions of a large segment of Dutch-Americans, consideration was given from time to time to exploring means for making politics and economics more attuned to Calvinist principles. Such movements were encouraged by developments taking place in the Netherlands, particularly through the influence of Abraham Kuyper (1827–1920). The latter, as a pastor and professor but especially as the author of numerous books and the editor of two newspapers, became one of the foremost publicists of strict orthodox Calvinism. He attempted to establish the authority of Christ and the Bible in every sphere of life, including not only the church and family but political and economic affairs as well. In 1878, Kuyper helped found the Calvinist Anti-Revolutionary State party and was its principal spokesman for almost forty-five years. He himself was active in politics, serving several terms in the States General and, from 1901 to 1905, as minister of home affairs and virtual prime minister. Through translations of Kuyper's works into English for those who could not read Dutch, and by means of a lecture tour of Dutch communities in the United States, he helped spread the idea of founding a Christian political party in this country. He also inspired the founding of Calvinist-oriented newspapers patterned after those in the Netherlands.

These developments in the United States, however, cannot be attributed entirely to Kuyper's influence. The idea of Calvinism as a life-and-world view, in which Christian principles must permeate all fields of human endeavor, was ingrained in the minds of many nineteenth-century immigrants and their descendants, thereby making it easier for Kuyper's views to take root. As early as 1858, for example, Dominie Scholte of Pella, Iowa, declared that "Christians whose Higher Law is the Bible . . . can exert a beneficial influence upon the community," adding that "no social or political position as such lies out of the sphere of action of a believer."[52]

In 1903, a group of Christian Reformed ministers and laymen of Grand Rapids, Michigan, founded an organization bearing the Latin title *Fas et Jus,* for the purpose of discussing politics and related matters in the light of Reformed theology.[53] It met with some success in translating Calvinist principles into political action at the local level. From this, it was but a natural step to establish a Christian political party at the national level patterned after the Anti-Revolutionary party in the Netherlands. Although the intention was to make it interdenominational, its greatest appeal was to members of the Christian Reformed Church. This movement, which got started in 1913, had only a brief existence, in part because of the outbreak of the First World War.

The idea of rebuilding the American political and social structure in terms of a kind of neo-Calvinism persisted among Dutch-Americans after World War I. In 1921, a group of Hollanders in Chicago established a newspaper, *The Daily Standard,* aimed at giving its readers not only the day by day news but also at propagating a Calvinist outlook on politics and society. Although it hoped to have a national appeal, it was almost entirely Christian Reformed in its inception and was patterned after similar newspapers in the Netherlands. Hampered by limited funds and an inexperienced staff, it lasted less than a year. Its chief obstacle, however, like that of the Christian Political party, was "the practical, pragmatic philosophy that governed American political thought; the average American voter does not take a philosophical, not to mention a theological, view of politics."[54]

Dutch-Americans also attempted to apply Calvinist principles to economics, especially in the area of labor relations. The most noteworthy of these efforts was the creation in 1931 of the Christian Labor Association, more commonly called the CLA, with headquarters in Grand Rapids, Michigan. It is perhaps the only example of Christian trade unionism in the United States today. Its aims, pursued within the framework of Christian precepts, were to establish an employment bureau to help unemployed workers find jobs, to obtain and uphold adequate wages, and to achieve employment insurance and old-age pensions. Initially, membership was restricted to confessing Christians, but the Wagner Act of 1935, which prohibited religious discrimination by unions, compelled the CLA to open its doors to anyone who wished to join. This adjustment in no way changed its basic commitment to biblical precepts, or affected its recognition that sin is the underlying basis of all discord in employer-employee relations.

From the beginning, the Christian Labor Association sought the support of all Christian churches and all ethnic groups. Members of the Christian Reformed Church, however, some of whom participated in Christian social action work in the Netherlands, have been its chief supporters, both as workers and as employers. An examination of its official paper, *The Christian Labor Herald*, a bimonthly that began publication in 1947, reveals an abundance of Dutch names among its members. In fact, membership corresponds largely to those geographical areas where Dutch communities are found.

The CLA over the years has been a conservative organization. This was particularly manifested in its favoring passage of the Taft-Hartley Act in 1947 and the Landrum-Griffin Act in 1959. Consequently, many workers have hesitated to join the CLA, fearing it would be too compromising in negotiations with employers. Membership is also small because many Christians, including members of the Christian Reformed Church, question the need for this type of labor organization. Such critics prefer that Christian workers give witness to their beliefs by joining existing "neutral" unions. Present membership is only approximately five thousand, with locals found in seven states: Pennsylvania, Ohio, Indiana, Illinois, Michigan, Minnesota, and California.[55]

❂     ❂     ❂     ❂

In a subject as large and complex as the Dutch in American politics, it is obvious that one can touch upon it only in a general way.[56] Enough has been stated, however, to show that persons of Dutch descent have seldom been passive in matters of government. As early as the New Netherland period, they showed themselves ready to oppose measures they considered adverse to their welfare. Because of the long time span involved and because of intermarriage with other ethnic groups, it is impossible to make judgments on the recent voting habits of Dutchmen whose American ancestry dates back to the colonial period. The historian is on safer ground in discussing the political thinking of immigrants and their descendants of the Great Migration. With respect to them, three main conclusions can be reached: first, they were determined to be American citizens; second, the great majority of them were conservative in their political outlook; and third, religion was a major factor in shaping that outlook.

## CHAPTER XIII

# A Century of Dutch Contributions to American Life

THE VAST MAJORITY OF DUTCH IMMIGRANTS AND THEIR DESCEN-
dants have been ordinary people, earning their living by the
sweat of their brow. Tens of thousands of them became factory
workers, helping supply the labor forces required for America's
growing industries. Many others became farmers, taming the
forests of Wisconsin and Michigan or breaking the prairie sod of
Iowa and the Dakotas. In addition to these nameless many,
there were individual Dutch-Americans in politics, science, the
humanities, the arts, and the business world who helped create a nation. Brief, biographical sketches of Dutch-Americans
of the last hundred years who have had distinguished careers
in these fields demonstrate how much they have contributed
to American culture.[1]

The interjection of material of a laudatory nature in an ethnic
study runs the risk of becoming unjustifiably chauvinistic. Pride
in one's formative background is legitimate; ethnic pomposity
is not. It will help in avoiding the latter to recall that there are
two parts to the hyphenated term "Dutch-Americans." As
Dutchmen, they normally possessed traits that had been brought
by them or their forebears from the "old country." Their ideas
and behavior patterns, however, were also shaped by the American environment—its vastness, its opportunities, its social mo-
bility, and so on. Therefore, it is frequently a moot question as
to how much of the achievement of a transplanted Hollander
or his descendant can be attributed to his "Dutchness" and how
much to his American experience.

The answer depends in part on the extent of his contact with
the homeland culture. Thus, in considering Francis Van der

Kemp as a scholar in the New York wilderness, it must be borne in mind that he was already a learned man in Holland before he came to the United States in 1788. Similarly, Henry Frankfort (b. 1897) was a noted historian and archaeologist prior to his leaving the Netherlands to join the staff of the Oriental Institute at the University of Chicago in 1938. So, too, William Kolff (b. 1911) had already achieved fame in the Netherlands for developing an artificial kidney before he came to the United States in 1950. Similarly, a nonimmigrant Dutch-American who was reared in a predominantly Dutch community in the United States would probably be heir to characteristic Dutch ways to a relatively significant extent.

The degree to which his ethnic background shaped the traits of a Dutch-American also depended on how long he and his ancestors had lived in the New World. It is doubtful, for example, if very much of Cornelius Vanderbilt's (b.1794) Dutch heritage survived the family's one hundred fifty years in America to assist his rise from a farm boy with little education to the possession of a fortune of over one hundred million dollars at the time of his death in 1877. The same can be said of the movie-making skill of Cecil B. De Mille (b. 1881), whose first American ancestors, Antonius De Mil and his wife Elizabeth Van der Hout De Mil, left a quiet bakery shop in Haarlem, the Netherlands, for New Amsterdam in 1658. Nor can the distinguished journalistic career of Walter Cronkite, anchorman of the CBS-TV evening news, be ascribed to any Dutch tradition that still might linger from the marriage in New Amsterdam in 1642 between his first American ancestors, Hercks Siboutszen Krankheydt and Wyntje Theunis. Naturally, too, the further back a person's American ancestry extends, the greater is the chance that his ethnic heritage will be "diluted" by intermarriage with those from other backgrounds. It is primarily for this reason that the emphasis in this chapter is on persons whose American experience extends back only a few generations.[2] Moreover, those selected are intended to give a representative, rather than a complete, picture of Dutch contributions to American life.

The number of Dutch immigrants who achieved national fame as politicians is small. Only two persons born in the Netherlands served in Congress during a one-hundred-sixty-year period extending from 1789 to 1949.[3] Several descendants of nineteenth- and twentieth-century Dutch immigrants, however, have had distinguished political careers at the national level. Gerrit John Diekema and Arthur Hendrick Vandenberg can be cited as examples.

Diekema was born in Holland, Michigan, in 1859 of Dutch immigrant parents. He graduated from the settlement's Hope College in 1881, and from the University of Michigan law school two years later. Most of his life was spent in his home town as a lawyer and banker, but politics was his chief interest. Diekema served six years as a member of the Michigan House of Representatives and two terms in the United States Congress. He became best known as a party organizer, having held several high positions in Republican state and national organizations. Because of his service to the GOP, and by reason of his Dutch background, President Hoover appointed him United States minister to the Netherlands in 1929, a position he was still holding at the time of his death in 1930.

Diekema exhibited several characteristics indicating his Dutch background. His father was a self-educated, God-fearing farmer, and Diekema freely acknowledged his father's influence on him. He also was a great admirer of Dominie Van Raalte. As a noted orator, his speeches were often filled with references to the glorious past of the Netherlands, and his addresses before Dutch-American audiences were sometimes delivered in the ancestral language. Diekema was a religious man, serving as superintendent of Sunday School in one of the Reformed churches of Holland for twenty-five years, and as leader of a large Men's Bible Class for twelve years. In his politics, he was conservative—at times, almost to the point of being reactionary.[4]

Arthur Hendrick Vandenberg was born at Grand Rapids, Michigan, in 1884, the son of a Dutch immigrant harness maker.[5] His mother was American-born, but of Dutch stock. He early decided on a career in journalism, and from 1906 to 1928 served as editor of the Grand Rapids *Herald*. Like Diekema, politics interested him at an early age, and he held several important posts in the state Republican organization before being appointed to fill a vacancy in the United States Senate in 1928.

Vandenberg was elected to this post a few months later, and was regularly reelected until his death in 1951. His career as a senator was distinguished from the beginning. After 1936, he was regularly mentioned as a possible presidential nominee for the Republican party.

Although Senator Vandenberg took a middle-of-the-road position on President Roosevelt's domestic legislation of the 1930's, he was for many years a confirmed isolationist in foreign policy, even opposing the Selective Service Act of 1940. Of the latter, he said, "Something precious goes out of the American way of life and something sinister takes its place under conscription." Pearl Harbor, however, changed him into an internationalist almost overnight, and he became one of the leading champions of a bipartisan foreign policy. As his party's principal spokesman on foreign affairs, he helped win Republican support for the United Nations, NATO, the Marshall Plan, and the Truman Doctrine. Dutch-Americans today can be truly proud that Vandenberg was one of them, and can only wonder what his influence on foreign policy would have been had he lived a few years longer.

New immigrants and their descendants were more active in state than national politics. John Meyers, for example, who was born in the Netherlands and was an important political figure among the Hollanders of the Chicago area during the late 1800's, served for a time as speaker of the lower house in the Illinois legislature. Frederic De Young, whose parents emigrated to Chicago in 1864, served in various public offices before becoming a justice of the Illinois Supreme Court (1924–34). Henry Hospers, who was Holland-born and became one of the guiding lights of the Dutch settlement in northwest Iowa, served as a state legislator for several terms. Similarly, Frank Le Cocq, Jr., son of immigrant parents and chief founder in 1882 of the Dutch settlement in Douglas County, South Dakota, became a member of the state legislature and also served as state railroad commissioner. Herman Liesveld, another Hollander, served two terms in the Nebraska state legislature during the 1880's. Frank Steunenburg, born of immigrant parents at Keokuk, Iowa, in 1861, became the fourth governor of Idaho (1896–1901).

Although few Dutch-Americans were attracted to socialism,

one of them, Daniel De Leon, achieved national prominence as a leader in the socialist movement. De Leon was born in 1852 in the Dutch colony of Curaçao, where his father served as surgeon in the colonial army. He received his early education there, but later moved to Amsterdam. In 1874, at the age of twenty-two, he emigrated to the United States, where, after studying law and political science at Columbia University, he busied himself briefly as a teacher. Very soon, however, he threw himself wholeheartedly into the socialist movement, and continued in this until his death in 1914. He became a leading force in the Socialist Labor party in 1890, and served as the editor of its paper, *The People*, for many years. He ran for governor of New York twice on the socialist ticket, as well as several times for the United States Congress. At Chicago, in 1905, together with Eugene Debs, he helped found the Industrial Workers of America.

De Leon's strong opposition to labor union leaders, whom he termed "fakers," frequently placed him at odds with more moderate socialists. His conversion to Marxism and the idea of class struggle helped bring about a split in the I.W.W. He wrote several works on socialism, one of the most notable being *Socialist Reconstruction of Society* (1905), in which he denounced the "robberburg of capitalism," and urged workers to unite for the overthrow of all exploitative systems—political as well as economic. His writings on socialist tactics won the admiration of Lenin, who once declared they contained the germ of the Soviet system.[6] Among Dutch-Americans, however, Daniel De Leon was a loner; his Dutch background was of little help in winning support among Hollanders for the socialist movement.

The contributions of Dutch-Americans in the advancement of science have been of great significance. This is perhaps nowhere better shown than in the field of physics. Cornelis Bol (b. 1885) came to the United States as a child when his parents emigrated to Montana. He left there in 1914, determined to pursue a career in science. That he succeeded is shown by his work as teacher and researcher at Stanford University from 1936 until his retirement in 1950. He is best known as the inventor of the Bol lamp, a tiny, mercury vapor lamp that gives off intense brilliance. Another noted research physicist was Robert J. Van de Graaf

(b. 1901), who joined the staff of the Massachusetts Institute of Technology in 1931. He is credited with building the first electrostatic generator, which became important in atom smashing. George E. Uhlenbeck (b. 1900) and Samuel A. Goudsmit (b. 1902), both trained in the Netherlands, became colleagues at the University of Michigan, where they achieved nationwide reputations as nuclear physicists.

By reason of the Netherlands' distinction in the training of astronomers, it was only natural that schools in the United States would draw upon Dutch universities for scientists in this field. These include, among others, Jan Schilt (b. 1894), Dirk Brouwer (b. 1902), and Bart Jan Bok (b. 1906), all of whom, after completing their training in the Netherlands, emigrated to the United States where their original research quickly attracted the attention of the scientific world. Schilt became chairman of the astronomy department at Columbia University and director of the Rutherford Observatory; Brouwer was a professor of astronomy and director of the observatory at Yale University; Bok, who was on the staff of Harvard University for many years, became head of the department of astronomy at the University of Arizona and director of the Steward Observatory.

Dutch-Americans who distinguished themselves in the field of chemistry include Izaak Maurits Kolthoff (b. 1894), who arrived in the United States in 1927 to become head of the department of analytical chemistry at the University of Minnesota. During his career, he published over seven hundred papers and articles on technical subjects. Peter J. W. Debye (b. 1884) came to America in 1940 to accept the chairmanship of the department of chemistry at Cornell University. He was already an established scholar before emigrating, having been awarded the Nobel Prize in chemistry in 1936.

Distinguished botanists include Arie Jan Haagen-Smit (b. 1900) and Frits W. Went (b. 1903). Both of these men were educated in the Netherlands, and arrived in the United States during the 1930's. Haagen-Smit, who taught at Harvard University and at the California Institute of Technology, became world-famous for his research on plant hormones. Went was attached to various institutions, the last being the Desert Research Institute of the University of Nevada, and became a widely recognized authority on the impact of climate on vegetation.

Medical science in the United States has also been ably served by persons of Dutch descent. Here, too, space permits mention of only a few names. Benjamin Spock (b. 1903), a descendant of James Spaak, who emigrated from the Netherlands and served in the Revolutionary War, became one of America's best-known pediatricians. His *Common Sense Book of Baby and Child Care* has sold over twenty million copies. William De Kleine (b. 1877), whose father emigrated to Michigan as a child, served as medical director of the American Red Cross from 1928 to 1941, and organized the Red Cross Blood Bank program during World War II. Joannes G. Dusser de Barenne (b. 1885) came to the United States in 1930 to direct the neurophysiological research laboratory at Yale University's School of Medicine. There he continued to publish innumerable scientific papers of the highest order, and was an inspiration to young physiologists who were just beginning their careers.

In veterinary medicine, there have been few equal in stature to Ralph R. Dykstra. Born in the Netherlands in 1879, he emigrated to the United States as a child. Immediately upon receiving his degree from Iowa State College in 1905, Dykstra joined the staff of the School of Veterinary Medicine at Kansas State College, serving as its dean from 1911 to 1948. He became especially well-known for his work in animal sanitation and disease control.

A discussion of Dutch-American men of science would be incomplete without mention of Paul De Kruif. Born in 1890 in Zeeland, Michigan, of immigrant parents, he attended the University of Michigan where he received a Ph.D. in biology in 1916. After a brief career as a bacteriologist, De Kruif turned to popular writing on medical and other scientific subjects. During his lifetime, he wrote thirteen books and more than two hundred magazine articles. Half of the latter were for *The Reader's Digest*, which he served as a contributing editor for more than twenty years. He also supplied much of the scientific material for Sinclair Lewis's novel *Arrowsmith*, which appeared in 1925, and collaborated with Sidney Coe Howard in writing

*Yellow Jack,* a 1934 Broadway hit that dramatized Dr. Walter Reed's fight against yellow fever. As a popularizer of medical science, De Kruif has had few peers. His best-known work, *Microbe Hunters* (1926), is about pioneers in bacteriology; it sold over a million copies, and was translated into eighteen languages.

American technology became the envy of the world during the twentieth century, and persons of Dutch descent played an important role in this growth. As was true in so many fields of activity, the American ancestry of some of these men goes back to the New Netherland period. Curtis Hussey Veeder (b. 1862), the descendant of a Hollander who came to America in 1642, was issued more than a hundred United States patents and nearly as many foreign patents on his inventions. Even more significant were the accomplishments of Lee De Forest (b. 1873), a descendant of Isaak De Forest, who left the Netherlands for New Amsterdam about the middle of the seventeenth century. Because of his achievements in electronics, especially the perfection of the vacuum tube, he has sometimes been called the "father of radio broadcasting." De Forest also did pioneer work in developing sound motion pictures and television.

In contrast to Veeder and De Forest, David Christiaan Henry (b. 1860) and Carl Lucas Norden (b. 1880) were Dutch immigrants. Henry arrived in 1884, and spent several years working as an engineer in various parts of the United States before organizing his own consulting firm at San Francisco in 1892. Specializing in waterworks, irrigation projects, and power construction, he served as a consulting engineer to several federal agencies as well as state and municipal bodies. He became particularly known as one of America's leading experts on dam-building, and was either the builder or a consulting engineer on most of the big dams constructed in the West during the decades prior to World War II, including Grand Coulee and Boulder.

Carl Norden was employed by various manufacturers after his arrival in the United States about 1900, before establishing his own practice in Brooklyn as a consulting engineer. In 1921, the United States Navy asked him to study the problems of precision bombing. As a consequence, he helped perfect in 1930 the Navy's Mark XV bombsight, commonly known as the

Norden bombsight, which did not become obsolete until the appearance of jet bombers. It was one of the military's most carefully guarded secrets, and enabled American planes during World War II to carry out high-altitude, daylight precision bombing as a substitute for the low-level, nighttime bombing used by the British. For the rights to this instrument, Norden charged the United States government the sum of one dollar. After the war, Norden continued to design military aviation devices, including radio-controlled target planes, launching equipment for aircraft carriers, and robot flying bombs.

Dutch-Americans have also made their mark in the social sciences. The field of history can be taken as an example. Henry Lucas (b. 1889) was the grandson of an immigrant who accompanied Van Raalte's band to Michigan in 1847. Educated in the colony's own Hope College, he received a Ph.D. in history from the University of Michigan and studied for a time in Holland and Belgium. In 1921, he accepted a position at the University of Washington, remaining there until his retirement in 1959. Lucas became an acknowledged authority on the history of Europe during the Renaissance and Reformation, and also did considerable research and writing on the history of the Dutch in America. Another Dutch-American who went far in the academic world and who was trained as a historian was Cornelis Willem De Kiewiet. Born in Holland in 1902, he became an authority on South Africa, where he lived for a time. In 1929, De Kiewiet came to the United States, joining the history department at the University of Iowa. In 1935, he went to Cornell University as a professor of history, where he remained until 1951, when he became president of the University of Rochester, a post he held until his retirement in 1961.

De Kiewiet was only one of many Dutch-Americans who served as college and university presidents. Clarence A. Dykstra (b. 1883), whose grandparents were immigrants, took his formal academic training in political science. After serving in various civic offices, including that of City Manager of Cincinnati, he became president of the University of Wisconsin in 1937. He relinquished this post in 1945 to become provost of the University of California at Los Angeles. Some indication of Dykstra's standing in the academic community is shown by his being awarded honorary degrees by some of the most prestigious schools in the United States, including Harvard, Johns Hopkins, Rutgers, and Northwestern.

Garret Droppers (b. 1860), whose grandfather emigrated from the Netherlands to Wisconsin in 1842, received an excellent education in economics at Harvard and the University of Berlin. After teaching economics for nine years at the University of Tokyo, he served as president of the University of South Dakota (1898–1906). Upon resigning the presidency, Droppers held various academic and civic positions before being appointed minister to Greece by President Woodrow Wilson in 1914. With the outbreak of World War I and the political strife existing in the Balkans when the war ended, his task as chief American diplomat in Greece was not an easy one. According to all accounts, however, Droppers served his country ably until ill health forced him to resign in 1920.

Other Dutch-Americans who served as college and university presidents include Charles Van Hise (University of Wisconsin, 1903–18); John Scholte Nollen, grandson of Dominie Scholte, founder of Pella, Iowa (Grinnell College, 1931–40); Barend H. Kroeze (Jamestown College, 1909–46); Harry D. Gideonse (Brooklyn College, 1939–66, and the New School of Social Research, 1966–); and Gerrit T. Vander Lugt (Carrol College, 1940–46). The last three individuals were Netherlands-born. Obviously, nearly all the presidents of the Dutch Reformed and Christian Reformed colleges and seminaries in the United States have also been persons of Dutch extraction.

Americans of recent Dutch descent have also distinguished themselves in the field of literature. In this, they have merely followed the footsteps of several writers whose American ancestry goes back to colonial days. The latter group includes several of the nineteenth century, such as Walt Whitman (1819–92), who was of mixed Dutch and English ancestry, and Herman Melville (1819–91), whose mother was a Gansevoort, one of the oldest Dutch families of New York State. Even more signifi cant among those whose American ancestry dates back to colonial days have been several in the twentieth century whose names have become immortal in the annals of American litera· ture. These include Van Wyck Brooks (b. 1886) and the Van

Doren brothers, Carl (b. 1885) and Mark (b. 1894). Van Wyck
Brooks, who was of Dutch blood from both his father and
mother, became one of America's leading authorities on American literature and winner of a Pulitzer Prize in 1937. The Van
Dorens descended from Pieter Van Doren, who settled in New
Netherland sometime before 1657. Famous as teachers, novelists,
poets, and literary critics, the Van Dorens were also recipients of
Pulitzer Prizes—Carl for his biography of Benjamin Franklin in
1939, and Mark for his *Collected Poems, 1922–1938* in 1940.

Hendrick Willem Van Loon became one of the best known
of the Dutch-American writers who emigrated from the Netherlands. Born in 1882, he came to the United States in 1903 at
the age of twenty-one. He was at various times in his life an
Associated Press correspondent in Europe and visiting lecturer
at schools in the United States and abroad. As a classmate and
good friend of Franklin Roosevelt, Van Loon was frequently a
guest at the White House. He is best known, however, as an
author, having written nearly forty books, all in a popular vein
and mostly in the field of history. His books have sold over six
million copies, and have been translated into more than twenty
languages. He was especially interested in Dutch history and
wrote frequently on that subject, but his best-known works
are *The Story of Mankind* (1921), *The Story of the Bible* (1923),
and *Van Loon's Geography* (1932).

Pierre Van Paassen (b. 1895) was also born and reared in
the Netherlands, emigrating to Canada in 1914 and later to
the United States. He worked at various jobs before becoming
a roving European correspondent for the New York *Evening
World* (1924–31) and the *Toronto Star* (1932–35). He covered
several major events during those years, such as the Italian invasion of Ethiopia and the Spanish Civil War. He also had interviews with many important personalities, including several
with Hitler and Mussolini. The author of many books and articles, his best-known work was *Days of Our Years* (1939), a
kind of autobiography in which he surveyed and passed judg-
ment on a wide variety of world events he had reported on as
a correspondent. It was a choice of the Book-of-the-Month Club
and became a spectacular best seller. A long-time supporter of
the Zionist movement and an advocate of Jewish statehood,

Jewish editors in the United States and Canada in 1934 voted Van Paassen one of the greatest Christian friends of Jews.

As was true of other ethnic groups, the problems that Dutch immigrants and their children experienced in adjusting to the American way of life were often portrayed in fiction. Arnold Mulder (b. 1885), for example, between 1913 and 1921 wrote four novels about life among the Dutch in Michigan, the best known being *The Dominie of Harlem* (1913) and *The Outbound Road* (1919). In general, his works describe the conflicts, both fancied and real, between the values of the first generation of Dutch immigrants and those of their offspring, who considered the life of their parents dull and too conservative, as well as often hypocritical. A reader need not venture far into Mulder's novels to know that his sympathies were obviously with the younger generation. *The Bells of Helmus* (1934), by Cobie De Lespinasse, was written in a spirit similar to that of Mulder's works, but the setting was the Dutch community of Orange City, Iowa, instead of the Michigan settlements. More sympathetic toward the immigrants was Sara Elizabeth Gosselink's *Roofs Over Strawtown* (1945), describing life among the Hollanders of early Pella, Iowa.

David Cornell De Jong was another Dutch-American author who frequently used his own experiences among the Dutch as subject matter for his writings. Born in the Netherlands in 1905, he came to the United States with his parents in 1918, settling at Grand Rapids, Michigan. In his lifetime, he wrote nine novels and an autobiography as well as numerous poems and short stories. His first novel, *Belly Fulla Straw* (1934), which was highly praised, described a Dutch immigrant family—father, mother, and four children—and the frustrations they experienced in becoming Americanized. *Old Haven* (1938), which has his boyhood province of Friesland for a setting, won a Houghton Mifflin Prize. His autobiography, *With a Dutch Accent* (1944), describes his early life in the Netherlands, and the humor and heartaches he later experienced as a boy trying to adjust to American ways. *The Saturday Review of Literature* stated that this book "deserves an honorable position alongside the autobiographies or thinly disguised autobiographical fiction of such adopted sons of America as Rolvaag, Lewisohn, Adamic, and McFee."[7]

Meindert De Jong (b. 1910), a brother of David, is the author of about twenty books for young people. His success as a writer of children's fiction is shown by his having received the Newbery Medal in 1955, the Hans Christian Andersen Children's Book Award in 1962, and the National Book Award in 1968. The last award was granted for his *Journey from Peppermint Street*, a 242-page account of the experiences of a nine-year-old boy from a fishing village in the Netherlands. A reviewer of it stated that "no other author so successfully plumbs the emotional depths of childhood" as does Meindert De Jong.[8]

One of the best-known contemporary Dutch-American literary figures is Peter De Vries. Born in Chicago in 1910 of immigrant parents, he grew up in a strict Calvinist environment that included a parochial high school education and four years at Calvin College in Grand Rapids, Michigan, from which he graduated in 1931. His first novel was published in 1939 and was well received. Other novels, together with short stories and miscellaneous writings, have appeared at irregular intervals. Since 1944, De Vries has also served on the editorial staff of *The New Yorker*. His best-known work, *The Tunnel of Love* (1954), a comic novel, not only became a best seller, but was adapted for the Broadway stage, where it ran for a year. It was also made into a motion picture, released in 1958. Also well received was *The Vale of Laughter* (1967), which Oscar Handlin termed De Vries' best book. *The Blood of the Lamb* (1962), which is at least partly autobiographical, is one of his most serious works. The first part of it contains considerable description about life among the stern Dutch Calvinists. After reading innumerable reviews of De Vries' books, one can only conclude that much of his success as a writer is due to an uncanny ability to mix humor, satire, and sophistication in the proper amounts.

Journalism, too, attracted the interest of some Dutch-Americans, and several of them achieved national fame. One of the most successful was Edward William Bok (b. 1863), who emigrated to America with his parents in 1869 at the age of six, settling in Brooklyn, New York. Because of poverty, he quit school at the age of thirteen to work for Western Union and later for various publishing firms. By virtue of his writing talents and managerial skills, he was made editor of the *Ladies Home Journal* in 1889, remaining in this position until 1919. Due to Bok's numerous innovations and high literary standards, its circulation doubled within a few years, and totaled over two million when he retired in 1919. Upon retirement, he was offered the post of ambassador to the Netherlands, but declined it, preferring to devote himself full-time to philanthropic causes. In his will, he bequeathed two million dollars to charities. The author of several books, Bok was awarded a Pulitzer Prize for his autobiography, *The Americanization of Edward Bok* (1920). It sold over one-quarter million copies and became a classic in American autobiographical literature.

Other important journalists include Cyrenus Cole (b. 1863) and Henry Fris (b. 1884). Cole, whose parents accompanied Scholte's immigrants to Pella, Iowa, in 1847, was an editorial writer for the *Des Moines Register* from 1891 to 1898, and thereafter until 1921 was closely associated with the Cedar Rapids *Republican* and *Evening Times*. He left this position to become a United States congressman in 1921, a position he held for twelve years. Cole also wrote several books, of which the best known, *I Remember, I Remember* (1936), is autobiographical and shows the writer's nostalgic feelings for his Dutch Calvinist upbringing. Fris, who was born in the Netherlands, was associated with various newspapers in Michigan, Wisconsin, Texas, and Arizona before joining the Hearst organization in 1928. Thereafter, he served first as publisher of the *Times-Union* of Albany, New York, and later of the *Sentinel* of Milwaukee, Wisconsin.

The mainstream of American life has also drawn from the Dutch-Americans for some of its musicians. In the twentieth century, these included opera singers, composers, conductors, and critics, as well as numerous instrumentalists. Gladys Swarthout, born in the small Missouri town of Deepwater in 1904, could trace her American ancestry to the New Netherland period. Endowed with a beautiful voice, she rose from singing in the church choir to feature billing for sixteen years (1929–45) with the Metropolitan Opera Company of New York. Miss Swarthout was blessed with beauty as well as a fine voice, and

*Current Biography* in 1944 stated that she "was one of the first singers to prove that a Metropolitan Opera star need not be fat, frumpy, or foreign." She also appeared in countless concerts and radio programs and several movies.

Carl Van Vechten, born at Cedar Rapids, Iowa in 1880, left the Middle West for New York, where his first American ancestor, Teunis Dircksen Van Vechten, had settled in 1638. Carl's fame in music stemmed not from his being a performer but from his being a music critic. In addition to serving in that capacity for various New York newspapers and publishers, he wrote several books about music, of which *The Music of Spain* (1918) is one of the best known.

Two Dutch-Americans, born and educated in the Netherlands, who achieved fame as musicians in recent decades were Richard Hageman and Hans Kindler. Hageman, who came to the United States in 1906, served as conductor of several orchestras, including that of the Metropolitan Opera from 1914 to 1926 and that of the Hollywood Bowl after 1938. He was best known, however, as a composer, and his works ranged from popular songs to operas. Hageman's compositions included innumerable motion picture scores for which he received several high awards from the film industry. Hans Kindler came to the United States in 1914, performing first as a cellist with various orchestras. Increasingly, however, he turned his attention to conducting. In 1931, he helped found the National Symphony Orchestra of Washington, D.C., and served as its conductor until his retirement in 1949. It became not only one of America's finest orchestras, but also one of the busiest; between 1932 and 1941, it gave two hundred sixty-three concerts in ninety-four cities outside Washington. Kindler also made many arrangements for orchestras and composed several original pieces.

Willem Van de Wall's fame as a musician was different from the usual. Born in Amsterdam in 1887 and educated at the Royal Conservatory of Music in The Hague, he was engaged as a harpist in concert and opera work in Europe before coming to the United States in 1909. In his adopted country, he performed with several nationally known orchestras and taught at various universities. He became especially famous, however, as a pioneer in the scientific use of music as therapy for mentally disturbed people as well as for sick persons and prison inmates. Much of Van de Wall's time from 1921 until his death in 1953 was spent in researching this very important subject and publishing the results of his findings.

A few Hollanders have also had influence on American art. Piet Mondrian (b. 1872) is best known for his totally abstract or nonrepresentational art, which came to be known as Neoplasticism or *De Stijl*. Because he spent only the last four years of his life (1940–44) in America, it is open to question whether Mondrian should be classified as a Dutch-American. There is, however, some justification for taking note of him here. His ideas had long been influential on American painting, design, sculpture, and architecture, and his "actual presence in the United States" after 1940, according to one authority, gave "a great impetus toward purely formal abstraction."[9] Furthermore, the artist himself, in an interview shortly before his death, expressed great admiration for the United States, declaring, "I feel here is the place to be, and I am becoming an American citizen."[10]

Willem De Kooning (b. 1904) came to America in 1926, shortly after graduating from an art academy in Rotterdam, his birthplace. Supporting himself at first as a housepainter and commercial artist, he devoted his spare moments to serious painting. About 1934, he began painting in an abstract style, and by the late 1940's was considered one of America's leading abstract expressionist painters. Some indication of De Kooning's fame is shown in his selection by the Museum of Modern Art in 1954 as one of two painters to represent contemporary American art at the twenty-seventh Biennale International Art Exhibition in Venice, Italy.

Saco Rienk De Boer (b. 1883) was engaged in a completely different type of art. Born and educated in the Netherlands, he came to the United States in 1908 at the age of twenty-five, becoming one of America's better-known city planners and landscape architects. For many years, De Boer served as a consultant to several cities in the West and Southwest, as well as to various public and private institutions and agencies.

Military service, too, has attracted persons of Dutch descent, and many of them have risen high in its ranks. Included among those of recent years are three men who became distinguished generals. James A. Van Fleet saw service in World Wars I and II, and was commander of United Nations Forces in Korea from 1951 to 1953. Alexander A. Vandergrift was Commandant of the Marine Corps (1944–47) and the first Marine Corps officer to hold the rank of permanent general. Hoyt S. Vandenberg was Chief of Staff of the United States Air Force from 1948 to 1953.

Cornelius Vanderbilt was not the only person of humble background with an American ancestry going back to the New Netherland period who made it big in the business world. A similar story of success was that of Gilbert C. Van Camp (1817–1900), whose first American ancestor emigrated from the Netherlands to New Jersey during the seventeenth century. Having a talent for invention and ingenuity, he began experimenting with the preservation of fruits, vegetables, and meats—first by means of cold storage and later by canning. In 1882, the Van Camp Packing Company was incorporated, which by the close of the century was using six million tin cans a year, and was shipping its products to every state in the union as well as to Europe. Upon his retirement in 1898, the business was taken over by his three sons. One of the latter, Frank (b. 1863), sold his interest in 1914 and moved to California, where he established the Van Camp Sea Food Company, which within a short time was grossing annual sales of over eleven million dollars.

Another famous manufacturer, who also was the descendant of a New Netherland immigrant, was John Manning Van Heusen (1869–1931). Best known today as a shirt manufacturer, he began his career as a clerk in an Albany bank. Having an inventive turn of mind, Van Heusen soon began making his living as an inventor and designer. During the period 1913–20, he obtained patents on collars, cuffs, neck bands, and other wearing apparel. A firm known as Van Heusen Products was soon organized, and its products were rapidly distributed throughout the world, especially the unique shirt collar which had the appearance of a laundered collar although it was starchless and very comfortable.

The success of men like Vanderbilt, Van Camp, and others was not without influence in convincing numerous inhabitants of the Netherlands between the Civil War and World War I that America was indeed the land of opportunity. Many of those who emigrated during that period tried to repeat the achievements of these men. Although their success was more limited, that of their sons and grandsons frequently gave ample proof that a person of humble background could reach the pinnacle of success in the United States through perseverance and hard work. A good example is John Dykstra (b. 1898), who came to the United States with his parents in 1904 at the age of four. His parents having settled at Detroit, Michigan, it was not surprising that he sought employment in the automotive industry. He began work at the age of sixteen as an apprentice die maker, but took night courses in mechanical engineering. After serving two years in World War I, he returned to his old job but also enrolled in correspondence courses in foremanship. He advanced rapidly to important executive positions with General Motors Corporation (1934–47) and thereafter with the Ford Motor Company. In 1961, John Dykstra reached the summit in the business world when he was elected sixth president of the Ford firm.[11]

The Hekman brothers, Henry (b. 1885), John (b. 1886), and Jelle (b. 1888), are also notable examples of Dutch immigrants who came to America as children and who made good in the world of business. Their father, Edsko, who had been a baker in the Netherlands, emigrated with his family in 1893. Unable to find work on his arrival in Michigan, he started a bakery in Grand Rapids in 1894, using a simple kitchen cook stove. With the help of his sons, the business grew rapidly, branching out to neighboring towns and also into other enterprises. In time, the Hekman Brothers Company comprised three nationally known firms—the Hekman Biscuit Company and the Hekman Furniture Company, both of Grand Rapids, and the Dutch Tea Rusk Company of Holland, Michigan. The Hekman Biscuit Company later became part of the United Biscuit Company, whose name was changed to the Keebler Company in 1965. The latter presently markets products in some forty-five states.[12]

Another remarkable family of Dutch-Americans who made good in the business world were the Nollens, sons of an immigrant father and grandsons of Dominie Henry Scholte, founder of Pella, Iowa. Gerard Scholte Nollen (b. 1880) became president of Bankers' Life Company of Des Moines in 1926. Within little more than a decade, the assets of this firm increased from $81,000,000 to $216,000,000, making it one of the largest insurance companies west of the Mississippi River. In 1921, a brother, Henry (b. 1866), became president of Equitable Life Insurance Company of Iowa, which was only slightly smaller than Bankers' Life.

CHAPTER XIV

# Epilogue

DUTCH-AMERICANS, ALTHOUGH NOT AS NUMEROUS AS SOME OTHER ethnic groups, constitute an important segment of the American population. Numerous geographical place-names in the eastern states and the existence of nearly one hundred Reformed churches that predate the Revolution are reminders that the Dutch were among the first to establish permanent settlements in the United States. By reason of the many generations that have passed since the first Hollanders came to American shores and the tens of thousands who arrived after the Civil War, Americans who are of at least partial Dutch descent can presently be numbered in the millions.

Dutch immigrants and their immediate descendants frequently clustered together, first in New Netherland and then elsewhere as the frontier was pushed steadily westward, thereby establishing numerous ethnic communities across the length and breadth of America. These included rural towns with an almost wholly Dutch population, and "racial" enclaves located in the cities. They were distinguished from other communities by the degree to which their inhabitants displayed certain characteristics, including conservatism, individualism, frugality, clannishness, and an unusual concern for religious matters. Although these traits were not always constant and present, and although they could also be found among other ethnic groups, writers from early colonial times to the present have associated them in a special way with Dutch-American communities.

Religion was of tremendous influence as a binding force in maintaining Dutch culture for long periods of time. Despite a sharp decline in emigration from Holland after the fall of New Netherland to the English in 1664, travelers more than a century later still noted the existence of Dutch traits in parts of the

[ 257 ]

Hudson Valley, Long Island, and northern New Jersey. Religion, with church services in the Dutch language, was the primary cause for the perpetuation of this identification. This religious influence also accounts in large part for the persistence of the basic features of Dutch life and thought among certain communities established during the nineteenth century.

Although traits such as conservatism and frugality have been traditionally associated with the Dutch, it is difficult to measure these characteristics exactly. A comparison with traits of inhabitants of the Netherlands is of some help, but is beset with difficulties. The complex historical development of the Netherlands since the time of the Middle Ages resulted in a patchwork pattern of social customs. Consequently, an immigrant who hailed from one province often carried in his "baggage" a different set of customs than did an immigrant from another province. Furthermore, because of the phenomenal changes that have taken place in the Netherlands since World War II, an examination of present-day Dutch society does not yield a dependable picture as to how Dutch-Americans of past generations thought and behaved. It is also a moot question whether certain traits of Dutch-Americans are inherent in the Dutch psyche or are to be ascribed to the stern moral and economic views associated with Calvinism.

Americanization has naturally altered the ideas and customs of Dutch immigrants and their progeny, which adds to the difficulty in being precise about Dutch-American traits and their origins. Although the process of change among immigrants was frequently slow and imperceptible, metamorphosis was inevitable. Separated from the land of their forebears and surrounded by an environment at variance to that of the Netherlands, they had to adjust to their new surroundings; to continue to think and act solely as Netherlanders would have limited their chance of success in the New World. President Theodore Roosevelt, proud of his Dutch descent, pointed out the need for such a mutation and its effect in an address on January 10, 1890, before the prestigious Holland Society of New York:

We of the old Holland blood of New York have just cause to be proud of the men of note in American history who have come from among us.... [But] the point on which I wish to insist, is, that the Hollanders could never have played such a part, could never have won honorable renown by doing their full share in shaping the destiny of the republic, had they remained Hollanders instead of becoming Americans.... Had they remained aliens in speech and habit of thought, Schuyler would have been a mere boorish provincial squire instead of a major-general in the Revolutionary army, Van Buren would have been a country tavern-keeper instead of President of the mightiest republic the world has ever seen, and Vanderbilt would have remained an unknown boatman instead of becoming one of the most potent architects of the marvelous American industrial fabric; while the mass of our people, not having become Americans, would ... have rusted into a condition of inert, useless, and contemptuously disregarded provincialism.[1]

Despite frequent clannishness and certain traits that are ascribed to them, the Dutch, unlike some other ethnic groups, have never been serious victims of persecution in the United States. Know-Nothingism before the Civil War was directed at immigrants in general, and not specifically against the Dutch. The same can be said about criticism of persons speaking anything other than English during World War I. It is true that expressions were and are occasionally heard which could be considered disparaging to the Dutch, such as "Dutch treat" and "Dutch bargain," implying that they are stingy and parsimonious, and "dunderhead" and "clodhopper," implying that they are also dull-witted and boorish. Dutch-Americans, however, apparently have not been sensitive to such slurs. Libraries, for example, are not asked to remove copies of Washington Irving's books from their shelves because they contain passages that lampoon the Dutch. Nor are businessmen asked to remove signs announcing a "Dutch auction." A leading department store in midtown Manhattan has had a "Dutch Treat Restaurant" for several years, and it is unlikely that its manager has ever had a complaint about the choice of name.

Undoubtedly, one of the reasons Dutch-Americans have been well-accepted in the United States stems from the reputation the mother country enjoys in the minds of many Americans. School-book stories such as those about the brave lad who put his finger in the dike have helped create in young minds a favorable impression (one might even say legend) about the Dutch; so, too, has John Lothrop Motley's exaggerated account of Holland's heroic struggle for independence from the tyranny of Spain during the Eighty Years' War. Certain "trademarks" commonly associated with the Netherlands, including tulips, windmills, wooden shoes, and canals add to the idealized portrait Americans have about the inhabitants of the Netherlands. To these stories and ideas can be added Holland's long-standing reputation for tolerance, by which Pilgrims from England, Huguenots from France, and Jewish victims of Nazi persecution were often given protection and sanctuary. No doubt, Holland's herculean task of reclaiming land from the sea, and her global commercial enterprises, have also added to this favorable image.

Nothing in this study has been intended to exaggerate the role of the Dutch in American life. The United States is truly a "nation of nations," and no one ethnic group has an exclusive claim to having made it a great country. Dutch-Americans, along with Italian-Americans, Swedish-Americans, Afro-Americans, and many other groups have all played significant roles. Although the formerly accepted concept of an American "melting pot" is being modified, there is still considerable truth to the motto *E pluribus unum*—"out of many, one." This is clearly revealed in noting that candidates for the offices of President and Vice-President during the past half century have been drawn from a variety of ethnic backgrounds, including Dutch, English, Greek, Indian, Irish, Jewish, and Polish. An examination of persons who have achieved distinction in business, education, science, and the arts would indicate similar ethnic diversity.

The Dutch in America have in many ways behaved like their neighbors. They have had certain likes and dislikes as well as prejudices and hang-ups; there have been a few great and near-great among them, but also some failures. They have shown a respect for law and order, a determination to succeed in business, a fond hope of obtaining a good education for their children, and a wish to lead a happy, family life. In short, the Dutch-Americans have had about the same hopes and aspirations that have characteristically motivated most people, regardless of their ethnic background.

# Tables

TABLE 1

DISTRIBUTION OF THE DUTCH POPULATION
IN THE UNITED STATES IN 1790

A study based on local registers, tax lists, genealogical diction-
aries, church records, census lists, etc., of the white population
of the United States in 1790 gives the following figures for
persons of Dutch birth or ancestry:

| State | White population | Dutch | Dutch percentage |
|---|---|---|---|
| Maine | 96,107 | 100 | 0.1 |
| New Hampshire | 141,112 | 100 | .1 |
| Vermont | 85,072 | 500 | .6 |
| Massachusetts | 373,187 | 600 | .2 |
| Rhode Island | 64,670 | 250 | .4 |
| Connecticut | 232,236 | 600 | .3 |
| New York | 314,366 | 55,000 | 17.5 |
| New Jersey | 169,954 | 28,250 | 16.6 |
| Pennsylvania | 423,373 | 7,500 | 1.8 |
| Delaware | 46,310 | 2,000 | 4.3 |
| Maryland | 208,649 | 1,000 | .5 |
| Virginia | 442,117 | 1,500 | .3 |
| North Carolina | 289,181 | 800 | .3 |
| South Carolina | 140,178 | 500 | .4 |
| Georgia | 52,886 | 100 | .2 |
| Kentucky and Tennessee | 93,046 | 1,200 | 1.3 |
| Area enumerated | 3,172,444 | 100,000 | 3.4 |

Source: "Report of the Committee on Linguistics and National
Stocks in the Population of the United States," *Annual Report
of the American Historical Association for the Year 1931* (1932),
I, pages 124–25. See also pages 363–79, 396–97.

TABLE 2

COMPARISON OF THE DUTCH POPULATION
IN THE UNITED STATES IN 1790 WITH
OTHER NATIONAL OR LINGUISTIC STOCKS

| Nationality | Total of area enumerated | Percentage |
|---|---|---|
| White population | 3,172,444 | 100.0 |
| English | 1,933,416 | 60.9 |
| Scotch | 260,322 | 8.3 |
| Irish (Ulster) | 190,075 | 6.0 |
| Irish (Free State) | 115,886 | 3.7 |
| German | 276,940 | 8.7 |
| Dutch | 100,000 | 3.4 |
| French | 54,900 | 1.7 |
| Swedish | 21,100 | .7 |
| Unassigned | 219,805 | 6.6 |

Source: *Ibid.*, pages 124–25.

TABLE 3

IMMIGRATION FROM THE NETHERLANDS
TO THE UNITED STATES SINCE 1821

By decades 1821–1970:

| | | | | |
|---|---|---|---|---|
| 1821–1830 | 1,078 | | 1901–1910 | 48,262 |
| 1831–1840 | 1,412 | | 1911–1920 | 43,718 |
| 1841–1850 | 8,251 | | 1921–1930 | 26,948 |
| 1851–1860 | 10,789 | | 1931–1940 | 7,150 |
| 1861–1870 | 9,102 | | 1941–1950 | 14,860 |
| 1871–1880 | 16,541 | | 1951–1960 | 52,277 |
| 1881–1890 | 53,701 | | 1961–1970 | 30,606 |
| 1891–1900 | 26,758 | | | |

Annual immigration since World War II:

| 1945 | 50 | 1955 | 3,555 | 1965 | 2,356 |
|---|---|---|---|---|---|
| 1946 | 355 | 1956 | 5,040 | 1966 | 1,924 |
| 1947 | 2,936 | 1957 | 14,958 | 1967 | 1,786 |
| 1948 | 3,999 | 1958 | 3,102 | 1968 | 2,051 |
| 1949 | 3,330 | 1959 | 4,278 | 1969 | 1,285 |
| 1950 | 3,080 | 1960 | 8,654 | 1970 | 1,342 |
| 1951 | 3,062 | 1961 | 7,362 | 1971 | 1,092 |
| 1952 | 3,060 | 1962 | 6,378 | 1972 | 979 |
| 1953 | 2,973 | 1963 | 4,086 | | |
| 1954 | 3,595 | 1964 | 2,039 | | |

Total 152 years 1821–1972: 353,524

Figures for 1821–67 represent alien passengers arrived; those for 1868–91 and 1895–97, immigrant aliens arrived; those for 1892–94 and 1898–1972, immigrant aliens admitted. Data is for fiscal years ending June 30. Source: United States Department of Justice, *Annual Report of the Immigration and Naturalization Service*, Table 13, for the years 1949, 1955, 1960, 1967, and 1972.

TABLE 4

DISTRIBUTION OF FOREIGN-BORN DUTCH
IMMIGRANTS BY STATE ACCORDING TO DECADE

| | 1850 | 1860 | 1870 | 1880 | 1890 |
|---|---|---|---|---|---|
| Alabama | 1 | 26 | 14 | 27 | 26 |
| Alaska | | | | | |
| Arizona | | | | | 17 |
| Arkansas | 2 | 4 | 71 | 66 | 87 |
| California | 63 | 439 | 452 | 694 | 760 |
| Colorado | | | | 115 | 192 |
| Connecticut | 19 | 70 | 99 | 122 | 121 |
| Delaware | 5 | 3 | 16 | 10 | 12 |
| Florida | 8 | 7 | 7 | 19 | 42 |
| Georgia | 11 | 27 | 42 | 36 | 29 |
| Hawaii | | | | | |
| Idaho | | | | | 23 |
| Illinois | 220 | 1,416 | 4,180 | 5,012 | 8,762 |
| Indiana | 43 | 450 | 873 | 1,368 | 1,157 |
| Iowa | 1,108 | 2,615 | 4,513 | 4,743 | 7,941 |
| Kansas | | 45 | 300 | 749 | 872 |
| Kentucky | 38 | 154 | 270 | 262 | 135 |
| Louisiana | 112 | 262 | 232 | 170 | 76 |
| Maine | 12 | 16 | 26 | 16 | 16 |
| Maryland | 106 | 376 | 236 | 362 | 122 |
| Massachusetts | 138 | 351 | 480 | 586 | 609 |
| Michigan | 2,542 | 6,335 | 12,559 | 17,177 | 29,410 |
| Minnesota | | 391 | 1,855 | 1,581 | 1,796 |
| Mississippi | 8 | 39 | 35 | 27 | 25 |
| Missouri | 189 | 769 | 1,167 | 1,122 | 740 |
| Montana | | | | | 103 |

Source: Data from the decennial reports of the United States Bureau of the Census.

TABLE 4 (*continued*)

## DISTRIBUTION OF FOREIGN-BORN DUTCH IMMIGRANTS BY STATE ACCORDING TO DECADE

| 1900 | 1910 | 1920 | 1930 | 1940 | 1950 | 1960 | 1970 |
|---|---|---|---|---|---|---|---|
| 42 | 127 | 83 | 95 | 80 | 87 | 144 | 184 |
|  |  |  |  |  |  | 52 | 57 |
| 23 | 41 | 69 | 100 | 99 | 204 | 529 | 727 |
| 69 | 145 | 116 | 80 | 70 | 82 | 44 | 129 |
| 1,015 | 2,304 | 4,592 | 8,897 | 9,754 | 12,270 | 23,513 | 27,993 |
| 260 | 710 | 853 | 810 | 683 | 568 | 966 | 948 |
| 153 | 304 | 444 | 548 | 522 | 654 | 1,132 | 1,390 |
| 69 | 20 | 37 | 56 | 38 | 58 | 250 | 236 |
| 52 | 85 | 357 | 476 | 683 | 1,196 | 3,132 | 3,790 |
| 38 | 52 | 78 | 67 | 63 | 101 | 287 | 348 |
|  |  |  |  |  |  | 90 | 137 |
| 50 | 261 | 439 | 341 | 324 | 296 | 383 | 396 |
| 11,916 | 14,402 | 14,344 | 14,828 | 11,634 | 8,973 | 7,734 | 5,825 |
| 1,678 | 2,131 | 2,018 | 1,992 | 1,617 | 1,525 | 1,729 | 1,530 |
| 9,388 | 11,337 | 12,471 | 10,135 | 7,840 | 6,078 | 4,335 | 3,087 |
| 875 | 906 | 675 | 513 | 332 | 262 | 323 | 432 |
| 136 | 140 | 150 | 112 | 124 | 96 | 152 | 147 |
| 78 | 113 | 260 | 220 | 212 | 263 | 367 | 389 |
| 22 | 27 | 50 | 41 | 52 | 66 | 69 | 122 |
| 220 | 203 | 314 | 343 | 333 | 520 | 912 | 1,269 |
| 993 | 1,597 | 2,071 | 1,890 | 1,728 | 1,723 | 1,902 | 2,118 |
| 30,406 | 33,471 | 33,499 | 32,128 | 24,722 | 20,215 | 20,395 | 15,095 |
| 2,717 | 3,542 | 5,380 | 4,832 | 4,153 | 3,512 | 2,649 | 2,354 |
| 41 | 34 | 31 | 32 | 39 | 58 | 88 | 51 |
| 812 | 988 | 906 | 706 | 532 | 456 | 451 | 440 |
| 316 | 1,054 | 1,675 | 1,253 | 941 | 786 | 748 | 530 |

TABLE 4 (*continued*)

## DISTRIBUTION OF FOREIGN-BORN DUTCH IMMIGRANTS BY STATE ACCORDING TO DECADE

| | 1850 | 1860 | 1870 | 1880 | 1890 |
|---|---|---|---|---|---|
| Nebraska | | | 180 | 753 | 1,149 |
| Nevada | | | 44 | 21 | 4 |
| New Hampshire | 1 | 8 | 5 | 11 | 10 |
| New Jersey | 357 | 1,328 | 2,944 | 4,281 | 7,924 |
| New Mexico | | | | | 46 |
| New York | 2,917 | 5,354 | 6,426 | 8,399 | 8,366 |
| North Carolina | 4 | 15 | 13 | 23 | 7 |
| North Dakota | | | | | 288 |
| Ohio | 348 | 1,756 | 2,018 | 2,455 | 1,514 |
| Oklahoma | | | | | 6 |
| Oregon | | 15 | 39 | 127 | 244 |
| Pennsylvania | 257 | 766 | 819 | 1,068 | 652 |
| Rhode Island | 12 | 14 | 45 | 51 | 44 |
| South Carolina | 9 | 25 | 32 | 16 | 7 |
| South Dakota | | | | | 1,428 |
| Tennessee | 57 | 50 | 100 | 66 | 47 |
| Texas | 14 | 76 | 54 | 228 | 130 |
| Utah | | | | | 254 |
| Vermont | 2 | 1 | 20 | 10 | 17 |
| Virginia | 65 | 81 | 231 | 125 | 68 |
| Washington | | | | | 227 |
| West Virginia | | | 174 | 19 | 22 |
| Wisconsin | 1,157 | 4,906 | 5,990 | 5,698 | 6,252 |
| Wyoming | | | | | 17 |
| District of Columbia | 4 | 12 | 23 | 71 | 32 |
| Western Territories | 19 | 79 | 218 | 404 | |
| Total | 9,848 | 28,281 | 46,802 | 58,090 | 81,828 |

TABLE 4 (*continued*)

## DISTRIBUTION OF FOREIGN-BORN DUTCH IMMIGRANTS BY STATE ACCORDING TO DECADE

| 1900 | 1910 | 1920 | 1930 | 1940 | 1950 | 1960 | 1970 |
|---|---|---|---|---|---|---|---|
| 885 | 872 | 846 | 620 | 468 | 319 | 258 | 174 |
| 3 | 44 | 36 | 44 | 47 | 77 | 130 | 222 |
| 21 | 48 | 177 | 163 | 107 | 145 | 115 | 186 |
| 10,261 | 12,698 | 12,737 | 14,762 | 11,841 | 10,580 | 10,928 | 8,575 |
| 99 | 86 | 70 | 64 | 65 | 68 | 226 | 235 |
| 9,414 | 12,652 | 13,772 | 14,909 | 13,842 | 13,393 | 13,132 | 11,421 |
| 17 | 28 | 115 | 201 | 213 | 307 | 521 | 576 |
| 317 | 709 | 903 | 658 | 474 | 341 | 241 | 167 |
| 1,719 | 2,278 | 2,529 | 2,235 | 1,772 | 1,530 | 2,233 | 1,909 |
| 85 | 230 | 176 | 166 | 116 | 105 | 249 | 388 |
| 324 | 618 | 917 | 1,002 | 938 | 1,010 | 1,178 | 1,566 |
| 637 | 1,231 | 1,338 | 1,289 | 1,206 | 1,219 | 1,781 | 1,919 |
| 69 | 143 | 138 | 138 | 118 | 120 | 144 | 227 |
| 6 | 19 | 30 | 24 | 24 | 42 | 126 | 170 |
| 1,566 | 2,656 | 3,218 | 3,068 | 2,008 | 1,547 | 1,055 | 574 |
| 52 | 78 | 58 | 56 | 48 | 75 | 108 | 182 |
| 262 | 424 | 554 | 578 | 548 | 699 | 1,333 | 1,522 |
| 523 | 1,392 | 1,980 | 2,325 | 1,857 | 2,336 | 3,905 | 2,640 |
| 20 | 25 | 32 | 34 | 23 | 29 | 101 | 198 |
| 72 | 99 | 335 | 264 | 235 | 342 | 716 | 1,031 |
| 632 | 2,157 | 3,097 | 3,484 | 3,250 | 3,230 | 3,495 | 3,911 |
| 22 | 60 | 66 | 42 | 47 | 61 | 49 | 89 |
| 6,496 | 7,379 | 7,473 | 6,260 | 4,956 | 4,152 | 3,678 | 2,730 |
| 18 | 79 | 130 | 101 | 93 | 64 | 29 | 48 |
| 42 | 64 | 127 | 151 | 203 | 293 | 308 | 186 |
| 94,931 | 120,063 | 131,766 | 133,133 | 111,064 | 102,133 | 118,415 | 110,570 |

# Notes and References

## CHAPTER I

1. One of the best single-volume histories of the Netherlands in English is Bernard H. M. Vlekke, *Evolution of the Dutch Nation* (New York, 1945). The best history in Dutch is J. A. van Houtte and others, eds., *Algemene Geschiedenis der Nederlanden*, 12 vols. (Utrecht, 1949–58).

2. George Edmundson, *History of Holland* (Cambridge, 1922), p. 110.

3. Johan Goudsblom, *Dutch Society* (New York, 1967), p. 20.

4. For a careful treatment of this subject, see N. W. Posthumus, ed., *The Netherlands during German Occupation*, Vol. 245 of *The Annals of the American Academy of Political and Social Science* (May, 1946).

5. William Petersen, *Some Factors Influencing Postwar Emigration from the Netherlands* (The Hague, 1952), pp. 10–11.

## CHAPTER II

1. On the early history of the Dutch in North America see the carefully documented study by Simon Hart, *The Prehistory of the New Netherland Company* (Amsterdam, 1959). Also of value are Van Cleaf Bachman, *Peltries or Plantations: The Economic Policies of the Dutch West India Company in New Netherland, 1623–1639* (Baltimore, 1969), pp. 3–24; Thomas J. Condon, *New York Beginnings: The Commercial Origins of New Netherland* (New York, 1968), pp. 3–35.

2. E. B. O'Callaghan and Berthold Fernow, eds., *Documents Relating to the Colonial History of the State of New York* (Albany, 1856–87), I, p. 11 (hereafter cited as *New York Colonial Documents*).

3. The charter of the West India Company, as drawn up in 1621 and including later amplifications, is found in Dutch and English in A. J. F. Van Laer, ed., *Van Rensselaer Bowier Manuscripts Being the Letters of Kiliaen Van Rensselaer, 1630–1643 . . .* (Albany, 1908), pp. 86–135. For an analysis of the organization and shortcomings of the Company see Bachman, *Peltries or Plantations*, pp. 25–43.

4. F. C. Wieder, *De Stichting van New York in Juli 1625* ('s Gravenhage, 1925), p. 11. It was not unusual for Dutch documents of this period to use the word Virginias in place of New Netherland.

5. J. Van Hinte, *Nederlanders in Amerika: Een Studie over Landverhuizers en Volkplanters in de 19^de en 20^ste Eeuw in de Vereenigde Staten van Amerika* (Groningen, 1928), I, p. 5.

6. On the difficulty of determining when the first permanent settlers came to New Netherland see C. A. Weslager, *Dutch Explorers, Traders and Settlers in the Delaware Valley 1609–1664* (Philadelphia, 1961), pp. 49–57; A. J. F. Van Laer, ed., *Documents Relating to New Netherland 1624–1626 in the Henry E. Huntington Library* (San Marino, Calif., 1924), pp. xii–xix.

7. Just as there is uncertainty as to when the first permanent settlement of New Netherland took place, so, too, there is debate on the location of the first settlements in the colony. See Van Laer, *Documents Relating to New Netherland*, pp. xix–xxiv; Bachman, *Peltries or Plantations*, p. 82.

8. Van Laer, *Documents Relating to New Netherland*, p. 40. See also pp. xxi–xxii.

9. J. Franklin Jameson, ed., *Narratives of New Netherland 1609–1664* (New York, 1909), p. 79.

10. The instructions for Fredericksz are found in Van Laer, *Documents Relating to New Netherland*, pp. 132–169. Wieder's *Stichting van New York* contains more than twenty drawings, with text, illustrating the design and appearance of the proposed fort.

11. Jameson, *Narratives of New Netherland*, pp. 84–85, 88.

12. A. Eekhof, *Jonas Michaelius Founder of the Church of New Netherland* (Leyden, 1926), p. 110.

13. *New York Colonial Documents*, I, pp. 37–38.

14. Jameson, *Narratives of New Netherland*, pp. 82–83, 89.

15. The settlements at Gowanus, Wallabout, and the Ferry were, under the Dutch, never anything more than small hamlets. Dominie Henricus Selyns, the Dutch Reformed minister at Breuckelen, wrote in October, 1660, that the "Ferry, the Walebacht, and Guyanes, all belong to Breuckelen. . . . I found at Breuckelen . . . thirty-one householders, and one hundred and thirty-four people." *Ibid.*, p. 407.

16. The "Charter of Freedoms and Exemptions" of 1629 (printed in 1630) is found in Dutch and English in *Van Rensselaer Bowier Manuscripts*, pp. 136–153.

17. H. T. Colenbrander, ed., *Verscheyden Voyagien van David Pietersz. de Vries 1618–1644* ('s Gravenhage, 1911), p. xxvii.

18. On Kiliaen Van Rensselaer and Rensselaerswyck see, in addi-

tion to *Van Rensselaer Bowier Manuscripts*, J. Spinoza Castella Jessurum, *Kiliaen Van Rensselaer van 1623 tot 1636* ('s Gravenhage, 1917); Samuel G. Nissenson, *The Patroon's Domain* (New York, 1937).

19. The revised "Charter of Freedoms and Exemptions" of 1640 is found in *New York Colonial Documents*, I, pp. 119–123.

20. Jameson, *Narratives of New Netherland*, p. 209.

21. *New York Colonial Documents*, XIII, pp. 207–208, 214, 232–233. For an excellent summary of the patroonships founded on the west bank of the lower Hudson and the settlements that arose within their bounds see Adrian C. Leiby, *The Early Dutch and Swedish Settlers of New Jersey* (Princeton, 1964), pp. 8–23.

22. On the rise and decline of Dutch power in Brazil see C. R. Boxer, *The Dutch in Brazil, 1624–1654* (Oxford, 1957).

23. The arrival in New Netherland of Jewish refugees from Brazil is discussed in Samuel Oppenheim, "The Early History of the Jews in New York, 1654–1664," *Publications* of the American Jewish Historical Society, XVIII (1909), pp. 1–91. See also the *New York Times*, September 21, 1970, p. 45.

24. On the sending of Dutch orphans to New Netherland see *New York Colonial Documents*, I, pp. 364, 556; II, p. 52; XIV, pp. 166, 175–176, 264, 296, 322, 434, 471.

25. Albert Cook Myers, ed., *Narratives of Early Pennsylvania, West-New Jersey and Delaware 1630–1707* (New York, 1912), p. 123.

26. The best history of New Sweden and its relations with the Dutch of New Netherland is Amandus Johnson, *The Swedish Settlements on the Delaware 1638–1664*, 2 vols. (Philadelphia, 1911).

27. A copy of the "Conditions" is found in *New York Colonial Documents*, I, pp. 629–636.

28. The *Prins Maurits* probably also carried some Waldensian refugees. For a brief account of the Waldenses who left Holland for the Delaware River colony see George B. Watts, *The Waldenses in the New World* (Durham, N.C., 1941), pp. 10–13.

29. *New York Colonial Documents*, II, p. 68.

30. Edward T. Corwin, ed., *Ecclesiastical Records of the State of New York* (Albany, 1901–16), I, pp. 402–403.

31. *New York Colonial Documents*, II, p. 115.

32. Numerous letters, some very lengthy and informative, pertaining to New Amstel are scattered throughout volume two of *New York Colonial Documents*. A good, well-documented account of New Amstel is found in Weslager, *Dutch Explorers in the Delaware Valley*.

33. On the life and ideas of Plockhoy and his settlement on the

Delaware see Leland Harder, "Plockhoy and His Settlement at Zwanendael," *Delaware History*, III (March, 1949), pp. 138–154.

34. The dates for the founding of these Long Island towns are approximate. It is impossible to give exact dates, not only because of uncertainty about when each group of settlers first arrived, but also because the dates for plotting a town and for its formal incorporation may differ by several years. For a history of the Dutch on Long Island during the New Netherland period see Henry R. Stiles, *The History of the County of Kings and the City of Brooklyn*, 2 vols. (New York, 1884); Thomas M. Strong, *The History of the Town of Flatbush* (New York, 1842).

35. Jameson, *Narratives of New Netherland*, p. 398.

36. When Kingston celebrated its 300th anniversary in 1952, Her Majesty, Queen Juliana of the Netherlands, visited the city in recognition of its Dutch origins. Also to celebrate the event, thousands of tulip bulbs, imported from the Netherlands, were planted in the fall of 1951.

37. *New York Colonial Documents*, XIII, pp. 202–204, 215–216, 219.

38. A copy of the notice to establish Nieuw Haarlem is found in James Riker, *Revised History of Harlem (City of New York), Its Origin and Early Annals* (New York, 1904), pp. 169–171.

### CHAPTER III

1. Dixon Ryan Fox, *Yankees and Yorkers* (Port Washington, N.Y., 1963), p. 33; Alexander C. Flick, ed., *History of the State of New York* (New York, 1933–37), II, p. 36; Charles R. Boxer, *The Dutch Seaborne Empire* (New York, 1965), p. 228.

2. A copy of the Provisional Regulations in Dutch and English is found in Van Laer, *Documents Relating to New Netherland*, pp. 2–19. A careful analysis of it and other regulations governing the first settlers of New Netherland is found in Wieder, *De Stichting van New York*, pp. 21–35.

3. Van Hinte, *Nederlanders in Amerika*, I, p. 39.

4. *New York Colonial Documents*, I, p. 213.

5. Jameson, *Narratives of New Netherland*, p. 230. See also p. 352.

6. Bernard H. M. Vlekke and Henry Beets, *Hollanders Who Helped Build America* (New York, 1942), p. 14.

7. Condon, *New York Beginnings*, p. vii.

8. Boxer, *The Dutch in Brazil, 1624–1654*; George Edmundson, "The Dutch in Western Guiana," *English Historical Review*, XVI (1901), pp. 640–675.

9. *New York Colonial Documents*, I, p. 158.

10. Bachman, *Peltries or Plantations*, pp. 63–71, 157–160.

11. Condon, *New York Beginnings*, pp. 105, 141; Eekhof, *Jonas Michaelius*, p. 130.

12. *New York Colonial Documents*, I, pp. 135–136.

13. Jameson, *Narratives of New Netherland*, p. 321.

14. Quoted in Allen W. Trelease, *Indian Affairs in Colonial New York: The Seventeenth Century* (Ithaca, N.Y., 1960), p. 74.

15. Van Hinte, *Nederlanders in Amerika*, I, p. 37; A. Eekhof, *De Hervormde Kerk in Noord-Amerika, 1624–1664* ('s Gravenhage, 1913), I, p. 72.

16. Fox, *Yankees and Yorkers*, p. 40.

17. Arnold Mulder, *Americans from Holland* (Philadelphia, 1947).

18. *Algemene Geschiedenis*, VI, p. 141. See also pp. 142–146; Paul Zumthor, *Daily Life in Rembrandt's Holland* (London, 1962), pp. 229, 238, 245–248; Boxer, *The Dutch Seaborne Empire*, pp. 65–71.

19. Vlekke and Beets, *Hollanders Who Helped Build America*, p. 18. On Dutch emigration to England see W. Cunningham, *Alien Immigrants to England* (London, 1897), pp. 193–220; J. F. Bense, *Anglo-Dutch Relations from the Death of William the Third* (The Hague, 1925), pp. 112–151. For Dutch emigration elsewhere on the continent see F. Dekker, *Voortrekkers van Oud Nederland*, 2 vols. (Den Haag, 1938–47).

20. By contrast, religious discrimination was significant in Dutch emigration to Michigan and Iowa during the 1840's.

21. B. H. Wabeke, *Dutch Immigration to America, 1624–1860* (New York, 1944), p. 16.

22. *New York Colonial Documents*, XIV, p. 216. See also I, pp. 106, 246; XIII, p. 205.

23. Vlekke and Beets, *Hollanders Who Helped Build America*, p. 28. See also American Council of Learned Societies, "Report of the Committee on Linguistics and National Stocks in the Population of the United States," *Annual Report of the American Historical Association for the Year 1931* (Washington, D.C., 1932), I, pp. 363–366.

24. Condon, *New York Beginnings*, p. 133.

25. Jameson, *Narratives of New Netherland*, p. 259.

26. On the claims and counterclaims of the Dutch and English to the Connecticut Valley and eastern Long Island see Fox, *Yankees and Yorkers*, pp. 42–85. The treaty of Hartford was never ratified in London because to have done so would have meant recognizing the boundary line of 1650, thereby also recognizing the legal ex-

istence of New Netherland—something the English government was determined to avoid.

27. *New York Colonial Documents*, XIV, p. 481.

28. Stuyvesant's defense of his actions in surrendering New Netherland, along with supporting documents and letters written on his behalf by citizens of the colony, are found in *New York Colonial Documents*, II, pp. 363–510.

29. On the fall of the Delaware region to Carr see Weslager, *Dutch Explorers in the Delaware Valley*, pp. 237–255.

30. The "Articles of Capitulation" are found in *New York Colonial Documents*, II, pp. 250–253.

31. C. de Waard, *De Zeeuwsche Expeditie naar de West onder Cornelis Evertsen den Jonge, 1672–1674* (The Hague, 1928) is devoted to the expedition that reconquered New Netherland in 1673.

32. *New York Colonial Documents*, II, pp. 526–527.

33. *Ibid.* Pp. 526–734 of this work contain numerous documents on the Dutch reoccupation of New Netherland.

34. Wabeke, *Dutch Immigration to America*, p. 71. The role that Rotterdam played in European emigration to America during the eighteenth century is discussed in C. te Lintum, "Emigratie over Rotterdam in de 18ᵈᵉ Eeuw," *De Gids*, Vierde Serie, IV (1908), pp. 323–335.

35. Quoted in Wabeke, *Dutch Immigration to America*, p. 61.

36. A discussion of the *Kort Bericht* and other promotional literature on Pennsylvania, published in Dutch, is found in Van Hinte, *Nederlanders in Amerika*, I, pp. 24–26. See also William I. Hull, *William Penn and the Dutch Quaker Migration to Pennsylvania* (Swarthmore, Penn., 1935), pp. 308–316.

37. Quakerism in Holland and William Penn's visits there are described in *ibid.*, pp. 58–122, 322–323, 393–394. It is possible that Penn's mother was Dutch. If true, it undoubtedly helped his acceptance into Dutch society. *Ibid.*, pp. 1–2.

38. Quoted in Samuel Whitaker Pennypacker, *The Settlement of Germantown Pennsylvania and the Beginning of German Immigration to North America* (Lancaster, Penn., 1899), pp. 156–157.

39. *Ibid.*, p. 172; Van Hinte, *Nederlanders in Amerika*, I, p. 26; C. Henry Smith, *The Story of the Mennonites* (Newton, Kansas, 1950), p. 261.

40. For a description of the Dutch atmosphere that prevailed for many years at Germantown see Chapter IV, "The Dutch Quaker Founders of Germantown," Hull, *William Penn and the Dutch Quaker Migration*, pp. 178–300. See also Smith, *Story of the Men-*

*nonites*, pp. 530–531, 537, 541, 543; Pennypacker, *The Settlement of Germantown*, pp. 69–70, 175–195, 216, 222.

41. Hull, *William Penn and Dutch Quaker Migration*, p. 209.

42. *Ibid.*, pp. 180–181. See also Pennypacker, *The Settlement of Germantown*, p. 103. A Netherlands historian attributed the practice of some German writers of depreciating the role played by the Dutch in the early settlement of Pennsylvania to a "Deutschland uber alles" mentality. Van Hinte, *Nederlanders in Amerika*, I, p. 26.

43. Quoted in Pennypacker, *The Settlement of Germantown*, p. 148.

44. The derivation of the term "Pennsylvania Dutch," is explained in John Joseph Stoudt, "Pennsylvania Dutch," *Historical View of Berks County* (Spring, 1974), pp. 60–63.

45. For a brief description of De Labadie and the Labadist sect in Holland see "Jean de Labadie," *Biographisch Woordenboek van Protestantsche Godgeleerden in Nederland*, V, pp. 456–467.

46. The journal kept by Jasper Danckaerts constitutes not only an important source of information about the Labadists but also about the manner of life among the colonial settlements he visited. Bartlett B. James and J. Franklin Jameson, eds., *Journal of Jasper Danckaerts 1679–1680* (New York, 1959).

47. For a discussion of the Dutch Labadists in America see Bartlett B. James, "The Labadist Colony in Maryland," *Johns Hopkins University Studies in History and Political Science*, Series XVII, No. 6 (Baltimore, 1899).

48. [Samuel Bownas], *An Account of the Life, Travels, and Christian Experiences in the Work of the Ministry of Samuel Bownas* (Stanford, Eng., 1805), pp. 95–96.

49. The Quaker poet John Greenleaf Whittier, in "Andrew Rykman's Prayer," recaptured some of the spiritual life of New Bohemia. Rykman apparently knew De Labadie personally and was among the Dutch Labadists who migrated to America. The poem is found in *The Complete Poetical Works of John Greenleaf Whittier* (Boston, 1894), pp. 539–541.

50. *Ecclesiastical Records*, II, p. 1232.

51. Bownas, *Account of the Life, Travels, and Christian Experiences*, p. 96.

CHAPTER IV

1. Thomas Melvin Banta, *A Frisian Family: The Banta Genealogy* (New York, 1893), pp. 49–50, 59; R. Brinckerhoff, ed., *The Family of Joris Dircksen Brinckerhoff* (New York, 1887), pp. 32–33, 46–48,

52, 133, 166, 171; A. Van Doren Honeyman, *Joannes Nevius and His Descendants A.D. 1627–1900* (Plainfield, N.J., 1900), pp. 172–173.

2. Percy Wells Bidwell and John I. Falconer, *History of Agriculture in the Northern United States 1620–1860* (Washington, D.C., 1925), pp. 70–71.

3. The memorandum is found in *New York Colonial Documents*, I, pp. 365–371.

4. For the early history of the manors that were established in parts of the Hudson Valley see Irving Mark, *Agrarian Conflicts in Colonial New York 1711–1775* (New York, 1940). An interesting account of Philipsburgh manor, together with several photographs, is found in Elvira Mulhern, "Master-Builder of Nieuw Netherlands, Philipse Castle Opens as a Dutch Shrine," *Knickerbocker Weekly*, July 5, 1943, pp. 18–22.

5. Helen Wilkinson Reynolds, *Dutch Houses in the Hudson Valley before 1776* (New York, 1965), p. 297. See also Brinckerhoff, *Family of Joris Dircksen Brinckerhoff*, p. 17.

6. Reynolds, *Dutch Houses in the Hudson Valley*, p. 320.

7. Scattered parcels of land, however, had been purchased along the Hudson River from the Indians during the New Netherland period, and there were a few farms in the vicinity of some of these villages before 1664. See *Van Rensselaer Bowier Manuscripts*, p. 832; Tercentenary Committee on Research, *Tercentenary Studies 1928: Reformed Church in America* (New York, 1928), pp. 285–286.

8. Reynolds, *Dutch Houses in the Hudson Valley*, p. 179.

9. Edward Tanjore Corwin, *A Manual of the Reformed Church in America* (New York, 1902), p. 994; Thomas Jefferson Wertenbaker, *The Founding of American Civilization: The Middle Colonies* (New York, 1963), p. 104.

10. Peter Kalm, *The America of 1750: Peter Kalm's Travels in North America*, ed. by Adolph B. Benson (New York, 1937), II, p. 602. See also I, pp. 350–359.

11. *Tercentenary Studies*, pp. 276–281.

12. Richard P. McCormick, *New Jersey from Colony to State 1609–1789* (Princeton, 1964), p. 81.

13. *Tercentenary Studies*, p. 176.

14. *Records of the Reformed Dutch Churches of Hackensack and Schraalenburgh, New Jersey* (New York, 1891).

15. Adrian C. Leiby, *The Revolutionary War in the Hackensack Valley: The Jersey Dutch and the Neutral Ground, 1775–1783* (New Brunswick, N.J., 1962), p. 9.

16. Corwin, *Manual of the Reformed Church*, pp. 706–707.

17. *New York Colonial Documents*, I, p. 366.

18. A general discussion of the early settlement of the Raritan Valley is found in Cornelius V. Vermeule, "Raritan Valley, Its Discovery and Settlement," *Proceedings of the New Jersey Historical Society*, XIII, New Series (July, 1928), pp. 282–298.

19. On the history of the Dutch Reformed congregations of Monmouth County, see George C. Beekman, *Early Dutch Settlers of Monmouth County, New Jersey* (Freehold, N.J., 1901), and A. I. Martin, ed., *Reformed Church of the Navasink* (New York, 1899).

20. *New York Colonial Documents*, II, p. 15; Amelia Stickney Decker, *The Ancient Trail: The Old Mine Road* (Trenton, N.J., 1942), pp. 8–10.

21. *Ibid.*, p. 11. See also Kalm, *Travels in North America*, II, p. 635.

22. J. H. Battle, ed., *History of Bucks County Pennsylvania* (Philadelphia, 1887), pp. 282, 470–474, 480–482. It is possible that some of the first Hollanders in Bucks County came from older Dutch settlements on the lower Delaware River or from the Minisink region.

23. *Ibid.*, pp. 484–485; *The Two Hundred and Fiftieth Anniversary of the North and Southampton Reformed Church* (n.p.: 1960), p. 7.

24. Brinckerhoff, *Family of Joris Dircksen Brinckerhoff*, pp. 32–33, 46–48, 166, 171; Honeyman, *Joannes Nevius and His Descendants*, pp. 167–171.

25. Brinckerhoff, *Family of Joris Dircksen Brinckerhoff*, p. 166.

26. *Ibid.*, pp. 47–48, 52, 160, 171; John A. Rodger, *The Story of a Century: A History of the Reformed Church of Owasco* (Owasco, N.Y., 1896).

27. For information on the Dutch in Kentucky, the writer relied on Percy Scott Flippen, "The Dutch Element in Early Kentucky," *Proceedings of the Mississippi Valley Historical Association*, IX, Part I (1915–16), pp. 135–150, and A. H. Scomp, *Historic Sketch of the Old Mud Meeting House* (Harrodsburg, Ky., 1900).

28. There are differences of opinion regarding exactly where the first Kentucky Dutch pioneers settled and how much land was included in the Low Dutch Tract. On this question, in addition to the above sources, see *Banta Genealogy*, pp. 50 ff.

29. As explained in the Preface, other ethnic strains were present among Dutch communities in colonial America. In the case of those in Kentucky, several families had Huguenot ties.

30. Scomp, *Old Mud Meeting House*, p. 30.

31. Shepard B. Clough and Charles W. Cole, *Economic History of Europe* (Boston, 1952), pp. 193–194.

32. Gilbert C. Fite and Jim E. Reese, *An Economic History of the United States* (Boston, 1965), p. 36.

33. *New York Colonial Documents*, II, p. 184.

34. Hector St. John de Crèvecoeur, *Sketches of Eighteenth Century America* (New Haven, 1925), pp. 137–145.

35. Jameson, *Narratives of New Netherland*, p. 79.

36. Bidwell and Falconer, *History of Agriculture*, pp. 28–31, 112.

37. McCormick, *New Jersey from Colony to State*, p. 87.

38. David Maldwyn Ellis, *Landlords and Farmers in the Hudson-Mohawk Region, 1790–1850* (New York, 1967), pp. 103–104.

39. *New York Colonial Documents*, III, p. 397.

40. James Thacher, *The American Revolution . . . Given in the Form of a Journal . . .* (Cincinnati, 1857), p.156. See also Thomas Anburey, *Travels through the Interior Parts of America in a Series of Letters* (London, 1789), II, p. 275; Andrew Burnaby, *Burnaby's Travels through North America* (New York, 1904), p. 104.

41. Hector St. John de Crèvecoeur, *Letters from an American Farmer* (London, 1945), p. 50; Crèvecoeur, *Sketches of Eighteenth Century America*, p. 141.

42. Kalm, *Travels in North America*, I, p. 118. See also p. 351.

43. Ellis, *Landlords and Farmers*, p. 97.

44. Burnaby, *Travels*, p. 117.

45. Philip L. White, *The Beekmans of New York in Politics and Commerce, 1647–1877* (New York, 1956); Virginia D. Harrington, *The New York Merchant on the Eve of the Revolution* (New York, 1935).

46. Flick, *History of the State of New York*, II, p. 396.

47. Kalm, *Travels in North America*, I, p. 342.

48. *Ibid.*, p. 343.

49. Alice P. Kenny, *The Gansevoorts of Albany: Dutch Patricians in the Upper Hudson Valley* (Syracuse, 1969), p. 22. See also p. 27.

CHAPTER V

1. Kalm, *Travels in North America*, I, p. 142. See also pp. 119, 343; II, p. 602.

2. Anburey, *Travels*, II, p. 275; Burnaby, *Travels*, p. 117; Thacher, *Journal*, p. 156; Isaac Weld, *Travels through the States of North America and the Provinces of Upper Low Canada during the Years 1795, 1796, and 1797* (London, 1807), II, pp. 372–373.

3. Martin Van Buren, *The Autobiography of Martin Van Buren*, edited by John C. Fitzpatrick, Vol. II of American Historical Association, *Annual Report for the Year 1918* (Washington, D.C., 1920),

p. 9. Frederick W. Bogert, Chairman of the Committee on Genealogy of the Holland Society, informed the writer (June 7, 1973), "I have noted a remarkable number of intermarriages between members of Dutch families down through as many as six generations."

4. *Ecclesiastical Records*, II, p. 829.

5. Myers, *Narratives of Early Pennsylvania*, p. 238.

6. On the role of Dutch women in colonial America see Alice Earle, *Colonial Days in Old New York* (New York, 1938), pp. 45–46, 154–171; Richard H. Amerman, "The Ladies of New Netherland," *De Halve Maen*, XXIX (January, 1955), pp. 5–6.

7. [Anne McVicar] Grant, *Memoirs of an American Lady, with Sketches of Manners and Scenery in America, as They Existed Previous to the Revolution* (New York, 1846), p. 62. See also p. 41. Earle, *Colonial Days in Old New York* indicates, however, that not all Dutch children were considerate of their elders, pp. 16 ff. Several Dutch nursery rhymes of the Colonial period with English translations are found in the *Yearbook* of the Holland Society (New York, 1890–91), pp. 235 ff.

8. Such decrees were issued by the Director General and his council in 1641, 1647, 1648, 1656, 1657, 1658, 1661, and 1663. Edmund Bailey O'Callaghan, *Laws and Ordinances of New Netherland 1638–1674* (Albany, 1868), pp. 25, 60–61, 93, 95, 98–99, 310–311, 342, 344, 415–416, 448.

9. *Ibid.*, pp. 258–259, 448–449.

10. Quoted in Irving Elting, *Dutch Village Communities on the Hudson River* (Baltimore, 1886) p. 29.

11. Quoted in Richard H. Amerman, "Golf . . . of Dutch or Scotch Origin?" *De Halve Maen*, XXXIII (July, 1958), p. 5.

12. Grant, *Memoirs*, p. 57.

13. Sarah Kemble Knight, *The Private Journal of Sarah Kemble Knight: Being the Record of a Journey from Boston to New York in the year 1704* (Norwich, Conn., 1901), p. 64.

14. John J. Birch, *The Pioneering Church of the Mohawk Valley* (Schenectady, N.Y., 1955), p. 190.

15. O'Callaghan, *Laws and Ordinances*, pp. 93–94. See also Earle, *Colonial Days in Old New York*, pp. 145–146.

16. Van Hinte, *Nederlanders in Amerika*, I, p. 48; Earle, *Colonial Days in Old New York*, pp. 283–284, 301–302.

17. Kalm, *Travels in North America*, II, p. 629.

18. *Ibid.*, I, p. 121.

19. Grant, *Memoirs*, p. 33. Kalm, *Travels in North America*, I, pp. 121, 341, made virtually the same observation of the Albany Dutch in 1749.

20. *New York Colonial Documents*, I, p. 368. It is interesting to note that some of the first Dutch homesteaders in the Middle West constructed similar temporary shelters about two centuries later. For more detailed information on the construction and appearance of Dutch houses than is contained in the following pages, see Wertenbacker, *The Middle Colonies*; Reynolds, *Dutch Houses in the Hudson Valley*; Weslager, *Dutch Explorers in the Delaware Valley*; Rosalie F. Bailey, *Pre-Revolutionary Dutch Houses and Families in Northern New Jersey and Southern New York* (New York, 1936); and Harold D. Eberlin, *The Architecture of Colonial America* (Boston, 1915).

21. Jameson, *Narratives of New Netherland*, p. 262.

22. Wertenbacker, *The Middle Colonies*, pp. 47–48. The use of brick by the Dutch residing north of Albany is described by Kalm, *Travels in North America*, I, p. 356; II, p. 611.

23. Wertenbacker, *The Middle Colonies*, p. 62. Leiby, *Early Dutch and Swedish Settlers*, pp. 86–87, also has some material on the combination house and barn arrangement.

24. Bailey, *Pre-Revolutionary Dutch Houses and Families*, p. 21.

25. Alexander Hamilton, *Hamilton's Itinerarium: Being a Narrative of a Journey from . . . May to September, 1774*, edited by Albert Bushnell Hart (Saint Louis, 1907), p. 87.

26. Quoted in Leiby, *The Revolutionary War in the Hackensack Valley*, p. 77. See also Thacher, *Journal*, p. 156.

27. Kalm, *Travels in North America*, I, p. 132.

28. Hamilton, *Itinerarium*, p. 87.

29. Kalm, *Travels in North America*, I, p. 356. See also II, p. 612.

30. *Ecclesiastical Records*, I, p. 398. For more detailed information on Dutch schools in the American colonies than is given in the following pages see William Heard Kilpatrick, *The Dutch Schools of New Netherland and Colonial New York* (Washington, D.C., 1912).

31. E. B. O'Callaghan, ed., *The Register of New Netherland, 1626 to 1674* (Albany, 1865), p. 129.

32. John A. Bogert, "New Amsterdam's First Schoolmaster," *De Halve Maen*, XXXIII (April, 1958), p. 7.

33. Nelson R. Burr, *Education in New Jersey 1630–1871* (Princeton, 1942), pp. 8–12.

34. Quoted in Strong, *The History of the Town of Flatbush*, pp. 115–116.

35. Grant, *Memoirs*, p. 27. The extent to which Dutch girls were educated is, however, open to question. See Kilpatrick, *The Dutch Schools*, pp. 198, 217–219; Earle, *Colonial Days in Old New York*, pp. 35–40.

36. Quoted in Richard P. McCormick, *Rutgers: A Centennial History* (New Brunswick, N.J., 1966), p. 8.

37. Eekhof, *Jonas Michaelius*, p. 71.

38. Corwin, *Manual of the Reformed Church*, p. 907.

39. For accounts of Steendam's life see John A. Bogert, "The Bard of New Amsterdam," *De Halve Maen*, XXXIII (October, 1958), pp. 5–6. Henry C. Murphy, *Anthology of New Netherland* (New York, 1865) contains translations of much of Steendam's poetry. On De Sille, see Ellis Lawrence Raesly, *Portrait of New Netherland* (New York, 1945), pp. 294–309. The best general source for other writers is *Dictionary of American Biography*, 20 vols. (New York, 1928–44).

40. Charles X. Harris, "Jacobus Gerritsen Strycker (c. 1619–1687): An Artist of New Amsterdam," *New York Historical Society Bulletin*, X (October, 1926), p. 86. Harris's article also contains several reproductions of Strycker's paintings.

41. Daniel M. Mendelowitz, *A History of American Art* (New York, 1960), p. 144.

42. James Truslow Adams, *Provincial Society 1690–1763* (New York, 1927), pp. 145–146.

43. *The Complete Encyclopedia of Antiques* (New York, 1962), p. 1291.

44. *Ibid.*

45. Hamilton, *Itinerarium*, p. 87; John Boyd Thacher, "Old Albany," The Dutch Settlers Society of Albany, *Year Book 1926–1927*, II, p. 7; R. R. Palmer, ed., *Atlas of World History* (New York, 1957), pp. 194–195 gives the population of selected cities at various periods in history.

46. *New York Colonial Documents*, I, pp. 191–192; *Van Rensselaer Bowier Manuscripts*, pp. 805–846; Leo Hershkowitz, "The Troublesome Turk: An Illustration of Judicial Process in New Amsterdam," *New York History*, XLVI (October, 1965), p. 300.

47. *Ecclesiastical Records*, IV, p. 2590.

48. Kenney, *The Gansevoorts of Albany*, p. 42.

49. Hamilton, *Itinerarium*, pp. 88–89. On the low regard he held for the culture of the Albany Dutch, including their medical doctors, see pp. 79–81, 84, 96. Although he was referring specifically to the Dutch of the Albany area, Hamilton considered this to be a general characteristic of Dutch colonists elsewhere.

50. Kalm, *Travels in North America*, II, p. 629.

51. *Ibid.*, p. 628.

52. Van Laer, *Documents Relating to New Netherland*, pp. 187, 207.

53. Eekhof, *Jonas Michaelius*, p. 111.

54. *New York Colonial Documents*, XIV, pp. 444, 471.

55. *Ibid.*, II, p. 51.

56. Myers, *Narratives of Early Pennsylvania*, p. 238.

57. Wayne Andrews, ed., "A Glance at New York in 1697: The Travel Diary of Dr. Benjamin Bullivant," *New York Historical Society Quarterly*, XL (January, 1956), p. 66.

58. Burnaby, *Travels*, p. 117. See also Thacher, *Journal*, p. 157; Anburey, *Travels*, II, p. 275.

CHAPTER VI

1. O'Callaghan, *Laws and Ordinances of New Netherland*, pp. 240, 247.

2. For an account of the *zienkentroosters* see Gerald F. De Jong, "The *Ziekentroosters* or Comforters of the Sick in New Netherland," *New York Historical Society Quarterly*, LIV (October, 1970), pp. 339–359.

3. In 1772, the American branch of the Dutch Reformed Church declared itself independent and became known as the Reformed Dutch Church. In 1867, its name was changed to the Reformed Church in America, by which designation it is still known today.

4. For a more detailed account of Megapolensis' life see Gerald F. De Jong, "Dominie Johannes Megapolensis: Minister to New Netherland," *New York Historical Society Quarterly*, LII (January, 1968), pp. 7–47.

5. Quoted in Isaac N. P. Stokes, *Iconography of Manhattan Island* (New York, 1915–28), IV, p. 55.

6. *Ecclesiastical Records*, I, p. 318.

7. Jameson, *Narratives of New Netherland*, pp. 259–260.

8. D. M. Ellis and others, *A Short History of New York State*, rev. ed. (Ithaca, N.Y., 1967), p. 63.

9. *Ecclesiastical Records*, I, p. 602.

10. *Ibid.*

11. On the events that led to the Ministry Act of 1693 and the charter of the New York City church in 1696, see John Webb Pratt, *Religion, Politics, and Diversity: The Church-State Theme in New York History* (Ithaca, N.Y., 1967), pp. 37–46.

12. *Ecclesiastical Records*, II, p. 1172.

13. Cornbury's religious policy is discussed in H. J. Westerling, "De Nederduitsch Gereformeerde Kerk in de Provincien New York en New Jersey onder het Engelsch Bwind," *Nederlandsch Archief voor Kerkgeschiedenis*, Nieuwe Serie, XVI (1920–21), pp. 209–212.

14. Wertenbacker, *The Middle Colonies*, p. 105.

15. *Ecclesiastical Records*, IV, pp. 2955–2956.

16. Kalm, *Travels in North America*, II, p. 621.

17. O'Callaghan, *Laws and Ordinances of New Netherland*, pp. 25, 60–61, 93, 95, 98–99, 310–311, 342, 344, 415–416, 448.

18. Andrews "A Glance at New York in 1697," p. 66.

19. Knight, *Journal*, p. 54.

20. Grant, *Memoirs*, pp. 29–30.

21. *Ecclesiastical Records*, I, p. 400.

22. *Ibid.*

23. *Ibid.*, II, pp. 907–908.

24. It is possible that Bartholf was one of the persons about whom Selyns was complaining in the above quotation. On Bartholf's influence see James Tanis, *Dutch Calvinistic Pietism in the Middle Colonies: A Study in the Life and Theology of Theodorus Jacobus Frelinghuysen* (The Hague, 1967), pp. 44–47.

25. *Tercentenary Studies*, p. 193.

26. Corwin, *Manual of the Reformed Church*, p. 473. See also Tanis, *Dutch Calvinistic Pietism*, pp. 46–47.

27. *Ecclesiastical Records*, IV, p. 2587.

28. Quoted in Tanis, *Dutch Calvinistic Pietism*, p. 82. For a less favorable estimate of Frelinghuysen see Herman Harmelink III, "Another Look at Frelinghuysen and His Awakening," *Church History*, XXXVII (December, 1968), pp. 423–438.

29. *Ecclesiastical Records*, IV, p. 2335. See also pp. 2401–2402.

30. *Ibid.*, I, p. 525.

31. *Ibid.*, III, p. 1661; IV, p. 2591.

32. *Ibid.*, III, p. 1719.

33. *Ibid.*, p. 1858.

34. Westerling, "De Nederduitsch Gereformeerde Kerk," p. 217.

35. Corwin, *Manual of the Reformed Church*, p. 104.

36. The term coetus (pronounced "see-tus") was sometimes used to designate a union of churches that did not enjoy as much autonomy as a regular classis. Such ecclesiastical bodies were occasionally established among Dutch Reformed churches outside the Netherlands, and were found at one time or another in northern Germany and Dutch possessions overseas, including Java, Surinam, and South Africa.

37. *Ecclesiastical Records*, IV, pp. 2706–2710.

38. Corwin, *Manual of the Reformed Church*, pp. 102–117.

39. It is possible that Ritzema opposed the transformation of the Coetus into a classis for selfish reasons. He was expecting an offer of the chair in Dutch theology at pro-Anglican King's College (now Columbia) which had been established in 1754, and might have

feared that the prospects for the professorship would be jeopardized by the creation of an American Classis, which would want its own divinity school. McCormick, *Rutgers: A Centennial History*, p. 3.

40. *Tercentenary Studies*, pp. 179–182, 314–316; *Ecclesiastical Records*, V, p. 3645.

41. *Ibid.*, VI, p. 3992.

42. *Ibid.*, p. 3995.

43. Westerling, "De Nederduitsch Gereformeerde Kerk," p. 217; *Ecclesiastical Records*, VI, p. 4134.

44. Although congregational support for the Conferentie party was declining, the number of ministers who adhered to it was still significant. Of the thirty-four ministers serving in the colonies in 1771, eleven belonged to the Conferentie group, thirteen to the Coetus group, and ten were neutral. Corwin, *Manual of the Reformed Church*, pp. 121–122.

45. For the deliberations that took place at the meetings of 1771 and 1772 see *Acts and Proceedings of the General Synod of the Reformed Protestant Dutch Church in North America*, I, pp. 5–27.

46. Henry S. Lucas, ed., *Dutch Immigrant Memoirs and Related Writings* (Assen, The Netherlands, 1955), I, p. 471.

47. A brief account of Rutgers and the Seminary is found in Burr, *Education in New Jersey*, pp. 19–39. For a more detailed account see McCormick, *Rutgers: A Centennial History*.

48. Hamilton, *Itinerarium*, p. 59. See also p. 86.

49. Wertenbacker, *The Middle Colonies*, p. 108. See also *Tercentenary Studies*, p. 61.

50. *Ecclesiastical Records*, IV, pp. 2340–2341. See also p. 2582; VI, pp. 3935–3936. Almost from the beginning, however, there had been a few ministers, such as Samuel Drisius (d. 1673), who occasionally preached an English sermon. A brief account of the language problem is found in Alexander J. Wall, "The Controversy in the Dutch Church in New York concerning Preaching in English, 1754–1768," *The New York Historical Society Quarterly*, XII (July, 1928), pp. 39–58.

51. *Ecclesiastical Records*, V, p. 3459. See also Corwin, *Manual*, p. 107.

52. *Ecclesiastical Records*, VI, p. 3854.

53. *Ibid.*, p. 3879.

54. Quoted in Benjamin C. Taylor, *Annals of the Classis of Bergen* (New York, 1857), pp. 304–306.

55. Virginia L. Redway. "James Parker and the 'Dutch Church,' " *Musical Quarterly*, XXIV (October, 1938), pp. 481–500; *Ecclesiasti-*

*cal Records*, VI, pp. 3872, 4010, 4076, 4110; *Acts and Proceedings of the General Synod*, I, p. 98.

56. Wertenbacker, *The Middle Colonies*, p. 116; Theodore B. Romeyn, *Historical Discourse Delivered on Occasion of the Re-Opening and Dedication of the First Reformed (Dutch) Church at Hackensack, N.J.*, May 2, 1869 (New York, 1870), p. xxvi.

57. Wertenbacker, *The Middle Colonies*, p. 116.

58. Quoted in Maud Esther Dilliard, *An Album of New Netherland* (New York, 1963), p. 15. See also *Dutch Immigrant Memoirs*, I, p. 471.

59. Charlton Laird, *Language in America* (New York, 1970), p. 314

60. Information on the etymology of these and other words of Dutch origin can be found in William Z. Shetter, "A Final Word on Jersey Dutch," *American Speech*, XXXIII (December, 1958), pp. 243–251; William H. Carpenter, "Dutch Contributions to the Vocabulary of English in America," *Modern Philology*, VI (July, 1908), pp. 53–68; L. G. Van Loon, *Crumbs from an Old Dutch Closet: The Dutch Dialect of Old New York* (The Hague, 1938).

61. Laird, *Language in America*, 315.

62. These and other similar expressions are described in Lester V. Berrey and Melvin Van den Bark, *The American Thesaurus of Slang*, 2nd ed. (New York, 1953); Harold Wentworth and Stuart Berg Flexner, *Dictionary of American Slang* (New York, 1967); Mitford M. Mathews, ed., *A Dictionary of Americanisms*, 2 vols. (Chicago, 1951).

CHAPTER VII

1. George Atkinson Ward, ed., *The Journal and Letters of Samuel Curwen 1775–1783* (New York, 1970), p. 26.

2. Howard C. Rice, Jr., ed., *Travels in North America in the Years 1780, 1781 and 1782* (Chapel Hill, N.C., 1963), II, p. 436.

3. Alice P. Kenney, "Private Worlds in the Middle Colonies: An Introduction to Human Traditions in American History," *New York History*, LI (January, 1970), p. 23.

4. Ellis, *Short History of New York State*, p. 118.

5. Leiby, *Revolutionary War in the Hackensack Valley*, p. 103.

6. Merrill Jensen, *The Founding of a Nation: A History of the American Revolution 1763–1776* (New York, 1968), p. 660.

7. Benjamin F. Thompson and Charles J. Werner, *History of Long Island* (Port Washington, N.Y., 1962), I, p. 281. See also William H. Nelson, *The American Tory* (Oxford, 1961), pp. 88, 90;

Wallace Brown, *The Good Americans: The Loyalists in the American Revolution* (New York, 1969), p. 231; Claude Halstead Van Tyne, *The Loyalists in the American Revolution* (New York, 1902), pp. 117–118.

8. Nelson, *The American Tory*, p. 89.

9. *Ibid.*, pp. 89–91.

10. Adrian C. Leiby, "The Conflict among the Jersey Dutch during the Revolution," *New Jersey in the American Revolution* (Trenton, N.J., 1970), p. 26.

11. Alice P. Kenney, "The Albany Dutch: Loyalists and Patriots," *New York History*, XLII (October, 1961), p. 342.

12. Kalm, *Travels in North America*, I, p. 346. See also II, p. 614. Kalm reported that the same feeling existed around Saratoga, I, p. 359.

13. Kenney, "The Albany Dutch," pp. 335–336, 339–344.

14. *Ibid.*, p. 336. See also Brown, *The Good Americans*, pp. 55–56.

15. Thomas Jones, *History of New York during the Revolutionary War* (New York, 1879), I, p. 45. Lorenzo Sabine in *Biographical Sketches of the Loyalists of the American Revolution with an Historical Introduction* (Boston, 1864), II, p. 214, states: "In the controversy which preceded the Revolution he [i.e., Ritzema] acted uniformly with the Loyalists."

16. Brown, *The Good Americans*, p. 71; Van Tyne, *The Loyalists in the American Revolution*, pp. 109, 115.

17. Larry R. Gerlach, "New Jersey in the Coming of the American Revolution," *New Jersey in the American Revolution*, p. 15. See also Leiby, *The Revolutionary War in the Hackensack Valley*, pp. 30, 50, 61.

18. Harrington, *The New York Merchant*, p. 348; Thomas Jefferson Wertenbacker, *Father Knickerbocker Rebels: New York City during the Revolution* (New York, 1948), pp. 12, 17–18, 82; Leiby, "The Conflict among the Jersey Dutch," pp. 26–28.

19. Nelson, *The American Tory*, p. 122.

20. For information on Van Schaack see Nelson, *The American Tory*, and William Allen Benton, *Whig-Loyalism: An Account of Political Ideology in the American Revolutionary Era* (Teaneck, N.J., 1969).

21. Nelson, *The American Tory*, p. 121.

22. *Ibid.*, p. 92; Brown, *The Good Americans*, pp. 227–229, 232.

23. The capture of André and the discovery of the incriminating papers he was carrying took place by accident. For a glamorized description of Paulding's role see "Turning the Revolutionary Tide: Two Netherlanders Saved West Point from Disaster," *Knickerbocker Weekly*, III (January 3, 1944), pp. 18–21. According to this article,

Notes and References     [ 287 ]

Isaac Van Wart, another of the three men who captured André, was also of Dutch extraction.

24. Brinckerhoff, *The Family of Joris Dircksen Brinckerhoff*, p. 36.

25. See, for example, the Appendix, in Abraham Messler, *Centennial History of Somerset County* (Somerville, N.J., 1878), pp. 1–5. Even Kinderhoek had its share of Patriots. Edward A. Collier, *A History of Old Kinderhoek* (New York, 1914), pp. 182–184.

26. Stephen J. Voorhies, *Historical Handbook of the Van Voorhees Family in the Netherlands and America* (n.p., 1935), p. 62.

27. John C. Fitzpatrick, ed., *The Writings of George Washington from the Manuscript Sources 1745–1799* (Washington, D.C., 1931–41), XXVII, p. 290.

28. *Ecclesiastical Records*, VI, pp. 4303–4304.

29. Thompson, *History of Long Island*, I, p. 281.

30. "Bergen-Hudson Patriots in Revolution," *De Halve Maen*, XXX (October, 1955), p. 7. See also Leiby, *The Revolutionary War in the Hackensack Valley*. Some idea of the number of Dutchmen in New Jersey who sided with the Loyalists can be obtained from E. Alfred Jones, *The Loyalists of New Jersey* (Newark, N.J., 1927). Of the 1,727 names of Loyalists listed there, seventy-three begin with the prefix "Van." Numerous also are other Dutch names, including Banta, Beekman, Bogert, Brinckerhoff, De Groot, De Mott, and Duryea.

31. Anburey, *Travels through the Interior Parts of America*, II, pp. 275–276.

32. Edward Tanjore Corwin, *Historical Discourse on Occasion of the Centennial Anniversary of the Reformed Dutch Church of Millstone* (New York, 1866), p. 50.

33. *Writings of George Washington*, XXIV, p. 389.

34. *Ibid.*, XV, p. 210; XXIV, pp. 390–391; XXV, pp. 346–347; XXVII, pp. 239–240.

35. Quoted in Willard D. Brown, *The History of the Reformed Church in America* (New York, 1928), p. 75.

36. *Acts and Proceedings of the General Synod*, I, p. 84.

37. Quoted in John P. Luidens, "The Americanization of the Dutch Reformed Church" (unpublished Ph.D. dissertation, University of Oklahoma, 1969), pp. 198–199.

38. Brown, *History of the Reformed Church*, p. 75.

39. For an account of Lydekker's life see John Wolfe Lydekker, "The Rev. Gerrit (Gerard) Lydekker 1729–1794," *Historical Magazine of the Protestant Episcopal Church*, XIII (December, 1944), pp. 303–314. References to his support of the Loyalist cause are also

found in John Wolfe Lydekker, *The Life and Letters of Charles Ingles* (London, 1936), pp. 195, 199, 211–212, 258–260.

40. *Acts and Proceedings of the General Synod*, I, p. 57. See also p. 69.

41. *Ibid.*, pp. 83–86. Similar references to the need to counteract public demoralization are found in the minutes of 1782 and 1783.

42. Wertenbacker, *Father Knickerbocker Rebels*, p. 18; Brown, *The Good Americans*, pp. 56–57. The Reverend John Livingston, perhaps the most eminent minister of the Dutch Reformed Church, wrote his colleague, the Reverend Eilardus Westerlo of Albany, on October 22, 1783, after the Revolution: "The common enemy to our religious liberties is now removed; and we have nothing to fear from the pride and domination of the Episcopal Hierarchy." Alexander Gunn, *Memoirs of the Rev. John. H. Livingston, 1746–1826* (New York, 1829), p. 258.

43. The Conferentie congregations at Hackensack and Schraalenburg, New Jersey, and at nearby Tappan, New York, for example, were strongly Loyalist. Leiby, "The Conflict among the Jersey Dutch," p. 29.

44. Friedrich Edler, *The Dutch Republic and the American Revolution* (Baltimore, 1911), pp. 32–33.

45. Charles Francis Adams, ed., *The Works of John Adams* (Boston, 1850–56), X p. 224. For a brief sketch of Van der Kemp's life in America see Harry F. Jackson, "Contributions to America of the Dutch Patriot Francis Adrian Van Der Kemp (1752–1829)," *New York History*, XLIII (October, 1962), pp. 371–384. For a longer account, see, by the same author, *Scholar in the Wilderness: Francis Adrian Van Der Kemp* (Syracuse, N.Y., 1936).

46. *The Works of John Adams*, VII, p. 104.

47. *Ibid.*, p. 342.

48. Edler, *The Dutch Republic and the American Revolution*, p. 43.

49. J. Franklin Jameson, "St. Eustatius in the American Revolution," *American Historical Review*, VIII (July, 1903), p. 688. See also p. 695.

50. For a discussion of various economic ventures undertaken in America after the Revolution by Netherlanders see Paul Demund Evans, *The Holland Land Company* (Buffalo, N.Y., 1924).

51. As quoted in Henry W. Kent, "Van Braam Houckgeest, an Early American Collector," *Proceedings of the American Antiquarian Society*, XL (1930), p. 161.

52. For an account of Troost's life see Henry Grady Rooker, "A Sketch of the Life and Work of Dr. Gerard Troost," *Tennessee Historical Magazine*, III (1932–33), pp. 3–19.

## CHAPTER VIII

1. The best account of what is discussed in this and in the following chapter is Henry S. Lucas, *Netherlanders in America: Dutch Immigration to the United States and Canada, 1789–1950* (Ann Arbor, Mich., 1955).

2. Mulder, *Americans from Holland*, p. 109.

3. *Dutch Immigrant Memoirs*, I, p. 17.

4. Because of differing theological views and personality clashes among the leaders, several years elapsed before the Seceders organized themselves into a denomination.

5. Mulder, *Americans from Holland*, p. 101.

6. Jacob Van der Meulen, *Hollanders: The Development of Their Objectives in Europe and America* (Zeeland, Mich., n.d.), p. 18. See also Lubbertus Oostendorp, *H. P. Scholte: Leader of the Secession of 1834 and Founder of Pella* (Franeker, The Netherlands, 1964), pp. 151–152, 162.

7. *Dutch Immigrant Memoirs*, I, p. 186.

8. Amry Vandenbosch, *The Dutch Communities of Chicago* (Chicago, 1927), pp. 8–9; Wabeke, *Dutch Immigration to America*, pp. 89–92.

9. J. C. Boogman, "The Netherlands in the European Scene, 1813–1913," in J. S. Bromley and E. H. Kossmann, eds., *Britain and the Netherlands in Europe and Asia* (London and New York, 1968), pp. 138–159; Wabeke, *Dutch Immigration to America*, pp. 91–92.

10. Quoted in Wabeke, *Dutch Immigration to America*, pp. 105–106.

11. *Ibid.*, p. 95. See also Henry Zylstra, "A Mid-Nineteenth Century Dutch View of American Life and Letters," *Publications of the Modern Language Association of America*, LVII (December, 1942), pp. 1108–1136.

12. *Dutch Immigrant Memoirs*, I, p. 132.

13. Henry S. Lucas, *1847 Ebenezer 1947: Memorial Souvenir of the Centennial Commemoration of the Dutch Immigration to the United States* (New York, 1947), p. 32.

14. Quoted in Wabeke, *Dutch Immigration to America*, p. 114.

15. The charter of the Utrecht Association was the most elaborate. In published form, it totaled sixteen pages and contained thirty-five articles. It has been reprinted in Henry S. Lucas, "De Artikelen van Scholte's Vereeninging ter Verhuizing naar de Vereenigde Staten," *Nederlandsch Archief voor Kerkgeschiedenis*, Nieuwe Serie, XXXVIII (1952), pp. 179–187.

16. Several of these articles from the *Christian Intelligencer* have been reprinted in *Dutch Immigrant Memoirs*, I, pp. 23–44.

17. *Ibid.*, pp. 361–362. See also p. 370.

18. *Ibid.*, p. 364.

19. *Ibid.*, p. 243. See also pp. 124, 292.

20. *Ibid.*, p. 68.

21. *Ibid.*, p. 185.

22. Quoted in Wabeke, *Dutch Immigration to America*, p. 131.

23. Henry Peter Scholte, *Eene Stem uit Pella*, translated by Jacob Van der Zee as "The Coming of the Hollanders to Iowa," in *The Iowa Journal of History and Politics*, IX (October, 1911), p. 531.

24. Oostendorp, *H. P. Scholte*, pp. 156–163.

25. Quoted in Scholte, *Eene Stem uit Pella*, p. 568.

26. Henry Beets, "H. P. Scholte's Leven en Streven in Noord-Amerika," *Nederlandsch Archief voor Kerkgeschiedenis*, Nieuwe Serie, XXIII (1930), p. 266.

27. M. Cohen Stuart, "An Eminent Foreigner's Visit to the Dutch Colonies of Iowa in 1873," translated by Jacob Ven der Zee, *Iowa Journal of History and Politics*, XI (April, 1913), p. 232.

28. *Ibid.*, translator's note, p. 228.

29. *Eighth Census of the United States: Population* (Washington, D.C., 1864), pp. 620–621.

30. Henry S. Lucas, "The First Dutch Settlers in Milwaukee," *Wisconsin Magazine of History*, XXX (December, 1946), p. 181.

31. The title of this newspaper was shortened to *De Nieuwsbode* in 1855. It ceased publication in 1861.

32. The Catholics in the Netherlands were not allowed to create an organization of bishops, nor were they permitted to establish a system of education conforming to their religious beliefs.

33. Quoted from *De Tijd* in Wabeke, *Dutch Immigration to America*, p. 138.

34. *Dutch Immigrant Memoirs*, I, p. 48.

35. *Ibid.*, II, p. 184.

36. The best treatment of the Dutch settlements in the Chicago area is Vandenbosch, *The Dutch Communities of Chicago*.

37. Ellery A. Handy, "The Dutch in Rochester," *The Rochester Historical Society Publication Fund Series*, XIV (Rochester, N.Y., 1936), pp. 64–73.

38. *Dutch Immigrant Memoirs*, II, p. 296.

39. *Ibid.*, pp. 285–290; Handy, "The Dutch in Rochester," pp. 65–66.

CHAPTER IX

1. Fite and Reese, *Economic History of the United States*, pp. 311, 350.

2. This was a significant figure when compared with the number who came to American shores during previous periods, and it compared favorably with that of some European countries, but lagged behind that of others, as is shown in the following table:

| | Number of immigrants arriving in the U.S. 1860–1910 | Population in 1900 | Percentage of immigrants to the 1900 population |
|---|---|---|---|
| Germany | 4,805,270 | 56,400,000 | 8.5 |
| Italy | 3,072,563 | 32,500,000 | 9.5 |
| Ireland | 2,255,612 | 4,500,000 | 50.1 |
| Sweden | 1,021,165 | 5,100,000 | 20.0 |
| France | 262,805 | 39,000,000 | 0.7 |
| Netherlands | 154,364 | 5,100,000 | 3.0 |
| Belgium | 93,934 | 6,700,000 | 1.4 |

Source: Francis J. Brown and Joseph S. Roucek, eds., *One America: The History, Contributions, and Present Problems of Our Racial and National Minorities*, rev. ed. (New York, 1945), p. 632; Palmer, *Atlas of World History*, p. 193.

3. *Sioux County Herald*, March 2, 1882.

4. Of the 2,735 Dutch and Flemish immigrants who came to the United States in 1919, 1,366 stated they were uniting with relatives and 543 were joining friends. *Annual Report of the Commissioner General of Immigration: 1919* (Washington, D.C., 1919), p. 92.

5. The Chicago, Milwaukee, and St. Paul Railroad gave two of its stations in North Dakota the names of The Hague and Zeeland in the hopes of encouraging Hollanders to settle in those areas.

6. J. Knuppe, *Land en Dollars in Minnesota: Inlichtingen voor Landverhuizers* (Rotterdam, 1883).

7. *Dutch Immigrant Memoirs*, II, p. 341.

8. The most complete account of the Dutch settlement in northwest Iowa is Charles L. Dyke, *The Story of Sioux County* (Orange City, Iowa, 1942).

9. Jacob Van der Zee, *The Hollanders of Iowa* (Iowa City, Iowa, 1912), pp. 154, 179; *De Volksvriend*, April 6, 1882.

10. On the Dutch in Minnesota, the writer relied heavily on Herman Borger's recollections in *Dutch Immigrant Memoirs*, II, pp. 195–203. This was supplemented by statistics from *Census Reports*

and "yearbooks" of the Reformed and Christian Reformed churches. A small Dutch settlement was also founded as early as 1856 in Fillmore County in the southeastern part of the state.

11. Detailed information on the Dutch in the Dakotas can be found in Gerald F. De Jong, "The Dutch in Emmons County," *North Dakota History*, XXIX (July, 1962), pp. 253–265.

12. *Dutch Immigrant Memoirs*, II, p. 340.

13. *De Wachter*, March 30, 1883.

14. Much of the information on life among the early Dutch settlers in the Dakotas was acquired from interviews conducted by the author during the summer of 1973 through the South Dakota Oral History Project; from the "Dutch Folder" in North Dakota Writers' Project Ethnic Interviews, found in the State Historical Library at Bismarck, N.D.; and from *Dutch Immigrant Memoirs*.

15. *Annual Report of the Commissioner General of Immigration: 1903* (Washington, D.C., 1903), p. 7.

16. Henry Van der Pol, Sr., *On the Reservation Border: Hollanders in Douglas and Charles Mix Counties* (Stickney, S.D., 1969), pp. 20–21.

17. *Dutch Immigrant Memoirs*, II, pp. 356–357.

18. "Dutch Folder" (North Dakota).

19. For a vivid account of the impression that the Dakota prairie made on a Dutch boy growing up in South Dakota during the latter part of the nineteenth century see Van der Pol, *On the Reservation Border*, pp. 169–172.

20. *Dutch Immigrant Memoirs*, II, p. 357.

21. Van Hinte, *Nederlanders in Amerika*, II, pp. 112–113.

22. Detailed information on the Dutch in Nebraska can be found in Gustav Adolph Bade, "A History of the Dutch Settlement in Lancaster County, Nebraska" (unpublished Master's dissertation, University of Nebraska, 1938).

23. *Dutch Immigrant Memoirs*, II, pp. 307–308.

24. On the Dutch in Montana, the writer relied primarily on Van Hinte, *Nederlanders in Amerika*, II, 252–263, and Lucas, *Netherlanders in America*, pp. 402–412.

25. This denomination and its relationship to the Dutch is discussed in Chapter XI.

26. M. Borduin, "Conrad, Mont.," *The Banner*, LXI (February 12, 1926), p. 91.

27. Van Hinte, *Nederlanders in Amerika*, II, pp. 237–245.

28. *Ibid.*, p. 250.

29. A nine-day visit among the Mormons of Utah by a Hollander in 1884 is described in A. Wormser, *Verspreide Geschriften: Hier een*

*Weinig, Daar een Weinig* (Milwaukee, Wisc., 1885), pp. 160–187.

30. For a detailed discussion of these projects see Van Hinte, *Nederlanders in Amerika,* II, pp. 181–217.

31. Quoted in *ibid.,* p. 212.

32. *The Banner,* LXII (June 24, 1927), p. 464.

33. This scheme is discussed in detail in Dorothy Roberts, "A Dutch Colony in Colorado," *Colorado Magazine,* XVII (1940), pp. 229–236.

34. Quoted in *ibid.,* pp. 230–231.

35. For a brief account, with photographs, of this railroad see I. T. W. L. Scheltema, "A Dutch-American Railroad: The Kansas City Southern," *Knickerbocker Weekly* (November 23, 1942), pp. 15–18.

36. Charles Boissevain, *Van 't Noorden naar 't Zuiden: Schetsen en Indrukken van de Vereenigde Staten van Noord-Amerika,* 2 vols. (Haarlem, The Netherlands, 1881–82), II, pp. 148, 283, 292.

37. There is a brief description of this colony in *Dutch Immigrant Memoirs,* II, pp. 290–294.

38. An attempt to found a Dutch colony in Shelby County, Alabama, never proceeded beyond the discussion stage. See F. E. Dykema, ed., "Effort to Attract Dutch Colonists to Alabama, 1869," *Journal of Southern History,* XIV (May, 1948), pp. 247–261.

39. The Nederland experiment is briefly discussed in Scheltema, "A Dutch-American Railroad."

40. A. Kuipers, *Redding en Toekonst voor den Nederlandschen Landbouwer . . . in Zuid-Oostelijk Texas* (n.p., 1897).

41. Henry Beets, "Our Frisian Settlement in Whitinsville, Mass.," *The Banner,* LXI (October 1, 1926), p. 605; Van Hinte, *Nederlanders in Amerika,* II, pp. 305–307. According to a study made by a professor of the University of Amsterdam, a rather pure Frisian language was still spoken at Whitinsville in 1967. *Leeuwarder Courant,* January 8, 1968.

42. Van Eeden considered asking Roosevelt to accept membership on the colony's board of directors, but he thought better of it when the President informed him he distrusted visionary men.

43. The best account in English of Van Eeden's life and his utopian colony in America is Lewis Leary, "Walden Goes Wandering: The Transit of Good Intentions," *The New England Quarterly,* XXXII (March, 1959), pp. 3–30.

CHAPTER X

1. Beginning about 1900, however, some interest was shown in Dutch emigration to Argentina, Brazil, and Canada. J. A. A. Hartland,

*De Geschiedenis van de Nederlandse Emigratie tot de Tweede Wereldoorlog* (The Hague, 1959), p. 12.

2. The number of immigrants entering the United States from other West European countries during the 1880's, with the corresponding percentage figure of their population in 1880, were as follows: Denmark, 88,132 (4.4%); Germany, 1,452,970 (3.2%); Ireland, 665,482 (12.9%); Switzerland, 81,988 (2.9%); France 50,464 (1.3%); and Sweden, 391,776 (8.5%). The immigration figures are found in Francis J. Brown and Joseph S. Roucek, editors, *One America: The History, Contributions, and Present Problems of Our Racial and National Minorities*, rev. ed. (New York, 1945), Table I, p. 632. The population figures from which the percentages were derived are found in Palmer, *Atlas of World History*, p. 193.

3. For a detailed account of the effects of the war on the Netherlands see Posthumus, "The Netherlands during German Occupation." See also "Holland Suffers Worst," *Knickerbocker Weekly*, IV (December 11, 1944), p. 22.

4. G. Beijer and J. J. Oudegeest, *Some Aspects of Migration in the Netherlands*, Publications of the Research Group for European Migration Problems, Vol. III (The Hague, 1952), pp. 5–6.

5. B. P. Hofstede, "Those Who Went and Those Who Stayed: Dutch Post-War Overseas Emigration," *Delta*, X (Spring/Summer, 1967), p. 49. For a synopsis of the operation of the Dutch Emigration Department and the various private organizations see *Het Koninkrijk der Nederlanden: Feiten en Cijfers over de Nederlandse Samenleving* (The Hague, 1971), Part 10, pp. 1–4.

6. Each spring from 1946 to 1951, a representative sample of the Dutch population was asked whether, if they had a choice, they would like to emigrate. The percentages replying in the affirmative were as follows:

| | | | |
|---|---|---|---|
| 1946 | 22% | 1949 | 29% |
| 1947 | 32% | 1950 | 25% |
| 1948 | 32.5% | 1951 | 26% |

Petersen, *Factors Influencing Postwar Emigration*, pp. 10–11. See also the *New York Times*, February 15, 1953, p. 26, c. 4. Such high percentages may seem strange but as late as 1971, a Gallup Poll indicated that 41 percent of the people in Great Britain would have liked to emigrate. The percentages for other countries included in the poll were West Germany, 27; Sweden, 18; the Netherlands, 16; and the United States, 12. For the United States this was an increase from 6 percent in 1954 and 4 percent soon after World War II. *New York Times*, March 21, 1971, p. 68, c. 3.

7. The study was published by the Government Printing and Publishing Office, The Hague, in four books: *De Gaande Man: Gronden van de Emigratiebeslissing* (1958); N. H. Frijda, *Emigranten/Niet-Emigranten* (1960); R. Wentholt, *Kenmerken van de Nederlands Emigrant: Een Analyse van Persoonlijke Achter Grond, Omstandigheden en Beweegredenen* (1961); and N. H. Frijda, *Emigranten Overzee: Resultaten van een Eerste Enquête onder een Groep Emigranten* (1962). These four books have been published in English in an abridged form in G. Beijer, ed., *Characteristics of Overseas Migrants* (The Hague, 1961).

8. J. E. Ellemers, "The Determinants of Emigration, An Analysis of Dutch Studies on Migration," *Sociologia Neerlandica*, II (Summer, 1964), p. 52. See also p. 53.

9. By 1951, however, the United States had slipped to third place, the first choice being Australia and the second, Canada. The decline was perhaps due to the quota system in the United States. Because it was much easier to obtain permission to enter Australia and Canada, it is possible that more and more Hollanders began listing these countries instead of the United States. Petersen, *Factors Influencing Postwar Emigration*, p. 11; *Emigratie*, 1964, p. 133.

10. *Annals of the American Academy of Political and Social Science*, Vol. 245, p. 70. See also Eduard Elias, "What the U. S. Means to Holland," *Knickerbocker Weekly*, V (July 30, 1945), p. 13.

11. B. W. Haveman, "Planned Emigration: The Solution of Holland's Population Problem," *Progress*, Vol. 45 (Summer, 1956), p. 118.

12. W. S. Bernard, "America's Immigration Policy: Its Evolution and Sociology," *International Migration*, III (1965), p. 235. A good summary of American immigration policy from colonial times to the Second World War is Chapter 19, "Closing the Gates," pp. 487–538 of Carl Wittke, *We Who Built America: The Saga of the Immigrant*, rev. ed. (Cleveland, 1964).

13. This figure initially was set at 3,153.

14. In 1961, the Netherlands Emigration Fund Foundation in Amsterdam awarded the Van Noort Medal to Congressman Francis Walter of Pennsylvania, Chairman of the House Immigration Committee, for his efforts on behalf of Dutch emigration to the United States.

15. The writer is grateful to Willem Wanrooy of Pasadena, California, and Ms. Greta Kwik of the Anthropology Department of Syracuse University for furnishing information on the Dutch-Indonesians. A good summary of the Dutch-Indonesians in the United

States is *Doubly Uprooted*, a pamphlet published by the American Immigration and Citizenship Conference (New York, 1965).

16. Richard F. Smith, "Refugees," *The New Immigration*, edited by Edward P. Hutchinson, *Annals of the American Academy of Political and Social Science*, Vol. 367 (September, 1966), p. 47. In some instances, however, Dutch ancestry was kept unmixed in Indonesia at least as long as five generations.

17. For an excellent account of the problems confronting many Eurasians in Indonesia in 1949 and the reasons why so many preferred retaining their Dutch citizenship see Paul W. Van der Veur, "Eurasian Dilemma in Indonesia," *Journal of Asian Studies*, XX (November, 1960), pp. 45–60. See also Tamme Wittermans and Noel P. Gist, "The Ambonese Nationalist Movement in the Netherlands: A Study in Status Deprivation," *Social Forces*, XL (May, 1962), pp. 309–317.

18. Despite the advantage that Dutch-Indonesians had with English and despite their possession of transferrable skills, they nevertheless regarded the language problem as their major difficulty on arrival in the United States, and securing a job commensurate with their experience and training as their second greatest problem.

19. Correspondence between the writer and Mr. Wanrooy dated August 1, 1973.

20. Great Britain and Germany, for example, which were two of the leading users of immigrant visas in 1965, were not even among the top ten in 1969, having been replaced by such countries as Greece and Portugal, neither of which were among the top ten in 1965. "Who can Immigrate at Present to the United States," *Migration News*, 1969, pp. 23–24.

21. Hofstede, "Those Who Went and Those Who Stayed," p. 54.

22. B. P. Hofstede, *Thwarted Exodus: Post-War Overseas Migration from the Netherlands* (The Hague, 1964), p. 164; Department of Justice *Annual Report: Immigration and Naturalization Service* for the years 1966–68, Table 8 (henceforth cited as *Annual Report*).

23. *Migration Today*, No. 6 (May, 1966), pp. 32–33; *Elsevier's Weekblad*, April 15, 1967; *Neuwe Rotterdamse Courant*, June 20, 1967.

24. Table 42a, "Persons Naturalized by Specific Countries of Former Allegiance," *Annual Report*, 1966–68.

25. Hofstede, *Thwarted Exodus*, p. 96.

26. For a survey of Dutch Catholic emigration see Jos. F. Van Campen, "Summary Report about the Emigration of the Catholics in the Netherlands," an unpublished report appearing in August, 1951.

Van Campen was General Director of the Catholic Emigration Foundation.

27. The comparability of the data from the two census reports is slightly limited in that the 1940 statistics are for Netherlands-born whites whereas the 1970 figures are for Netherlands-born irrespective of race.

28. Table 42a, *Annual Report*, 1966–71. Beginning with the 1972 *Annual Report*, the Netherlands is no longer separately classified. See also *Emigratie*, 1955, p. 46; 1961, p. 36; 1962, p. 38; H. W. M. de Haas, "Nederlanders Vinden Toekomst in Californie," *De Tijd-Maasbode*, November 22, 1965.

29. Table 42a, *Annual Report*, 1966–71.

30. Some of the remarks that follow were derived from Cn, "Emigratie vroeger . . . en nu," *Emigratie*, No. 7 (Voorjaar 1960), pp. 8–10.

31. John Witte, *DIS*, I (May, 1970), p. 19. Mr. Witte is secretary of the Dutch Immigrant Society.

32. The writer is grateful to Marten Flipse, Chairman of the Board of Dutch Club AVIO, for furnishing him with information about this organization. The term AVIO stands for "Alle Vermaak Is Ons."

33. Most of the Utah members live in the Salt Lake City area, and their strong presence there can be explained by membership in the Mormon Church.

34. Correspondence between the writer and Case Deventer of Holland, Michigan, dated September 27, 1972.

## CHAPTER XI

1. The Reformed Church in America, as noted in Chapter VI, was called the Reformed Dutch Church before 1867. To avoid confusion, the term Reformed Church will be used throughout this chapter regardless of the time period being discussed.

2. Elton M. Eenigenburg, *A Brief History of the Reformed Church in America* (Grand Rapids, Mich., n.d.), pp. 62–63.

3. *Dutch Immigrant Memoirs*, I, p. 453.

4. As quoted in Henry Beets, *De Chr. Geref. Kerk in N.A.: Zestig Jaren van Strijd en Zegen* (Grand Rapids, Mich., 1918), p. 71.

5. At first the new denomination was called the Holland Reformed Church, which was changed to True Reformed Church in 1861, and to Holland Christian Reformed Church in America in 1880. A decade later, the word "Holland" was dropped from the title, as were the words "in America" in 1904.

6. The story of these New Jersey congregations is discussed in Henry Beets, "De Afscheiding van de Geref. Holl. Kerk in Noord-Amerika in 1822, in hare Wortelen, Voorloopers en Leiders," *Nederlandsch Archief voor Kerkgeschiedenis*, Nieuw Serie, XIII (1917), pp. 340–368.

7. The Christian Reformed Church is, however, a member of the Reformed Ecumenical Synod, an ecumenical movement with a Reformed constituency.

8. The Reformed Church has long permitted women to vote in congregational meetings, and recently permitted them to serve in the consistory. Despite considerable opposition, steps were also taken in 1973 to permit ordination of women. The Christian Reformed Church, on the other hand, has thus far only permitted women the right to vote in congregational meetings.

9. For an excellent summary of the differences between Reformed congregations in the East and those in the West see Donald J. Bruggink, "Differences within Our Church," *The Church Herald*, January 16, 1970, pp. 12–13.

10. *Dutch Immigrant Memoirs*, I, p. 504.

11. *Ibid.*, pp. 249–250. See also p. 68.

12. Although a newly elected town council ignored the plebiscite, attendance at the theater was so low it soon closed. *Life*, April 19, 1948, pp. 97–100; *Time*, April 12, 1948, p. 27. For similar developments in South Dakota see George W. Heeringa, "The Christian Reformed Church in South Dakota" (unpublished M.A. dissertation, University of South Dakota, Vermillion, 1955), pp. 95–97.

13. On the Dutch atmosphere that still prevails at Prospect Park, see the articles by Bert Nawyn in *Paterson News*, April 17 and April 19, 1973. According to the tax rolls of 1973, 658 of the 1,161 parcels of property in the borough were owned by persons with Dutch names.

14. Of these, about 10,000 Reformed and 75,000 Christian Reformed members belonged to churches located in Canada.

15. The writer is grateful to the Reverends W. C. Lamain and Gise J. Van Baren of Grand Rapids, Michigan, for information respectively about the Netherlands Reformed Congregations and the Protestant Reformed Churches in America.

16. On Dutch Catholic colonies see Van Hinte, *Nederlanders in Amerika*, II, pp. 280–281, 295–308; *Dutch Immigrant Memoirs*, II, pp. 145–187; Lucas, *Netherlanders in America*, pp. 444–459, 522–528.

17. *Dutch Immigrant Memoirs*, II, p. 153.

18. *Ibid.*, p. 179. See also Wabeke, *Dutch Emigration to North America 1624–1860*, p. 140.

19. By 1875, the orthodox Reformed element in the Netherlands, with support from the Catholics, had received permission from the government to establish their own schools, and even received state subsidies for their maintenance.

20. Eenigenburg, *Brief History of the Reformed Church*, p. 88. Rutgers at this time was still a Reformed Church college.

21. *Gedenkboek van het Vijftigjarig Jubileum der Christelijke Gereformeerde Kerk* (Grand Rapids, Mich., 1907), p. 81.

22. Lefferts A. Loetscher, ed., *Twentieth Century Encyclopedia of Religious Knowledge* (Grand Rapids, Mich., 1955), II, p. 949.

23. Handy, "The Dutch in Rochester," p. 70; correspondence between the writer and the Reverend Dr. Peter Y. De Jong of Sioux Center, Iowa, August 3, 1973.

24. *The Banner*, September 5, 1924, p. 574.

25. *Ibid.*, October 1, 1926, p. 605. See also December 24, 1926, p. 821, for Zillah, Washington.

26. R. T. Kuiper, *A Voice from America about America*, translated by E. R. Post (Grand Rapids, Mich., 1970), p. 67. The pace of acculturation in the cities varied, however, according to the number of Dutch inhabitants. It was, of course, slowest in a city like Grand Rapids, Michigan, where there was only limited interaction between Dutch and non-Dutch townsmen because of the large number of Hollanders residing there.

27. For an analysis of the acculturation of a large Dutch community see John A. Jakle and James O. Wheeler, "The Changing Residential Structure of the Dutch Population in Kalamazoo, Michigan," *Annals of the Association of American Geographers*, Vol. 59 (September, 1969), pp. 441–460.

28. For detailed discussions of the Dutch press in the United States see Henry Beets, "Hollandsche Couranten en Tijdscriften in de Ver. Staten," *Gereformeerede Amerikaan*, XX (December, 1916), pp. 514–522; Lucas, *Netherlanders in America*, pp. 529–541; Van der Zee, *Hollanders of Iowa*, pp. 245–255.

29. Mulder, *Americans from Holland*, p. 214.

30. By 1916, for example, Holland, Michigan, had published at one time or another eleven different newspapers as well as several magazines.

31. The writer is currently composing a detailed article on the reaction of the Dutch-Americans to the Boer War.

32. It is true that after World War II and again in 1953, when the Netherlands experienced one of its worst floods in history, Dutch-Americans sent large quantities of clothing and food to aid suffering and destitute Hollanders. It must be noted, however, that although

these relief programs were participated in by the younger generation, the initiative was almost entirely in the hands of first- and second-generation Dutch Americans.

33. In many communities, however, certain Dutch words and expressions continued to be generously mixed with English for many years. For a brief discussion of this see Dorothy De Lano Vander Werf, "Evidences of Old Holland in the Speech of Grand Rapids," *American Speech*, XXXIII (December, 1958), pp. 301–304.

34. This date is used because it marks the *final* transfer of New Netherland to England by the Treaty of Westminster of the previous year.

35. There had been other schools besides Columbia and Calvin offering such courses before 1949, but lack of interest led to their discontinuance. This subject is carefully treated in Walter Lagerway, "Universitair Nederlands Onderwijs in de Verenigde Staten," *De Nederlandistiek in het Buitenland*, edited by W. Thys and J. M. Jalink ('s Gravenhage, 1967), pp. 141–152. See also Walter Lagerwey, "Growing Interest for Dutch," *DIS* (June, 1971), pp. 15–17.

## CHAPTER XII

1. Mulder, *Americans from Holland*, p. 233.

2. Jameson, *Narratives of New Netherland*, pp. 324, 337, 338, 342; *Colonial Documents of New York*, I, p. 453.

3. Political developments in New Netherland are discussed in Morton Wagman, "The Struggle for Representative Government in New Netherland" (unpublished Ph.D. dissertation, Columbia University, 1969).

4. *Ecclesiastical Records*, II, p. 1042.

5. The best account of the Leisler Troubles is Jerome R. Reich, *Leisler's Rebellion: A Study of Democracy in New York 1664–1720* (Chicago, 1953).

6. Carl Lotus Becker, *The History of Political Parties in the Province of New York 1760–1776* (Madison, Wisc., 1909), pp. 12–15. There were, however, political factions among these families.

7. Louis Adamic, *A Nation of Nations* (New York, 1945), p. 101.

8. E. Wilder Spaulding, *New York in the Critical Period 1783–1789* (New York, 1932), p. 32; *Dictionary of American Biography*, XX, p. 598. Alexander Hamilton, one of the authors of the *Federalist Papers*, was a son-in-law of Schuyler.

9. As quoted in Hans Koningsberger, "Holland and the United States," a pamphlet published by the Netherlands Information Service, p. 4.

10. See especially *Federalist Papers* numbers 20, 39, and 75.

11. The antirent movement is discussed in Ellis, *Landlords and Farmers in the Hudson-Mohawk Region*, pp. 225–312.

12. Edward Morse Shepard, *Martin Van Buren* (Boston, 1888), p. 12.

13. Van Buren, *Autobiography*, p. 9.

14. *Dutch Immigrant Memoirs*, II, p. 156. See also pp. 158–159.

15. Scholte, *Eene Stem uit Pella*, p. 38.

16. *Dutch Immigrant Memoirs*, II, p. 290.

17. William Schrier, "Gerrit J. Diekema: Orator," *Michigan History*, XXXI (December, 1947), pp. 370, 374.

18. D. H. Kromminga, *The Christian Reformed Tradition: From the Reformation till the Present* (Grand Rapids, Mich., 1943), p. 135.

19. Scholte, *Eene Stem uit Pella*, pp. 2–3, 12–13.

20. Kuiper, *A Voice from America*, pp. 64–65.

21. Lucas, *Netherlanders in America*, p. 542.

22. Van der Zee, *Hollanders of Iowa*, p. 226.

23. Oostendorp, *H. P. Scholte*, p. 183. Despite its English title, the *Pella Gazette* published some articles in Dutch, but was primarily English.

24. For a brief account of this incident see Gerald F. De Jong, "General Synod and the Slavery Crisis of 1855," *Church Herald*, June 12, 1970, pp. 12–14.

25. Oostendorp, *H. P. Scholte*, pp. 183–186. Despite Scholte's efforts on behalf of Lincoln, most Iowa Hollanders still voted for the Democrats in 1860. On Scholte's being offered the post of Minister to Austria and the later withdrawal of the offer, see Leonora Scholte, "A Stranger in a Strange Land," *Iowa Journal of History and Politics*, XXXVII (April, 1939), pp. 179–180.

26. Wynand Wichers, "The Dutch Churches in Michigan during the Civil War," *Publications of the Michigan Civil War Centennial Observance Commission* (n.p., 1965), p. 10.

27. Adamic, *A Nation of Nations*, p. 106; *Dutch Immigrant Memoirs*, II, pp. 124–127, 135, 136; Handy, "The Dutch in Rochester," pp. 71–72.

28. *Dutch Immigrant Memoirs*, II, p. 124.

29. Robert Ernst, "Rufus King, Slavery, and the Missouri Crisis," *New York Historical Society Quarterly*, XLVI (October, 1962), p. 359. See also Simeon F. Moss, "The Persistence of Slavery and Involuntary Servitude in a Free State 1685–1866," *Journal of Negro History*, XXXV (July, 1950), p. 292.

30. Christobelle Van Deventer, *The Van Deventer Family* (Columbia, Mo., 1943), pp. 234–238. Persons of Dutch descent living

south of the Mason-Dixon line even had the distinction of furnishing a general to the Confederate side, Earl Van Dorn of Mississippi. For a recent biography of him see Robert G. Hartje, *Van Dorn: The Life and Times of a Confederate General* (Nashville, Tenn., 1967).

31. As quoted in Van der Zee, *Hollanders of Iowa*, p. 227. The quote is from the *Pella Gazette*, April 30 and August 6 and 13, 1857.

32. Vandenbosch, *Dutch Communities of Chicago*, "Notes of the Publishing Committee," p. 101.

33. Lucas, *Ebenezer*, p. 19.

34. Edgar Eugene Robinson, *They Voted for Roosevelt: The Presidential Vote 1932–1944* (Stanford, Cal., 1947), p. 109. A 1967 biographical study of a Michigan politician states, "Today a republican label is a certain guarantee of victory for a candidate in any Holland local or state political contest." Charles Warren Vander Hill, "Gerrit J. Diekema: A Michigan Dutch-American Political Leader, 1859–1930" (unpublished Ph.D. dissertation, University of Denver, 1967), p. 20.

35. Holland, the largest town in the county, had a population of less than 30,000 in 1970.

36. Michael Barone and others, *The Almanac of American Politics: The Senators, the Representatives—Their Records, States and Districts* (Boston, 1972), p. 371. Pages 378–379 discuss the provincial Republicanism of the Dutch in neighboring Ottawa County. See also the *New York Times*, October 20, 1973, p. 33, c. 1.

37. Richard Jensen, *The Winning of the Midwest: Social and Political Conflict, 1888–1896* (Chicago, 1971), p. 298.

38. Vandenbosch, *Dutch Communities of Chicago*, p. 51.

39. Bade, "A History of the Dutch Settlement in Lancaster County, Nebraska," pp. 154–155.

40. Richard M. Scammon, ed., *America at the Polls: A Handbook of American Presidential Election Statistics 1920–1964* (Pittsburgh, 1965), pp. 150–162. Goldwater polled 66 percent of the Sioux County vote.

41. Correspondence between the writer and the Reverend J. Peter Vosteen of Whitinsville, Massachusetts, April 18, 1973.

42. Based upon correspondence between the writer and various Dutch-Americans residing in these states.

43. Correspondence between the writer and Mr. Fred Troost of Mira Loma, California, May 8, 1973.

44. Correspondence between the writer and Mr. James Albers of Upland, California, May 11, 1973.

45. Correspondence between the writer and the Reverend Edward G. Cooke of West Sayville, New York, March 20, 1973.

46. Paul Kleppner, *The Cross of Culture: A Social Analysis of Midwestern Politics 1850–1900* (New York, 1970), p. 59.

47. Vandenbosch, *Dutch Communities of Chicago*, p. 59.

48. Andrew R. Baggaley, "Religious Influence on Wisconsin Voting," *The American Political Science Review*, LVI (March, 1962), p. 70.

49. A two-party trend has, however, emerged in recent years in the town of Pella itself, although the rural precinct is still traditionally Democratic. For a careful study of the Dutch voting pattern of the Pella Dutch, including reasons why Scholte was unable to get his fellow Dutchmen to change to his way of thinking when he switched from the Democrats to the Republicans in 1859, see Robert P. Swierenga, "The Ethnic Voter and the First Lincoln Election," *Civil War History*, XI (March, 1965), pp. 27–43, reprinted in Frederick C. Luebke, ed., *Ethnic Voters and the Election of Lincoln* (Lincoln, Nebraska, 1971), pp. 129–150.

50. Vandenbosch, *Dutch Communities of Chicago*, pp. 58–59.

51. The special election held in February, 1974, to fill Ford's seat saw two Dutchmen named Vander Veen and Vander Laan pitted against each other. Vander Veen's upset victory was the first GOP congressional loss in the district since 1912.

52. As quoted in Oostendorp, *H. P. Scholte*, pp. 186–187.

53. The title connotes the idea of a kind of universal law or natural order in which justice, ethics, behavior, etc., are all attuned to divine law—in this case, biblical law as interpreted by Calvinists. There is a good discussion of it and related matters in Henry Zwaanstra, *Reformed Thought in a New World* (Kampen, The Netherlands, 1973).

54. Lucas, *Netherlanders in America*, p. 571. There had, however, been similar papers, all weeklies, before this. Ate Dykstra, who emigrated from Friesland to Michigan in 1891 and was strongly influenced by Kuyper's writings, published a pro-labor newspaper at Grand Rapids, Michigan, in the Dutch language from 1892 to 1900.

55. The best accounts of the Christian Labor Association are Joseph Gritter, "History of the CLA," *The Christian Labor Herald*, XXVI–XXVII (December, 1965–June, 1966), and Bob Repas, "History of the Christian Labor Association," *Labor History*, V (Spring, 1964), pp. 168–182. The writer is grateful to Mr. Don Leep, Secretary of the CLA, for making information available to him.

56. To date, there has been little examination of the overall voting habits of Dutch-Americans. This is in sharp contrast with numerous studies of the voting practices of Italian, Jewish, Polish, Irish, German, and several other ethnic groups residing in the United States. See, for example, the extensive bibliographies on these groups in

Lawrence H. Fuchs, ed., *American Ethnic Politics* (New York, 1968), pp. 275–299, and Mark R. Levy and Michael S. Kramer, *The Ethnic Factor: How America's Minorities Decide Elections* (New York, 1972), pp. 242–244.

CHAPTER XIII

1. The writer, in composing this chapter, relied on all the basic reference works and aids. These are too numerous to mention for each person described, but include works of a general nature such as *Current Biography, Who's Who in America, Directory of American Scholars,* and *Dictionary of American Biography* as well as special guides dealing with art, literature, and music. A variety of miscellaneous sources of information were also used, including reviews of books written by Dutch-American authors, obituary notices in the *New York Times,* and personal correspondence.

2. The intermarriage problem, although very important, must not be exaggerated. The Dutch in America have tended to be clannish. It will be recalled that President Van Buren's eldest son was the first Van Buren in six generations to marry outside the Dutch line. Even in the twentieth century, there are Dutch communities in which, until recent years, it was unusual for a Hollander to marry a non-Hollander.

3. This is a small figure, but compared to several other ethnic groups who emigrated to America in much larger numbers, the Dutch percentage was by no means low. The Italian-born, for example, numbered only three and the Swedish-born only five. Murray G. Lawson, "The Foreign-Born in Congress, 1789–1949: A Statistical Summary," *American Political Science Review,* LI (December, 1957), pp. 1183–1189.

4. For a careful study of Diekema's life, see Vander Hill, "Gerrit J. Diekema."

5. His grandfather also emigrated to America, settling first in New York State.

6. Lenin suggested in 1920 that some of De Leon's works be translated into Russian, to which he himself would append some notes. Louis Fischer, *The Life of Lenin* (New York, 1964), p. 433.

7. *Saturday Review of Literature*( XXVII (February 19, 1944), p. 24.

8. *The Horn Book Magazine,* XLIV (December, 1968), p. 688.

9. Samuel M. Green, *American Art: A Historical Survey* (New York, 1966), p. 585.

10. As quoted in Michel Seuphor, *Piet Mondrian: Life and Work* (New York, n.d.), p. 188.

11. His father, Theodore, was also a success in the automotive industry. Trained as a coppersmith in the Netherlands, upon arrival in Detroit he soon was assigned to body work with the Hudson Motor Car Company. Innovations that he introduced into metal-stamping techniques led to one-piece body and fender panels. This was of such significance to the automotive industry that the *New York Times* took notice of his death in 1952.

12. Because of his long experience in the food industry, Edward J. Hekman, a grandson of Edsko and a former president of the Keebler Company, was named administrator of the Food and Nutrition Service when it was established in July, 1969, by President Richard Nixon.

CHAPTER XIV

1. *Yearbook of the Holland Society, 1890–91*, pp. 67–69.

# Selected Bibliography

BOOKS AND DISSERTATIONS

AMERICAN COUNCIL OF LEARNED SOCIETIES. "Report of the Committee on Linguistics and National Stocks in the Population of the United States." *Annual Report of the American Historical Association for the Year 1931.* Vol. I. Washington, D.C.: Government Printing Office, 1932.

ANBUREY, THOMAS. *Travels through the Interior Parts of America in a Series of Letters.* 2 vols. London: William Lane, 1789.

BACHMAN, VAN CLEAF. *Peltries or Plantations: The Economic Policies of the Dutch West India Company in New Netherland, 1623–1639.* Baltimore: Johns Hopkins, 1969.

BADE, GUSTAV ADOLPH. "A History of the Dutch Settlement in Lancaster County, Nebraska." Unpublished Master's dissertation, University of Nebraska, 1938.

BAILEY, ROSALIE F. *Pre-Revolutionary Dutch Houses and Families in Northern New Jersey and Southern New York.* New York: William Morrow, 1936.

BANTA, THOMAS MELVIN. *A Frisian Family: The Banta Genealogy.* New York: n.p., 1893.

BATTLE, J. H., ed. *History of Bucks County Pennsylvania.* Philadelphia: A. Warner & Co., 1887.

BEEKMAN, GEORGE C. *Early Dutch Settlers of Monmouth County, New Jersey.* Freehold, N.J.: Moreau Bros., 1901.

BEETS, HENRY. *De Chr. Geref. Kerk in N.A.: Zestig Jaren van Strijd en Zegen.* Grand Rapids, Mich.: Grand Rapids Printing Company, 1918.

BEIJER, G., ed. *Characteristics of Overseas Migrants.* The Hague: Government Printing Office, 1961.

BEIJER, G., and J. J. OUDEGEEST. *Some Aspects of Migration in the Netherlands.* Publications of the Research Group for European Migration Problems, Vol. III. The Hague: Government Printing Office, 1952.

BOISSEVAIN, CHARLES. *Van 't Noorden naar 't Zuiden: Schetsen en Indrukken van de Vereenigde Staten van Noord-Amerika.* 2 vols. Haarlem, The Netherlands: H. D. Tjeenk Willink, 1881–82.

BOXER, CHARLES R. *The Dutch Seaborne Empire*. New York: Knopf, 1965.

BRINCKERHOFF, R., ed. *The Family of Joris Dircksen Brinckerhoff*. New York: Richard Brinckerhoff Publisher, 1887.

BROWN, FRANCIS J., and JOSEPH S. ROUCEK, eds. *One America: The History, Contributions, and Present Problems of Our Racial and National Minorities*. Rev. ed. New York: Prentice Hall, 1945.

BROWN, WALLACE. *The Good Americans: The Loyalists in the American Revolution*. New York: William Morrow, 1969.

BRUINS, ELTON J. *The Americanization of a Congregation*. Grand Rapids, Mich.: William B. Eerdmans, 1970.

BURNABY, ANDREW. *Burnaby's Travels through North America*. Reprint of the 3rd ed. of 1798, with introduction and notes by Rufus Rockwell Wilson. New York: A. Wessels Company, 1904.

BURR, NELSON R. *Education in New Jersey 1630–1871*. Princeton: Princeton University Press, 1942.

COLE, CYRENUS. *I Remember, I Remember*. Iowa City: State Historical Society, 1936.

CONDON, THOMAS J. *New York Beginnings: The Commercial Origins of New Netherland*. New York: New York University Press, 1968.

CORWIN, EDWARD T., ed. *Ecclesiastical Records of the State of New York*. 7 vols. Albany: J. B. Lyon, 1901–16.

—————. *Manual of the Reformed Church in America*. 4th ed., rev. New York: Board of Publication of the Reformed Church, 1902.

CRÈVECOEUR, HECTOR ST. JOHN DE. *Sketches of Eighteenth Century America*. Edited by Henri L. Bourdin and others. New Haven: Yale University Press, 1925.

DILLIARD, MAUD ESTHER. *An Album of New Netherland*. New York: Twayne Publishers, 1963.

DYKE, CHARLES L. *The Story of Sioux County*. Orange City, Iowa: n.p., 1942.

EARLE, ALICE. *Colonial Days in Old New York*. New York: Empire State Book Co., 1938.

EDLER, FRIEDRICH. *The Dutch Republic and the American Revolution*. Johns Hopkins University Studies in Historical and Political Science, Series XXIX, No. 2. Baltimore: Johns Hopkins Press, 1911.

EEKHOF, A. *De Hervormde Kerk in Noord-America, 1624–1664*. 2 vols. 's Gravenhage, The Netherlands: Martinus Nijhoff, 1913.

—————. *Jonas Michaelius Founder of the Church of New Netherland*. Leyden, The Netherlands: A. W. Sijthoff, 1926.

EENIGENBURG, ELTON M. *A Brief History of the Reformed Church in America*. Grand Rapids, Mich.: Douma Publications, n.d.

ELLIS, DAVID MALDWYN. *Landlords and Farmers in the Hudson-Mohawk Region, 1790–1850.* New York: Octagon Books, 1967.

ELLIS, DAVID MALDWYN, and others. *A Short History of New York State.* Rev. ed. Ithaca, N.Y.: Cornell University Press, 1967.

"Emigration Conditions in Europe." 61st Congress, 3d Session, *Senate Documents,* No. 748, Vol. 12. Washington, D.C.: Government Printing Office, 1911.

EVANS, PAUL DEMUND. *The Holland Land Company.* Buffalo, N.Y.: Buffalo Historical Society, 1924.

FLICK, ALEXANDER C., ed. *History of the State of New York.* 10 vols. New York: Columbia University Press, 1933–37.

FOX, DIXON RYAN. *Yankees and Yorkers.* 2nd ed. Port Washington, N.Y.: Ira J. Friedman, 1963.

FUCHS, LAWRENCE H., ed. *American Ethnic Politics.* New York: Harper Torchbooks, 1968.

*Gedenkboek van het Vijftigjarig Jubileum der Christelijke Gereformeerde Kerk A.D. 1857–1907.* Grand Rapids, Mich.: H. Verhaar, 1907.

GRANT, [ANNE MCVICAR]. *Memoirs of an American Lady, with Sketches of Manners and Scenery in America, as They Existed Previous to the Revolution.* New York: D. Appleton & Co., 1846.

HAMILTON, ALEXANDER. *Hamilton's Itinerarium: Being a Narrative of a Journey from . . . May to September, 1774.* Ed. by Albert Bushnell Hart. Saint Louis: William K. Bixby, 1907.

HANSEN, MARCUS LEE. *The Atlantic Migration, 1607–1860.* New York: Harper Torchbooks, 1961.

HART, SIMON. *The Prehistory of the New Netherland Company.* Amsterdam: City of Amsterdam Press, 1959.

HARTLAND, J. A. A. *De Geschiedenis van de Nederlandse Emigratie tot de Tweede Wereldoorlog.* The Hague: n.p., 1959.

*Het Koninkrijk der Nederlanden: Feiten en Cijfers over de Nederlandse Samenleving.* The Hague: Government Printing Office, 1971.

HOFSTEDE, B. P. *Thwarted Exodus: Post-War Overseas Migration from the Netherlands.* The Hague: Martinus Nijhoff, 1964.

HONEYMAN, A. VAN DOREN. *Joannes Nevius and His Descendants A.D. 1627–1900.* Plainfield, N.J.: Honeyman & Co., 1900.

HULL, WILLIAM I. *William Penn and the Dutch Quaker Migration to Pennsylvania.* Swarthmore College Monographs on Quaker History, No. 2. Swarthmore, Penn.: Swarthmore College, 1935.

HUTCHINSON, EDWARD P., ed. "The New Immigration." *Annals of the American Academy of Political and Social Science.* Vol. 367 (September, 1966).

HYMA, ALBERT. *Albertus C. Van Raalte and His Dutch Settlements in the United States.* Grand Rapids, Mich.: William B. Eerdmans, 1947.

JAMESON, J. FRANKLIN, ed. *Narratives of New Netherland 1609–1664.* New York: Charles Scribner's Sons, 1909.

JOHNSON, AMANDUS. *The Swedish Settlements on the Delaware 1638–1664.* 2 vols. Philadelphia: University of Pennsylvania Press, 1911.

JONES, MALDWYN ALLEN. *American Immigration.* Chicago: University of Chicago Press, 1960.

KALM, PETER. *The America of 1750: Peter Kalm's Travels in North America.* Ed. by Adolph B. Benson. 2 vols. New York: Wilson-Erickson, 1937.

KENNEY, ALICE P. *The Gansevoorts of Albany: Dutch Patricians in the Upper Hudson Valley.* Syracuse: Syracuse University Press, 1969.

KILPATRICK, WILLIAM HEARD. *The Dutch Schools of New Netherland and Colonial New York.* Washington, D.C.: Government Printing Office, 1912.

KROMMINGA, D. H. *The Christian Reformed Tradition: From the Reformation till the Present.* Grand Rapids, Mich.: William B. Eerdmans, 1943.

KUIPER, R. T. *A Voice from America about America.* Translated by E. R. Post. Grand Rapids, Mich.: William B. Eerdmans, 1970.

KUIPERS, A. *Redding en Toekomst voor den Nederlandschen Landbouwer . . . in Zuid-Oostelijk Texas.* N.p.: n.p., 1897.

LEIBY, ADRIAN C. *The Early Dutch and Swedish Settlers of New Jersey.* Princeton: Van Nostrand, 1964.

————. *The Revolutionary War in the Hackensack Valley: The Jersey Dutch and the Neutral Ground, 1775–1783.* New Brunswick, N.J.: Rutgers University Press, 1962.

LUCAS, HENRY S., ed. *Dutch Immigrant Memoirs and Related Writings.* 2 vols. Assen, The Netherlands: Van Gorcum, 1955.

————. *Netherlanders in America: Dutch Immigration to the United States and Canada, 1789–1950.* Ann Arbor, Mich.: University of Michigan Press, 1955.

LUIDENS, JOHN PERSHING. "The Americanization of the Dutch Reformed Church." Unpublished Ph.D. dissertation, University of Oklahoma, 1969.

MCCORMICK, RICHARD P. *New Jersey from Colony to State 1609–1789.* Princeton: Van Nostrand, 1964.

MULDER, ARNOLD. *Americans from Holland.* Philadelphia: J. B. Lippincott, 1947.

MURPHY, HENRY C. *Anthology of New Netherland.* New York: n.p., 1865.

MYERS, ALBERT COOK, ed. *Narratives of Early Pennsylvania, West-New Jersey and Delaware 1630–1707.* New York: Charles Scribner's Sons, 1912.

NELSON, WILLIAM H. *The American Tory.* Oxford: Clarendon Press, 1961.

NISSENSON, SAMUEL G. *The Patroon's Domain.* New York: Columbia University Press, 1937.

O'CALLAGHAN, EDMUND BAILEY, ed. *Laws and Ordinances of New Netherland 1638–1674.* Albany: Weed, Parsons and Company, 1868.

O'CALLAGHAN, EDMUND BAILEY, and BERTHOLD FERNOW, eds. *Documents Relating to the Colonial History of the State of New York.* 15 vols. Albany: Weed, Parsons and Company, 1856–87.

OOSTENDORP, LUBBERTUS. *H. P. Scholte: Leader of the Secession of 1834 and Founder of Pella.* Franeker, The Netherlands: T. Wever, 1964.

PENNYPACKER, SAMUEL WHITAKER. *The Settlement of Germantown Pennsylvania and the Beginning of German Immigration to North America.* Pennsylvania-German Society Proceedings and Addresses, Vol. IX. Lancaster, Penn.: Pennsylvania German Society, 1899.

PETERSEN, WILLIAM. *Some Factors Influencing Postwar Emigration from the Netherlands.* Publications of the Research Group for European Migration Problems, Vol. VI. The Hague: Martinus Nijhoff, 1952.

POSTHUMUS, N. W., ed. *The Netherlands during German Occupation. Annals of the American Academy of Political and Social Science.* Vol. 245 (May, 1946).

PRATT, JOHN WEBB. *Religion, Politics, and Diversity: The Church-State Theme in New York History.* Ithaca, N.Y.: Cornell University Press, 1967.

RAESLY, ELLIS LAWRENCE. *Portrait of New Netherland.* New York: Columbia University Press, 1945.

REICH, JEROME R. *Leisler's Rebellion: A Study of Democracy in New York 1664–1720.* Chicago: University of Chicago Press, 1953.

REYNOLDS, HELEN WILKINSON. *Dutch Houses in the Hudson Valley before 1776.* New York: Dover Publications, 1965.

SCAMMON, RICHARD M., ed. *America at the Polls: A Handbook of American Presidential Election Statistics 1920–1964.* Pittsburgh: University of Pittsburgh Press, 1965.

STOKES, ISAAC N. P. *Iconography of Manhattan Island.* 6 vols. New York: R. H. Dodd, 1915–28.

TANIS JAMES. *Dutch Calvinistic Pietism in the Middle Colonies: A Study in the Life and Theology of Theodorus Jacobus Frelinghuysen.* The Hague: Martinus Nijhoff, 1967.

TENZYTHOFF, GERRIT J. "The Netherlands Reformed Church: Stepmother of Michigan Pioneer Albertus Christiaan Van Raalte." Unpublished Ph.D. dissertation, University of Chicago, 1968.

TERCENTENARY COMMITTEE ON RESEARCH. *Tercentenary Studies 1928: Reformed Church in America.* New York: Published by the Church, 1928.

THOMPSON, BENJAMIN F., and CHARLES J. WERNER. *History of Long Island.* 3rd ed. 3 vols. Port Washington, N.Y.: Ira J. Friedman, 1962.

TRELEASE, ALLEN W. *Indian Affairs in Colonial New York: The Seventeenth Century.* Ithaca, N.Y.: Cornell University Press, 1960.

VANDENBOSCH, AMRY. *The Dutch Communities of Chicago.* Chicago: The Knickerbocker Society, 1927.

VANDER HILL, CHARLES WARREN. "Gerrit J. Diekema: A Michigan Dutch-American Political Leader, 1859–1930." Unpublished Ph.D. dissertation, University of Denver, 1967.

VAN DER MEULEN, JACOB. *Hollanders: The Development of Their Objectives in Europe and America.* Zeeland, Mich.: First Reformed Church, n.d.

VAN DER POL, HENRY, SR. *On the Reservation Border: Hollanders in Douglas and Charles Mix Counties.* Stickney, S.D.: Argus Printers, 1969.

VAN DER ZEE, JACOB. *The Hollanders of Iowa.* Iowa City: State Historical Society, 1912.

VAN HINTE, J. *Nederlanders in Amerika: Een Studie over Landverhuizers en Volkplanters in de 19de en 20ste Eeuw in de Vereenigde Staten van Amerika.* 2 vols. Groningen, The Netherlands: P. Noordhoff, 1928.

VAN HOUTTE, J. A., and others, eds. *Algemene Geschiedenis der Nederlanden.* 12 vols. Utrecht, The Netherlands: W. De Haan, 1949–58.

VAN LAER, A. J. F., ed. *Documents Relating to New Netherland 1624–1626 in the Henry E. Huntington Library.* San Marino, Calif.: Henry E. Huntington Library and Art Gallery, 1924.

————, ed. *Van Rensselaer Bowier Manuscripts Being the Letters of Kiliaen Van Rensselaer, 1630–1643 . . .* Albany: University of the State of New York, 1908.

VAN LOON, L. G. *Crumbs from an Old Dutch Closet: The Dutch Dialect of Old New York.* The Hague: Martinus Nijhoff, 1938.

VLEKKE, BERNARD H. M. *Evolution of the Dutch Nation.* New York: Roy Publishers, 1945.

VLEKKE, BERNARD H. M., and HENRY BEETS. *Hollanders Who Helped Build America.* New York: American Biographical Company, 1942.

WABEKE, B. H. *Dutch Immigration to America, 1624–1860.* New York: Netherlands Information Bureau, 1944.

WERTENBAKER, THOMAS JEFFERSON. *The Founding of American Civilization: The Middle Colonies.* New York: Cooper Square Publishers, 1963.

WESLAGER, C. A. *Dutch Explorers, Traders and Settlers in the Delaware Valley 1609–1664.* Philadelphia: University of Pennsylvania Press, 1961.

WHITE, PHILIP L. *The Beekmans of New York in Politics and Commerce, 1647–1877.* New York: New York Historical Society, 1956.

WITTKE, CARL. *We Who Built America: The Saga of the Immigrant.* Rev. ed. Cleveland: Press of Case Western Reserve University, 1964.

WORMSER, A. *Verspreide Geschriften: Hier een Weinig, Daar een Weinig.* Milwaukee: Yewsdale, 1885.

ZUMTHOR, PAUL. *Daily Life in Rembrandt's Holland.* London: Weidenfeld and Nicolson, 1962.

ZWAANSTRA, HENRY. *Reformed Thought in a New World.* Kampen, The Netherlands: J. H. Kok, 1973.

### ARTICLES AND PAMPHLETS

AMERICAN IMMIGRATION AND CITIZENSHIP CONFERENCE. "Doubly Uprooted." New York: American Immigration and Citizenship Conference, 1965.

ANDREWS, WAYNE, ed. "A Glance at New York in 1697: The Travel Diary of Dr. Benjamin Bullivant." *New York Historical Society Quarterly,* XL (January, 1956), pp. 55–73.

BEETS, HENRY. "Hollandsche Couranten en Tijdscriften in de Ver. Staten." *Gereformeerde Amerikaan,* XX (December, 1916), pp. 514–522.

BRUGGINK, DONALD J. "Differences within Our Church." *The Church Herald,* January 16, 1970, pp. 12–13.

CARPENTER, WILLIAM H. "Dutch Contributions to the Vocabulary of English in America." *Modern Philology,* VI (July, 1908), pp. 53–68.

COLENBRANDER, H. T. "The Dutch Element in American History." *Annual Report of the American Historical Association for the Year 1909*, pp. 193–201.

DE JONG, GERALD F. "Dominie Johannes Megapolensis: Minister to New Netherland." *The New York Historical Society Quarterly*, LII (January, 1968), pp. 7–47.

————. "The Dutch in Emmons County." *North Dakota History*, XXIX (July, 1962), pp. 253–265.

————. "The Dutch Reformed Church and Negro Slavery in Colonial America." *Church History*, XXXX (December, 1971), pp. 423–436.

DYKEMA, F. E., ed. "Effort to Attract Dutch Colonists to Alabama, 1869." *Journal of Southern History*, XIV (May, 1948), pp. 247–261.

FLIPPEN, PERCY SCOTT. "The Dutch Element in Early Kentucky." *Proceedings of the Mississippi Valley Historical Association*, IX, Part I (1915–16), pp. 135–160.

GERLACH, LARRY R. "New Jersey in the Coming of the American Revolution." *New Jersey in the American Revolution*. Papers presented in the First Annual New Jersey Historical Symposium held December 6, 1969, at Rutgers University. Trenton: New Jersey Historical Commission, 1970. Pp. 8–20.

HANDY, ELLERY A. "The Dutch in Rochester." *The Rochester Historical Society Publication Fund Series*, XIV. Rochester, N.Y.: Published by the Society, 1936. Pp. 64–73.

HARDER, LELAND. "Plockhoy and His Settlement at Zwanendael." *Delaware History*, III (March, 1949), pp. 138–154.

HARMELINK, HERMAN, III. "Another Look at Frelinghuysen and His 'Awakening.'" *Church History*, XXXVII (December, 1968), pp. 423–438.

HARRIS, CHARLES X. "Jacobus Gerritsen Strycker (c. 1619–1687): An Artist of New Amsterdam." *New York Historical Society Quarterly Bulletin*, X (October, 1926), pp. 83–91.

HOFSTEDE, B. P. "Those Who Went and Those Who Stayed: Dutch Post-War Overseas Emigration." *Delta*, X (Spring/Summer, 1967), pp. 42–54.

HOSPERS, HENRY. "Diary of a Journey from the Netherlands to Pella, Iowa, in 1849." Translated by Jacob Van der Zee. *Iowa Journal of History and Politics*, X (July, 1912), pp. 363–382.

JACKSON, HARRY F. "Contributions to America of the Dutch Patriot Francis Adrian Van Der Kemp (1752–1829)." *New York History*, XLIII (October, 1962), pp. 371–384.

JAKLE, JOHN A., and JAMES O. WHEELER. "The Changing Residential

Structure of the Dutch Population in Kalamazoo, Michigan." *Annals of the Association of American Geographers*, LIX (September, 1969), pp. 441–460.

JAMES, BARTLETT B. "The Labadist Colony in Maryland." *Johns Hopkins University Studies in History and Political Science*, Series XVII, No. 6. Baltimore: Johns Hopkins Press, 1899.

KENNEY, ALICE P. "Dutch Patricians in Colonial Albany." *New York History*, XLIX (July, 1968), pp. 249–283.

———. "Private Worlds in the Middle Colonies: An Introduction to Human Traditions in American History." *New York History*, LI (January, 1970), pp. 4–31.

———. "The Albany Dutch: Loyalists and Patriots." *New York History*, XLII (October, 1961), pp. 331–350.

KNUPPE, J. "Land en Dollars in Minnesota: Inlichtingen voor Landverhuizers." Rotterdam: Van Hengel & Eeltjes, 1883.

LAGERWAY, WALTER. "Universitair Nederlands Onderwijs in de Verenigde Staten." *De Nederlandistiek in het Buitenland*. Edited by W. Thys and J. M. Jalink. 's Gravenhage: n.p., 1967. Pp. 141–152.

LEIBY, ADRIAN C. "The Conflict among the Jersey Dutch during the Revolution." *New Jersey in the American Revolution*. Papers presented in the First Annual New Jersey Historical Symposium held December 6, 1969, at Rutgers University. Trenton: New Jersey Historical Commission, 1970. Pp. 21–32.

LUCAS, HENRY S. "De Artikelen van Scholte's Vereeniging ter Verhuizing naar de Vereenigde Staten." *Nederlandsch Archief voor Kerkgeschiedenis*, Nieuwe Serie, XXXVIII (1938), pp. 179–187.

———. "Character of the Michigan Hollander." *The Michigan Alumnus, Quarterly Review*, LVIII (Summer, 1952), pp. 284–296.

MCKINLEY, A. E. "Transition from Dutch to English Rule." *American Historical Review*, VI (1900), pp. 693–724.

MAISEL, ALBERT Q. "The Hollanders among Us." *Reader's Digest*, October, 1955, pp. 171–176.

OPPENHEIM, SAMUEL. "The Early History of the Jews in New York, 1654–1664." *Publications* of the American Jewish Historical Society, XVIII (1909), pp. 1–91.

PUTNAM, RUTH. "The Dutch Element in the United States." *Annual Report of the American Historical Association for the Year 1909*, pp. 205–218.

ROBERTS, DOROTHY. "A Dutch Colony in Colorado." *Colorado Magazine*, XVII (1940), pp. 229–336.

SCHELTEMA, I. T. W. L. "A Dutch-American Railroad: The Kansas

City Southern." *Knickerbocker Weekly*, November 23, 1942, pp. 15–18.

SCHOLTE, HENRY PETER. *Eeene Stem uit Pella*. Translated by Jacob Van der Zee as "The Coming of the Hollanders to Iowa." *Iowa Journal of History and Politics*, IX (October, 1911), pp. 528–574.

—————. *Tweede Stem uit Pella*. Translated by Robert P. Swierenga as "A Place of Refuge." *Annals of Iowa*, XLI (1968), pp. 321–357.

SCHRIER, W. "Gerrit J. Diekema: Orator." *Michigan History*, XXXI (December, 1947), pp. 367–379.

SHETTER, WILLIAM Z. "A Final Word on Jersey Dutch." *American Speech*, XXXIII (December, 1958), pp. 243–351.

STUART, M. COHEN. "An Eminent Foreigner's Visit to the Dutch Colonies of Iowa in 1873." Translated by Jacob Van der Zee. *Iowa Journal of History and Politics*, XI (April, 1913), pp. 221–247.

SWIERENGA, ROBERT P., ed. and trans. "A Dutch Immigrant's View of Frontier Iowa." *Annals of Iowa*, XXXVIII (1965), pp. 81–118.

—————. "The Ethnic Voter and the First Lincoln Election." *Civil War History*, XI (March, 1965), pp. 27–43. Reprinted in Frederick C. Luebke, ed. *Ethnic Voters and the Election of Lincoln*. Lincoln, Nebr.: University of Nebraska Press, 1971. Pp. 129–150.

SYRETT, HAROLD C. "Private Enterprise in New Amsterdam." *William and Mary Quarterly*, XI (October, 1954), pp. 536–550.

TE LINTUM, C. "Emigratie over Rotterdam in de 18ᵈᵉ Eeuw." *De Gids*, Vierde Serie, IV (1908), pp. 323–335.

TEN HOOR M. "Dutch Colonists and American Democracy." *Michigan History*, XXXI (December, 1947), pp. 353–366.

VANDER WERF, DOROTHY DE LANO. "Evidences of Old Holland in the Speech of Grand Rapids." *American Speech*, XXXIII (December, 1958), pp. 301–304.

WALL, ALEXANDER J. "The Controversy in the Dutch Church in New York Concerning Preaching in English, 1754–1768." *The New York Historical Society Quarterly*, XII (July, 1928), pp. 39–58.

# Index

Went, Frits W., 243
Werkman, W. E., 162
Westchester County, N. Y., 51, 53
Westerlo, Reverend Eilardus, 79-80, 112, 288n42
Western Theological Seminary, 204
West India Company, 11, 12, 16, 17, 18, 28, 29, 30, 32, 49, 51, 63, 87, 89, 90
Westminster, Treaty of (1674), 38
Whitefield, George, 96
Whitinsville, Mass., 169, 206, 229
Willemstadt (formerly Fort Orange), 38
William I, King of the Netherlands, 129, 132
William the Silent, 2, 152, 227
Wiltwyck, 26, 53. *See also* Kingston

Wisconsin, 136, 140, 142-56, 151, 152, 155, 201, 202, 222, 226, 238
World War One, 7, 205, 206, 223
World War Two, 7, 173, 174, 175, 177, 184, 193, 210
Wormser, Reverend Andreas, 160
Wyckhoff, Reverend Isaac, 136
Wynkoop, 58

Yates, Abraham, 219
Yonkers, N. Y., 27, 51
York County, Penn., 49, 58-60, 84
Yorke, Sir Joseph, 125

*Ziekentrooster*, 76, 88
Zijlstra, Douwe, 162
Zonne, Reverend Pieter, 143
Zwijndrecht Brothers, 163